THE PLAYS OF

ANTON CHEKHOV

ALSO BY PAUL SCHMIDT

Meyerhold at Work
The Complete Works of Arthur Rimbaud
The Collected Works of Velimir Khlebnikov
Night Life (poems)
Winter Solstice (poems)

THE PLAYS OF

ANTON CHEKHOV

A NEW TRANSLATION BY
PAUL SCHMIDT

HarperFlamingo
An Imprint of HarperCollinsPublishers

A hardcover edition of this book was published in 1997 by HarperCollins Publishers.

First HarperFlamingo edition published 1998.

Designed by Alma Hochhauser Orenstein

The Library of Congress has catalogued the hardcover edition as follows:

Chekhov, Anton Pavlovich, 1860–1904.
    [Plays. English]
    The plays of Anton Chekhov / a new translation by Paul Schmidt. — 1st ed.
      p. cm.
    Contents: Swan song—The bear—The proposal—Ivanov—The seagull—
A reluctant tragic hero—The wedding reception—The festivities—Uncle
Vanya—Three sisters—The dangers of tobacco—The cherry orchard.
    ISBN 0-06-018705-0
    1. Chekhov, Anton Pavlovich, 1860–1904—Translations into English.
I. Schmidt, Paul, 1934– . II. Title.
PG3456.A19S36 1997
891.72'3—dc20   96-42456

ISBN 0-06-092875-1 (pbk.)

98 99 00 01 02 ❖/RRD 10 9 8 7 6 5 4 3 2

CONTENTS

Introduction   1

SWAN SONG   9
THE BEAR   19
THE PROPOSAL   35
IVANOV   51
THE SEAGULL   109
A RELUCTANT TRAGIC HERO   165
THE WEDDING RECEPTION   175
THE FESTIVITIES   191
UNCLE VANYA   207
THREE SISTERS   257
THE DANGERS OF TOBACCO   323
THE CHERRY ORCHARD   331

INTRODUCTION

The death of a doctor often seems a contradiction—an individual who can save other people's lives cannot save his own. Anton Chekhov was a doctor, a practicing physician, who died at the age of forty-four of tuberculosis. He had repeatedly refused to recognize his own illness, even after he began to cough blood. Someone else had to make the diagnosis.

We know Chekhov as a writer of short stories and plays, but we should remember that healing the sick was his foremost occupation. It helps us to understand the compassion for human beings that suffuses his work. He worked tirelessly for most of his life as a country doctor, often treating patients without payment.

What kind of man was he, this doctor who introduced into European playwriting something never before seen and never reproduced since? He was certainly not the rickety-looking invalid we see in photos taken just before his early death, nor was he the crotchety fussbudget whom Stanislavsky portrays in his memoirs—among the bases for almost a century of misreadings and misstagings of Chekhov's plays.

His plays are not "tragedies"; it was Stanislavsky who called them that. Chekhov called them comedies, except for *Three Sisters*, the only one of the plays that contains what might be called tragic elements; he called it a "drama." Chekhov, after all, began his career as a comic writer; comedy was what he knew best. And if any one author ever had a sense of the human comedy, the heartbreaking ridiculousness of our everyday behavior, it was Chekhov.

No, the Chekhov who wrote these plays was above all a master at the craft of writing, which he learned by writing continually, every day, for over twenty-five years. He was a professional writer, a man of wit and humor. A real *mensch*, a man who loved life, traveling, parties, and champagne, he was a great lover of women (although he managed to avoid marriage until the last possible moment). And he was an indefatigable worker for the betterment of society, without ever pontificating on the evils of that society. In 1890, he traveled across Siberia to the island of Sakhalin, on Russia's Pacific coast, which the government was settling as a convict colony. The trip was as much a vacation for Chekhov as anything else. "I'm not going for observations and impressions," Chekhov wrote to his friend Shcheglov. "All I want to do is live six months differently than the way I'm living now." Yet the notes from his trip, which he published in 1895 as *The Island of Sakhalin*, were to galvanize the government into a series of measures to improve the chaotic conditions he described.

During the cholera epidemic of 1892, he was responsible for setting up treatment facilities over a wide range of territory near his home in Melikhovo, and he spent months on the road ensuring that the facilities were in place and functioning.

Maxim Gorky's descriptions of Chekhov are usually renderings of what Gorky wanted to see in him, but one of his statements rings true: "Beautifully simple himself, he loved everything simple, real, and sincere." The thrust of Chekhov's development as a man and an artist was always toward greater and greater simplicity. Simplicity was his touchstone for art. He hated pretentiousness and fuss. He objected to Stanislavsky's stagings because they were too busy, too artfully "real." He made fun of actors who emoted and exaggerated.

"Beautifully simple" is a provocative description of his plays as well. What kind of plays are these? How do they work? In what sense can we call them simple? Why should they have moved the audiences of the world so profoundly for the past hundred years?

We have to begin where Chekhov did—with a professional writer's attempt to write a successful play. He was, after all, an extremely successful and well-known writer of stories, which he wrote easily and constantly. But he loved theater, and his playwriting career was a willed and difficult endeavor to learn a craft he admired.

He was no innovator when he began. His earliest long plays—the *Platonov* text, *The Wood Demon, Ivanov*—all follow the conventional patterns of the popular melodramas of the Russian commercial stage. All Chekhov's plays are based on the traditional themes of middle-class melodrama: hopeless love, money, marriage, and who owns the house. In that sense he was a playwright of his time, trying to write the kind of plays audiences wanted. It's important to remember that in his lifetime his most popular plays, and the ones that made money, were the one-act comic "sketches" he wrote over a period of five years. These he wrote easily and quickly, because the comic sketch was the genre with which he began as a writer. But when we look at the longer plays, and especially the various drafts and rewritings, we see him struggling to reinvent the craft of playwriting, to free himself from the theatrical conventions of the theater of his time. (One of my reasons for including *Ivanov* in this collection is to show the kind of melodramatic scenes Chekhov later abandoned.)

Chekhov was surely influenced by the Symbolist movement. Although we can imagine his ironic raised eyebrow at some of the vapors Symbolism gave rise to, he was very interested in the work of writers like Strindberg and Maeterlinck, playwrights whom his age referred to as "decadent." On November 2, 1895, while he was working on *The Seagull*, he wrote to his friend Suvorin: "Why don't you try staging Maeterlinck at your theater? If I were a director of your theater, in two years I would make a Decadent Theater of it—or try to. It would perhaps be a strange one, but it would at least have a recognizable identity." Chekhov's major plays are more and more influenced by Symbolist technique: they become increasingly plotless, in conventional terms; his dialogue is often like Maeterlinck's, consisting of mutually incomprehensible pieces of dialogue, phrases repeated and repeated until they become mere sound effect, lacking sense. The interplay between action and stillness, sound and silence; human actions viewed against the background of nature—a lake, a forest, a garden, an orchard: these fundamental devices of Maeterlinck's plays become fundamental for Chekhov as well.

The Cherry Orchard is a play in which, essentially, nothing happens; the only plot element is resolved at the end of Act Three, when Lopákhin buys the estate—an action that takes place well offstage. There is tantalizing evidence of the play Chekhov might have written after *The Cherry Orchard* had he lived: a scene set on an explorer ship frozen in the polar ice, the characters including the ghost of the woman loved by both heroes. This is the realm of Symbolist writing, a long way from the gunshots of the early plays. It is interesting, in fact, to trace Chekhov's move away from melodrama in his use of guns: all the major plays have guns onstage, but they occupy a progressively less central role. In *Platonov* the hero is shot to death; in *The Wood Demon*, *Ivanov*, and *The Seagull*, the heroes shoot themselves; in *Uncle Vanya*, an attempted murder becomes farcical when the shooter misses; in *Three Sisters*, the gunshots and the Baron's death are kept offstage; in *The Cherry Orchard*, the guns are in the hands of comic characters, who never fire them.

But none of this should distract us from the fundamental comedic nature of his plays. His comic sketches, of course, are meant to be played farcically, and it seems to me they are rarely given enough weight in studies of Chekhov as a playwright. They are a fundamental part of his dramaturgy; all his plays have moments of real (and quite deliberate) humor—not always in the boffo sense of the comic sketches, but in a quiet, understated mode. We smile and laugh at the follies and absurdities of human beings just like ourselves. But formally as well, the plays are comedies. Take, for example, Act Three of *The Cherry Orchard*, which is composed as a series of vaudeville turns, beginning with old Firs and his wobbly cross with a seltzer bottle (that stock comedic prop!), through Trofímov's pratfall down the stairs after his grand melodramatic exit, Carlotta's tricks, and Lopákhin's entrance to a slapstick whack over the head.

Over and over, we see Chekhov reducing action and dialogue to their simplest terms, to ensure his audiences' identification with their own lives. He wanted the people onstage to be recognizably normal for the audience and to speak a language that the audience understood was theirs.

And he succeeded. Surely the enduring qualities of the last plays is to be found in their perceptions of the realities of human behavior as it manifests itself not in rhetoric but in the everyday reaches of human speech. The silences of missed opportunity, the nonsense phrase that suddenly seems laden with meaning, the jealousies and envies and despairs that drive people to drink instead of expressing their feelings—all are revealed in an increasingly fragmentary language. The commonplace words and phrases in the plays function as replacements for the passions that unite or separate us. Melodrama put these passions onstage, tore them to tatters with artificial rhetoric, removed them to the realm of fantasy. Chekhov moved the passions off the stage, as it were, and his characters refer to them obliquely, uncomprehendingly. What Chekhov accomplished, in a kind of miraculous progression through those four last plays, was gradually to cut away the melodramatic moments of the "plot," or shift them offstage, leaving finally only his characters' helpless, unheeding responses to those moments.

And suddenly the whole fabric of nineteenth-century theater col-

lapses. The rule of causality, the idea that every act is subject to con-
sequences, that morality is a matter of rectitude or retribution—all
that vanishes. Chekhov's characters pull actions and phrases out of
the air (as happens in reality) and let them loose. His characters are
unaware of, or ignore, the effect of what they say and do. Chekhov's
own description of what he was up to is best: "What happens onstage
should be just as complicated and just as simple as things are in real
life. People are sitting at a table having dinner, that's all, but at the
same time their happiness is being created, or their lives are being
torn apart."

It is this that makes the language of his plays so crucial. There are
no great poetic passages in these plays; the long hopeful speeches
about the future are spoken by ineffectual characters. Chekhov's language is *ordinary* language—flat, banal, unremarkable. It is this quality of Chekhov's language that I have tried to make clear in these
translations. I hope they will provide students with a clear text for
their first reading of Chekhov. Above all, I hope these translations
will provide actors and directors with a clear sense of how the plays
are meant to work and how they should sound.

I want to emphasize that this is an American translation, not simply another "English" translation. I believe it's crucial to make the
distinction. We tend to think we and the Britons share a common
tongue, but in the theater, where language as it is spoken is
paramount, it's always clear that we speak two different dialects—
mutually understandable, true, but each with its own accents, idioms,
and emotive speech rhythms. For a long time we relied on British
translations of Chekhov, and so we tended to think he spoke the language of Shaw and Galsworthy, and we tended to equate his characters with theirs. But when British translations are played on the
American stage, his characters sound like English aristocrats. That,
coupled with the common American perception of English locutions
as somehow "upper class," gives a totally false idea of the Russian
context. What Chekhov created belongs in fact to a different world.

I believe, too, that most theater texts need continual retranslating.
While the language of the original remains fixed in time, the language of every audience changes enough in forty or fifty years to
make a new translation necessary. And faster even than language,
theatrical sensibilities change. The "skies of gray" that Gershwin
found in Chekhov productions in the 1920s have cleared a little; the
moody "Russian soul" our parents went to Chekhov to observe turns
out to be remarkably like our own. And we in America no longer

admire the autumnal melancholy, the wistful nostalgia for gentility, that so many productions, here as well as in England, have laid upon Chekhov's plays.

A particular reason for me to translate these plays is that I am an actor and a playwright who happens to be a Russian scholar. Most of the published translations of Chekhov are done either by native Russians, whose English is often awkward and stilted, or by Russian scholars, whose English is often formal and unidiomatic. The others are "versions" or "adaptations" done by playwrights who know no Russian; they work either by comparing existing translations or by hiring a Russian to help them. Inevitably their sense of what Chekhov actually wrote is extremely attenuated. And when they are playwrights with a strong dramatic language of their own, Chekhov's style and nuance are usually subordinated to theirs.

The task of the translator of Chekhov, as I see it, is to write a play in English that will produce, when staged, an effect such as the original may be said to have had on a Russian audience. I have to try to re-create in American English a voice that resounds within the American language the way Chekhov's voice resounds within Russian. In other words, I have to be aware of the linguistic *choices* Chekhov makes. What other expression might he have used here? What associations does a particular word conjure up for a Russian audience? What makes Chekhov's choice—of word, phrase, or idiom—unique and uniquely his?

Above all, whatever language I speak as a translator must be a language the audience can recognize as *theirs*. And if it isn't contemporary language, it must at least be recognizable as part of the audience's history, part of what they already know. Theater, I believe, works only if the actors speak the same language as the audience. That language must be as natural in the actor's mouth as it is in the audience's ear.

This volume contains twelve of the sixteen plays Chekhov wrote. I hesitate to call it the complete plays, but in a real sense it is. The twelve plays in this volume are the plays that Chekhov himself saw through the long process of theatrical production, that he rewrote, edited for publication, and saw into print. So they form the legitimate canon of Chekhov's dramatic work, as he intended it. The four omitted texts are *Tatiana Repina*, a short play that Chekhov wrote as a private joke for his friend Suvorin; *On the Main Road* and the *Platonov* text, two drafts that Chekhov abandoned; and *The Wood Demon*, which he later cut up and used as the basis for *Uncle Vanya*.

The Wood Demon is sometimes performed as a "lost masterpiece." It was never lost, nor is it a masterpiece. All in all, I think we must respect Chekhov's own opinion of *The Wood Demon*: "I hate that play and I'm trying to forget it. Whether it's the way it was written or the way it was directed, I don't know, but I would take it as a real insult if anybody dragged it out and staged it again."

A brief note on Russian names. All Russians have a given name and a last name, as Americans do, but they also have, as a kind of middle name, a patronymic: that is, a name that incorporates their father's name. Many English names, in fact, were originally patronymics, like Johnson, Williamson, Thomson, Davidson; in the course of time they became family names. But Russians still use the patronymic in both masculine and feminine forms as a fixed part of a name. So, for example, Andréy Sergéyevich Prózorov is Andréy, the son of Sergéy Prózorov; his sister is Ólga Sergéyevna. Russians who know each other only casually, or who have just been introduced, address and refer to each other by name and patronymic. These names are frequently used in the texts of the plays, sometimes in a contracted form; that is, Iván Románich instead of Iván Románovich.

The translations are made from the Russian texts with notes and variants as published in volumes 11, 12, and 13 of *Anton Chekhov: Complete Works and Letters*, 34 volumes (Moscow: Nauka, 1978). I have provided some notes for the five main plays; I hope they help to make things clear for directors and actors, and help to answer the kinds of textual questions that arise in rehearsals.

There are two books I can recommend as background reading. Richard Gilman's *Chekhov's Plays: An Opening into Eternity* (New Haven: Yale, 1995) is a sensitive analysis of the major plays. *Letters of Anton Chekhov* (New York: Harper & Row, 1977), translated by Michael Heim with commentary by Simon Karlinsky, restores previous cuts made in the letters and provides a detailed, intelligent history of Chekhov's life and writings. This is a fundamental reference for any serious study of Chekhov's plays, and should be required reading for all directors and actors of Chekhov. I owe a debt of gratitude to the directors who commissioned and first staged these translations: Libby Appel, Joumana Rizk, Joseph Hanreddy, Elizabeth LeCompte, Peter Sellars, Barbara Damashek, and above all Carey Perloff, whose encouragement and trust have kept me translating.

SWAN SONG

A DRAMATIC SKETCH IN ONE ACT

1887

CHARACTERS

Vasíly Vasílich Svetlovídov, an actor, about 68 years old

Nikíta Ivánich, the prompter, an old man

The action takes place on the stage of a theater in the provinces, late at night, after the show.

The empty stage of a second-rate provincial theater. Right, several crude unpainted doors leading to the dressing rooms; left and rear, piles of backstage junk. Center stage, an overturned stool. It's night. The stage is dark.

Enter from a dressing room Svetlovídov, costumed as Calchas from Offenbach's La Belle Hélène, *with a candle in his hand.*

SVETLOVÍDOV: Well, if that isn't ... *(A loud laugh)* What a joke! I fell asleep in the dressing room! The performance is over, everybody's gone home, and I slept through it all like a baby! Silly old fart. I must be getting old. Had a few too many, and I just sat there and went to sleep. Very smart. Brilliant performance. *(Shouts)* Yégorka! Yégorka! Where are you, goddamn it? Petrúshka! They must've gone home.... God damn 'em. Yégorka! *(Picks up the stool, sits down on it, and sets the candle on the floor)* There's nobody here. Just an echo. I gave each of them a big fat tip today, and now when I need them they're gone. Bastards probably locked up the theater, too. *(Shakes his head)* Ohh, God! I'm still drunk. I drank too much at the benefit today, all that beer and wine. Jesus. I smell like a brewery. My mouth feels like it's got twenty tongues in it.... Ohh! I feel awful.

(Pause.)

... really stupid. I've gotten to be an old drunk! I got shit-faced at the benefit, and I don't even know whose benefit it was. I feel like someone kicked me in the kidneys, my back is killing me, I've got the shakes ... cold all over, just like the grave. You don't give a damn about your health, do you? Asshole. You're too old for this anymore.

(Pause.)

You're old ... you can't pretend anymore. No getting away from it this time. Your life is over. Sixty-eight years down the drain, just like that. And it won't come back. The bottle's almost empty, just a little bit left in the bottom. Dregs, that's what it is. That's just the way it is, Váska, my boy, that's just the way it is. Ready or not, it's time for your final role. The death scene. The undiscovered bourne. *(Stares straight ahead)* I've been an actor for forty-five years, and this is the first time I've ever been onstage in the middle of the night. Yes. The first time. Curious. It's so dark out there.... *(Crosses down to the edge of the stage)* Can't see a thing. Well, the prompter's box, a little, and the stage boxes, and the conductor's podium ... All the rest is darkness. A bottomless black hole, just like the grave, and death out there, waiting ... Brr! It's cold! There's a wind coming from somewhere.... You could scare up a ghost out of this darkness. God, I'm scaring myself. My skin's starting to crawl.... *(Shouts)* Yégorka! Petrúshka! Where the fucking goddamn hell are you? *(Beat)* I've got to stop using language like that, I've got to stop drinking, I'm an old man, I'm going to die.... Most people get to be sixty-eight, they start going to church again, they start getting ready ... ready to die. And you—look at you. God! Swearing, getting drunk ... Look at this stupid costume—how could I want people to see me like this? I better go change.... I'm scared.... If I stay here the rest of the night, I'll die. *(Starts to exit to the dressing room)*

> *(Enter Nikíta Ivánich from the dressing room door farthest upstage. He wears a long white dressing gown. Svetlovídov sees him, shrieks with horror, and staggers backward.)*

Who's that? Who're you? What do you want? *(Stamps his feet)* Who *is* that?

NIKÍTA IVÁNICH: It's just me.

SVETLOVÍDOV: Who're you?

NIKÍTA IVÁNICH: *(Moving slowly toward him)* Me. Nikíta Ivánich. The prompter. Vassíly Vasílich, it's me!

SVETLOVÍDOV: *(Falls onto the stool, shaking and breathing heavily)* Oh, my God ... Who? Is that you? Is that you, Nikíta? Wha ... what are you doing here?

NIKÍTA IVÁNICH: I've been sleeping nights in one of the dressing rooms. Only, please, don't say anything to the manager.... I haven't got any other place to go.

SVETLOVÍDOV: It's just you, Nikíta. Oh, my God, my God. I thought ... *(Beat)* They had sixteen curtain calls tonight, and bouquets of flowers, and who knows what all, but nobody took the trouble to wake up an old man and help him home. I'm an old man, Nikíta. I'm sixty-eight ... and I'm sick. I don't have any strength left. *(Grabs Nikíta's hand and starts to cry)* Don't leave me, Nikíta! I'm old, I'm sick, I'm going to die.... I'm scared! I'm so scared!

NIKÍTA IVÁNICH: *(Gently, respectfully)* Vasíly Vasílich, it's time for you to go home.

SVETLOVÍDOV: No, no, I can't! I haven't got a home! I can't! I can't!

NIKÍTA IVÁNICH: Oh, dear. Did you forget where you live?

SVETLOVÍDOV: I won't go back there—I can't! I'll be all alone, Nikíta. I haven't got anybody—no wife, no children, no family. I'm all alone; I'm like the wind in an empty field. . . . I'm going to die, and no one will remember me. . . . It's awful to be alone. No one to hug you, keep you warm, put you to bed when you're drunk. . . . Who do I belong to? Does anybody need me? Does anybody love me? Nobody loves me, Nikíta!

NIKÍTA IVÁNICH: *(Almost in tears)* The audience loves you, Vasíly Vasílich!

SVETLOVÍDOV: The audience? Where are they? They've gone home to bed and forgotten all about me. No, nobody needs me, nobody loves me. No wife, no children . . .

NIKÍTA IVÁNICH: Now, now, what are you getting all upset about . . . ?

SVETLOVÍDOV: I'm a human being, aren't I? I'm still alive, aren't I? I've got blood in my veins, not water. And I come from a good family, Nikíta, a very good family. Before I got involved in show business I was in the army. I was an officer—I was an artillery officer. You should have seen me when I was young. I was so good-looking, I was clean-cut, strong, full of energy, full of life! Oh, my God, where did it all go? And what an actor I was, Nikíta, huh? *(Gets up, leaning on Nikíta's arm)* Where did it go, all that? My God, I . . . Tonight I looked out into that darkness, and it all came back to me, everything! That darkness swallowed up forty-five years of my life, Nikíta. But what a life! I look out into that darkness and I can see it all again, just like I see you now! My youth, my confidence, my talent, the women who loved me . . . the women who loved me, Nikíta!

NIKÍTA IVÁNICH: Vasíly Vasílich, I think it's time for bed.

SVETLOVÍDOV: When I was a young actor, and just beginning to feel how good I was, I remember, there was this one woman. . . . She loved me for my acting! She was tall, beautiful, elegant, young, innocent. She burned with a pure flame, like the dawn light in summer! One look from those blue eyes, that magic smile, you couldn't resist! I remember one time, I stood before her, just like I'm standing before you now. She was so beautiful that day, so beautiful, and she was looking at me—I'll never forget that look, not to my dying day. Her eyes like velvet, full of love, full of passion, the dazzle of her youth! I wanted her, I was mad for her, I fell to my knees in front of her. . . . *(His voice starts to trail off)* And she said, you have to choose. Me or the theater. *(Beat)* Give up the theater! You understand? She wanted me to give up the theater! She could make love to an actor, but marry one—never! And I remember that day; I was playing . . . oh, it was some awful part, nothing but clichés, and I was out there onstage . . . and all of a sudden my eyes were opened! And I realized then there was no holy art of acting, it was all lies and pretending, and I was just a toy, a slave to other people's pleasure, a clown! Just a cheap clown! That's when I realized what the audience was after, what they wanted from me! And after that I never believed the applause, the bouquets of flowers, the glowing reviews. It's true, Nikíta! They applaud me, they buy my photographs, but we are strangers to one another, and they think of me as trash, as a whore! They want to get to know me because I'm a celebrity—it flatters them—but they wouldn't lower themselves to let me marry one of their sisters or daughters! And I don't believe their applause! *(Falls back onto the stool)* I just don't believe them anymore!

NIKÍTA IVÁNICH: Vasíly Vasílich, you're scaring me. . . . You look just awful! Let's you and me go home. Come on now. . . .

SVETLOVÍDOV: That's when I finally found out what it was all about, Nikíta. I understood what they were like, and that knowledge has cost me dear! After that—after that girl—I rushed off without any direction, didn't care what my life was like, never thought ahead. I played cheap parts, cynical parts, I played the joker, I seduced anyone I could get my hands on . . . But what an actor I was, what an artist! And then I let my art go, I got vulgar and commercial, I lost the divine spark. . . . That black hole out there swallowed me up! I didn't realize it until now, but now, just now, when I woke up, I looked back, and I saw those sixty-eight years! I'm old! My life is over! I have sung my swan song! *(Sobs)* I've sung my swan song!

NIKÍTA IVÁNICH: Vasíly Vasílich! Don't be so upset. Just calm down, you poor man, just calm down. . . . Oh, my God! *(Shouts)* Petrúshka! Yégorka!

SVETLOVÍDOV: But what talent! What power! You can't imagine the power of my voice, of my emotions—how sexy I was, like a vibrating chord! *(Pounds his chest)* In here! Right in here! I had it all! I'm all right—just let me get my breath. . . . Listen, Nikíta,

just listen! *(Excited)* This is from *King Lear,* you remember, on
the heath, the storm, the rain, thunder and lightning ...
Vroooom! Psssssssh! The heavens open, then comes:
"Blow, winds, and crack your cheeks! Rage! Blow!
  You cataracts and hurricanoes, spout
  till you have drenched our steeples, drowned the cocks!
  You sulf'rous and thought-executing fires,
  vaunt-couriers of oak-cleaving thunderbolts,
  singe my white head! And thou, all-shaking thunder,
  strike flat the thick rotundity o' the world,
  crack Nature's molds, all germens spill at once
  that make ungrateful man!"
(Impatient) Quick, the Fool! Give me the Fool's lines! I don't
have much time!

NIKÍTA IVÁNICH: *(Acts the Fool's part)* "Oh, nuncle, court holy water
  in a dry house is better than this rain water out o' door. Good
  nuncle, in; ask thy daughters' blessing! Here's a night pities neither wise men nor fools!"

SVETLOVÍDOV:
  "Rumble thy bellyful! Spit, fire! Spout, rain!
  Nor rain, wind, thunder, fire are my daughters.
  I tax not you, you elements, with unkindness.
  I never gave you kingdom, called you children ..."
Not bad, huh? What power! What talent! What an artist!
Another one now, something ... something from the old days!
(Gives a long, happy laugh) Something from *Hamlet*! I'll start.
Where? Oh, I know. . . . *(Acts Hamlet)*
"Oh, the recorders! Let me see one. To withdraw with you—why
do you go about to recover the wind of me ... ?"

NIKÍTA IVÁNICH: "O my lord, if my duty be too bold, my love is too
  unmannerly."

SVETLOVÍDOV: "I do not well understand that—will you play upon
  this pipe?"

NIKÍTA IVÁNICH: "My lord, I cannot."

SVETLOVÍDOV: "I pray you."

NIKÍTA IVÁNICH: "Believe me, I cannot."

SVETLOVÍDOV: "I do beseech you."

NIKÍTA IVÁNICH: "I know no touch of it, my lord."

SVETLOVÍDOV: "It is as easy as lying; govern these ventages with your
  finger and thumb, give it breath with your mouth, and it will dis-
  course most eloquent music. . . ."

NIKÍTA IVÁNICH: ". . . I have not the skill!"

SVETLOVÍDOV: "Why, look you now, how unworthy a thing you make of me! You would play upon me, you would seem to know my stops, . . . and there is much music, excellent voice in this little organ, yet cannot you make it speak. 'Sblood, do you think I am easier to be played on than a pipe? Call me what instrument you will, . . . you cannot play upon me."

Bravo! Encore! Who says I'm old? I'm not old—that's all a fantasy! I can feel my strength coursing through my veins—it's my youth, my strength, my life! Nikíta, I'm not old—you can tell, can't you? Talent doesn't grow old! Wait a minute, I'm a little dizzy. . . . Oh, God . . . am I going crazy?

(The sound of a door opening.)

What's that?

NIKÍTA IVÁNICH: It must be Petrúshka and Yégorka coming back. Talent, Vasíly Vasílich! You have a great talent!

SVETLOVÍDOV: *(Shouts, turning toward the sound)* Here I am, my brave warriors! *(To Nikíta)* Come on, let's go get dressed. I'm not old—that was all a fantasy, just a momentary weakness. *(Laughs joyfully)* What are you crying for? You poor old man, what are you crying for? You mustn't do that. You really mustn't. *(Hugs him, with tears in his eyes)* You mustn't cry. When you're an artist, when you've got talent, then you never get old, you're never alone, never sick—even death seems a petty thing. . . . *(Weeps)* What am I talking about talent, Nikíta? No, we've sung our swan song. I'm just a squeezed-out old lemon, a melting icicle, a rusty nail, and you . . . you're just an old theater mouse. You're the prompter. Come on, let's go.

(They start off.)

Talent? No . . . The only thing I ever played in Shakespeare was Fortinbras—and I'm getting a little old for that. Oh, yes. You remember that speech from Othello, Nikíta?
                    ". . . Oh, now forever,
farewell the tranquil mind! Farewell content!
Farewell the plumed troop and the big wars
that make ambition virtue! Oh, farewell,
farewell the neighing steed, and the shrill trump,
the spirit-stirring drum, the ear-piercing fife,

the royal banner and all quality,
pride, pomp and circumstance of glorious war!"
NIKÍTA IVÁNICH: That's talent! You've got it! Real talent!
SVETLOVÍDOV: And this one:
"Our revels now are ended. . . . We are such stuff
as dreams are made on, and our little life
is rounded with a sleep . . . "

(His voice fades as he goes out with Nikíta.)

THE CURTAIN FALLS SLOWLY.

THE BEAR

A COMIC SKETCH IN ONE ACT

1888

CHARACTERS

Yeléna Ivánovna Popóva, a widow with dimples and a large estate

Grigóry Stepánovich Smírnoff, landowner, in his thirties

Luká, an elderly servant

The action takes place in Popóva's living room.

Popóva's living room. Popóva, dressed completely in black, sits staring at a photograph. Luká, her old servant, tries to talk sense to her.

LUKÁ: It's just not right, missus. You're letting yourself fall to pieces. Cook and the maid have gone berry picking, every living thing is out enjoying the sunshine, even your cat, now, he's out there trying to catch himself a bird, and here you sit, shut up in the house all day long, like some kind of nun. That's no fun. You listen to what I'm saying, now! It's been a whole year since you left the house!

POPÓVA: I shall never leave this house. Why should I? My life is over. He's dead and buried, and so am I, buried here within these four walls. We're both dead.

LUKÁ: I never heard the like! Your husband's dead. Well, God rest him, he's not coming back. You mourned him good and proper; now it's time to move on. You can't sit here wearing black and crying for the rest of your life. I lost my old woman, too, a while back, I cried for a month, and that was that. No need to sit around for years singing hymns; she wasn't worth it. (*Sighs*) You haven't seen your neighbors in months, you don't go out, and you tell us not to let anybody in. We're all living like spiders in the dark here, if you'll excuse the expression. My livery jacket's got moth holes. Fine, if there was nobody around worth seeing, but the whole county's crawling with eligible young men. There's a regiment in the next town, all those good-looking officers, melt in your mouth, most of them, and they have a dance every Friday night, and the band gives a concert every afternoon. Oh, missus, take a look at yourself—you're still a juicy young thing, you're still beautiful, you can go out and enjoy life. But a beautiful face won't last forever, you know. You wait—ten years from now you're going to want to go swanning after those officers, and it'll be too late.

POPÓVA: (*Firmly*) I must ask you never to talk to me like this again! When my husband died, life lost all meaning for me. You know that. I may look like I'm alive, but I'm not. I swore I'd wear black and shut myself up here until the day I die, didn't I? And I will. He'll see how much I loved him.... Oh, I know he treated me badly—I don't have to tell you about it. He was mean and . . . and even unfaithful. But I intend to be faithful to the grave and show him what *real* love means.

LUKÁ: That's just a lot of talk. You'd do better to go out and take a walk, or have me hitch up Toby and go visit the neighbors.

POPÓVA: Oh! *(Bursts into hysterical tears)*

LUKÁ: Missus! What is it? For God's sake, what's the matter?

POPÓVA: Toby! He used to love Toby so! He'd ride all over the neighborhood on him. What a horseman! Remember how grand he looked in the saddle? Oh, Toby, Toby! Go tell them he gets extra oats today.

LUKÁ: *(Sighs)* Don't worry, I will.

(The doorbell rings. And keeps ringing.)

POPÓVA: *(Exasperated)* Now who's that? Go tell whoever it is I am not at home! To anyone!

LUKÁ: Whatever you say, missus. *(Goes out)*

POPÓVA: *(To the photograph)* You see what real love means, Nicky? My love will last as long as I do, right to my last heartbeat. *(Laughs, almost crying)* And I hope you're ashamed of yourself! You see what a good girl I am, what a faithful wife? I locked myself up here and will be faithful to you till the day I die, while you . . . I hope you're ashamed, you little pig. You were mean to me, you cheated on me, you left me alone for weeks at a time—

(Enter Luká; he's upset.)

LUKÁ: Missus, there's someone wants to see you. Says it can't wait.

POPÓVA: Didn't you tell him that my husband is dead and that I see no one?

LUKÁ: I did, but he doesn't want to listen, says it's very important.

POPÓVA: And I said I see no one!

LUKÁ: That's what I told him, but he's . . . he's kind of a wild man— he started shouting and pushed his way into the house. He's in the dining room right now.

POPÓVA: All right, all right, tell him all right. Really! The nerve of some people!

(Luká goes out.)

Why must people be so difficult? Why can't they just leave me alone? *(Sighs)* Oh, I may have to go join a nunnery after all. *(Thinks)* I wonder what kind of nun I'd make. . . .

(Enter Smírnoff, trailed by Luká.)

SMÍRNOFF: *(To Luká)* You dingbat, stop trying to talk me out of here! Idiot! *(Sees Popóva; suddenly very dignified)* Ah, madam. Let me introduce myself: Grigóry Stepánovich Smírnoff, Field Artillery, retired. I own a place over in the next county. Sorry to disturb you, but this is important—

POPÓVA: *(Doesn't offer him her hand)* What can I do for you?

SMÍRNOFF: I had the pleasure of knowing your late husband, and as it happens, he left me two IOUs—the total comes to twelve hundred rubles. Now, I have a mortgage payment due tomorrow, so I have to ask you, madam, to pay up. And I'm afraid I need the money today.

POPÓVA: Twelve hundred? What did my husband owe you the money for?

SMÍRNOFF: I sold him a couple of loads of oats.

POPÓVA: *(With a sigh, to Luká)* Now don't forget what I told you, Luká. You make sure Toby gets his extra oats.

(Luká goes out.)

(To Smírnoff) If my husband owed you the money, then of course I'll pay it, but you'll have to excuse me—I don't have any cash on me today. My manager will be back from town the day after tomorrow, and he'll see that you get paid. But today, I'm afraid, I cannot help you. It's exactly seven months today that my husband died, and I'm in a sad mood. I'm in no condition to talk about money.

SMÍRNOFF: *(Annoyed)* And I'm in a sad mood too, because if I don't meet my mortgage payment tomorrow, they'll foreclose on my property! I'll lose my shirt!

POPÓVA: You'll have your money the day after tomorrow.

SMÍRNOFF: I need the money today, not the day after tomorrow.

POPÓVA: Excuse me; I've already said I cannot pay you today.

SMÍRNOFF: And I've already said I can't wait till the day after tomorrow.

POPÓVA: What can I do? I don't *have* the money!

SMÍRNOFF: That means you won't pay me?

POPÓVA: It means I *can't* pay you!

SMÍRNOFF: I see. Is that your final word?

POPÓVA: That is my final word.

SMÍRNOFF: You've made up your mind?

POPÓVA: I've made up my mind.

SMÍRNOFF: Thank you very much. I won't forget this. *(Shrugs)* Am I supposed to take all this lying down? On my way here, I met my accountant. "Why are you always so down in the dumps?" he asks me. Well, excuse me, he should know! I'm desperate for money! I got up at dawn yesterday and rode around to everyone I know who owes me money, and not a one of them came across! I ran in more circles than a hunting dog, spent the night in some godforsaken fleabag hotel, and finally I get here, fifty miles from home, expect to get paid, and what do I get? "A sad mood"! What kind of mood do you think that puts *me* in?

POPÓVA: I think I made myself perfectly clear: I'll pay you as soon as my manager gets back from town.

SMÍRNOFF: I came to see you, not your manager! What the hell— excuse my language—do I want with your manager?

POPÓVA: My dear sir, I will not have such language in my house, nor will I tolerate that tone of voice! I refuse to listen to any more of this! *(Storms out)*

SMÍRNOFF: I don't believe this! "It's seven months today my husband died, and I'm in a sad mood. . . ." What's that got to do with me? I have to make a mortgage payment! Fine, your husband's dead, your manager's gone to town, you're in a mood or whatever— what do you expect me to do? Flap my wings and fly away from my creditors? Run around banging my head into a brick wall? I go see Grúzdeff, he's not home. I go see Yarosévich, he hides. I go see Kurítsyn, we get into a fight; I damn near threw him out his own window. I go see Mazútov, he's sick. And now this one has "a sad mood." Not a one of them paid me! What a bunch of dead-beats! And it's all because I'm such a soft touch, I'm a sucker for a hard-luck story! I'm too nice for my own good! Well, it's time to get a little tough. Nobody's going to fool around with me like this, goddamn it! I'm not moving; I'm staying put until she pays up! Oh, boy, am I mad! Look at me—I'm quivering mad! Mad through and through, goddamn it! Mad enough to get nasty! *(Shouts)* Hey, you!

   (Enter Luká.)

LUKÁ: What do you want?

SMÍRNOFF: A glass of water. Or better yet, a beer.

   (Luká goes out.)

What kind of logic is that? Here's a man so desperate for money he's ready to hang himself, and she can't pay him because—excuse me very much—she's "in no condition to talk about money." Talk about petticoat logic! This is why I don't like women and hate talking to them. I'd rather light a campfire on a powder keg than talk to a woman. Makes my skin crawl, they make me so mad! All I have to do is see one of those romantic creatures coming, my leg muscles start cramping up. I want to start shouting for help.

(Enter Luká.)

LUKÁ: *(Brings Smírnoff a glass of water)* The missus is sick; she says she can't see anybody!
SMÍRNOFF: Get out of here!

(Luká goes out.)

She's sick and she can't see anybody! That's fine; she doesn't have to see me. I'll just stay right here until I get my money, that's all. She stays sick for a week, I stay here for a week. She's sick for a year, I stay here for a year. I want my money, lady! Your black dress and your dimples don't impress me. I've seen plenty of dimples before! *(Goes to the window and shouts)* Hey, Semyón, unhitch the horses! We're not leaving just yet! I'm staying right here! Tell them in the stable to give my horses some oats! And watch it, you nitwit—you've got the trace horse tangled again! You just wait till I get ... oh, forget it. *(Moves away from the window)* Jesus, what a mess. Hottest day of the year, nobody wants to pay me, couldn't sleep the whole night, and now I've got to deal with some wacky widow and her moods. It's enough to give a man a headache. I need a drink, that's what I need. *(Yells)* Hey, you!

(Enter Luká.)

LUKÁ: What do you want?
SMÍRNOFF: A shot of vodka!

(Luká goes out; Smírnoff falls into a chair and looks himself over.)

Oof, I'm a mess. Dirt, mud on my boots, I need a shave, my hair needs combing, straw sticking out of my pockets. The lady must have thought I was out to rob her. *(Yawns)* Not too polite, I guess, showing up like this, but what the hell ... I'm not a guest, I'm a bill collector; nobody says I have to dress right. . . .

(Enter Luká; he gives Smírnoff a glass of vodka.)

LUKÁ: You take too many liberties, you know that . . . ?

SMÍRNOFF: *(Angry)* What?

LUKÁ: Oh, nothing. I just . . . Nothing.

SMÍRNOFF: Who do you think you're talking to? Just shut up, will you?

LUKÁ: *(Aside, as he goes out)* How're we going to get rid of him . . . ?

SMÍRNOFF: Oh, I'm mad! I am so mad! Mad enough to blow up the world! Mad enough to get nasty! *(Shouts)* Hey, you!

(Enter Popóva.)

POPÓVA: *(Not looking at him)* My dear sir, I have lived so long in retirement I have grown unused to the human voice. I cannot stand shouting. I must earnestly beg you to respect my solitude.

SMÍRNOFF: Pay me my money and I'll go.

POPÓVA: I have told you in no uncertain terms that I have no money here at the moment and you will have to wait until the day after tomorrow.

SMÍRNOFF: And I also told you in no uncertain terms that I need the money today, not the day after tomorrow. If you don't pay me today, I might as well hang myself by the day after tomorrow.

POPÓVA: But what can I do, since I don't have the money?

SMÍRNOFF: You mean you're not going to pay me? Is that what you mean?

POPÓVA: I can't!

SMÍRNOFF: In that case, I stay right here until I get it. *(Sits down)* You're going to pay me the day after tomorrow? Fine. I'll be sitting right here! *(Jumps up)* Look, don't you believe I have a mortgage payment due tomorrow? You think I'm joking?

POPÓVA: I asked you not to shout! You're not in a stable.

SMÍRNOFF: I didn't ask you about a stable! What I asked you was, Don't you believe I have a mortgage payment due tomorrow?

POPÓVA: You haven't the faintest idea of how to behave in a lady's presence.

SMÍRNOFF: I do so know how to behave in a lady's presence!

POPÓVA: No, you do not! You are ill-mannered and vulgar! No gentleman would speak like this in front of a lady!

SMÍRNOFF: Oh, well, excuse me! Just how would he speak in front of a lady? In French? *(With a nasty lisp)* Madame, je vous prie . . . How charmed I am to know that you reject to pay me my money! Ah, *pardon,* I seem to be upsetting you! Lovely weather we're having! And my, my, don't you look lovely in black! *(Makes a fake bow)*

POPÓVA: You're being very stupid and not funny.

SMÍRNOFF: *(Mocking)* Stupid and not funny! I don't know how to behave in a lady's presence! Woman, I have seen more ladies in my time than you have seen sparrows in yours! I have fought three duels because of ladies, I have walked out on twelve ladies, and nine ladies have walked out on me! So there! Oh, I used to be an idiot, got crushes on them, sweet-talked, cast my pearls before— Well ... Bow, click my heels, fall in love, suffer, sigh in the moonlight, freeze up, melt into puddles—I did it all. I could rattle on for hours about women's rights: I spent half my life hanging around women, but not anymore! No, thank you very much! No more wool over my eyes! I've had it! Dark eyes, red lips, dimples in the cheeks, moonlight, sighs of passion—no, sir, I wouldn't give you two cents for any of it now. Present company excepted, of course, but all women are pretentious, affected, gossipy, hateful, liars to the marrow of their bones, vain, petty, merciless, they can't think straight, and as for this part here *(slaps his forehead)* ... well—excuse my frankness—a sparrow has ten times more brains than any philosopher in skirts. Take a good look at anyone of these romantic creatures: petticoats and hot air, divine transports, the whole works; then take a look at her soul. Pure crocodile. *(Grabs the back of a chair; the chair cracks and breaks)* And the worst part is, this crocodile thinks she has a monopoly on the tender emotion of love! Goddamn it, has any woman ever known how to love anything except her lapdog? She's in love, all she can do is snivel and whine. A man in love, now, he suffers and sacrifices, but a woman, her love shows up how? She swishes her skirt and gets a firm grip on your nose. You're a woman, unfortunately, but at least you know what I mean, what woman's nature is like. Tell me honestly: have you ever seen a woman who was faithful and true? No, you haven't! The only honest and faithful women are old or ugly.

POPÓVA: Excuse me, but would you mind telling me just who you think *is* faithful and true? Men?

SMÍRNOFF: Well, of course, men.

POPÓVA: Men! *(A mean laugh)* Men are faithful and true in love! Well, spread the good news! *(Hotly)* How dare you say that? Men faithful and true? Let me tell you a thing or two! Of all the

men I know or have ever known, my dear departed husband
was the best. I loved him passionately, with all my heart and
soul, the way only a young and sensitive girl can love; I gave him
my youth, my happiness, my life, my money; I lived and
breathed for him, I worshiped him, he was my idol, and ... and
what do you think he did? This best of all possible men betrayed
me in the worst possible way: he cheated on me every chance he
got. After he died I found boxes and boxes of love letters in his
desk! And when he was alive he'd leave me alone for weeks on
end. And he flirted with other women right in front of me, he
deceived me, he spent all my money, he laughed at me when I
objected. And despite everything, I loved him, and I will be
faithful to his memory. Even though he's dead, I am faithful
and unshakable. I have buried myself within these four walls,
where I shall mourn him forever. I shall wear black until the
day I die.

SMÍRNOFF: *(A sneering laugh)* Black? Don't make me laugh! How
dumb do you think I am? I know exactly why you go around in
that Mardi Gras outfit and why you've buried yourself within
these walls! Of course! It's all so romantic, so mysterious!
You're waiting for some shavetail army lieutenant to come riding by, or some sentimental schoolboy with a bad complexion,
and he'll look up at your window and think: Ah! There dwells
the mysterious Tamara, who loved her husband so much she
buried herself within four walls.... I know all about your little
games.

POPÓVA: *(Flares up)* What? How dare you even suggest anything of
the kind!

SMÍRNOFF: You buried yourself alive, but you didn't forget to powder
your nose!

POPÓVA: How dare you!! How dare you speak to me like this!

SMÍRNOFF: Don't yell at me—I'm not your manager. But I'm a man,
not a woman, and I'm used to calling a spade a spade. And please
stop shouting.

POPÓVA: I'm not shouting—you are! Will you please go away and
leave me alone!

SMÍRNOFF: Pay me my money and I'll go!

POPÓVA: I will not give you any money!

SMÍRNOFF: You will too!

POPÓVA: I will not! You won't get one red cent from me! Now please
go away!

SMÍRNOFF: I do not have the pleasure of being either your husband or your fiancé, so please stop making scenes for my benefit. *(Sits down)* I hate that.

POPÓVA: *(Snorting with anger)* You dare sit down?

SMÍRNOFF: Exactly.

POPÓVA: Will you please go!

SMÍRNOFF: Just give me my money! *(Aside)* Oh, am I mad! Am I mad!

POPÓVA: Of all the nerve! I want nothing more to do with you! Please leave!

(Pause.)

You're still here? You haven't left?

SMÍRNOFF: No.

POPÓVA: No?

SMÍRNOFF: No.

POPÓVA: All right! *(Rings)*

(Enter Luká.)

Luká, will you please show this gentleman out?

LUKÁ: *(Goes over to Smírnoff)* Please leave, sir. The lady asked you to. She doesn't want you here.

SMÍRNOFF: *(Leaps to his feet)* And you shut up! Who do you think you're talking to? I'll make a tossed salad out of you!

LUKÁ: *(Clutches his heart)* Oh, my God! Oh, mother of God! *(Falls into an armchair)* I'm dying! I'm dying! I can't breathe!

POPÓVA: Dásha! Where's Dásha? *(Screams)* Dásha! Pelégea! Dásha! *(Rings frantically)*

LUKÁ: They all went off berry picking. There's nobody else in the house! Oh, I'm dying! Water!

POPÓVA: Will you get out of here?

SMÍRNOFF: Can't you be a little more polite?

POPÓVA: *(Makes a fist and stamps her foot)* You peasant! You bear! You vulgar bear! Monster! You . . . *radical*!

SMÍRNOFF: What? What did you call me?

POPÓVA: I said you were a bear!

SMÍRNOFF: *(Moves toward her)* And just who said you could insult me like that?

POPÓVA: You're right, I am insulting you! What about it? You think I'm afraid of you?

SMÍRNOFF: You think, just because you're some kind of romantic heroine, that gives you the right to insult me with impunity? Is that it? Oh, no! This is a matter for the field of honor!

LUKÁ: Oh, my God! Oh, my God! Water!

SMÍRNOFF: Time to choose weapons!

POPÓVA: And just because you've got big fists and a bull neck, you think I'm afraid of you? You . . . you bear!

SMÍRNOFF: To the field of honor! Nobody insults me like that, not even a woman!

POPÓVA: (Trying to shout him down) Bear! Bear! Bear!

SMÍRNOFF: It's about time we got rid of old prejudices about only men needing to defend themselves on the field of honor! If it's equality you want, then it's equality you get! I challenge you to a duel!

POPÓVA: You want to fight a duel! Good! Let's fight!

SMÍRNOFF: Right this minute!

POPÓVA: Right this minute! My husband had a set of pistols; wait here, I'll go get them. (Starts out and immediately returns) God-damn you! You have no idea what a pleasure it will be for me to put a bullet through your thick head! (Goes out)

SMÍRNOFF: I'll shoot her like a sitting duck! I'm not a schoolboy any-more, I'm no sentimental puppy—I don't care if she is the weaker sex!

LUKÁ: Oh, please, sir! (Falls to his knees) Please don't do this, please just leave, please. I'm an old man, my heart won't stand all the excitement! Please don't shoot her!

SMÍRNOFF: (Pays no attention to him) I'll shoot her—that's real equal-ity; that'll emancipate her! Equality of the sexes at last! But what a woman! (Imitates her) "Goddamn you! You have no idea what a pleasure it will be to put a bullet through your thick head!" Yes, what a woman! She got all flushed; her eyes were flashing fire; she accepted my challenge without even thinking! By God, that's the first time this has ever happened to me!

LUKÁ: Oh, please, sir, please go! Just go away!

SMÍRNOFF: Now, that's a woman I understand! That's a real woman! She's not one of your sissies, nothing wishy-washy about her; she's all flint and firepower! I'm almost sorry to have to kill her!

LUKÁ: (Cries) Please, sir, please, just go! Please!

SMÍRNOFF: I definitely like this woman! Definitely! So she has dim-ples—I still like her. I'm almost ready to tell her to forget about the money. And I'm not mad anymore. . . . What an astonishing woman!

(Enter Popóva; she carries a pair of dueling pistols.)

POPÓVA: Here're the pistols. But before we have our duel, will you please show me how to use the damn things? I've never even touched one before.

LUKÁ: Oh, God have mercy on us all! I'm going to get the gardener and the coachman.... Why did this have to happen to us ...? *(Goes out)*

SMÍRNOFF: *(Looks over the pistols with a professional eye)* You see, there are several different makes of weapon. You've got your Mortimer, now—that's a special dueling pistol, percussion action. But what you have here are Smith and Wesson revolvers, triple action, with an extractor and central sights. Beautiful pieces! Must have cost at least ninety rubles the pair. Now look, you hold the pistol like this.... *(Aside)* What amazing eyes she's got! What a little spitfire!

POPÓVA: Like this?

SMÍRNOFF: That's it, that's the way. Next you cock the piece, like this ... and you take aim.... Move your head back a little. Stretch out your arm ... that's the way. Then you press your finger on this little thing here, and that's all there is to it. Main thing is, keep your cool and take slow, careful aim. Try not to let your hand shake.

POPÓVA: Right.... We shouldn't shoot indoors—let's go outside.

SMÍRNOFF: All right, let's go outside. Only I warn you, I intend to shoot into the air.

POPÓVA: Oh, that's the last straw! Why?

SMÍRNOFF: Because ... because ... It's none of your business why!

POPÓVA: Are you getting scared? Is that it? Aha, that's it! Oh no, you won't get out of this so easily! Come on, we're going outside! I won't rest until I put a bullet through that head of yours—that head I hate so! What's the matter, are you a coward?

SMÍRNOFF: That's it, I'm a coward.

POPÓVA: You're lying! Why don't you want to fight?

SMÍRNOFF: Because ... because ... because I like you.

POPÓVA: *(Sarcastic laugh)* He likes me! He dares to tell me he likes me! *(Points to the door)* Just go.

SMÍRNOFF: *(Puts down the pistol in silence, takes his hat, and starts out; at the door, he stops and turns. They look at each other in silence for a moment; then he goes hesitantly toward Popóva)* Listen ... are you still mad? I was crazy myself until just a minute ago, but you know ... how can I put it? Well, the fact is, I ... you see, the fact is, nothing like this ever happened to me before.... *(Shouts)* Well, goddamn it, is it my fault I like you? *(Grabs a chair behind his back; the chair cracks and breaks)* Why do you have such fragile furniture! I like you! You understand? I ... I think I'm in love with you!

POPÓVA: Get away from me! I hate you!

SMÍRNOFF: God, what a woman! I've never seen anything like her in my entire life! I'm done for! I'm caught in her mousetrap!

POPÓVA: Get away from me, or I'll shoot!

SMÍRNOFF: Go ahead, shoot! You don't know how happy that will make me, to die with your beautiful eyes upon me, die from a gun in your silky little hand. . . . Oh, I'm out of my mind! Look, you'd better think this over fast and decide right away. Once I leave here, we'll never see each other again. Make up your mind. I own a lot of land, I'm from a good family, I've got an income of ten thousand a year. . . . I can put a bullet through a coin in the air at twenty paces. . . . I've got the best horses you'll ever see. . . . Will you marry me?

POPÓVA: *(Angry, she waves the pistol)* Marry you? I intend to shoot you! On the field of honor!

SMÍRNOFF: I'm out of my mind! I don't understand what's happening. . . .

POPÓVA: On the field of honor!

SMÍRNOFF: I'm out of my mind! I'm in love! I'm behaving like an idiot schoolboy! *(Grabs her hand; she shrieks with pain)* I love you! *(Falls to his knees)* I love you, the way I've never loved anyone before! I walked out on twelve women, nine walked out on me, but I never loved one of them the way I do you! My mind has turned to jelly, my joints have turned to sugar, I'm on my knees like a dope, and I'm asking for your hand. . . . Oh, the shame, the shame! I haven't been in love for six years, I swore I never would again, and all of a sudden I'm head over heels! I'm asking you to marry me! Yes or no? Will you? Yes or no? No? Fine! *(Gets up and heads quickly toward the door)*

POPÓVA: Wait a minute . . .

SMÍRNOFF: *(Stops)* Well?

POPÓVA: Nothing, just go! No, I mean, wait. . . . No, go away! Go away! I hate you! I mean, no, don't go! Oh, you make me so mad! *(Throws the pistol on the floor)* My finger's all swollen up from that damn thing! *(Starts tearing her handkerchief)* Well, what are you waiting for? Just get out of here!

SMÍRNOFF: All right, then. Goodbye.

POPÓVA: Yes, yes, just go! *(Screams)* Where are you going? Wait a minute. . . . Oh, come on back. Oh, I'm so mad! Stay away from me! Stay away from me!

SMÍRNOFF: *(Crosses to her) You're* mad? *I'm* mad! I fell in love like a schoolboy, got down on my knees, I even got goose bumps. . . . *(Roughly)* I love you! That's all I needed, to fall in love with you! Tomorrow I've got to pay the mortgage, start cutting hay, and now you— *(Grabs her around the waist)* I'll never forgive myself for this—

POPÓVA: Get away from me! Get your hands off me! I . . . I hate you! I want to fight the d-d-duel!

(A long kiss. Enter Luká with a shovel, the gardener with a rake, the coachman with a pitchfork, some farmworkers with sticks.)

LUKÁ: *(Sees the couple kissing)* Oh, my God. . . .

(Pause.)

POPÓVA: *(Shyly)* Luká, go out to the stable and tell them Toby doesn't get extra oats anymore.

CURTAIN.

THE PROPOSAL

A COMIC SKETCH IN ONE ACT

1888

CHARACTERS

Stepán Stepánich Chubukóv, a landowner

Natália Stepánovna (Natásha), his daughter

Iván Vassílievich Lómov, their neighbor

The action takes place in Chubukóv's farmhouse.

A room in Chubukóv's farmhouse. Enter Lómov, wearing a tail-coat and white gloves. Chubukóv goes to meet him.

CHUBUKÓV: By God, if it isn't my old friend Iván Vassílievich! Glad to see you, boy, glad to see you. *(Shakes his hand)* This is certainly a surprise, and that's a fact. How are you doing?

LÓMOV: Oh, thanks a lot. And how are you? Doing, I mean?

CHUBUKÓV: We get by, my boy, we get by. Glad to know you think of us occasionally and all the rest of it. Have a seat, boy, be my guest, glad you're here, and that's a fact. Don't want to forget your old friends and neighbors, you know. But why so formal, boy? What's the occasion? You're all dressed up and everything—you on your way to a party, or what?

LÓMOV: No, I only came to see you, Stepán Stepánich.

CHUBUKÓV: But why the fancy clothes, boy? You look like you're still celebrating New Year's Eve!

LÓMOV: Well, I'll tell you. *(Takes his arm)* You see, Stepán Stepánich, I hope I'm not disturbing you, but I came to ask you a little favor. This isn't the first time I've, uh, had occasion, as they say, to ask you for help, and I want you to know that I really admire you when I do it. . . . Er, what I mean is . . . Look, you have to excuse me, Stepán Stepánich, this is making me very nervous. I'll just take a little drink of water, if it's all right with you. *(Takes a drink of water)*

CHUBUKÓV: *(Aside)* He wants me to lend him some money. I won't. *(To him)* So! What exactly are you here for, hm? A big strong boy like you.

LÓMOV: You see, I really have the greatest respect for you, Stepán Respéctovich—excuse me, I mean Stepán Excúsemevich. What I mean is—I'm really nervous, as you can plainly see. . . . Well, what it all comes down to is this: you're the only person who can give me what I want and I know I don't deserve it of course that goes without saying and I haven't any real right to it either—

CHUBUKÓV: Now, my boy, you don't have to beat about the bush with me. Speak right up. What do you want?

LÓMOV: All right, I will. I will. Well, what I came for is, I came to ask for the hand of your daughter Natásha.

CHUBUKÓV: *(Overjoyed)* Oh, mama! Iván Vassílievich, say it again! I don't think I caught that last part!

LÓMOV: I came to ask—

CHUBUKÓV: Lover boy! Buddy boy! I can't tell you how happy I am and everything. And that's a fact. And all the rest of it. *(Gives him a bear hug)* I've always hoped this would happen. It's a longtime dream come true. *(Sheds a tear)* I have always loved you, boy, just like you were my own son, and you know it. God bless you both and all the rest of it. This is a dream come true. But why am I standing here like a big dummy? Happiness has got my tongue, that's what's happened, happiness has got my tongue. Oh, from the bottom of my heart ... You wait right here, I'll go get Natásha and whatever.

LÓMOV: *(Intense concern)* What do you think, Stepán Stepánich? Do you think she'll say yes?

CHUBUKÓV: Big, good-looking fellow like you—how could she help herself? Of course she'll say yes, and that's a fact. She's like a cat in heat. And all the rest of it. Don't go away, I'll be right back. *(Exit)*

LÓMOV: It must be cold in here. I'm starting to shiver, just like I was going to take an exam. The main thing is, you have to make up your mind. You just keep thinking about it, you argue back and forth and talk a lot and wait for the ideal woman or for true love, you'll never get married. Brr ... it's cold in here. Natásha is a very good housekeeper, she's kind of good-looking, she's been to school ... What more do I need? I'm starting to get that hum in my ears again; it must be my nerves. *(Drinks some water)* And I can't just *not* get married. First of all, I'm already thirty-five, and that's about what they call the turning point. Second of all, I have to start leading a regular, normal life. There's something wrong with my heart—I've got a *murmur*; I'm always nervous as a tick, and the least little thing can drive me crazy. Like right now, for instance. My lips are starting to shudder, and this little whatsit keeps twitching in my right eyelid. But the worst thing about me is sleep. I mean, I don't. I go to bed, and as soon as I start falling asleep, all of a sudden something in my left side goes *drrrk!* and it pounds right up into my shoulder and my head. . . . I jump out of bed like crazy and walk around for a while and then I lie down again and as soon as I start falling asleep all of a sudden something in my left side goes *drrrk!* And that happens twenty times a night—

(Enter Natásha.)

NATÁSHA: Oh, it's you. It's just you, and Papa said go take a look in the other room, somebody wants to sell you something. Oh, well. How are you anyway?

LÓMOV: How do you do, Natásha?

NATÁSHA: You'll have to excuse me, I'm still in my apron. We were shelling peas. How come you haven't been by to see us for so long? Sit down. . . .

(They both sit.)

You feel like something to eat?

LÓMOV: No, thanks. I ate already.

NATÁSHA: You smoke? Go ahead if you want to; here's some matches. Beautiful day today, isn't it? And yesterday it was raining so hard the men in the hayfields couldn't do a thing. How many stacks you people got cut so far? You know what happened to me? I got so carried away I had them cut the whole meadow, and now I'm sorry I did—the hay's going to rot. Oh, my! Look at you! What've you got on those fancy clothes for? Well, if you aren't something! You going to a party, or what? You know, you're looking kind of cute these days. . . . Anyway, what are you all dressed up for?

LÓMOV: *(A bit nervous)* Well, you see, Natásha . . . well, the fact is I decided to come ask you to . . . to listen to what I have to say. Of course, you'll probably be sort of surprised and maybe get mad, but I . . . *(Aside)* It's awful cold in here.

NATÁSHA: So . . . so what did you come for, huh? *(Pause)* Huh?

LÓMOV: I'll try to make this brief. Now, Natásha, you know, we've known each other for a long time, ever since we were children, and I've had the pleasure of knowing your entire family. My poor dead aunt and her husband—and as you know, I inherited my land from them—they always had the greatest respect for your father and your poor dead mother. The Lómovs and the Chubukóvs have always been on very friendly terms, almost like we were related. And besides—well, you already know this—and besides, your land and mine are right next door to each other. Take my Meadowland, for instance. It lies right alongside of your birch grove.

NATÁSHA: Excuse me. I don't mean to interrupt you, but I think you said "my Meadowland." Are you saying that Meadowland belongs to you?

LÓMOV: Well, yes; as a matter of fact, I am.

NATÁSHA: Well, I never! Meadowland belongs to us, not you!

LÓMOV: No, Natásha. Meadowland is mine.

NATÁSHA: Well, that's news to me. Since when is it yours?

LÓMOV: What do you mean, since when? I'm talking about the little pasture they call Meadowland, the one that makes a wedge between your birch grove and Burnt Swamp.

NATÁSHA: Yes, I know the one you mean. But it's ours.

LÓMOV: Natásha, I think you're making a mistake. That field belongs to me.

NATÁSHA: Iván Vassílich, do you realize what you're saying? And just how long has it belonged to you?

LÓMOV: What do you mean, how long? As far as I know, it's always been mine.

NATÁSHA: Now wait just a minute. Excuse me, but—

LÓMOV: It's all very clearly marked on the deeds, Natásha. Now, it's true there was some argument about it back a ways, but nowadays everybody knows it belongs to me. So there's no use arguing about it. You see, what happened was, my aunt's grandmother let your grandfather's tenants have that field free of charge for an indefinite time in exchange for their making bricks for her. So your grandfather's people used that land for free for about forty years and they started to think it was theirs, but then, when it turned out what the real situation was—

NATÁSHA: My grandfather and my great-grandfather both always said that their land went as far as Burnt Swamp, which means Meadowland belongs to us. So what's the point of arguing about it? I think you're just being rude.

LÓMOV: I can show you the papers, Natálya Stepánovna!

NATÁSHA: Oh, you're just teasing! You're trying to pull my leg! This is all a big joke, isn't it? We've owned that land for going on three hundred years, and all of a sudden you say it doesn't belong to us. Excuse me, Iván Vassílich, excuse me, but I can't believe you said that. And believe me, I don't care one bit about that old meadow: it's only twelve acres, it's not worth three hundred rubles, even, but that's not the point. It's the injustice of it that hurts. And I don't care what anybody says—injustice is something I just can't put up with.

LÓMOV: But you didn't listen to what I was saying! Please! Your grandfather's tenants, as I was trying very politely to point out to you, made bricks for my aunt's grandmother. Now, my aunt's grandmother just wanted to make things easier and—

NATÁSHA: Grandmother, grandfather, father—what difference does it all make? The field belongs to us, and that's that.

LÓMOV: That field belongs to me!

NATÁSHA: That field belongs to us! You can go on about your grandmother until you're blue in the face, you can wear fifteen fancy coats—it still belongs to us! It's ours, ours, ours! I don't want anything that belongs to you, but I do want to keep what's my own, thank you very much!

LÓMOV: Natálya Stepánovna, I don't care about that field either; I don't need that field; I'm talking about the principle of the thing. If you want the field, you can have it. I'll give it to you.

NATÁSHA: If there's any giving to be done, I'll do it! That field belongs to me! Iván Vassílich, I have never gone through anything this crazy in all my life! Up till now I've always thought of you as a good neighbor, a real friend—last year we even lent you our threshing machine, which meant that we were threshing *our* wheat in November—and now all of a sudden you start treating us like Gypsies. *You'll* give *me* my own field? Excuse me, but that is a pretty unneighborly thing to do. In fact, in my opinion, it's downright insulting!

LÓMOV: So in your opinion I'm some kind of claim jumper, you mean? Look, lady, I have never tried to take anybody else's land, and I'm not going to let anybody try to tell me I did, not even you. *(Runs to the table and takes a drink of water)* Meadowland is mine!

NATÁSHA: You lie! It's ours!

LÓMOV: It's mine!

NATÁSHA: You lie! I'll show you! I'll send my mowers out there today!

LÓMOV: You'll what?

NATÁSHA: I said I'll have my mowers out there today, and they'll hay that field flat!

LÓMOV: You do, and I'll break their necks!

NATÁSHA: You wouldn't dare!

LÓMOV: *(Clutches his chest)* Meadowland is mine! You understand? Mine!

NATÁSHA: Please don't shout. You can scream and carry on all you want in your own house, but as long as you're in mine, try to behave like a gentleman.

LÓMOV: I tell you, if I didn't have these murmurs, these awful pains, these veins throbbing in my temples, I wouldn't be talking like this. *(Shouts)* Meadowland is mine!

NATÁSHA: Ours!

LÓMOV: Mine!

NATÁSHA: Ours!

LÓMOV: Mine!

(Enter Chubukóv.)

CHUBUKÓV: What's going on? What are you both yelling for?

NATÁSHA: Papa, will you please explain to this gentleman just who owns Meadowland, him or us?

CHUBUKÓV: Lover boy, Meadowland belongs to us.

LÓMOV: I beg your pardon, Stepán Stepánich, how can it belong to you? Think what you're saying! My aunt's grandmother let your grandfather's people have that land to use free of charge, temporarily, and they used that land for forty years and started thinking it was theirs, but it turned out what the problem was—

CHUBUKÓV: Allow me, sweetheart. You're forgetting that the reason those people didn't pay your granny and all the rest of it was because there was *already* a real problem about just who *did* own the meadow. And everything. But nowadays every dog in the village knows it belongs to us, and that's a fact. I don't think you've ever seen the survey map—

LÓMOV: Look, I can prove to you that Meadowland belongs to me!

CHUBUKÓV: No you can't, lover boy.

LÓMOV: I can too!

CHUBUKÓV: Oh, for crying out loud! What are you shouting for? You can't prove anything by shouting, and that's a fact! Look, I am not interested in taking any of your land, and neither am I interested in giving away any of my own. Why should I? And if it comes down to it, lover boy, if you want to make a case out of this, or anything like that, I'd just as soon give it to the peasants as give it to you. So there!

LÓMOV: You're not making any sense. What gives you the right to give away someone else's land?

CHUBUKÓV: I'll be the judge of whether I have the right or not! The fact is, boy, I am not used to being talked to in that tone of voice and all the rest of it. I am twice your age, boy, and I'll ask you to talk to me without getting so excited and whatever.

LÓMOV: No! You think I'm just stupid, and you're making fun of me! You stand there and tell me my own land belongs to you, and then you expect me to be calm about it and talk as if nothing had happened! That's not the way good neighbors behave, Stepán

Stepánich! You are not a neighbor, you are a u*surper*!

CHUBUKÓV: I'm a *what*? What did you call me?

NATÁSHA: Papa, you send our mowers out to Meadowland right this very minute!

CHUBUKÓV: You, boy! What did you just call me?

NATÁSHA: Meadowland belongs to us, and I'll never give it up—never, never, never!

LÓMOV: We'll see about that! I'll take you to court, and then we'll see who it belongs to!

CHUBUKÓV: To court! Well, you just go right ahead, boy, you take us to court! I dare you! Oh, now I get it, you were just waiting for a chance to take us to court and all the rest of it! And whatever! It's inbred, isn't it? Your whole family was like that—they couldn't wait to start suing. They were always in court! And that's a fact!

LÓMOV: You leave my family out of this! The Lómovs were all decent, law-abiding citizens, every one of them, not like some people I could name, who were arrested for embezzlement—your uncle, for instance!

CHUBUKÓV: Every single one of the Lómovs was crazy! All of them!

NATÁSHA: All of them! Every single one!

CHUBUKÓV: Your uncle was a falling-down drunk, and that's a fact! And your aunt, the youngest one, she used to run around with an architect! An architect! And that's a fact!

LÓMOV: And your mother was a hunchback! *(Clutches his chest)* Oh, my God, I've got a pain in my side ... my head's beginning to pound! Oh, my God, give me some water!

CHUBUKÓV: And your father was a gambler and a glutton!

NATÁSHA: And your aunt was a tattletale; she was the worst gossip in town!

LÓMOV: My left leg is paralyzed. ... And you're a sneak! Oh, my heart! And everybody knows that during the elections, you people ... I've got spots in front of my eyes. ... Where's my hat?

NATÁSHA: You're low! And lousy! And cheap!

CHUBUKÓV: You are a lowdown two-faced snake in the grass, and that's a fact! An absolute fact!

LÓMOV: Here's my hat! My heart! How do I get out of here ... where's the door? I think I'm dying ... I can't move my leg. *(Heads for the door)*

CHUBUKÓV: *(Following him)* And don't you ever set foot in this house again!

NATÁSHA: And you just take us to court! Go ahead, and see what happens!

(Exit Lómov, staggering.)

CHUBUKÓV: *(Walks up and down in agitation)* He can go to hell!

NATÁSHA: What a creep! See if I ever trust a neighbor again after this!

CHUBUKÓV: Crook!

NATÁSHA: Creep! He takes over somebody else's land and then has the nerve to threaten them!

CHUBUKÓV: And would you believe that wig-worm, that chicken-brain, had the nerve to come here and propose? Hah? He proposed!

NATÁSHA: He proposed what?

CHUBUKÓV: What? He came here to propose to you!

NATÁSHA: To propose? To me? Why didn't you tell me that before!

CHUBUKÓV: That's why he was all dressed up in that stupid coat! What a silly sausage!

NATÁSHA: Me? He came to propose to me? Oh, my God, my God! *(Collapses into a chair and wails)* Oh, make him come back! Make him come back! Oh, please, make him come back! *(She has hysterics)*

CHUBUKÓV: What's the matter? What's the matter with you? *(Smacks his head)* Oh, my God, what have I done! I ought to shoot myself! I ought to be hanged! I ought to be tortured to death!

NATÁSHA: I think I'm going to die! Make him come back!

CHUBUKÓV: All right! Just stop screaming! Please! *(Runs out)*

NATÁSHA: *(Alone, wailing)* What have we done? Oh, make him come back! Make him come back!

CHUBUKÓV: *(Reenters)* He's coming, he's coming back and everything, goddamn it! You talk to him yourself this time; I can't. . . . And that's a fact!

NATÁSHA: *(Wailing)* Make him come back!

CHUBUKÓV: I just told you, he *is* coming back. Oh, God almighty, what an ungrateful assignment, being the father of a grown-up girl! I'll slit my throat, I swear I'll slit my throat! We yell at the man, we insult him, we chase him away . . . and it's all your fault. It's your fault!

NATÁSHA: No, it's your fault!

CHUBUKÓV: All right, I'm sorry, it's my fault. Or whatever.

(Lómov appears in the doorway.)

This time you do the talking yourself! *(Exit)*

LÓMOV: *(Entering, exhausted)* I'm having a heart murmur, it's awful, my leg is paralyzed . . . my left side is going *drrrk!*

NATÁSHA: You'll have to excuse us, Iván Vassílich—we got a little bit carried away. . . . Anyway, I just remembered, Meadowland belongs to you after all.

LÓMOV: There's something wrong with my heart—it's beating too loud. . . . Meadowland is mine? These little whatsits are twitching in both my eyelids. . . .

NATÁSHA: It's yours—Meadowland is all yours. Here, sit down.

(They both sit.)

We made a mistake.

LÓMOV: It was always just the principle of the thing. I don't care about the land, but I do care about the principle of the thing.

NATÁSHA: I know, the principle of the thing. . . . Why don't we talk about something else?

LÓMOV: And besides, I really can prove it. My aunt's grandmother let your grandfather's tenants have that field—

NATÁSHA: That's enough! I think we should change the subject. *(Aside)* I don't know where to start. . . . *(To Lómov)* How's the hunting? Are you going hunting anytime soon?

LÓMOV: Oh, yes, geese and grouse hunting, Natásha, geese and grouse. I was thinking of going after the harvest is in. Oh, by the way, did I tell you? The worst thing happened to me! You know my old hound Guesser? Well, he went lame on me.

NATÁSHA: Oh, that's terrible! What happened?

LÓMOV: I don't know; he must have dislocated his hip, or maybe he got into a fight with some other dogs and got bit. *(Sighs)* And he was the best hound dog, not to mention how much he cost. I got him from Mirónov, and I paid a hundred and twenty-five for him.

NATÁSHA: *(Beat)* Iván Vassílich, you paid too much.

LÓMOV: *(Beat)* I thought I got him pretty cheap. He's a real good dog.

NATÁSHA: Papa paid only eighty-five for his hound dog Messer, and Messer is a lot better than your old Guesser!

LÓMOV: Messer is better than Guesser? What do you mean? *(Laughs)* Messer is better than Guesser!

NATÁSHA: Of course he's better! I mean, he's not full grown yet, he's still a pup, but when it comes to a bark and a bite, nobody has a better dog.

LÓMOV: Excuse me, Natásha, but I think you're forgetting something. He's got an underslung jaw, and a dog with an underslung jaw can never be a good retriever.

NATÁSHA: An underslung jaw? That's the first I ever heard of it!

LÓMOV: I'm telling you, his lower jaw is shorter than his upper.

NATÁSHA: What did you do, measure it?

LÓMOV: Of course I measured it! I grant you he's not so bad on point, but you tell him to go fetch, and he can barely—

NATÁSHA: In the first place, our Messer is a purebred from a very good line—he's the son of Pusher and Pisser, so that limp-foot mutt of yours couldn't touch him for breeding. Besides which, your dog is old and ratty and full of fleas—

LÓMOV: He may be old, but I wouldn't take five of your Messers for him. How can you even say that? Guesser is a real hound, and that Messer is a joke, he's not even worth worrying about. Every old fart in the county's got a dog just like your Messer—there's a mess of them everywhere you look! You paid twenty rubles, you paid too much!

NATÁSHA: Iván Vassílich, for some reason you are being perverse on purpose. First you think Meadowland belongs to you, now you think Guesser is better than Messer. I don't think much of a man who doesn't say what he knows to be a fact. You know perfectly well that Messer is a hundred times better than that . . . that dumb Guesser of yours. So why do you keep saying the opposite?

LÓMOV: You must think I'm either blind or stupid! Can't you understand that your Messer has an underslung jaw?

NATÁSHA: It's not true!

LÓMOV: He has an underslung jaw!

NATÁSHA: (Shouting) It's not true!

LÓMOV: What are you shouting for?

NATÁSHA: What are you lying for? I can't stand any more of this. You ought to be getting ready to put your old Guesser out of his misery, and here you are comparing him to our Messer!

LÓMOV: You'll have to excuse me, I can't go on with this conversation. I'm having a heart murmur.

NATÁSHA: This just goes to prove what I've always known: the hunters who talk the most are the ones who know the least.

LÓMOV: Will you please do me a favor and just shut up. . . . My heart is starting to pound. . . . (Shouts) Shut up!

NATÁSHA: I will not shut up until you admit that Messer is a hundred times better than Guesser!

LÓMOV: He's a hundred times worse! I hope he croaks, your
Messer. . . . My head . . . my eyes . . . my shoulders . . .

NATÁSHA: And your dumb old Guesser doesn't need to croak—he's
dead already!

LÓMOV: Shut up! *(Starts to cry)* I'm having a heart attack!

NATÁSHA: I will not shut up!

(Enter Chubukóv.)

CHUBUKÓV: Now what's the matter?

NATÁSHA: Papa, will you please tell us frankly, on your honor, who's
a better dog: Guesser or Messer?

LÓMOV: Stepán Stepánich, I just want to know one thing: does your
Messer have an underslung jaw or doesn't he? Yes or no?

CHUBUKÓV: Well? So what if he does? What difference does it
make? Anyway, there isn't a better dog in the whole county, and
that's a fact.

LÓMOV: But don't you think my Guesser is better? On your honor!

CHUBUKÓV: Now, loverboy, don't get all upset; just wait a minute.
Please. Your Guesser has his good points and whatever. He's a
thoroughbred, got a good stance, nice round hindquarters, all the
rest of it. But that dog, if you really want to know, boy, has got
two vital defects: he's old and he's got a short bite.

LÓMOV: You'll have to excuse me, I'm having another heart murmur.
Let's just look at the facts, shall we? All I'd like you to do is just
think back to that time at the field trials when my Guesser kept
up with the count's dog Fresser. They were going ear to ear, and
your Messer was a whole half mile behind.

CHUBUKÓV: He was behind because one of the count's men whopped
him with his whip!

LÓMOV: That's not the point! All the other dogs were after the fox,
and your Messer was chasing a sheep!

CHUBUKÓV: That's not true! Now listen, boy, I have a very quick
temper, as you very well know, and that's a fact, so I think we
should keep this discussion very short. He whopped him because
none of the rest of you can stand watching other people's dogs
perform! You're all rotten with envy! Even you, buddy boy, even
you! The fact is, all somebody has to do is point out that somebody's dog is better than your Guesser, and right away you start
in with this and that and all the rest of it. I happen to remember
exactly what happened!

LÓMOV: And I remember too!

CHUBUKÓV: *(Mimics him)* "And I remember too!" What do you remember?

LÓMOV: My heart murmur . . . My leg is paralyzed . . . I can't move . . .

NATÁSHA: *(Mimics him)* "My heart murmur!" What kind of hunter are you? You'd do better in the kitchen catching cockroaches instead of out hunting foxes! A heart murmur!

CHUBUKÓV: She's right—what kind of hunter are you? You and your heart murmur should stay home instead of galloping cross-country, and that's a fact. You say you like to hunt; all you really want to do is ride around arguing and interfering with other people's dogs and whatever. You are *not*, and that's a fact, a hunter.

LÓMOV: And what makes you think you're a hunter? The only reason you go hunting is so you can get in good with the count! My heart! You're a sneak!

CHUBUKÓV: I'm a what? A sneak! *(Shouts)* Shut up!

LÓMOV: A sneak!

CHUBUKÓV: You young whippersnapper! You puppy!

LÓMOV: You rat! You rickety old rat!

CHUBUKÓV: You shut up, or I'll give you a tailful of buckshot! You snoop!

LÓMOV: Everybody knows your poor dead wife—oh, my heart!—used to beat you. My legs . . . my head . . . I see spots . . . I'm going to faint, I'm going to faint!

CHUBUKÓV: And everybody knows your housekeeper has you tied to her apron strings!

LÓMOV: Wait wait wait . . . here it comes! A heart attack! My shoulder just came undone—where's my shoulder? I'm going to die! *(Collapses into a chair)* Get a doctor! *(Faints)*

CHUBUKÓV: Whippersnapper! Milk sucker! Snoop! You make me sick! *(Drinks some water)* Sick!

NATÁSHA: What kind of a hunter are you? You can't even ride a horse! *(To Chubukóv)* Papa! What's the matter with him? Papa! Look at him, Papa! *(Screeching)* Iván Vassílich! He's dead!

CHUBUKÓV: I'm sick! I can't breathe . . . give me some air!

NATÁSHA: He's dead! *(Shakes Lómov's shoulders)* Iván Vassílich! Iván Vassílich! What have we done? He's dead! *(Collapses into the other chair)* Get a doctor! Get a doctor! *(She has hysterics)*

CHUBUKÓV: Oh, now what? What's the matter with you?

NATÁSHA: *(Wailing)* He's dead! He's dead!

CHUBUKÓV: Who's dead? *(Looks at Lómov)* Oh, my God, he *is* dead!

Oh, my God! Get some water! Get a doctor! *(Puts glass to Lómov's mouth)* Here, drink this.... He's not drinking it.... That means he's really dead ... and everything! Oh, what a mess! I'll kill myself! I'll kill myself! Why did I wait so long to kill myself? What am I waiting for right now? Give me a knife! Lend me a gun! *(Lómov stirs)* I think he's going to live! Here, drink some water. That's the way.

LÓMOV: Spots ... everything is all spots ... it's all cloudy.... Where am I?

CHUBUKÓV: Just get married as soon as you can and then get out of here! She says yes! *(Joins Lómov's and Natásha's hands)* She says yes and all the rest of it. I give you both my blessing and whatever. Only please just leave me in peace!

LÓMOV: Huh? Wha'? *(Starts to get up)* Who?

CHUBUKÓV: She says yes! All right? Go ahead and kiss her.... And then get the hell out of here!

NATÁSHA: *(Moaning)* He's alive.... Yes, yes, I say yes....

CHUBUKÓV: Go ahead, give him a kiss.

LÓMOV: Huh? Who?

   (Natásha kisses him.)

Oh, that's very nice.... Excuse me, but what's happening? Oh, yes, I remember now.... My heart ... those spots ... I'm so happy, Natásha! *(Kisses her hand)* My leg is still paralyzed....

NATÁSHA: I'm ... I'm very happy too.

CHUBUKÓV: And I'm getting a weight off my shoulders. Oof!

NATÁSHA: But all the same—you can admit it now, can't you?— Messer is better than Guesser.

LÓMOV: He's worse!

NATÁSHA: He's better!

CHUBUKÓV: And they lived happily ever after! Bring on the champagne!

LÓMOV: He's worse!

NATÁSHA: Better! Better! Better!

CHUBUKÓV: *(Tries to make himself heard)* Champagne! Bring on the champagne!

   CURTAIN.

Ivanov

A DRAMA IN FOUR ACTS

1889

CHARACTERS

Nikolái Ivánov, a member of the County Council

Anna, his wife, born Sarah Abramson

Count Matvéy Shabélsky, his maternal uncle

Pável Lébedev, president of the County Council

Zinaída, his wife

Sásha, their daughter, in her twenties

Yevgény Lvov, a young local doctor

Martha Babákina, a young widow, the daughter of a well-to-do
businessman, who has her own property

Dimítry Kósykh, an employee of the tax office

Mísha Bórkin, a distant cousin of Ivánov, who manages his estate

Avdótya Nazárovna, an old woman with no known occupation

Yégorushka, a poor relation of the Lébedevs

First Guest, a young man

Second Guest, a middle-aged man

Third Guest, an older man

Pyótr, Ivánov's valet (nonspeaking role)

Gavríla, Lébedev's butler (nonspeaking role)

Guests and servants

The action takes place in a rural district in central Russia.

ACT ONE

The garden of Ivánov's country house. Left, the front of the house and the veranda. One of the windows is open. In front of the terrace is a broad semicircular space from which tree-lined walks lead left and right. Right, garden benches and small tables. On one of the tables, a lamp is burning. Evening; it is growing dark. As the curtain rises, we hear music from the house, a duet for cello and piano. Ivánov sits by the table and reads. Bórkin appears at the end of one of the tree-lined walks, wearing heavy boots and carrying a rifle; he's been drinking. When he sees Ivánov, he sneaks up close to him and points the rifle in his face.

IVÁNOV: *(Sees Bórkin, gives a start, and jumps to his feet)* Mísha, for God's sake! You scared the hell out of me! I'm upset as it is, and you come around playing your stupid tricks! *(Sits)* All right, I'm scared. Does that make you happy?

BÓRKIN: *(Laughs)* OK, OK, I'm sorry. *(Sits down next to him)* I won't do it anymore, I promise. *(Takes off his cap)* It's hot. You may not believe this, but I've just done ten miles in three hours. Wore myself out. Feel how my heart is beating. . . .

IVÁNOV: *(Reads his book)* Later.

BÓRKIN: No, feel it now. *(Takes Ivánov's hand and places it on his chest)* Hear it? Tum-tum-tum-tum-tum-tum. That means I have a heart condition. I could die any minute now. So, what do you think . . . will you be sorry if I die?

IVÁNOV: I'm trying to read. Can we talk about it later?

BÓRKIN: No, I'm serious. Will you be sorry if I die? Huh, Nikolái? Will you? Will you be sorry if I die?

IVÁNOV: Stop bothering me!

BÓRKIN: Just tell me. Will you be sorry?

IVÁNOV: I'm already sorry—sorry you're drunk! It's not very attractive, Mísha.

BÓRKIN: *(Laughs)* Am I drunk? How *surprising* . . . Actually, there's nothing surprising about it. I ran into the assistant prosecutor in town, and we tossed off about eight vodkas. But I have to admit, drinking is bad for you. Huh, what do you think? It's bad for you, isn't it? Isn't it?

IVÁNOV: I can't take any more of this. Mísha, you're really being obnoxious!

BÓRKIN: OK, OK, I'm sorry, I'm sorry! The hell with you—you can sit here all by yourself. *(Gets up and starts off)* God, these crazy people, you can't even have a little conversation with them.... *(Comes back)* Oh, yeah, I almost forgot. I need eighty-two rubles.

IVÁNOV: What for?

BÓRKIN: I have to pay the workmen tomorrow.

IVÁNOV: I haven't got eighty-two rubles.

BÓRKIN: Oh, that's good! *(Mimics him)* "I haven't got eighty-two rubles." So what am I going to pay the workmen with? You tell me.

IVÁNOV: I don't know! I haven't got any money right now. Wait till the first; I get paid then.

BÓRKIN: The workmen don't get paid on the first; they get paid tomorrow morning!

IVÁNOV: What do you expect me to do about it now? Go on, keep nagging—you'll nag me to death. Why do you always do this? You come around and bother me just when I'm reading—

BÓRKIN: I asked you, What am I going to pay the workmen with? Oh, what's the use! *(Makes a dismissive gesture)* You gentlemen farmers, you're all alike. Scientific farming methods ... Two thousand acres, and not a cent in your pocket. What do you want me to do—sell the horse and carriage? Sure, why not! I already sold the oats in the field; might as well sell the rye too. *(Starts walking rapidly back and forth)* You think I won't? Huh? Just don't push me.

(In the house, the music stops.)

SHABÉLSKY *(Offstage)* I can't play with you. You have no ear and an exasperating technique.

ANNA: *(Appears in the open window)* What's going on out there? Is that you, Mísha? What are you marching around like that for?

BÓRKIN: Trying to talk sense into your friend Nicholas here. *Voilà.* Enough to make anybody start marching.

ANNA: Mísha, I want some hay brought up to the croquet lawn; don't forget to tell them.

BÓRKIN: *(A derisive wave of the hand)* Oh, leave me alone, will you?

ANNA: How rude! Will you please not take that tone with me? How do you expect women to like you, if you get mad and talk like that to them? *(To Ivánov)* Nikolái ... *(Laughs)* Shall we go romp in the hay?

IVÁNOV: You shouldn't stand in the open window, Anna. You'll catch cold. Get back inside, will you? *(Shouts)* Somebody close that window!

(Anna leaves the window, and someone shuts it.)

BÓRKIN: You have a loan payment to Lébedev due in two days. Don't forget.

IVÁNOV: I haven't forgotten. I'm going over there tonight; I'll ask him for an extension. *(Looks at his watch)*

BÓRKIN: When are you going?

IVÁNOV: Right now.

BÓRKIN: *(Excited)* Wait a minute, wait a minute! Today's Sásha's birthday, isn't it? Tsk, tsk, tsk, and I almost forgot. My head's like a sieve. *(Begins to prance around)* I'm on my way, I'm on my way ... *(Sings)* I'm on my way! I tell you, Nikolái, I know you're upset—you're always having a fit about something, you're depressed—but you and me, goddamn it! We could do great things together! And I'd do anything for you, you know that. If you asked me to, I'd even marry Martha Babákina for her money and then give you half. Hell, all of it—I'd give you all her money!

IVÁNOV: Oh, stop babbling.

BÓRKIN: No, I'm serious, I'll do it. You want me to marry old Martha? We'll split the money. *(Beat)* Why the hell do I even talk to you? *(Mimics him)* "Oh, stop babbling." You know what your trouble is? You're a nice guy, you're very smart, but you haven't got any get-up-and-go. You're neurotic—all you do is whine. . . . If you'd act like a normal human being, you could be a millionaire in a year! Now look: if I had two thousand three hundred rubles, I could turn it into twenty thousand in two weeks! You think I'm babbling? This is not babbling. You just give me two thousand three hundred rubles, and inside a week I'll give you twenty thousand. How? They're selling a strip of land by the river, right across from our property. They want two thousand three hundred for it. We buy that strip, and then we own both sides of the river! And if we own both sides of the river, we can build a dam! See what I mean? And a mill. And as soon as word gets out that we're building a dam, everybody living downstream will start raising a ruckus, and then we've got 'em! "You don't want a dam, you have to pay up." See what I mean?

IVÁNOV: Mísha, that's extortion. Will you please drop all this talk? Otherwise I'm going to get really angry.

BÓRKIN: *(Sits down at the table)* Just what I figured! You won't do anything yourself, and now you won't let me do anything either.

(Shabélsky and Lvov come out of the house.)

SHABÉLSKY: You're a doctor, hm? You know the difference between a doctor and a lawyer? A lawyer robs you blind, but a doctor robs you blind and kills you while he's at it. Present company excepted, of course.... *(Sits on a bench)* Cheats, all of them. Con men. Maybe in some never-never land you'll find an exception to my rule, but I doubt it. In my lifetime I have spent something like twenty thousand on doctors' bills, and I never met one I wouldn't call a professional criminal.

BÓRKIN: *(To Ivánov)* That's it, isn't it? You won't do anything yourself, and now you won't let me do anything either. Which is why we have no money.

SHABÉLSKY: Let me emphasize, I'm not talking about present company. And I'm sure there are other exceptions, but still and all ... *(Yawns)*

IVÁNOV: *(Closes his book)* Well, Doctor, what do you think?

DOCTOR LVOV: *(Glances up at the window)* Just what I told you this morning: she has *got* to go to a warmer climate. To the Crimea. As soon as possible. *(Begins to pace up and down)*

SHABÉLSKY: *(Starts to laugh)* The Crimea! Wonderful idea! Mísha, what about you and me? Shall we go take the cure? What a system! Our poor pale Ophelia starts coughing and hacking ... because she's got nothing better to do, you understand. And wham! Medical science to the rescue! And what's your prescription? Start with a good-looking young doctor, follow up with a trip to the Crimea, then add a good-looking young Crimean—

IVÁNOV: *(To Shabélsky)* Just drop it, will you, please? *(To Lvov)* To go to the Crimea you need money. And even if I could come up with it ... you know she categorically refuses to go.

DOCTOR LVOV: You're right, she does.

(Pause.)

BÓRKIN: Look, Doctor, is she that sick? That she has to go to the Crimea, I mean?

DOCTOR LVOV: *(Glances up at the window)* Yes. She has tuberculosis.

BÓRKIN: Sheesh ... Oh, that's terrible! Well, you know, I've noticed it lately: she looks like she's not long for this world.

DOCTOR LVOV: Don't talk so loud. She can hear you inside.

(Pause.)

BÓRKIN: *(With a sigh)* Ah ... The life of man is like a flower in the field: along comes a goat, takes a bite, and it's all over. ...

SHABÉLSKY: It's all a lot of fool doctor's tricks. *(Yawns)* Fools! Con men!

BÓRKIN: I've been trying to teach Nikolái here how to make a little money. He just won't listen. Look at him: the picture of depression and boredom—sad, bitter, angry ...

SHABÉLSKY: *(Gets up and stretches)* Ah, but you, you're a tower of wisdom—you can teach us all how to live. ... Why don't you ever teach me anything? Come on: you're so smart, teach me a thing or two. I'm looking for the answer to everything.

BÓRKIN: I'm going swimming. See you all later. *(To Shabélsky)* There are always twenty answers to everything. I could teach you how to get twenty thousand by the end of the week. *(Starts to leave)*

SHABÉLSKY: *(Follows him)* How? Wait a minute—tell me how. ...

BÓRKIN: If I were in your shoes, I could have thirty thousand, maybe more. ...

(Bórkin and Shabélsky leave.)

IVÁNOV: *(Beat)* Stupid people, stupid talk, stupid questions—it's driving me crazy, Doctor. I lose my temper, I start acting petty and childish, I can't sleep, I get headaches, and there's no way out of it. No way at all.

DOCTOR LVOV: Nikolái Alexéyich, I have to talk seriously with you.

IVÁNOV: Then go ahead. Talk.

DOCTOR LVOV: It's about your wife. *(Sits down)* Yes, she refuses to go to the Crimea. But she'd go if you went with her.

IVÁNOV: *(Thinks a bit)* If we both go, that costs twice as much. Besides, I can't get away from work. I've already used up all my leave.

DOCTOR LVOV: All right. Let's suppose that's the case. There's more. The best medicine for tuberculosis is absolute rest. And your wife cannot get a minute's rest around here. Your attitude constantly upsets her! Excuse me for ... but I'm upset myself. Look, I'll tell you straight out: what's killing her is your attitude.

(Pause.)

Nikolái Alexéyich, I'd hoped I could think better of you!

IVÁNOV: You're right. I know, it's all true. It probably is all my fault. But my mind is a mess; there's a lethargy in my soul. I don't understand other people, I don't understand myself. *(Glances up at the window)* They can hear us in there—let's go take a walk. *(Both men stand)* You're a good friend. I'd tell you the whole story from the beginning, but it's long and complicated; it'd take all night. *(They start off)* She's a remarkable woman, Anna, really extraordinary. She converted to Christianity so she could marry me, left her father and mother; they cut her off without a cent— and they have plenty, believe me. And if I asked her for a hundred more such sacrifices, she'd do it without batting an eye. And then there's me. Nothing extraordinary about me, and I haven't sacrificed a thing. Frankly, Doctor, it's . . . *(Beat)* Well, the fact is, I married her because I was passionately in love with her, and I promised to love her forever, but now it's five years later. She still loves me, but I . . . *(Beat; throws up his hands)* You tell me she hasn't long to live, and I don't feel a thing—no love, no compassion, just a feeling of emptiness, fatigue. You probably look at me and think: What a monster; but something's happened to me, here inside me, I don't know what it is. . . .

> *(They stroll off down one of the paths; as they go, Shabélsky appears, roaring with laughter.)*

SHABÉLSKY: I swear to God, he's not just a crook, that Bórkin, he's a genius! A virtuoso! He deserves a monument. He combines all the worst aspects of modern life: doctor, lawyer, merchant, thief. *(Sits on the lowest step of the veranda)* And he never went to school a day in his life. Just think what a masterful sonofabitch he'd be if he had a smattering of culture and a liberal education! "You could have twenty thousand by the end of the week," he tells me. "You've got one big ace up your sleeve," he says, "and that's your title. Any woman would marry you just to be a countess." *(Roars with laughter)* "She gets a title, and you get title to her money."

> *(Anna opens the window and looks out.)*

"You want me to fix you up with old Martha?" *Qui est-ce que c'est,* this Martha? Oh, yes, that one, Martha Balabálkina—no, what is her name? Babákina . . . anyway, the one who looks like a cleaning lady.

ANNA: Is that you, Count?

SHABÉLSKY: What is it?

(Anna laughs.)

(With a Yiddish accent) So vot's so funny?

ANNA: I was trying to remember one of your jokes. Remember, last night at dinner? What was it? A thief . . . something about a horse . . .

SHABÉLSKY: There are three things nobody needs: a converted Jew, a convicted thief, and a constipated horse.

ANNA: *(Laughs)* Even your jokes have a nasty edge to them. You're a nasty man. *(Seriously)* I mean it, Count. You're really very malicious. You hurt people . . . and you bore them. You're always quarreling and complaining; you think everyone's out to take advantage of you. Honestly, have you ever said anything good about anybody?

SHABÉLSKY: What is this, an interrogation?

ANNA: We've been living under the same roof for the last five years, and I've never once heard you express a good opinion of anything. You're full of bitterness and contempt; you make fun of everyone. What have people ever done to you? Or do you think you're better than the rest of us?

SHABÉLSKY: Not at all. I'm just as much a sonofabitch as the next man. I'm a worn-out old has-been, and ill-mannered to boot. I never say anything good about myself either. Who am I? What am I? I used to be rich, I could do more or less what I wanted to, I was more or less happy. . . . And now? I'm a hanger-on for handouts, a jester without a face. I whine and complain, and people laugh at me. I laugh, they shake their heads and say, Too bad, the old man's losing it. But mostly they pay no attention to me whatsoever.

ANNA: *(Quietly)* There it is again. . . .

SHABÉLSKY: What?

ANNA: The owl. Didn't you hear him? He cries like that every night. It's bad luck.

SHABÉLSKY: Let him cry. Things can't get any worse than they are now. *(Stretches)* Ah, Sarah, my dear, if I could win a couple of thousand in the lottery, I'd show you a thing or two. You wouldn't see me around here anymore. I'd get out of this hellhole, away from your charity, and never show up again till Judgment Day.

ANNA: Suppose you did win . . . what would you do?

SHABÉLSKY: *(Thinks for a bit)* First thing, I'd go to Moscow, go to a Gypsy restaurant, listen to the music. Then . . . then I'd head for

Paris. I'd rent an apartment, start going to the Russian church ...

ANNA: What else?

SHABÉLSKY: I'd go every day and sit on my wife's grave. Just sit and think. I'd sit there until I keeled over. My wife's buried in Paris. ...

(Pause.)

ANNA: What a boring day. Shall we play another duet?

SHABÉLSKY: Why not? Go lay out the music.

(Anna goes inside. Ivánov and Doctor Lvov appear on the garden path.)

IVÁNOV: You see, Doctor, you just graduated last year; you're still young and full of fight. But I'm thirty-five, which gives me the right to offer you a little advice. Never marry a Jew, a neurotic, or an intellectual. Find yourself an unremarkable woman, someone ordinary and dull. Try to make your life a cliché. Don't try to be a hero, don't tilt at windmills, don't bang your head against a stone wall. And I hope to God you never get involved with all this scientific agriculture, all these government programs. Just curl up in your shell and do whatever little job God has assigned you. That way you'll have a normal honest agreeable life. Look at the life I've led. Boring. Boring. All the mistakes, the injustices, the stupidities ... *(Sees Shabélsky; irritated)* Every time I turn around, Uncle, there you are! Can't a man have a private conversation around here?

SHABÉLSKY: *(Complaining)* Oh, for God's sake, can't a man get a moment's rest around here? *(Jumps up and goes into the house)*

IVÁNOV: *(Calling after him)* Look, I'm sorry, I'm sorry! *(To Lvov)* Why did I go and insult him like that? I'm coming apart at the seams. I've got to do something about myself, I've got—

DOCTOR LVOV: *(Upset)* Nikolái Alexéyich, I've listened to you talk and talk, and I ... Excuse me, but I'm not going to pull any punches. Your tone of voice, the things you say—you are soulless and egotistical, you are a cold, heartless ... Someone very close to you is dying, dying *because* she's close to you, and you—you don't love her, you just put on this facade ... Look, I'm not much good at expressing myself, but I ... well, frankly, I don't like you. I don't like you at all.

IVÁNOV: All right, you don't like me. Maybe you see me as I really am. And all this is probably my fault. *(Listens)* They're getting the horses hitched. I have to go dress. *(Walks toward the house, then stops)* You know, Doctor, you don't like me and you tell me so to my face. I respect that. *(Goes into the house)*

DOCTOR LVOV: Damn, I can't talk to him without losing my temper! And I wanted to talk things over with him. But the minute I open my mouth, something in here *(He slaps his chest)* starts churning and choking me. I hate that pompous hypocrite with all my heart. There he goes . . . and his poor wife can't live without him, he's like the air she breathes; she keeps begging him to spend just one evening at home with her, just one, and he . . . he just . . . He says he can't breathe in his own house, he feels cramped, if he had to spend a night at home he'd shoot himself out of boredom. He needs space, he says. Yes, to think up some new way to cause her grief.

(Ivánov comes out of the house, wearing a hat and coat; Shabélsky and Anna come with him.)

SHABÉLSKY: Really, Nicholas, you're being inhuman! You go off every evening and leave the two of us alone here! We're so bored we go to bed by eight o'clock. What kind of life is that? It's outrageous. How come you get to go and we never do?

ANNA: Let him alone, Count. Just let him go if he wants. . . .

IVÁNOV: *(To his wife)* You're sick—how can you go out? You're sick and you shouldn't be out in the open air after sundown. Ask the doctor here. You're not a child, Anna—you have to be reasonable. *(To Shabélsky)* What do you want to go for?

SHABÉLSKY: I'd go anywhere, to hell and back, a nest of crocodiles, just to get out of here! I'm bored! All I do here is get in other people's way. You leave me behind so she won't be left all alone, but all I do is drive her crazy!

ANNA: Let him go, Count, if that's what makes him happy.

IVÁNOV: Anna, why take that tone? You know I don't go over there because it makes me happy! I have to discuss my loan payment.

ANNA: You don't have to make excuses. Just go if you want to. Who's stopping you?

IVÁNOV: For God's sake, let's not snap at each other!

SHABÉLSKY: *(Plaintively)* Nicholas, Nicky dear, please take me with you! You know how entertaining I find all those idiots. And I haven't been out of this house since Easter!

IVÁNOV: *(Irritably)* All right, all right, come along! I'm tired of the whole lot of you!

SHABÉLSKY: I can come? Oh, *merci, merci! (Takes him by the arm)* Do you think I could borrow your straw hat?

IVÁNOV: Yes, only make it snappy, will you?

> *(Shabélsky runs into the house.)*

You make me sick, the whole lot of you! *(Beat)* Oh, God, what am I saying? Anna, I don't mean to talk to you like this. I never used to. Goodbye, Anna. I'll be back after midnight.

ANNA: Nicky . . . dear . . . stay home tonight.

IVÁNOV: *(Upset)* My darling wife, my sweet unhappy wife, please . . . don't try to keep me from going out nights. I know, I'm being cruel, I'm being unfair, but please, just let me be unfair, will you? I go crazy all alone here! As soon as the sun goes down, I get depressed. Don't ask me why; I swear to God I don't know! I'm depressed here at home, I get to the Lébedevs' and it's worse, so I come back here, and I'm depressed all over again, and it goes on like that all night. I'm really at my wit's end. I—

ANNA: Nicky, if only you'd stay . . . We could talk, the way we used to do, have supper by the fire, then read. . . . And that old grouch and I have practiced lots of duets for you. . . . *(Puts her arms around him)* Please stay!

> *(Pause.)*

I don't understand you. This has been going on for a whole year now. Why have you changed?

IVÁNOV: I don't know, I don't know. . . .

ANNA: And why don't you ever want me to go out with you evenings?

IVÁNOV: All right—if you really want to know, I'll tell you. I hope this doesn't sound cruel, but it's better to be honest. . . . When I get depressed like this, I . . . I start not loving you. And I want to run away from you. All I can say is, I have to get out of this house!

ANNA: You're depressed . . . yes, I understand. But you know what, Nicky? Just try, like you used to—try to sing, and laugh, and get mad at something. Please stay. We'll have a lovely time, have a few drinks, and you'll see—your depression will be gone, just like that. You want me to sing for you? Or we can go to your study, the way we used to, and sit in the dark, and you can tell me all about your depression. Your eyes are so full of hurt! Let me look into them, I'll start crying, and then we'll both feel better.

(Laughs, but then begins to cry) Oh, Nicky, what's happening to us? The flowers come back every spring—why can't happiness? *(Beat)* It doesn't, though, does it . . . ? All right—if you're going, just go. . . .

IVÁNOV: Just say a prayer for me, Anna. *(Starts off, stops, thinks a moment)* No, I can't! *(Leaves)*

ANNA: Just go. . . . *(Sits down by the table)*

DOCTOR LVOV: *(Pacing up and down)* Anna Petróvna, you must remember: once it strikes six o'clock, I want you to go to your room and stay there until morning. The damp evening air is very bad for you.

ANNA: Whatever you say, *Sir.*

DOCTOR LVOV: "Sir"? This is a serious matter!

ANNA: Well, I don't want to be serious. *(Coughs)*

DOCTOR LVOV: You see? You're already starting to cough.

(Shabélsky comes from the house in a coat and straw hat.)

SHABÉLSKY: Where's Nikolái? Are the horses ready? *(Goes to Anna and kisses her hand)* Good night, my darling! *(Makes a funny face; with a Yiddish accent)* Oy, gevelt! Vot have I done? *(Rushes off)*

DOCTOR LVOV: Clown!

(Pause; in the distance, someone is playing an accordion.)

ANNA: What a bore. *(Beat)* Listen, the cook and the coachman are having a party, and I . . . I . . . I'm all by myself. Doctor, why are you pacing up and down like that? Come sit down!

DOCTOR LVOV: I can't sit down.

(Pause.)

ANNA: Listen, they're playing "Snowbird." *(Sings)*
"Snowbird, snowbird, where've you been?
Down in the valley where the grass is green . . ."

(Pause.)

Doctor, do you still have your father and mother?

DOCTOR LVOV: My mother. My father's dead.

ANNA: Do you miss her?

DOCTOR LVOV: I don't have time to miss anybody.

ANNA: The flowers come back every spring; why not happiness? Who told me that? I can't remember. Maybe it was Nikolái who said it. *(Listens)* There's that owl again!

DOCTOR LVOV: Forget the owl.

ANNA: You know, Doctor, I'm beginning to think that fate has cheated me somehow. There are lots of people no better than I am, and they're happy, . . . they've never had to pay for their happiness. But I've had to pay for everything, every single thing! Why have I had to pay so much? Dear Doctor, you're all so careful with me, so considerate, you're afraid to tell me the truth, and you think I don't know what's the matter with me. But I know what I've got. I know perfectly well what I've got. But it's a boring topic of conversation. *(Yiddish accent)* Oy, gevelt! Vot have I done? *(Beat)* Do you know any good jokes?

DOCTOR LVOV: No.

ANNA: Nikolái does. *(Beat)* Oh, why can't people respond to love with love? And why is the truth always paid for in lies? How long do you think my mother and father are going to hate me? They live about twenty miles from here, and I can feel their hatred night and day, even when I'm asleep. And what can I do about Nikolái's depression? He says it's only at night he doesn't love me, when he feels depressed. I understand; I think he's probably right; but suppose . . . suppose he stopped loving me altogether? I know that couldn't happen, really—but what if it did? No, I can't think that. *(Sings)* "Snowbird, snowbird, where've you been?" *(Shivers)* What a scary thought . . . You aren't married, Doctor, are you? So there's lots you don't understand.

DOCTOR LVOV: I am amazed. *(Sits down beside her)* You amaze me! Now look: will you please explain something, just to help me to understand? How is it that an intelligent, honest woman like you, almost a saint, can let herself be treated so badly? What are you doing in this cuckoos' nest? What have you got in common with that cold, inhuman— Sorry, let's leave your husband out of it. What have you got in common with this useless, vulgar household? My God! That crazy old count, that crook Mísha—how did you get involved with these people?

ANNA: *(Laughs)* That's exactly the way he used to talk . . . exactly like it. Only his eyes are larger than yours, and whenever he started talking intensely about anything, they used to burn like live coals. . . . *(Beat)* Go on, go on, don't stop. Talk to me.

DOCTOR LVOV: *(Stands, makes an impatient gesture)* What is there to say? You should go in.

ANNA: You keep saying Nikolái is this or that or the other. How can you possibly know what he's like? You've only known him for the last six months; you can't get to know a man in that short a time. He's a remarkable man, Doctor. I'm sorry you didn't meet him a few years ago. Now he's always depressed, won't talk, doesn't do anything; but then ... What a delight he was! I fell in love the first time I saw him! *(Laughs)* I took one look, and snap! I was caught in his trap! And he said, Come on, let's go away together. . . . So I cut myself off from everything, like cutting rotten leaves from a plant, and I went. . . .

(Pause.)

Only now it's different. Now he spends all his time at the Lébedevs', he's seeing other women, and I just ... I sit here in the garden and listen to the owl cry.

(The sound of the watchman on his rounds.)

Do you have any brothers, Doctor?
DOCTOR LVOV: No.

(Anna bursts into tears.)

What is it? What's the matter?
ANNA: *(Gets up)* I can't stand it, Doctor. I'm going.
DOCTOR LVOV: Going? Going where?
ANNA: Wherever he went. I'm going to follow him. Tell them to get the horses ready, will you? *(Goes toward the house)*
DOCTOR LVOV: You can't go out like this—
ANNA: Leave me alone, it's none of your business. I can't stand this, and I'm going. Tell them to get my horses, please! *(Runs into the house)*
DOCTOR LVOV: That's it—I can't be responsible for treating anyone under these circumstances! It's bad enough they don't pay me, but I get involved, I let my feelings run away with me. No, I just can't! I've had enough! *(Goes into the house)*

CURTAIN.

ACT TWO

The Lébedev drawing room. French doors up center lead to the garden; two doors, right and left. Expensive antique furniture. Chandeliers, candelabra, paintings, all hung with dust covers.

Zinaída sits on the sofa; on either side of her, in armchairs, two elderly men (one of them the Third Guest); younger men (one of them the First Guest) sit on side chairs. Upstage near the garden door, a card table; Kósykh, Avdótya Nazárovna, Yegórushka, and the Second Guest are playing bridge. Gavríla stands by the door at right. A Parlormaid carries around a tray of snacks. During the act, guests circulate constantly from the garden through the door at right. Enter Babákina from doorway right; she crosses to Zinaída.

ZINAÍDA: *(Delightedly)* Martha! Darling!

BABÁKINA: How are you, Zinaída? And it's Sásha's birthday! Well, I congratulate *you* . . .

(The two women kiss.)

and I hope to God . . .

ZINAÍDA: Thank you, my sweet! I'm delighted you could come. How are you feeling these days?

BABÁKINA: Quite well, thanks. *(Sits down beside her on the sofa)* Ah, and here are our young people!

(The younger guests rise and bow.)

FIRST GUEST: *(Laughs)* Young people? What does that mean—that you're old?

BABÁKINA: *(Sighing)* Ah, well . . . I'm no longer as young as I once was. . . .

FIRST GUEST: *(A polite laugh)* What a thing to say! You'd take a prize over any young girl I know.

(Gavríla brings Babákina a cup of tea.)

ZINAÍDA: *(To Gavríla)* What are you doing? I told you always to serve the tea with preserves—the gooseberry preserves. They're over there somewhere. . . .

BABÁKINA: No, this is fine; much obliged, I'm sure. Please don't make a fuss. . . .

(Pause.)

FIRST GUEST: *(To Babákina)* Did you come by way of Mushkíno?

BABÁKINA: No, by way of Zaimíshch. The road's better.

FIRST GUEST: Oh, I agree.

KÓSYKH: Two spades.

YEGÓRUSHKA: Pass.

AVDÓTYA NAZÁROVNA: Pass.

SECOND GUEST: Pass.

BABÁKINA: Did you know, Zína, they've raised the price of lottery tickets! Can you imagine? It now costs two hundred seventy for the grand prize drawing, and almost two hundred fifty for the others! I never heard of such a thing!

ZINAÍDA: *(Sighs)* Well, I suppose if you're rich . . .

BABÁKINA: You mustn't be tempted, darling! It's too risky an investment!

THIRD GUEST: As I see it, *madame,* all investments are risky these days. Mutual funds yield extremely small dividends, and the stock market is extremely dangerous. My belief, *madame,* is that a man with money to invest nowadays, *madame,* faces more problems than one with—

BABÁKINA: *(Sighs)* Isn't that the truth!

(The First Guest yawns.)

Well! Do we yawn in front of ladies nowadays?

FIRST GUEST: I beg your pardon, *madame.* I . . . I couldn't quite control it.

(Zinaída rises and goes out right. A long silence.)

YÉGORUSHKA: Two diamonds.

AVDÓTYA NAZÁROVNA: Pass.

SECOND GUEST: Pass.

KÓSYKH: Pass.

BABÁKINA: *(To herself)* God, how boring! I'll die before this is over!

(Zinaída comes back through the door right, arm in arm with Lébedev.)

ZINAÍDA: *(Quietly)* What were you doing, sitting all by yourself like that? What a prima donna you are! Sit here with your guests!

LÉBEDEV: *(Yawning)* Oh, God. Purgatory. *(Sees Babákina)* Well, if it isn't my own little bonbon! My Turkish delight! *(Kisses her hand)* How's my precious today?

BABÁKINA: Quite well! Much obliged, I'm sure!

LÉBEDEV: Well, thank God! Thank God for that! *(Sits in an armchair)* Well, well. *(Beat)* Gavríla!

(Gavríla brings him a tray with a large shot of vodka and a glass of water. He tosses off the vodka and then drinks the water.)

FIRST GUEST: Here's to your good health!

LÉBEDEV: My good health! That's a laugh! Well, I'm not dead yet; I suppose I'm grateful for that. *(To his wife)* Zína, where's our birthday girl?

KÓSYKH: *(Whining)* Oh, for God's sake! Will somebody please explain to me why we didn't take even one trick? *(Gets up)* Why the hell do we always lose?

AVDÓTYA NAZÁROVNA: We always lose because of you! If you don't know how to play, stay out of the game! What gives you the right to lead someone else's suit? And then you get stuck with your stupid ace!

(They both leave the card table and cross downstage toward the others.)

KÓSYKH: *(Practically in tears)* I was holding diamonds: ace, king, queen, a run of eight diamonds, the ace of spades, and one little heart—just one, goddamn it! And she couldn't even make one little slam! I bid no-trump—

AVDÓTYA NAZÁROVNA: *(Interrupting)* I was the one who bid no-trump! You bid two no-trump!

KÓSYKH: This is disgraceful! Excuse me, but you had . . . I had . . . I mean, you had . . . *(To Lébedev)* Pásha, you be the judge! I was holding diamonds: ace, king, queen, a run of eight diamonds—

LÉBEDEV: *(Covering his ears)* Please! Leave me out of this, will you? Please!

AVDÓTYA NAZÁROVNA: *(Screams)* I was the one who bid no-trump!

KÓSYKH: *(Angry)* I'll be damned if I ever sit down to play with that old sturgeon again! *(Runs out into the garden)*

(The Second Guest runs after him; Yegórushka remains alone at the card table.)

AVDÓTYA NAZÁROVNA: Oh, he makes me so mad! Sturgeon! Sturgeon yourself!

BABÁKINA: Now, now, dear, don't get yourself all worked up.

AVDÓTYA NAZÁROVNA: *(Seeing Babákina for the first time; clasps her hands together)* Oh, she's here! My beautiful angel, the light of my life! Here she is. Oh, I must be blind as a bat—I never even noticed you come in. . . . *(Kisses her shoulder and sits down beside her)* Let me look at you! My, my! Beautiful as ever! Spit, spit. There. That'll protect you from the evil eye.

LÉBEDEV: She's at it again! *(To Avdótya Nazárovna)* Never mind the evil eye: you should think about finding her a new husband.

AVDÓTYA NAZÁROVNA: Oh, I will, I will! I won't rest until I get her married off, and Sásha too, I promise! Won't rest as long as there's life in these old bones! *(Sighs)* Except that nowadays ... where are you going to find eligible young men these days? Take a look at this bunch here! All huddled up like wet roosters!

THIRD GUEST: I find your metaphor remarkably inappropriate. Roosters indeed! If the young men of today, *madame,* refuse to get married, it's society, so to speak, that's to blame, the social attitudes—

LÉBEDEV: Please, please! No social attitudes! I don't want to hear about social attitudes. Can't stand that kind of talk!

(Enter Sásha; she crosses to her father.)

SÁSHA: It's a beautiful evening, and here you all are, sitting around in this stuffy room!

ZINAÍDA: Sásha dear, where are your manners? Here's Martha Babákina.

SÁSHA: I'm sorry! *(Goes to greet Babákina)*

BABÁKINA: Are you getting too good for the rest of us, Sásha? You haven't once been to see me. *(They exchange kisses)* Happy birthday, dear.

SÁSHA: Thank you. *(Sits down next to her father)*

LÉBEDEV: *(To Avdótya Nazárovna)* You're right about the young men these days, though. It's a problem finding a suitable man for a young girl to marry. Young men nowadays are spoiled. They're overeducated. They've forgotten the social graces, how to dance, how to make polite conversation. . . . They don't even know how to drink like a man.

AVDÓTYA NAZÁROVNA: Oh, they know how to drink, believe me! Just let me—

LÉBEDEV: Well, of course, everyone knows how to drink—even a horse knows how to drink. I'm talking about knowing how to drink like a man! Now, in my day we used to study hard all day long, and then, come evening, we'd head out to the bright lights and carry on until dawn! Dance, have fun with the ladies, that kind of thing. We'd argue, tell stories, talk till we couldn't talk anymore. But nowadays ... *(Makes a dismissive gesture)* I don't understand them. There's only one outstanding young man in the whole county, and he's already married. *(Sighs)* And it seems to be driving him crazy. . . .

BABÁKINA: Who's that?

LÉBEDEV: Ivánov.

BABÁKINA: Yes, he's a lovely man. *(Makes a face)* But he's so unhappy!

ZINAÍDA: Well, of course, darling! How can you expect him to be happy? *(Sighs)* The poor man made a dreadful mistake! He married that Jewish girl, hoping, I suppose, that her parents would give him a mountain of money, but it turned out just the opposite. The moment she converted, her parents disowned her; they refused to see her ever again. So he never got a cent. Of course, now he's sorry, but it's a bit late for that. . . .

SÁSHA: Mama, that's not true!

BABÁKINA: *(Annoyed)* Sásha! Why do you say it's not true? Everybody knows it! Why would he have married a Jew if he hadn't expected to make some money out of it? Aren't there plenty of Russian girls? He made a mistake, dear, that's all there is to it. *(Bitchy)* And my Lord, he certainly lets her know it now! "Your mother and father cheated me," he says. "I want you out of this house right now!" But where is the poor girl supposed to go? Her mother and father won't take her back. . . . I suppose she could get work as a domestic somewhere, but of course she hasn't the faintest idea of work. She's never had to do any. If it weren't for the count, he'd have done her in long ago.

AVDÓTYA NAZÁROVNA: What I heard was, he locks her up in the cellar and makes her eat nothing but garlic! And she has to eat and eat until she throws up!

(Everybody laughs.)

SÁSHA: Papa, that's a lie and you know it!

LÉBEDEV: Well, what difference does it make? Let them talk; that's all they know how to do. *(Shouts)* Gavríla!

(Gavríla brings the tray with another vodka and water.)

ZINAÍDA: The poor man has ruined himself, and she's the reason. Besides, darling, his financial affairs are a disaster! If he didn't have Mísha Bórkin to take care of the farm, he and that Jew of his wouldn't have a thing to eat. *(Sighs)* And the torments he's put us through! Absolute torments, darling! God knows how we manage. Would you believe that he has owed us nine thousand for the last three years?

BABÁKINA: *(Horrified)* Nine thousand!

ZINAÍDA: Yes! It was my dear softhearted husband who lent it to him. He still doesn't understand that there are people you can lend money to and people you just *can't*. And I'm not even talking about the principal, God knows. But you'd think he could at least make the interest payments on time!

SÁSHA: *(Hotly)* Mama, you've been over this a thousand times already!

ZINAÍDA: What business is it of yours? Why do you always stick up for him?

SÁSHA: *(Stands)* How can you talk this way about a man who never did you any harm?

THIRD GUEST: Sásha—if you'd allow me a word or two? I admire Ivánov, I've always considered it an honor to know him, but speaking frankly *entre nous,* the man's an adventurer.

SÁSHA: Is that what you think? Congratulations.

THIRD GUEST: And I can offer the following fact as evidence, a fact that was related to me by his second in command, or perhaps we should say his *attaché,* his friend Bórkin. Two years ago, during the anthrax epidemic, he bought up cattle and insured them—

ZINAÍDA: Yes, yes, yes! I remember! I heard that too!

THIRD GUEST: —insured them, as I said. Bear that in mind. Then he exposed them to the virus and collected the insurance money.

SÁSHA: That's ridiculous! Just ridiculous! Nobody bought any cattle and infected them! It was that Bórkin who thought up the idea and went around bragging he was going to do it! The only thing Ivánov is guilty of is not having the guts to get rid of that Bórkin and of trusting people too much! They've cheated him out of everything he has!

LÉBEDEV: That's enough, Sásha! Calm down!

SÁSHA: But why are they making up these ridiculous stories? It's so boring! Ivánov, Ivánov, Ivánov—that's all you people ever talk about! *(Starts for the door, then turns)* You surprise me! *(To the younger guests)* You really surprise me! Aren't you bored, sitting here listening to all that gossip? The air in here is stifling! Say something amusing, go flirt with the girls, do something alive! If Ivánov is all you've got to talk about, you'd do better to start dancing. It might liven up the party!

LÉBEDEV: *(Laughs)* That's it, that's my girl—you tell 'em!

SÁSHA: No, I'm serious. Do me a favor. At least once in your lives, just for the fun of it, say something witty, something brilliant, something shocking or vulgar, anything, as long as it makes someone laugh! Be different! I don't care what it is—just something intense, something alive, so we young women can look at you at least once in our lives and say: "Yes!" If you want us to like you, why don't you try to be likable? Oh, gentlemen, you're doing it all wrong! Wrong! Wrong! Look at you! You—

(Shabélsky and Ivánov appear in the doorway right.)

SHABÉLSKY: Who's making a speech? You, Sásha? *(Laughs and takes her hand)* Happy birthday, my angel. I hope you have a long life and no reincarnation.

ZINAÍDA: Nikolái! Count!

LÉBEDEV: Is it the count? It is! *(Goes to greet him)*

SHABÉLSKY: *(Notices Zinaída and Babákina, stretches out his arms)* Two rich ladies on a single sofa! What a lovely sight! *(Kisses Zinaída)* Good evening, Zína! *(To Babákina)* Good evening, my little pompom!

ZINAÍDA: Delighted to see you! You come to see us so rarely, Count. *(Shouts)* Gavríla, tea! Sit down, won't you? *(Stands, crosses to the door right and returns immediately, with a worried look on her face)*

(Sásha sits back down where she was, and Ivánov greets the group.)

LÉBEDEV: *(To Shabélsky)* This is a real surprise, by God. To what urge do we owe the honor? *(Kisses him)* Count, why haven't you been to see us? *(Takes him by the arm and crosses downstage)* You're mad at us, or what?

SHABÉLSKY: How was I supposed to get here, on a broomstick? I don't have my own horses, and Nikolái won't take me with him; he tells me to stay home and keep Sarah from getting bored. If you want to see me, send your carriage to pick me up.

LÉBEDEV: *(Makes a deprecating gesture with his hands)* Oh, yes, I'm sure! Zína would have a fit if I lent out the horses. My old friend, my dearest, oldest friend, you mean more to me than anyone else in the world! You and I are the only ones of our group who've made it to old age! "In you I see the struggles of my youth, my suffering and my perished hopes...." No, but seriously ... I think I'm going to cry. *(Embraces Shabélsky)*

SHABÉLSKY: Oof, that's enough, that's enough! You smell like a brewery.

LÉBEDEV: Oh, Count, you can't imagine how bored I am without my old friends! I'm ready to hang myself out of boredom. *(Softly)* Zína's gotten so mercenary with all her loans, she's driven away all the decent people, and you can see for yourself what's left. A bunch of idiots. Doodkin, Boodkin ... I don't even know their names. Here, have a cup of tea.

(Gavríla brings Shabélsky his tea.)

ZINAÍDA: *(Fretfully, to Gavríla)* What are you doing? I told you always to serve the tea with preserves—gooseberry preserves ... they're over there somewhere.

SHABÉLSKY: *(Chuckling, to Ivánov)* What did I tell you? *(To Lébedev)* On the way over, I made a bet with him: the minute we set foot in the house, Zína would bring out the gooseberry jam!

ZINAÍDA: Oh, Count, you're always making fun of me! *(Sits down)*

LÉBEDEV: She put up twenty quarts of it this year—she's got to get rid of it somewhere.

SHABÉLSKY: *(Sits by the table)* Still raking it in, Zína? You must be a millionaire by now, no?

ZINAÍDA: *(Sighs)* Yes, to look at us from the outside, you'd think nobody had more money than us. But it's all just talk. . . .

SHABÉLSKY: Oh, yes, we know, we know! You're a lousy business-woman! *(To Lébedev)* Tell the truth, Pásha. Have you got a million yet?

LÉBEDEV: Don't ask me. That's Zína's department.

SHABÉLSKY: And my juicy little pom-pom will soon be a millionaire too! By God, you're getting better-looking all the time! That's always a sign you've got money!

BABÁKINA: Much obliged, I'm sure, Count. But please spare me your jokes.

SHABÉLSKY: My dear millionaire, it was no joke. That was a cry from the heart. A superfluity of feeling loosened my tongue. I love you both endlessly, you and Zína. *(Exuberantly)* Oh, joy! Oh, rapture! I can't see either of you without—

ZINAÍDA: You haven't changed; you're the same as you always were. *(To Yégorushka)* Yégorushka, put those candles out! The game's over; why waste them?

(Yégorushka jumps to attention, puts out the candles, and sits back down.)

(To Ivánov) And your wife, Nikolái? How's her health?

IVÁNOV: Bad. The doctor said today she definitely has TB.

ZINAÍDA: Really? What a pity! *(Sighs)* And we're all so fond of her. . . .

SHABÉLSKY: Nonsense! Nonsense! That's nonsense! She hasn't got TB. That doctor's a quack! He wants to keep on seeing her, so he thought up TB as an excuse. It's a good thing her husband's not jealous. *(Ivánov makes an impatient gesture)* And I don't believe a thing Sarah says either. I have never once in my entire life trusted a doctor, a lawyer, or a woman. All you get from them is nonsense—nonsense, quackery, and tomfoolery!

LÉBEDEV: *(To Shabélsky)* I'm surprised at you, Matvéy. You're a likable man, but the minute you open your mouth you put your foot in it. Hoof-in-mouth disease. I swear to God.

SHABÉLSKY: What do you want me to do, go around shaking hands with fools and criminals?

LÉBEDEV: And where exactly do you see fools and criminals?

SHABÉLSKY: Of course, I'm not speaking about present company, but—

LÉBEDEV: "But"! There you go again. This is all a put-on.

SHABÉLSKY: A put-on, is it? You only think so because you have no worldview, no philosophy of life.

LÉBEDEV: What do you mean, no worldview? I could drop dead anytime—that's my worldview. You and I, my boy, we're too old to worry about philosophy. That's just the way it is. . . . *(Shouts)* Gavríla!

(Gavríla brings the usual vodka and water.)

SHABÉLSKY: You've been indulging in a little too much Gavríla. Look at your nose—it's turning red!

LÉBEDEV: Who cares? I'm not about to go out and get married.

ZINAÍDA: It's been ages since Doctor Lvov came to visit. He must have forgotten us.

SÁSHA: That's because I don't like him. He's such a paragon of virtue! He can't ask for a glass of water or light a cigarette without showing off his extraordinary honesty. What a bore!

SHABÉLSKY: He's a narrow-minded prig, that doctor. All he cares about is that people think he's honest!

IVÁNOV: I must say I find him tiresome. Still, he's a sympathetic character. He's very sincere.

SHABÉLSKY: Oh, fine! Sincere! The other evening, he comes up to me and without any preamble announces, "Count, I don't like you at all." Well, thank you very much, I'm sure! And it's all just intellectual prejudice. Of course he hates me; that's natural. I know that already—why say it to my face? I may be a silly individual, but after all, I am a man of a certain age. . . . His honesty is just lack of compassion.

LÉBEDEV: Now, now, now. You were young once yourself. You know how it is—

SHABÉLSKY: Yes, I was young and I was stupid, I used to go around calling people dishonest, but I never called a man a thief to his face. I had some manners, after all. But that idiot doctor of yours lives in a world of his own. He thinks it would be heroic to punch me out in public—all in the name of his principles and his grandiose ideas about humanity.

LÉBEDEV: Young people are always difficult. I had an uncle who was a follower of Hegel. He'd invite a whole houseful of people, get drunk, get up on a table, and start yelling at his guests: "You're all ignorant! It's you who're the forces of evil! The dawn of a new life!" And on and on and on and on and on. And he'd keep lecturing them—

SÁSHA: What did the guests do?

LÉBEDEV: Nothing. They went on drinking.

(Enter Bórkin from the door right. He is somewhat overdressed, carries a package, and hums and does a few dance steps. There is a general chorus of welcome.)

(The following three speeches overlap.)

THE LADIES: Mísha! Mikhaíl Mikhaílich!

LÉBEDEV: Michél Michélich! What a surprise!

SHABÉLSKY: The life of the party!

BÓRKIN: Here I am! *(Crosses to Sásha)* Noble signorina, allow me to congratulate the universe on the birthday of such a lovely flower as yourself. And as a sign of my admiration, I take the liberty of offering you these. *(Gives her the package)* Firecrackers and Roman candles, of my own manufacture. And may they light up the night the way you light up the shadows of this kingdom of darkness! *(Makes a theatrical bow)*

SÁSHA: Thank you.

LÉBEDEV: *(Bursts out laughing; to Ivánov)* Why don't you get rid of that Judas?

BÓRKIN: *(To Lébedev)* Pável Kiríllich! *(To Ivánov)* Hi, boss. *(Sings)* Voilà little Nicky, hee hee hee . . . *(Goes around saying hello to every-one individually)* Zinaída Sávishna, dear lady . . . Martha

Yégorevna, divine as always! . . . And the venerable Avdótya Nazárovna! . . . His exalted highness the count!

SHABÉLSKY: *(Bursts out laughing)* The life of the party! The minute he comes in, the atmosphere improves. Did you notice that?

BÓRKIN: There, I think that's everybody. Oof, I'm worn out. Well, now, ladies and gentlemen, what's new? Any new scandals? *(To Zinaída, eagerly)* Oh, I forgot to tell you: I was on my way over here—*(To Gavríla)* Gavríla, bring me a cup of tea, will you? Only no gooseberry preserves! *(To Zinaída)* I was on my way over here, and I saw some of the locals gathering kindling near your willow trees by the river. Why don't you start charging them for that?

LÉBEDEV: *(To Ivánov)* Why don't you get rid of that Judas?

ZINAÍDA: *(Startled)* You're right, of course! Why didn't I ever think of that!

BÓRKIN: *(Starts doing stretching exercises)* I can't sit still even for a minute. Martha, my darling, I'm in great shape, aren't I? I'm positively bursting with health! Zína, how about let's get a game going, something different. . . . *(Sings)* "Once more here before you . . ." What would you like? Hide-and-seek, charades? The fireworks? Or shall we dance?

THE LADIES: *(Applauding)* No, fireworks! The fireworks! *(They begin exiting to the garden)*

SÁSHA: *(To Ivánov)* What are you looking so depressed about?

IVÁNOV: I've got a headache, Sásha. And I'm bored.

SÁSHA: Come on into the parlor.

(They go out right; everyone goes out into the garden except Zinaída and Lébedev.)

ZINAÍDA: That's what I like to see, that young man. The minute he got here, everybody started having a good time. *(Turns down the light in a large lamp)* No need to keep the lights on here, now that they're all out in the garden.

LÉBEDEV: *(Crosses to her)* Zína, we should offer people something to eat, a little supper. . . .

ZINAÍDA: All these candles . . . No wonder people think we're rich. *(Blows them out)*

LÉBEDEV: *(Following her)* Look, Zína, we've got to give them something to eat. You know what young people are like, hungry all the time. Zína . . .

ZINAÍDA: The count didn't finish his tea. I hate to see all that sugar going to waste. *(Goes out left)*

LÉBEDEV: Oh, for God's sake . . . *(Goes out into the garden)*

(Sásha and Ivánov enter from right.)

SÁSHA: They're all out in the garden.

IVÁNOV: It's just the way things are, Sásha. There was a time I worked hard and thought a lot about things, but I was never tired; nowadays I do nothing and think about nothing, but I'm exhausted in body and soul. My conscience bothers me day and night, but I can't figure out exactly what I've done wrong. And then there's my wife's illness, and hopelessness, and our squabbles and gossip and stupid conversations and that idiot Bórkin. I hate my own house; living there is worse than torture. I tell you frankly, Sásha, I've gotten to where I can't stand to be around my wife, and the woman loves me dearly. You and I are old friends; I can tell you all this without you getting angry. I came over here to relax, but now I'm bored here too, and I want to go home. Excuse me. I'll just slip out quietly.

SÁSHA: I do understand you, Nikolái. You're unhappy because you're lonely. You need someone around you who can love you and understand you. You need to change your life, and love is the only thing that can do that.

IVÁNOV: Be serious, Sásha! I'm a worn-out old rooster; the last thing I need is a new love affair. God deliver me from that! No, my little psychiatrist, love is not the answer. I swear to you by all that's holy, I could put up with everything—my depression, my neuroses, my financial disasters, and losing my wife, and getting old ahead of my time, and being lonely—but I cannot stand my own contempt for myself. I'm intelligent, I'm in the prime of life, and I could die of shame when I realize that I'm turning into some kind of Hamlet, a completely superfluous man. It fills me with shame! It torments my pride, it weighs me down, and I suffer. . . .

SÁSHA: *(Joking, but almost in tears)* You and I should run away to America, Nikolái.

IVÁNOV: I'm too worn out to get through that door, and you talk to me about America. . . . *(They cross to the door to the garden)* It must be terribly hard for you, Sásha, living here! When I look at the people who surround you here, I get terrified: who are you going to marry?

(Zinaída enters left, carrying a jar of preserves.)

Excuse me a moment, Sásha. I'll catch up with you later.

(Sásha goes out into the garden.)

Zinaída Sávishna, I have to ask you a favor. . . .

ZINAÍDA: What is it, Nikolái?

IVÁNOV: *(Hesitates)* Well, you see, the problem is, my loan payment is due in two days. I'd be eternally grateful to you if you could give me an extension, or let me add this interest payment to the principal. I simply don't have any money at the moment. . . .

ZINAÍDA: *(Shocked)* Nikolái, that's quite impossible! What kind of businesswoman would that make me? No, don't even think of it. And please, you mustn't upset me like this!

IVÁNOV: I'm very sorry. Excuse me. *(Goes out into the garden)*

ZINAÍDA: God, what a state he's gotten me in! I'm shaking all over. *(She goes out left)*

(Kósykh enters left and crosses the stage.)

KÓSYKH: I was holding diamonds: ace, king, queen, a run of eight diamonds, the ace of spades, and one little heart, just one, goddamn it to hell! And she couldn't even make one little slam! *(Goes out stage right)*

(Avdótya Nazárovna and the First Guest come in from the garden.)

AVDÓTYA NAZÁROVNA: I could kill her! What a skinflint! I could just kill her! Is this her idea of a joke? I've been here since five o'clock, and all she's served us is some stale herring! What a household! What hospitality!

FIRST GUEST: It's so boring around here! I feel like banging my head against the wall. What ridiculous people! I'm so bored and hungry I could eat a wolf!

AVDÓTYA NAZÁROVNA: I could just kill her!

FIRST GUEST: I'm going to have one more drink and then go home.

AVDÓTYA NAZÁROVNA: Let's go find us a drink. . . .

FIRST GUEST: Shh! They'll hear us! I think there's some schnapps in the dining room cabinet. Let's go find Yégorushka; he'll know where it is. Shh!

(They go out left. Anna and Doctor Lvov enter at right.)

ANNA: It's all right. They'll be glad to see us. There's no one here. They must all be out in the garden.

DOCTOR LVOV: I wish you'd tell me why you brought me over here to see these vultures. This is no place for you and me! Honest people should stay away from this house.

ANNA: My honest friend, may I point out that it's hardly attractive to drive all this way with a lady and talk about nothing but your own honesty. Maybe you're honest, but you're also boring. You should never talk to women about your good qualities; let them find out for themselves. When my Nikolái was your age and in the company of ladies, he'd be singing and telling jokes, but all of them managed to get a very clear idea of his good qualities.

DOCTOR LVOV: Please, don't talk to me about your Nikolái. I understand his qualities only too well.

ANNA: You're a nice man, but you don't understand a thing. Let's go out into the garden. Nikolái would never say things like that. "I'm an honest man! I can't stand this place! They're all vultures! Owls! Crocodiles!" The menagerie never bothered him. And if he got upset, he'd say things like, "I was unfair today" or "Anna, I really pity that man!" That's what he'd say. But you . . .

(They go out into the garden as Avdótya Nazárovna and the First Guest enter left.)

FIRST GUEST: Nothing in the dining room, so it must be in the pantry. We'll have to find Yegórushka. This way.

AVDÓTYA NAZÁROVNA: I could just kill her!

(They go out right, as Babákina and Bórkin run in from the garden. Shabélsky follows them, prancing and wiping his hands.)

BABÁKINA: It's so boring! *(Bursts out laughing)* It's so boring! They all walk around as if they'd swallowed a yardstick! My bones are bored stiff! *(Begins to hop up and down)* I've got to get the blood flowing again!

(Bórkin grabs her around the waist and kisses her on the cheek.)

SHABÉLSKY: *(Bursts out laughing and begins to clap his hands)* Damn, what fun! *(Starts to cough uncontrollably)* More or less . . .

BABÁKINA: Let me go—take your hands off me, you naughty man! Or the count will think God knows what! Stop it!

BÓRKIN: My soul's angel, my heart's precious jewel! *(Kisses her)* Lend me two thousand three hundred rubles!

BABÁKINA: No, no, no . . . If it's money you want, much obliged, I'm sure, but no, no, no! And take your hands away!

SHABÉLSKY: *(Prances around them)* My little pom-pom . . . What a garden of delights!

BÓRKIN: *(Stops laughing)* That's enough. Let's be serious and talk business for a bit. Answer me directly, answer yes or no, no tricks now, listen! *(Points to Shabélsky)* Here's a man who needs money, three thousand a year at the very least. You need a husband. Would you like to be a countess?

SHABÉLSKY: *(Laughing)* What a cynic you are!

BÓRKIN: Do you want to be a countess? Yes or no?

BABÁKINA: *(Agitated)* Mísha, you're inventing all this. Really, you can't talk about these things so suddenly like this. If the count wants to, he can . . . well . . . ask me himself. I don't know, this is all so sudden. . . .

BÓRKIN: Don't confuse the issue. This is a business deal. Yes or no?

SHABÉLSKY: *(Smiles and rubs his hands)* What the hell, I *should* do this myself, really. How about it? Hah? My little pom-pom? *(Kisses her cheek)* Divine! My little tomato!

BABÁKINA: Stop, stop—you've got me all upset. . . . Leave me alone! Leave me alone! *(Beat)* No, don't go yet!

BÓRKIN: Quick! Yes or no? There's no time to waste!

BABÁKINA: I'll tell you, Count. Why don't you come visit me for a few days. You'll enjoy yourself, I promise, not like around here. . . . Come tomorrow. *(To Bórkin)* And will you please stop making jokes?

BÓRKIN: *(Angry)* Who's making jokes? This is a serious business!

BABÁKINA: Oh, stop, stop . . . Oh, I feel faint! I'm going to faint! A countess! I'm going to faint! Hold me up!

> *(Bórkin and Shabélsky laugh and kiss her on the cheeks, then grab her by the arms and drag her offstage right, as Ivánov and Sásha run in from the garden.)*

IVÁNOV: *(Clasps his head in despair)* No, Sásha! You mustn't say that! You mustn't! Please, Sásha, you mustn't say that!

SÁSHA: *(Passionately)* I love you! I'm crazy about you! If I can't be with you, I'll never know happiness ever again! You're everything to me!

IVÁNOV: Why? Why? My God, I just don't understand. . . . Sásha, stop saying that!

SÁSHA: When I was a girl, you were my only joy. I loved you, I loved your soul, I loved you more than I loved myself. And now . . . I love you, Nikolái. I'll go anywhere with you: to the ends of the earth, I'll follow you to the grave, only for God's sake let's go, let's go now. I'm suffocating. . . .

IVÁNOV: *(Breaks into a laugh of happiness)* Is this really happening? Could this be the beginning of a new life? A way out? Yes, Sásha, yes! You're mine! *(Pulls her to him)* My youth, my innocence . . .

> *(Anna enters from the garden, sees Ivánov and Sásha, and stops stock-still.)*

Let's live! Yes! Let's begin all over again!

> *(He kisses her. After the kiss they look around and see Anna.)*

(Horrified) Sarah!

CURTAIN.

ACT THREE

Ivánov's study. A desk with a disorderly collection spread out on it: papers, books, official documents, knickknacks, a revolver; also a lamp, a carafe of vodka, a plate with herring, slices of bread, and cucumber pickles. On the walls, pictures, maps, rifles, pistols, daggers, riding crops, etc. It is noon. Shabélsky and Lébedev sit on either side of the desk. Bórkin straddles a chair in the middle of the room. Pyótr stands by the door.

LÉBEDEV: The French know exactly what they want: they want to beat hell out of Germany. But Germany, now, that's another story, let me tell you. The Germans have their eyes on more than France.

SHABÉLSKY: Don't be ridiculous! The way I see it, they're all cowards, French *and* Germans. They'll never fight.

BÓRKIN: What's the point of fighting? You know what I'd do? I'd round up every stray dog I could find, inject it with rabies, and let them all loose in enemy territory. I'd have everyone foaming at the mouth within a month.

SHABÉLSKY: Sheer genius.

LÉBEDEV: Goddamn, Michél, you are a funny man! *(Stops laughing)* Well, gentlemen, you know what the song says: "Don't talk about your heroes and forget about your booze . . ." *Repetátur!* *(Pours out three glasses of vodka)* Here's to our very good health.

(They all drink and have a bite to eat.)

Ah, herring! The snack of kings!

SHABÉLSKY: No, pickles are better.

LÉBEDEV: And caviar goes good with vodka too, you know. Best way I know to fix it, you take a quarter pound of pressed caviar, the green parts of two spring onions, some olive oil, mix it all up like this, and sprinkle a little lemon juice on top. Heaven!

BÓRKIN: You know what else is good with vodka? Fried smelts. Only you have to know how to cook them right. Crisp enough to crackle. Yum, yum!

SHABÉLSKY: We had a delicious dish last night at Babákina's: white mushrooms. With onions, I think, and bay leaf, and a lot of different spices.

LÉBEDEV: What do you say, gentlemen? *Repetátur!*

(They all drink another glass of vodka.)

Here's to everybody's good health. *(Looks at his watch)* I don't think I can wait any longer for Nikolái. I've got to go. And by the way, would you mind telling me, why the hell you're spending all this time at Martha Babákina's?

SHABÉLSKY: *(Gesturing to Bórkin)* It's him; he wants me to marry her.

LÉBEDEV: Marry her? How old are you?

SHABÉLSKY: Sixty-two.

LÉBEDEV: Oh, the perfect age for marriage! You and Martha will make a lovely couple.

BÓRKIN: We're not after Martha; we're after her money.

LÉBEDEV: Martha's money? Dream on! You can't get blood from a stone.

BÓRKIN: Wait till he marries her and gets his hands on her money— you'll see what you can get out of a stone. You'll drool with envy. . . .

SHABÉLSKY: Our genius here is convinced I'm going to do what he tells me and go get myself married—

BÓRKIN: What do you mean? Are you backing out already?

SHABÉLSKY: You're crazy. I never backed in.

BÓRKIN: Well, thanks a lot! You mean you've been leading me on all this time? "Yes, I'll get married . . . no, I won't get married . . ." Make up your goddamn mind. And in the meantime I gave her my word. So now you're *not* going to marry her?

SHABÉLSKY: *(Shrugs)* I can't believe he's serious. What a character!

BÓRKIN: *(Indignant)* Then why did you trifle with the affections of an honest woman? What kind of behavior do you call that? You know she's crazy to be a countess; she can't sleep or eat.

SHABÉLSKY: *(Snaps his fingers)* All right, then, suppose I did it? Hah? Just for spite? Just went ahead and did it? That'd be a hoot, wouldn't it?

(Enter Doctor Lvov.)

LÉBEDEV: Ah, the disciple of Asclepius! What a signal honor! *(Shakes hands with Lvov and sings)* "Doctor, dear Doctor, come save my poor child . . ."

DOCTOR LVOV: Isn't Ivánov back yet?

LÉBEDEV: Not yet. And I've been waiting over an hour.

(Doctor Lvov begins to pace impatiently.)

What about Anna Petróvna? How's she doing?

DOCTOR LVOV: Bad.

LÉBEDEV: *(Sighs)* Would it be all right if I went up to see her for a moment?

DOCTOR LVOV: No, please, not now. She's sleeping.

(Pause.)

LÉBEDEV: Such a lovely woman, really lovely . . . *(Sighs)* That time she fainted, at our house, on Sásha's birthday, I remember looking at her face and thinking, poor thing, she's not long for this world. But I could never figure out why she fainted. I walked in and there she was, on the floor, white as a sheet, with Nikolái kneeling beside her—he was as white as she was—and Sásha standing there in tears. Sásha was upset for a week afterwards. So was I.

SHABÉLSKY: *(To Lvov)* Would the high priest of science be so good as to answer a question? Who was it discovered that whenever a woman is suffering from a chest ailment, it's important to have a young doctor in constant attendance? An amazing discovery! Is that what you call hands-on healing?

(Lvov starts to answer, thinks better of it, makes a dismissive gesture, and leaves the room.)

Did you see the way he looked at me?

LÉBEDEV: Well, why did you insult him like that?

SHABÉLSKY: *(Irritably)* Well, why does he have to lie? "She's got TB, there's no hope, she's going to die . . ." It's all lies! I can't stand to hear him lie!

LÉBEDEV: What makes you think he's lying?

SHABÉLSKY: *(Stands and paces)* I refuse to tolerate the idea that a person can just die like that, all of a sudden, for no reason. And please let's change the subject!

(Enter Kósykh. He's in a hurry and out of breath.)

KÓSYKH: Is Nikolái here? Oh, hello. *(Shakes hands with everybody)* Is he here?

BÓRKIN: No, not yet.

KÓSYKH: *(Sits down, then jumps up again)* Well, I'm off, then. I can't wait. *(Drinks a glass of vodka and eats a bit of herring)* I've got errands to do. . . . What a day! I'm completely worn out.

LÉBEDEV: What have you been doing?

KÓSYKH: I was playing cards at Barabánov's. Lost my shirt. *(Starts to whine)* There I was, holding hearts the whole time. . . . *(Turns to Bórkin, who moves away from him)* He plays a diamond, I play a heart, he plays another diamond, and I never take a single trick.

LÉBEDEV: *(Covers his ears)* Spare me! For the love of Christ, spare me!

KÓSYKH: *(To Shabélsky)* You understand? I had the ace, queen, and six of clubs, the ace, ten, and three of spades—

SHABÉLSKY: *(Waving him away with his hands)* Please! I don't want to listen to any of this!

KÓSYKH: And then—disaster! I lose the ace of spades on the first round—

SHABÉLSKY: *(Grabs the revolver from the desk)* Get out! Get out before I shoot!

KÓSYKH: *(Makes a dismissive gesture)* What's the matter, won't anybody listen to me? It's like living in Australia around here! Nobody to tell your troubles to, nobody cares about anybody else. We all live separate lives, don't we? All right, I'm going. . . . It's getting late. *(Grabs his hat)* Time is money, right? *(Shakes Lébedev's hand)* I pass!

(They all laugh. Kósykh goes out and nearly collides in the doorway with Avdótya Nazárovna.)

AVDÓTYA NAZÁROVNA: *(With a shriek)* Watch it! You damn near knocked me off my feet!

EVERYONE: Aha! Here she is! The inescapable presence!

AVDÓTYA NAZÁROVNA: And here you all are! I've been searching the

whole house. Hello hello hello! How are all my bright boys?
(Greets them all individually)

LÉBEDEV: What are you doing here?

AVDÓTYA NAZÁROVNA: I'm here on business, dear. *(To Shabélsky)*
This concerns Your Lordship, I'm afraid. My instructions were to
say hello, inquire after your health, and ask where you've been all
this time. My dear friend and yours says to tell you if you don't
come by to see her tonight, she'll cry her little eyes out. Get him
alone, she says, and whisper it to him secretly. But why should I
whisper? We're all friends here. I'm not trying to rob the hen-
house; this is all about love, legal love, and mutual accommoda-
tion. *(Sees the vodka)* Ah. You know I never drink, but an occasion like this, I think I deserve one!

LÉBEDEV: I'll have one with you. *(Pours two glasses)* You old magpie,
you're still the life of the party. *(To the others)* I've known this old
woman for thirty years, maybe more—

AVDÓTYA NAZÁROVNA: I've lost count myself. I've buried two husbands, and I'm ready for a third, only nobody wants an old lady
with no money. And the eight kids I've got ... *(Takes the glass of
vodka)* Well, here's hoping. We've got a nice thing going here;
let's see if we can finish it right. The two of them will live happily
ever after, and we'll all be tickled pink every time we see them.
Here's to loving wisely ... *(Drinks)* That vodka's very strong!

SHABÉLSKY: *(Bursts out laughing; to Lébedev)* You know, the funniest
part is how seriously they all take this business: they think I'm
actually going to ... Amazing! *(Stands)* Suppose I do it—what do
you say, Pásha, hmm? Goddamn it, I *will*, I—

LÉBEDEV: Talk sense, Count, will you? You and I ought to be thinking about measuring our coffins. It's too late now for Martha and
her money.

SHABÉLSKY: No, I'm going to do it! By God, I'm going to do it!

(Enter Ivánov and Doctor Lvov.)

DOCTOR LVOV: All I ask is five minutes of your time.

LÉBEDEV: Nicky! *(Goes to meet Ivánov, hugs him)* Hello! My dear boy,
I've been waiting for you a whole hour already.

AVDÓTYA NAZÁROVNA: My little darling! Welcome home!

IVÁNOV: *(Bitterly)* You people have done it again—you've turned my
study into a tavern! How many times have I asked you not to do
this.... *(Crosses to the desk)* Look, vodka spilled all over my
papers; crumbs, pickles ... It's disgusting!

LÉBEDEV: Sorry, Nicky, I'm sorry—forgive me, won't you? Now you and I have some very important business to discuss—

BÓRKIN: So have I.

DOCTOR LVOV: Nikolái Alexéyich, may I *please* speak with you!

IVÁNOV: *(Gestures toward Lébedev)* He wants to speak with me too, you know. Just wait a minute, I'll talk to you later. *(To Lébedev)* What is it?

LÉBEDEV: *(To the others)* Gentlemen, I really must speak to him in private. . . .

(Shabélsky goes out with Avdótya Nazárovna, Bórkin follows, then Doctor Lvov.)

IVÁNOV: Pásha, look, I know how you drink, you're an alcoholic, fine, but for God's sake, please don't get my uncle started. He never used to drink like this. It's very bad for him.

LÉBEDEV: *(Taken aback)* Dear boy, I didn't know, I simply didn't realize . . .

IVÁNOV: I don't want that old infant to die. He doesn't mean anything to you, but I . . . What did you want?

(Pause.)

LÉBEDEV: Well . . . You see, my boy . . . my dear dear boy . . . I don't know where to begin, to make this less embarrassing. . . . Nicky, I'm so ashamed I'm starting to blush, I can't find the right words, but look, dear boy, put yourself in my position. . . .

IVÁNOV: What is it?

LÉBEDEV: My wife sent me. Do me a favor, please: pay her the interest on your loan! You won't believe the way she torments me—I can't get her off my back! For the love of God, just pay her! And get her off your back too!

IVÁNOV: Pásha, you know I don't have any money right now.

LÉBEDEV: I know, I know, but what do you expect me to do? She won't wait. If she decides to take you to court, Sásha and I will never be able to look you in the face again.

IVÁNOV: Now I'm the one who's ashamed. Pásha, I feel like crawling into a hole, but where am I supposed to get it? Just tell me where! The only thing I can see to do is wait till autumn, when I sell my wheat crop.

LÉBEDEV: *(Wails)* But she won't wait!

(Pause.)

IVÁNOV: I know this is terrible, it puts you in an awkward situation ... but what kind of situation do you think I'm in? *(Paces and thinks)* I can't think of a way out. I haven't got anything left to sell. ...

LÉBEDEV: Can't you go see Millbach and ask him for it? He owes you sixteen thousand.

(Ivánov gestures hopelessly.)

Look, Nicky, suppose I ... Oh, I know you'll get angry, but ... humor an old drunk, will you? Just as a friend ... Think of me as a friend, just a friend. We're both educated men, liberals, we share the same ideas, the same interests. ... We both graduated from Moscow University! Our alma mater! *(Takes out his wallet)* Now, I've got a little money saved up; nobody at home knows anything about it. Take it as a loan. ... *(Takes out money and places it on the table)* Forget your pride; just be a friend. ... I'd take it from you, I swear to God. ...

(Pause.)

Here's eleven hundred, right here on this table. You go see her today, you give it to her yourself. "Here you are, Zinaída Sávishna, I hope this makes you happy." Only for God's sake don't let on I gave it to you, or she'll make gooseberry jam out of me! *(Beat; he sees the look on Ivánov's face)* Oh, Nicky, I'm sorry! *(Grabs the money and sticks it back in his pocket)* I'm really sorry. I was only joking. Christ, I'm sorry!

(Pause.)

I know. ... *(Sighs)* You're going through a dark period, all this shame and sorrow. ... You know, my dear, life is like a samovar. It sits peacefully on the kitchen shelf, very cool, but every once in a while somebody drops in a few hot coals, and pssh! Pssh! *(Beat)* I don't know what's the point of that comparison, but it's all I could think of ... : *(Sighs)* What upsets me is what people are saying. ... Where did all these stories come from? People are accusing you of all sorts of things; they're just waiting for the police to come and arrest you.

IVÁNOV: It's all just gossip. Look, I'm getting a headache—

LÉBEDEV: That's because you think too much.

IVÁNOV: I don't think at all anymore.

LÉBEDEV: Why don't you just forget about all this and come visit.

Sásha loves you, she understands you. She's a wonderful girl, Nicky. She doesn't take after her mother, doesn't take after me.... Sometimes I look at her and I wonder how a red-nosed old soak like me wound up with a treasure like that.

(Pause.)

IVÁNOV: Pásha, please. Leave me alone for a while.....
LÉBEDEV: I understand, I understand. *(Glances hastily at his watch)* I understand. *(Hugs Ivánov)* I have to stop at the dedication ceremony at the school. *(Goes to the door)*
IVÁNOV: Pásha! *(Stops him; beat)* Pásha, what's the matter with me?
LÉBEDEV: I've been wanting to ask you that myself, but you know, I felt embarrassed. I don't know, my boy. I think maybe you're worn out with all these troubles, but then of course I know the kind of man you are: you'd never let ... I mean, you're not a defeatist. But there's something else going on, Nicky; I don't know what it is.....
IVÁNOV: I don't know either. Sometimes I think ... No, it's not that.

(Pause.)

What I wanted to say was ... You know, I used to have a hired man, Semyón—you remember him. And once—it was harvest time, he wanted to show off for the girls, show how strong he was, and he tried to shoulder two bales of rye. Well, he tore a muscle or something inside, and he died soon after. And I feel as if I've torn something inside too. First there was high school, then university, then trying to farm this place, trying to start a school, all those projects.... I didn't believe the things everyone else believed, I didn't get married the way everyone else did, I took risks, I threw my money away—well, *you*'re aware of that. I went through a lot of emotional ups and downs, but I was happy! I worked harder than anyone in the neighborhood! And all that, Pásha, was like those bales of rye. I tried to shoulder the whole thing at once, and it broke my back. When we're twenty we're all heroes, we think we can do everything, and then suddenly we're thirty and we're worn out, useless. How do you account for that? Maybe I'm wrong, maybe it's not ... No, it's not, it really isn't.... I'm sorry, Pásha, I'm keeping you. I didn't mean to be such a bore.
LÉBEDEV: *(Excited)* You know what it is? It's this environment, the atmosphere around here—it's destroying you!

IVÁNOV: That's a silly thing to say, Pásha. And it's been said before.

LÉBEDEV: It *is* silly, isn't it? You're right. All right, I'm leaving, I'm leaving. . . . *(Leaves)*

IVÁNOV: I'm a monster. And I'm good for nothing. You have to be a worn-out old alcoholic like Pásha in order to think I'm still worth something. God, how I hate myself! I hate myself with a passion. I hate the sound of my voice, my footsteps, my hands, these clothes, the things I keep thinking. . . . Funny, isn't it? And depressing. Less than a year ago I still felt fine, I was strong, I was full of energy, I worked hard, I could do anything with these hands. . . . I could talk, even make the country people understand me; I could cry when I saw others suffering; I got upset and angry in the presence of evil. I knew what inspiration meant; I knew the joy and poetry of those long, quiet nights when you sit working, or sit and let dreams crowd your brain. I had faith; I could look straight into the future as if into my own mother's eyes. . . . And now—oh, my God. I'm worn out, I've lost my faith, I spend days and nights doing nothing. My hands and feet, my brain, they're no longer part of me. My fields are dying, my woodlands are all cut down. *(Starts to cry)* My own land looks at me like an orphan. I have no future; nothing moves me; my soul sinks at the thought of tomorrow. And my life with Sarah? I swore I would love her forever, swore we'd be happy together, I told her we'd have a glowing future, a life she'd never dare dream of. And she believed me. And for the last five years what's happened? She's sinking beneath the weight of all the sacrifices she's made, her conscience is killing her, and yet she's never once questioned me, God knows, she's never made the slightest reproach. . . . And I've stopped loving her. Why? How did it happen? I don't under-stand. And now she's dying, and I run away because I can't bear to look at her pale face, her wasted body, the pleading in her eyes. . . . I'm a complete coward. I'm ashamed, I'm so ashamed!

(Pause.)

And Sásha, who's just a girl . . . she says she loves me. . . . I'm an old man, and she intoxicates me; I forget the rest of the world, I'm like someone enthralled by a piece of music, and I shout: "Yes! A new life! Happiness!" And the next day I no longer believe in that life or that happiness any more than I believe in ghosts. What's the matter with me? What is this bottomless pit I'm hurl-ing myself into? What's the matter with my nerves? If my sick wife annoys me, or one of the servants disturbs me, or my gun won't fire . . . I lose my temper, I yell, I don't recognize myself—

(Enter Lvov.)

DOCTOR LVOV: Nikolái Alexéyich, you and I must have a talk! Right now!

IVÁNOV: Doctor, if you and I go on with these talks day after day, we'll have no energy for anything else.

DOCTOR LVOV: Would you mind for once hearing me out?

IVÁNOV: I hear you out every day, and I still have no idea what you're getting at. What exactly is it you want from me?

DOCTOR LVOV: I have been expressing myself clearly and precisely. You can't understand me? That's because you are completely heartless.

IVÁNOV: My wife is about to die? I know that. I am unforgivably guilty where she is concerned, I know that. You are an honest man who always speaks his mind. I know that too. What else do you want me to know?

DOCTOR LVOV: You people are heartless! This woman is dying! And you, the man for whom she sacrificed everything—her religion, her family—you abandon her every night and rush off to Lébedev's, and your reasons are only too obvious to everyone—

IVÁNOV: Look, I haven't been over there in two weeks. . . .

DOCTOR LVOV: *(Pays no attention)* I say things as I see them! You need her to die so you can move on to new conquests. Fine. But can't you at least wait? Let nature take its course, let her die gently, don't keep hurting her with your outrageous cynicism—or are you afraid you'll lose that Lébedev girl and her dowry? Is that why you want your wife dead right away, instead of next month, or next year?

IVÁNOV: You're such a smart man, aren't you? According to you, I'm like an open book. Right? I married Anna hoping to get a large dowry. My plan didn't succeed, there was no dowry, and now I'm trying to get rid of her so I can marry someone else—and get the dowry this time round. Right? How simple, how obvious! Man is such a simpleminded machine! No, Doctor, each of us is much too complicated for anyone to judge another on external impressions. Don't be so sure of yourself all the time.

DOCTOR LVOV: You think I can't see right through you?

IVÁNOV: You and I are never going to agree, that's clear. For the last time, I ask you: what do you want from me? *(Annoyed)* And with whom exactly do I have the honor of speaking: my wife's doctor or the state prosecutor?

DOCTOR LVOV: I am your wife's doctor, and you are killing her! I
knew people were sometimes stupid, unbalanced, crazy ... but
until I met all you people here, I never imagined they could be
consciously criminal, deliberately evil. I used to respect people, I
used to love them, but whenever I look at you—

IVÁNOV: We've been through all this!

DOCTOR LVOV: Have we?

(Enter Sásha, in riding clothes. Lvov looks at her and shrugs.)

Well. Now I think we do understand each other. *(Goes out)*

IVÁNOV: *(Taken aback)* Sásha! What are you doing here?

SÁSHA: I came to see you. *(Beat)* Hello. You didn't expect me? Why
haven't you been to see us all this time?

IVÁNOV: Sásha, this is madness! If my wife knows you're here, it will
destroy her!

SÁSHA: She won't know. I came in the back way. And I'll go in a
minute. I worry about you: are you all right? And why haven't
you been to see me all this time?

IVÁNOV: My wife is miserable as it is, she's dying, and you show up
like this! Sásha, Sásha, you're being thoughtless and cruel!

SÁSHA: What else could I do? You haven't been to see us for two
weeks; you don't answer my letters. It was driving me crazy.
I kept imagining you were sick, or dying.... I can't sleep
at night. All right, I'm going. At least tell me there's nothing
wrong.

IVÁNOV: Everything's wrong. I make myself miserable, other people
make me miserable.... I just can't take it anymore! And now
you're here! This is all so sick, so crazy! Sásha, I'm so full of guilt!

SÁSHA: You love to talk like this, don't you? Full of guilt? For what?
What have you got to be guilty about?

IVÁNOV: I don't know, I don't know. ...

SÁSHA: Are you guilty because you don't love your wife anymore?
Maybe you don't. No one can control the way he feels; you didn't
stop loving her on purpose. Guilty because she saw us kissing that
time? That was an accident; you didn't do it on purpose—

IVÁNOV: *(Interrupting her)* And so on and so on ... Fall in love with
you, fall out of love with her, can't control my emotions—it's all
so trite, just empty phrases. ...

SÁSHA: It wears me out, talking to you. *(Beat; she examines a drawing
of a dog on the wall)* What a lovely drawing. Did the dog sit for his
portrait?

IVÁNOV: Yes. And our little love affair, that's trite too, more empty phrases. "His nerve had failed him; he had lost his way; then *she* appeared, full of hope and courage, and her love restored him." That's lovely, but it only happens that way in novels. In real life—

SÁSHA: It happens in real life too.

IVÁNOV: You have a very poor sense of real life, you know that? All my whining inspires a kind of religious fervor in you: you think you've discovered another Hamlet in me. But the way I see it, this craziness of mine is a farce and nothing more. You ought to be laughing your head off at my affectations; instead you want to help! You want to save me! God, how I hate myself today! This mood of mine has to change, I can't go on like this! Or I'll start breaking things! Or else—

SÁSHA: Good. That's exactly what you ought to do. Break something, smash something, start screaming at the top of your lungs! You're angry at me, and I know it was stupid, coming here like this. All right, get mad, yell at me, stamp your feet. Why not? Go on, get mad. . . .

   (Pause.)

Well?

IVÁNOV: *(Smiles)* You're very funny.

SÁSHA: At last! We're smiling! How wonderful! You think you can bring yourself to smile again?

IVÁNOV: *(Laughs)* Whenever you start to save me from myself, or try to knock some sense into my head, you get this innocent look on your face, incredibly innocent—your eyes get bigger and bigger, as if you were watching a shooting star. Hold on a minute— you've got something on your shoulder. *(He brushes some dust from her shoulder)* An innocent man is an idiot. But you women manage to make innocence seem warm and sweet and normal instead of idiotic. You all have this quirk: if a man's strong and well and happy, you ignore him completely, but the minute he loses his grip, begins to fall, you fall all over him. Is it really worse to be married to a strong, successful man than to play nursemaid to a sniveling failure?

SÁSHA: Much worse!

IVÁNOV: Why?

SÁSHA: Any girl would rather love a failure than someone success- ful, because every girl is looking for a love that requires her to *do something*. You understand? Something she can share, an *active* love. Men have their work, so love for them is always secondary. They'll talk to a woman, take a stroll around the garden, enjoy her company, shed a tear on her grave—and that's it. But for a woman, love is her whole life. I say I love you, that means I dream of keeping you safe from despair, and I'd follow you to the ends of the earth. You're on top, I'm on top. You're on bottom, I'm on bottom. For instance, my greatest pleasure would be to spend the whole night doing your accounts for you, or watch all night long to see that no one disturbed your sleep, or walk a hundred miles at your side. I remember one time about three years ago—it was during the harvest—you stopped by our house. You were exhausted, all dusty and sunburned, and you asked for something to drink. I brought you a glass of water, but you were already asleep on the couch, dead to the world. You slept the whole day through, and I stood guard by the door so no one would wake you. And how wonderful I felt! The more you have to *do* for love, the better it is. I mean, the more you feel it.

IVÁNOV: An active love ... Hmm. That's silly; it's just schoolgirl talk—or maybe that's the way things are supposed to be.... *(Shrugs)* Who knows? *(Relieved, happy)* Sásha, I swear to you, I am a decent human being! You be the judge: You know I love to talk and argue, but not once have I ever said: "Women are no good" or "Women are asking for trouble." I swear to God, I was grateful they were there, that's all! That's all! Oh, sweetheart, how good you are, what a relief it is to talk to you! And I'm such a stupid idiot! I go around upsetting people, I do nothing but complain. *(Laughs)* Poor me! Boo-hoo! *(Suddenly moves away from her)* Sásha, you've got to go! We forgot!

SÁSHA: Yes, I've got to go. Goodbye. I'm afraid your honest doctor may decide it's his duty to tell Anna Petróvna I'm here. Now, you listen to me: Go up and see your wife. Sit down beside her and stay there. Sit for a year if you have to, ten years, if that's how long it takes. Do what you promised to do. Have some pity for her, ask her forgiveness, weep with her. You've got to. But the most important thing: don't neglect your work.

IVÁNOV: Now I feel the same as I did before—as if I'd eaten a poison mushroom. The same as before!

SÁSHA: God will give you strength. You don't have to think about me at all. Write me a note in a week or two; I'd be very grateful for that. And I'll write you back.

(Bórkin opens the door and glances in.)

BÓRKIN: Nikolái Alexéyich, can I come in? *(Sees Sásha)* Oh, I'm sorry, I didn't know . . . *(Comes into the room) Bonjour! (Bows)*

SÁSHA: *(Embarrassed)* Hello . . .

BÓRKIN: You've put on some weight! Looks good on you!

SÁSHA: *(To Ivánov)* I've got to go, Nikolái. Goodbye. *(Leaves)*

BÓRKIN: What a looker! I'm all prose, and she's all poetry. *(Sings)* "You came to me like a bird on the wing . . ."

> *(Ivánov is extremely upset; he paces around the stage. Bórkin sits down.)*

She has something the other girls don't, Nicholas. She does, doesn't she? Something special . . . transcendental, I guess. *(Sighs)* Fact is, of course, she's the richest catch in the neighborhood, but her mama's such a twisted old bat no one wants to get involved. Once she's dead, Sásha will get it all, but until then the only dowry her mother's willing to give is ten thousand, *maybe,* and she'd better be damn grateful for that much. *(Reaches in his coat pocket)* How about a smoke? *(Takes out a cigar case)* De las Mejores. Best cigars on the market.

IVÁNOV: *(Goes up to Bórkin; he is livid with rage)* Get out of here! Right this minute! I don't ever want to see your face in my house again!

> *(Bórkin stands, drops his cigar.)*

Out! Right now!

BÓRKIN: Nicholas, what's the matter? What are you getting mad at me for?

IVÁNOV: What for? Where did you get those cigars? You think I don't know where you take the old man every day? And why?

BÓRKIN: *(Shrugs)* What do you care where I take him?

IVÁNOV: You bastard! All your crazy projects that upset the whole neighborhood, and everybody blames me for them! They think I'm a crook because of you! We have absolutely nothing in common, and I demand that you leave my house! Right now! *(Paces frantically)*

BÓRKIN: I know you don't mean any of this; you're just upset. So I'm not mad at you. Go ahead, insult me some more. *(Picks up the cigar)* Only drop the melancholy hero bit, will you? You're not a schoolboy anymore.

IVÁNOV: What did I just tell you? *(Threatens him)*

(Enter Anna Petróvna.)

BÓRKIN: Now see what you've done. Here's your wife. I'll be going. *(Leaves)*

(Ivánov stops beside the table and lowers his head.)

ANNA: *(After a pause)* What was she doing here?

(Pause.)

I asked you: What was she doing here?

IVÁNOV: Please, Anna, don't ask. . . .

(Pause.)

This is all my fault. Completely my fault. You can punish me any way you want to, I'll do anything you want, but . . . don't ask me. Please. I haven't got the strength to go into it.

ANNA: *(Angrily)* I want to know why she was here!

(Pause.)

So that's what you are! I understand everything now. I finally see the kind of man you are—dishonest, a cheat . . . Remember how you came and lied to me: you told me you loved me, and I believed you, and I left my mother and my father and my religion, and I followed you. And you lied to me, about truth, about honor, your fine projects, and I believed every word of it—

IVÁNOV: Anna, I have never lied to you—

ANNA: I have lived with you for five years, I've suffered because I gave up my own religion—that's why I'm sick—but I loved you and I never left you, not for one minute. You were my idol. And what's the result? I now find out that you've been deceiving me, and flaunting it in front of everybody!

IVÁNOV: Anna, that's not true. I've made an enormous mistake, true, but I've never lied to you in my entire life. You have no right to accuse me of that.

ANNA: Oh, I understand it all now. You married me because you thought my parents would forgive me and give me a huge dowry . . . that's what you thought.

IVÁNOV: Oh, God, my God! Anna, I can't stand this! *(Begins to cry)*

ANNA: You just shut up and listen! And when you found out there wasn't going to be any money, you began a new game with someone else. Oh, I remember everything, I understand everything. *(Starts to cry)* You've never loved me, you've never been faithful! Never!

IVÁNOV: Sarah, that's a lie! Go ahead, say whatever you want, but don't lie about what I've done!

ANNA: You are a low, dishonest human being! You owe money to the Lébedevs, and you're trying to get out of paying them by seducing their daughter, seducing her just the way you seduced me! I'm right, aren't I?

IVÁNOV: For God's sake, will you please stop it? *(Breathing heavily)* I'm out of control. . . . I'm so angry now, I—I'll say something you'll regret.

ANNA: You've always cheated on me, right out in the open, and not just me! All your dishonest behavior, and you kept blaming it all on Bórkin, but now I know—I know who's really to blame!

IVÁNOV: Shut up, Sarah, just shut up! And leave me alone! Before I say something we'll both regret. No, I'll say it—I *want* to say it! *(Screams at her)* You goddamn Jew!

ANNA: I will not shut up! You've cheated on me for too long. I am *not* going to shut up now—

IVÁNOV: I told you to shut up! *(Struggles with himself)* For the love of God—

ANNA: Go on over to the Lébedevs'! Now you can start cheating on her!

IVÁNOV: And you—you're dying! You're going to die! The doctor says you'll be dead before . . . before . . .

ANNA: *(Sits down; her voice changes)* When did he say that?

(Pause.)

IVÁNOV: *(Clutches his head)* What have I done? Oh, my God, what have I done? *(Sobs out loud)*

CURTAIN.

ACT FOUR

About a year has elapsed between the end of Act Three and the beginning of Act Four.

Drawing room in the Lébedev mansion. An arch separates the drawing room from a salon in the rear. Doors right and left. Antique bronzes, family portraits. Floral decorations for a wedding. On the piano a violin, and near it a cello. During the entire fourth act, guests in evening clothes stroll back and forth in the salon. Enter Doctor Lvov.

DOCTOR LVOV: *(Looks at his watch)* It's past four. They ought to be starting soon. So, this is it. The triumph of truth and justice! He never managed to swindle Sarah, so he tortured her to death, and now he's ready to start on another one. Hypocrite! He'll lie to this one too, until he gets her money, then bury her next to poor Sarah. It'll be the same sordid story. . . .

  (Pause.)

No, not yet it won't. I am an honest man; my job is to open the eyes of those who will not see. And once I've done my duty, I intend to leave this miserable place forever! *(Thinks)* But what can I do? Make a scene in front of everybody? Challenge him to a duel? God, I can't think straight anymore. What? A duel?

  (Enter Kósykh.)

KÓSYKH: *(Delighted to see Lvov)* Guess what? Yesterday I bid a little slam and made a grand slam, all on clubs. Only that Barabánov ruined the whole thing for me, same as last time! We're playing, right? I bid no-trump. He—

DOCTOR LVOV: You'll have to excuse me. I don't play cards, so I'm afraid I can't share your emotion. Will the ceremony start soon?

KÓSYKH: I think so. They're trying to calm down Zína. She's having a screaming fit because of the dowry.

DOCTOR LVOV: And not because of her daughter?

KÓSYKH: Oh, no, because of the dowry. Well, it *is* too bad. Once he's married to her daughter he won't have to pay back the money he owes her, and of course she can't sue a family member over a personal loan.

  (Babákina, elaborately dressed, makes a grand entrance. Kósykh tries to hide a snicker. She looks around.)

BABÁKINA: Stupid!

  (Kósykh pokes her in the side and bursts out laughing.)

Peasant! *(Goes out)*

KÓSYKH: *(Still laughing)* That silly woman's lost her mind! She was perfectly all right until she started thinking of herself as a countess; now you can't get near her! *(Mimicking her)* "Peasant!"

DOCTOR LVOV: *(Upset)* Listen ... Tell me honestly: what do you think of Ivánov?

KÓSYKH: Not much. He plays cards like a shoemaker. Last year, just before Easter, I'll tell you what happened. We sit down to a game—me, him, the count, and Bórkin. I lead—

DOCTOR LVOV: *(Interrupting)* I mean, is he ... is he a good person?

KÓSYKH: Him? He's one slick customer, believe you me. So's the count. They're two of a kind—both of them got a nose for a fat profit. First he married that Jewish girl, couldn't get her money, so now he's trying to pick Zína's pockets. He will, too; bet you anything he'll have the whole Lébedev fortune before the year is out. Just like the count and poor Babákina. They'll take the money and start living it up, see if they don't. What's the matter, Doctor, you not feeling well? You look awful.

DOCTOR LVOV: No, I'm fine. I had too much to drink yesterday.

(Enter Lébedev and Sásha.)

LÉBEDEV: We can talk here. *(To Lvov and Kósykh)* All right, you two, go flirt with the ladies in the other room. We want to have a little talk in private.

KÓSYKH: *(Kisses his fingers as he passes Sásha)* What a beauty! Queen of Trumps!

LÉBEDEV: Animal! Out, out, get out!

(Exit Lvov and Kósykh.)

Sit down, Sásha—no, over here.... *(Sits and looks around)* Now, Sásha, I want you to listen very carefully. I'm your father, remember. Well, now ... your mother wanted me to tell you—no, she insisted that I tell you ... You understand, now, this is all your mother's idea, not mine—

SÁSHA: Please, Papa, get to the point!

LÉBEDEV: You're to get a dowry of fifteen thousand rubles cash. That's all settled and agreed upon. No, wait, listen to me! That's just the beginning. You get a dowry of fifteen thousand cash, but ... seeing that Nikolái still owes your mother nine thousand, we're subtracting that amount from the fifteen thousand. So. Now, besides that—

SÁSHA: Why are you telling me all this?

LÉBEDEV: Your mother told me to.

SÁSHA: Can't you leave me alone? I don't need your dowry! I never asked for it, and I don't want it!

LÉBEDEV: I don't know what you're getting mad at me for!

SÁSHA: Just leave me alone! All this money talk! You're really being insulting!

LÉBEDEV: *(Losing his temper)* Oh! You get me so angry, the two of you, I could kill someone—or kill myself! Your mother won't shut up, she nags and complains, squeezes her last cent, and you—you're supposed to be the smart one, for God's sake, an emancipated woman, and you won't even listen, you just insult your own father! And before I came in here to be insulted, I was out there *(Points to the door)* being drawn and quartered! Neither of you even tries to understand me! *(Heads for the door, then stops)* All the same, I don't like this! I don't like this one bit!

SÁSHA: What don't you like?

LÉBEDEV: None of it!

SÁSHA: None of *what*?

LÉBEDEV: What is this, some kind of interrogation? I don't like the whole business. I . . . I don't even want to take part in this wedding! *(Crosses to her and speaks lovingly)* Sásha dear, forgive me. Maybe this marriage is a good idea, maybe it's full of ideals and honest and aboveboard, but something is wrong here, something is very wrong! It's not like an ordinary wedding. You're a young girl, you're fresh, innocent, beautiful, and he . . . he's a widower, and his life's coming apart at the seams. I'm sorry, I just don't understand him. *(Kisses her)* Sásha darling, there's something . . . forgive me, but there's something indecent about all this. And people have been talking. That Sarah of his dies, and all of a sudden he wants to marry you, just like that. *(Hastily)* But what do I know? I'm just an old woman, that's all, babbling away. Don't pay any attention to me. Listen to your own heart, not to the rest of us.

SÁSHA: No, Papa. I . . . I feel the same way. There's something . . . something not right somewhere. Not right at all! If you only knew how awful I feel! It's unbearable! And I feel awkward and guilty even talking about it. Papa dear, please, help me—oh, dear God, help me. . . . Tell me what to do!

LÉBEDEV: What is it? What's the matter?

SÁSHA: I'm terrified! I've never felt like this before, ever! *(Glances around)* It's as if I don't understand him, as if I'll never understand him! The whole time we've been engaged, he's never once smiled or looked me straight in the eyes; he's always complaining, saying he's sorry, talking about being guilty; his hands are always shaking. . . . I can't stand much more of it. There are even times when I . . . when I think I don't love him as much as I should. He comes over to see me, he talks to me, and I start getting bored. What does it all mean, Papa? I'm so scared!

LÉBEDEV: Oh, sweetheart, you're my only child—listen to your old father. Tell him you won't marry him.

SÁSHA: *(Terrified)* What? What are you saying?

LÉBEDEV: I mean it, Sásha. It will cause a scandal, the whole neighborhood will gossip, but better to put up with a scandal than ruin your entire life!

SÁSHA: No, Papa, don't say that! Don't say it! I won't listen. You mustn't even think that. He's a good man, he's unhappy, and no one understands him, but I will, I'll love him and understand him and help him to stand on his own two feet again. I'll do my duty. I've made up my mind.

LÉBEDEV: Your duty? You're acting crazy!

SÁSHA: Look, we've said enough. I've told you something I didn't want to admit to anyone—even myself. Let's just forget it.

LÉBEDEV: I don't understand any of this. Either I'm getting stupid in my old age or you're all getting smarter, but I don't understand anything anymore! Not a goddamn thing!

   (Enter Shabélsky.)

SHABÉLSKY: The hell with them all! Me included!

LÉBEDEV: What's the matter?

SHABÉLSKY: I swear to God, I'm about to do something to make you all hate me as much as I hate myself! I told Bórkin to tell them I'm getting married. *(Laughs)* They're all sonsabitches; I might as well be one too!

LÉBEDEV: Matvéy, you're getting boring. If you don't shut up, they'll shut you up—in the crazy house. Sorry, I mean it.

SHABÉLSKY: What makes a crazy house any worse than this house? Fine, let them—let them shut me up. Anyplace they like. I've never met a worse bunch of people—petty, destructive, useless— and I'm as bad as the rest of them. I don't believe a word I say anymore—

LÉBEDEV: Matvéy, for God's sake! Stop it, will you? Better yet, get your hat and go home. This is a wedding party, everybody's having a good time, and you go around croaking like an old crow. Please!

(Shabélsky collapses on the piano and bursts into tears.)

Matvéy, what's the matter? My God, Count ... Matty ... Matty, what's the matter? Come on, that's a good boy, come on, stop it now, stop it. . . . Did I say something? I'm sorry, I'm such an idiot, just an old drunk. . . . Here, have a drink of water. . . .

SHABÉLSKY: No, I'm fine, it's all right. *(Raises his head)*

LÉBEDEV: What are you crying for?

SHABÉLSKY: It's all right. I—

LÉBEDEV: No, come on, tell me: what's the matter?

SHABÉLSKY: When I saw the cello, I started thinking about that poor Jewish girl. . . .

LÉBEDEV: *Today* you start thinking about her? Look, I'm sorry for her, sorry she's dead, but this is hardly the time and place—

SHABÉLSKY: We used to play duets together. . . . She was such a lovely woman!

(Sásha bursts into tears.)

LÉBEDEV: Now what's the matter with *you?* Stop crying! My God, they're both hysterical; what am I supposed to ... what if someone comes in?

SHABÉLSKY: Pásha, it doesn't matter how old you are, as long as you have hope. But I don't! I haven't got any hope left! None at all!

LÉBEDEV: *(Sighs)* You're right, actually. You haven't got a thing. No children, no money, no job ... Well, that's how things work out sometimes. *(To Sásha)* But you? What have you got to cry about?

SHABÉLSKY: Pásha, give me some money. I'll give it back when we both get to heaven. I want to go to Paris, go see my wife's grave. Please, be a friend. . . .

LÉBEDEV: *(Embarrassed)* Look, believe me, I haven't got a cent—believe me! Oh, all right, all right—I mean, I can't promise, but I'll see what I can do. I ... *(Mutters)* They're going to drive me crazy!

(Enter Babákina.)

BABÁKINA: What's become of my cavalier? Count, you left me all alone! How could you? Bad boy! *(Whacks him with her fan)*

SHABÉLSKY: *(In disgust)* Just leave me alone! I hate you!

BABÁKINA: What? *What?*

SHABÉLSKY: Just leave me alone!

BABÁKINA: *(Drops into an armchair)* Oh! *(Begins to cry)*

(Enter Zinaída, in tears.)

ZINAÍDA: *(In tears)* They're here . . . the groom's party. It's time for the wedding. . . . *(Bursts out sobbing)*

SÁSHA: *(Imploringly)* Mama!

LÉBEDEV: Oh, fine, now they're all crying! It's a quartet! What are you trying to do, rain us out? Matty! Martha! Look, you'll make *me* start! I swear to God— *(Bursts out crying)* Oh, Lord!

ZINAÍDA: *(To Sásha)* I mean nothing to you anymore, do I? You don't want me to be happy, all you want is my blessing. Well, fine. You have it. . . .

(Enter Ivánov, in a dress coat and white gloves.)

LÉBEDEV: Oh, no! This is all we need!

SÁSHA: What are you doing here?

IVÁNOV: I'm sorry, everyone. I need to talk to Sásha for a moment. Alone.

LÉBEDEV: You can't! You're not supposed to see the bride before the ceremony! Anyway, it's time to leave for the church!

IVÁNOV: Pásha, I beg you . . .

(Lébedev shrugs; he goes out, followed by Shabélsky, Zinaída, Babákina.)

SÁSHA: *(Tense)* What do you want?

IVÁNOV: I'm so angry I'm ready to explode! But I'm going to speak very calmly. Listen. Just now, when I was getting dressed for the wedding, I looked at myself in the mirror, and . . . and I'm old! My hair's getting gray! Sásha, it's time to stop all this nonsense— it's not too late! You're young, you're innocent, and I—

SÁSHA: You've already said all this. I've heard it all before, and I'm sick of it! Just go to the church; you're keeping everyone waiting.

IVÁNOV: No; I'm going home, and you're going to apologize to your family, because there's not going to be any wedding. I don't care what you tell them. It's time to be sensible. I've been playing Hamlet, you've been playing Ophelia, and it's time for us both to stop.

SÁSHA: *(Angry)* Don't take that tone with me! I don't intend to listen!

IVÁNOV: Well, I intend to talk! And go on talking!

SÁSHA: Why did you come whining here today? You make a laughingstock of everything!

IVÁNOV: A laughingstock? Yes! I want the whole world to laugh at me! I looked at myself in the mirror, and it was like a bomb going off in my head! What melancholy! What a noble mind is here o'erthrown! All I need now is to start writing cheap poetry! Whining, moaning about everything, boring people to death, knowing I'm a has-been! Thanks, but no thanks! I still have a little pride and some conscience left! On my way over here, I kept laughing at myself, and everything was laughing too, making fun of me: the birds, the trees—

SÁSHA: You're not angry—you're crazy!

IVÁNOV: You think so? No, I'm not. It's just that now I see things as they are, and my mind is as clear as your conscience. We love each other, yes, but we are not getting married! I can rant and rave as much as I like, but I have no right to ruin your life! I poisoned my wife's final days with my whining. Since we've been engaged, you've aged five years and forgotten how to laugh. Your father used to have a clear sense of life, and now thanks to me he says he can't understand people anymore. I spread boredom, irritation, disgust, everywhere I go. You have to understand, I've always been a realist, but I've always loved life! And now I'm a whining cynic and I'm beginning to hate life! I can't help myself. I curse my fate and whine, and everyone who hears me starts to hate life too. What pretentiousness! You'd think I was doing life a favor by living! The hell with it.

SÁSHA: But listen to what you're saying! You say you hate whining this way—that means you're ready to change, to start life over again! That's a positive step!

IVÁNOV: I don't see anything positive about it. And what kind of a life am I going to start? My life is over! I'm all washed up! It's time for both of us to face it! *(Sarcastically)* Start life over again!

SÁSHA: Nikolái, please, just listen to yourself! Who says your life is over? Why are you being so cynical? I'm not going to listen to any more of this. Just go to the church, please!

IVÁNOV: My life is over!

SÁSHA: Stop shouting like that—people will hear you!

IVÁNOV: If an intelligent, well-intentioned, educated man for no reason at all starts whining and sliding into a depression and there's nothing he can grab onto, then nothing can save him. Tell me what can save me! Nothing works! I can't drink—it gives me a headache. I refuse to start writing lousy poems. I won't pray to some higher power to save me—I don't believe in all that. Weakness is weakness, and laziness is laziness. What else can I call them? My life is over—over! And talking doesn't help anymore! *(Looks around)* Listen. If you love me, help me. Say you won't marry me, say it right now! Please!

SÁSHA: Oh, Nikolái, if you only knew how you've worn me out, how much pain you make me feel! You're a good person, you're intelligent; how can you put me through all this? Not a day goes by but it's something else, each thing harder than the last.... No woman could put up with it. I wanted a love I could share, an active love, but this ... this is torture!

IVÁNOV: And once we're married it will all get worse. Don't do it! Leave me! It isn't love that motivates you; it's stubbornness! You understand that? You set yourself the goal of saving me no matter what; you flattered yourself you'd be successful.... And now you're ready to give me up: only false emotion keeps you from doing it. Do you understand that?

SÁSHA: What strange, cruel logic you use! How can I leave you? You have no family, no friends.... You're ruined, they've taken away all your property, people say awful things about you....

IVÁNOV: It was stupid of me, coming here. I should have done what I set out to do....

(Enter Lébedev.)

SÁSHA: *(Runs to him)* Papa—oh, my God, he's crazy! He came over here just to torment me! He wants me to leave him, he says he doesn't want to ruin me. Tell him I don't want his noble gesture! I know what I'm doing!

LÉBEDEV: I don't understand anything.... What noble gesture?

IVÁNOV: There isn't going to be any wedding!

SÁSHA: There is too! Papa, tell him there is too going to be a wedding!

LÉBEDEV: Now wait a minute, wait a minute, will you? Why don't you want there to be a wedding?

IVÁNOV: I explained it all to her, but she refuses to understand.

LÉBEDEV: No, don't explain to her, explain to me, and explain so that *I* can understand! All this is driving me crazy! All right, then, all right, what am I supposed to do now? Challenge you to a duel, or what?

IVÁNOV: There's no need for a duel. All you need to do is keep an open mind and hear me out.

SÁSHA: *(Upset, begins to pace)* This is terrible! Just terrible! He's acting like a child!

LÉBEDEV: Listen, Nikolái. According to you, this is all very psychological, but according to me, it's a scandal! My boy, will you listen to me? Calm down! Things in this world aren't all that complicated. The ceiling's white, my boots are black. You love Sásha, she loves you. You love her, stay. You don't love her, go, we won't make a fuss. It's as simple as that! You're both intelligent people, you're well-educated, you're well-fed, thank God, what more do you need? You don't have any money? Money isn't everything. Of course, I understand: your land is mortgaged, you can't make the mortgage payments, I understand, I understand; her mother won't give you any money, fine, you can do without. Sásha says she doesn't want a dowry; it's about her principles and Schopenhauer or something. . . . *(Beat)* I'll tell you what. I have ten thousand in the bank. *(Looks around)* Nobody knows a thing about it . . . my grandmother left it to me. It's yours. Take it, only with one condition: give the count a couple of thousand. . . .

(Guests begin to assemble in the salon.)

IVÁNOV: Pásha, you can't talk me out of it. I'm following my conscience.

SÁSHA: And I'm following *my* conscience! You can say whatever you like; I'm not leaving you. Papa, give us your blessing! Right now! I'll go get Mama. . . . *(Goes out)*

LÉBEDEV: I don't understand any of this. . . .

IVÁNOV: My poor friend, I'm not going to try to explain myself. You wouldn't understand. Am I an honorable man or a monster? Am I sane or psychotic? I was young once, and passionate and intelligent; I loved, I hated, I had faith—in my own way, not like the rest of them. And I worked harder than ten men. I had no idea of my physical limits, no judgment, no knowledge of life—I took on a burden that pulled a muscle and broke my back. I thought youth alone was enough, I was intoxicated with work, I refused to recognize my own limits. There was no other possibility, was there? I mean, there are only a few of us, and there's so much work to be done . . . so much! My God, so much to be done! And after all that, you see how life has treated me? By the time I was thirty, I felt like life was a sick hangover, I felt like an old man in an old bathrobe. I'm beaten down, my soul is sluggish, stagnant, I'm tormented, torn apart, ripped to pieces, without anything to believe in—no love, no goals. I move through the human race like a shadow, and I don't know who I am, why I'm alive, what it is I want. I think love is foolish, I think sex is ridiculous, I think there's no point in work, I think poetry and passionate speeches are vulgar and out of date. And I can't find a way out! I'm thirty-five and I'm already worn out—my pride torments me, my anger suffocates me! *(Staggers)* Just look at me! I can barely stand. . . . Where's Matvéy? Have him take me home.

VOICES OFF: Here's the best man! For the double wedding!

(Enter Shabélsky, Bórkin, after them Lvov and Sásha.)

SHABÉLSKY: Look at me! In a secondhand dress coat, no gloves, and all these repulsive little people making snide remarks and cruel jokes about me.

BÓRKIN: *(In a dress coat, carrying flowers for the grooms)* Whew! Where is he? *(To Ivánov)* We're all waiting at the church, and here you are having one of your intellectual discussions. You're not supposed to see the bride before the ceremony; you're supposed to be there first with me, and then she arrives—didn't anyone ever tell you that?

LVOV: *(To Ivánov)* You're still here? Nikolái Alexéyevich Ivánov, I hereby declare, in front of these witnesses, that you are a bastard! A coward and a bastard!

IVÁNOV: *(Coldly)* Thank you very much.

(General confusion.)

BÓRKIN: *(To Lvov)* Sir, you are being insulting! I hereby challenge you to a duel!

LVOV: And you, sir . . . I consider it beneath me not only to fight with you, sir, but even to talk with you! As for Ivánov, he can demand satisfaction whenever he pleases.

SHABÉLSKY: And I, sir, will fight with you as well!

SÁSHA: *(To Lvov)* What are you insulting him for? What for? Excuse me, but I want an answer! What for?

LVOV: I didn't insult him without proof! I came here as an honest man to make you see what kind of person he is, and I beg you to listen to what I have to say.

SÁSHA: What? What have you got to say? That you're an honest man? We all know that! You'd do better to tell me honestly if you really understand yourself or not! You come in here like an honest man and insult him and nearly kill me in the process. You've been following him around like a shadow, and you were so sure you were doing your duty, being an honest man! You've meddled in his private life, you've slandered and judged him whenever you could, you've sent anonymous letters to me and everyone we know! All that cruel and petty behavior, and you keep on thinking you are such an honest man!

IVÁNOV: *(Laughs)* This isn't a wedding, it's a debating society! Bravo!

SÁSHA: *(To Lvov)* Do you understand yourself or not? What stupid, heartless people! *(Takes Ivánov's hand)* Come on, Nikolái, let's get out of here! Papa, let's go!

IVÁNOV: Go where? Stop, I've got to end all this! I still have some strength left! This is the old Ivánov talking! *(Takes a gun from his pocket)*

SÁSHA: *(Screams)* Nikolái, for the love of God!

IVÁNOV: I've been slipping down this incline forever, but it's time to stop. Time to take my leave. Out of the way, everybody, please! Thank you, Sásha!

SÁSHA: *(Screams)* Nikolái, for the love of God! Don't do it!

IVÁNOV: Leave me alone! *(Runs offstage and shoots himself)*

CURTAIN

IVÁNOV: NOTES

Page 56. "Yes. She has tuberculosis." Tuberculosis, or consumption, as it was called, was the leading cause of death for all age groups in the Western world from the end of the eighteenth century until the early twentieth century. It was the disease that killed Chekhov. The consumptive heroine expiring palely in her lover's arms—Violetta in *La Traviata* and Mimi in *La Bohème,* to name two famous ones—was no operatic cliché. Patients with tuberculosis were thought to do better in warmer regions, and the Crimea, on the Black Sea, has a salubrious climate and has long been a summer vacation resort. The other great center for tuberculosis "cures" was Nice, on the French Riviera. Chekhov himself, after his tuberculosis was diagnosed, spent the winter of 1897 in Nice. After his return to Russia, he sold his farm at Melikhovo and moved to Yalta in the Crimea, where he built himself a house.

Page 68. "Spit spit. There. That'll protect you from the evil eye." Avdótya Nazárovna is a matchmaker, and both her occupation and her manner of speaking would seem more at home in an Ostrovsky play. Her conversation is full of folksy expressions.

Page 77. "... some kind of Hamlet, a completely superfluous man." In 1850,

Turgenev wrote a novel called *The Diary of a Superfluous Man*. The term "superfluous man," and Turgenev's description of him as an ineffectual idealist hero, became a cliché of nineteenth-century Russian criticism, which used the term to criticize the Russian society that presumably produced such men. In 1860, Turgenev wrote an essay called "Hamlet and Don Quixote," in which he divided intellectuals into two types: self-conscious, introspective, and ineffectual Hamlets; and energetic, active Quixotes. Ivánov's early reference to tilting at windmills and his reference to Hamlet here must be read against the background of this essay. Ivánov tells us in essence that he used to be a Quixote and has now become a Hamlet, a superfluous man. But Chekhov is attempting to lay this literary cliché to rest; Ivánov's problems are more deeply psychological and not simply conditioned by the banality or oppression of his milieu. Chekhov himself wrote a long analysis of Ivánov in a letter to his friend Suvorin (Letter 14, in *Letters of Anton Chekhov,* translated by Michael Heim and annotated by Simon Karlinsky).

Page 81, 82. *"Repetátur!"* Latin. It means, roughly, "Time for another."

Page 89. "I'm a monster." This long speech of Ivánov's attempts to lay out his predicament but gets him no closer to an understanding of what is causing his self-hatred and depression.

Page 96. "You goddamn Jew!" Anti-Semitism has always been endemic in Russia. The conversation of Zinaída and Babákina in Act Two sets the tone for it, and even Ivánov, when pushed to a point of anger, as here, reverts to the atavistic attitude. By Chekhov's time, many of the rules restricting Jews to certain areas and certain professions had been removed, and Jews began to be assimilated into the general population. But the old fears and hatreds are as alive in Russia today as they were then.

THE SEAGULL

A COMEDY IN FOUR ACTS

1895

CHARACTERS

Irína Nikoláyevna Arkádina, an actress; her married name is Tréplev

Konstantín Gavrílovich Tréplev, her son, in his twenties

Pyótr Nikoláyevich Sórin, her brother

Nína Mikháilovna Zaréchnaya, nineteen, daughter of a wealthy neighbor

Ilyá Afanásyevich Shamráyev, a retired army lieutenant who manages
Sórin's farm

Paulína Andréyevna, his wife

Másha, his daughter

Borís Alexéyevich Trigórin, a novelist

Yevgény Sergéyevich Dorn, the local doctor

Semyón Semyónovich Medvedénko, a schoolteacher

Yákov, the hired man

The Cook

The Maid

The action takes place at Sórin's farm.

Between Acts Three and Four, two years go by.

ACT ONE

The back lawn at Sórin's farm. A broad path lined with trees leads toward the lake in the distance; a small stage has been set up in the middle of the path, with the curtain drawn, so the lake is hidden. Bushes to the right and left of the little stage. A few chairs, a small table. It's just after sunset. On the little stage, behind the curtain, Yákov and another workman are busy; sounds of coughing and hammering. Enter Mása and Medvedénko, returning from a walk.

MEDVEDÉNKO: Why do you always wear black?

MÁSHA: Because I'm in mourning for my life. I'm not happy.

MEDVEDÉNKO: Why not? *(Perplexed)* I don't understand why not. You're in good health; your father is ... well, he's not rich, but he's pretty well off. I'm in a lot worse shape than you. I make twenty-three rubles a month, that's before payroll deductions, and I'm not in mourning. *(Sits)*

MÁSHA: It has nothing to do with money. You can be poor and still be happy.

MEDVEDÉNKO: Well, maybe in theory, but it doesn't work out that way. There's me, my mother, my two sisters, and my little brother. I'm the wage earner, and all I get is those twenty-three rubles. How am I supposed to buy a drink? Or sugar for tea? Or cigarettes, even? I can't do it.

MÁSHA: *(Looks at the stage)* It's about time for the performance to start.

MEDVEDÉNKO: Yeah ... Konstantín wrote a play, and that Zaréchny girl is starring in it. They're in love. Tonight their souls will be united in a unique artistic endeavor. But your soul and my soul can't find a way to get united! I love you, I love you so much I can't stay away, every day I walk over here—it's five miles over and five miles back—and all I get from you is indifferentism. But I can see why. I haven't got any money, and I have all this family to support. Who'd want to marry a man who hasn't got enough to eat?

MÁSHA: That's not the reason. *(Takes a pinch of snuff)* I know you love me; I'm touched. I just don't love you back, that's all. *(Holds out the snuffbox)* Want some?

MEDVEDÉNKO: No, thanks.

(Pause.)

MÁSHA: It's so muggy. It'll probably rain later on. All you ever do is talk and talk about money. You think there's nothing worse than being poor, but I think it's a thousand times better to go around in rags and beg on the street than . . . Oh, you wouldn't understand.

(Enter Sórin and Konstantín.)

SÓRIN: *(Walks with a cane)* I don't know, my boy, I just don't feel right in the country. I'll never get used to living here. Last night I went to bed at ten, and I woke up this morning at nine, and it felt like my brain was stuck to my skull! Or something. *(Laughs)* And today after lunch I fell asleep again, didn't mean to, and now I'm exhausted. I had a nightmare. Or something.

KONSTANTÍN: You should go live in town. *(Sees Másha and Medvedénko)* Look, we'll call you when it's time, but right now I don't want anybody out here. Do you mind?

SÓRIN: *(To Másha)* Másha, would you please ask your papa to see that the dog gets tied up tonight? Otherwise he just barks. My sister didn't sleep a wink the whole night.

MÁSHA: You can ask my *father* yourself. I don't intend to. Sorry. *(To Medvedénko)* Come on, let's go.

MEDVEDÉNKO: *(To Konstantín)* Don't forget to let us know when it starts.

(Exit Másha and Medvedénko.)

SÓRIN: That means he'll bark all night long again. It's always the same story: I can't ever live in the country the way *I* want. Used to be I'd take a month off, come out here to do nothing, just relax. Or something. But the minute I got here they'd be after me with this and that. . . . After a day of it, I'd be ready to leave. *(Laughs)* The only time I ever felt relaxed was the day I left! Only now I'm retired, I haven't got any other place to go. That's it, I guess. Just go on living, whether you feel like it or not.

YÁKOV: Konstantín Gavrílovich, we're going down to take a dip in the lake.

KONSTANTÍN: All right, but be back in ten minutes, will you? *(Looks at his watch)* We've got to start soon.

YÁKOV: Don't worry, we will.

KONSTANTÍN: *(Checks over the stage)* Now, this is what I call a theater! A curtain, two wings, right and left, and then nothing. No set. Empty space! The curtain opens, all you see is the lake and the far horizon. And the curtain will open at exactly eight-thirty, just as the moon rises.

SÓRIN: That's wonderful!

KONSTANTÍN: Of course, if Nína's late, the whole effect will be ruined. She should have been here by now. Her father and her stepmother keep her locked up, almost. Getting her out of the house is like getting her out of prison. *(Fixes Sórin's tie)* Your hair's a mess; so is your beard. You should have shaved. . . .

SÓRIN: *(Combs his beard with his fingers)* Tragedy of my life. Even when I was your age, I always looked as if I'd been up all night drinking. Never had any luck with women either. *(Sits)* Why is your mother so irritable?

KONSTANTÍN: Why? She's bored. *(Sits beside him)* She's also jealous. She already hates me, she hates my play, she hates this performance tonight because she's afraid her writer friend might like Nína. She's never read my play, but she hates it already.

SÓRIN: *(Laughs)* Oh, you're just imagining things!

KONSTANTÍN: She's angry because Nína's the star of the show and she isn't. *(Looks at his watch)* She's a psychological textbook, my mother. She's talented, no question about that. And smart. She can recite all of Nekrásov's poetry by heart, she's a wonderful nurse if anybody gets sick, she is, really; but just try talking about Eleonora Duse when she's around! Oh, no. You're supposed to talk about *her,* write about *her,* applaud *her,* tell *her* she was divine in *Camille*, or in a piece of trash like *The Fumes of Life*. And here she is in the country, where nobody knows who she is, so she's bored and then she gets mean, and of course it's all our fault. And she's superstitious—she won't light three on a match, she's terrified of the number thirteen. And she's stingy. I happen to know for a fact she has seventy thousand in the bank in Odéssa, but go ask her for a loan and she has hysterics!

SÓRIN: You see, you've made up your mind she won't like your play, and you're all upset already. Just calm down. Your mother adores you.

KONSTANTÍN: *(Picks a daisy and tears off the petals)* She loves me, loves me not. Loves me, loves me not. Loves me, loves me not. *(Laughs)* See? My mother doesn't love me. Well, why should she? She wants to lead a glamorous life, make love to that man, and dress like an eighteen-year-old . . . and then there's me. I'm twenty-five years old; I'm a constant reminder she's not so young anymore. When I'm not around, she's only thirty-two; when I'm around, she's forty-three. That's why she hates me. Besides, I can't stand her kind of theater. She *loves* The Theater, she thinks she's serving the cause of humanity, she thinks she's a high priestess of Art, but what I think is, that kind of theater is tired, it's all worn out. It's so restrictive! The curtain goes up, the lights come on, you're in a room with three walls, and there they are, these servants of art, and all they do is show us how people eat, drink, make love, walk, and wear clothes! And then they try to draw some kind of moral, some nice *easy* little moral, something you wouldn't mind having around the house. You go, they give you the same stuff over and over and over . . . and it makes me sick! I want to run away from it all, the way Maupassant ran away from the Eiffel Tower, he thought it was so ugly and vulgar.

SÓRIN: But we need theater! Can't do without it!

KONSTANTÍN: What we need are new forms! We need new forms, and if we can't have them, then we're better off with no theater at all. *(Looks at his watch)* I love my mother, I really do, but just look at her! She smokes, she drinks, she flaunts her affair with that writer of hers, her name is always in the papers, and I hate all that. *(Beat)* And I guess sometimes it's just my ego talking. I mean, I'm just an ordinary mortal, aren't I? Sometimes I'm sorry she's a great actress, and I think if she were just an ordinary woman I'd be happier. Oh, Uncle . . . it's awful! She has all these famous people at her parties, writers and actors, and I'm the only one there who isn't famous, and they only tolerate me because I'm her son. And who am I? I left the university after my third year, I'm not talented, I haven't got a cent to my name, my birth certificate says I'm from Kíev and I was "born into the middle class." Why? Because my father was from Kíev and he was "born into the middle class"; he just happened to be a famous actor! So there I am with all those actors and writers, and finally someone is kind enough to talk to me, but I know they think I'm a nobody, and I just want to die!

SÓRIN: *(Beat)* That writer of hers—what's he like? I can't figure him out. He never says a thing.

KONSTANTÍN: He's all right. Kind of ordinary. Doesn't say much. He's not dumb, though; he's not even forty yet and he's already rich and famous, he can have anything he wants. So now he only drinks beer and only goes for older women. *(Beat)* I don't know what to say about his writing. . . . He's got talent and charm, but . . . well, who wants to read Trigórin after Tolstóy or Zola?

SÓRIN: I just love writers. There was a time, all I ever wanted was two things: get married and be a writer. And I never did either one. Yes. Well, it must be nice to be a writer, even if you're not famous. I suppose.

KONSTANTÍN: *(Listens)* I hear somebody coming. . . . *(Hugs his uncle)* It's her! Oh, I can't live without her! Even the sound of her footsteps is perfect! I'm so happy I'm out of my mind! *(Goes to greet Nína, as she enters)* Oh, my darling, my dream . . .

NÍNA: *(Out of breath)* I'm not late . . . I'm not, am I?

KONSTANTÍN: *(Kisses her hand)* No, no, no . . .

NÍNA: I've been worried all day—I was afraid my father wouldn't let me come. But he and my stepmother just left. The sky was getting dark, and the moon was starting to rise, so I ran as fast as I could! *(Laughs)* And I'm so glad I'm here! *(Shakes Sórin's hand warmly)*

SÓRIN: *(Laughs)* Your pretty eyes look like they've been crying! Now, now, now . . . mustn't do that . . .

NÍNA: It's just that I . . . See, I'm still out of breath. I can't stay more than a half hour, so we have to hurry. Don't make me late—I just can't be late, I just can't. My father doesn't know I'm here.

KONSTANTÍN: It's all right; it's time to start anyway. I'll go get everybody.

SÓRIN: No, I'll go. Or something. *(Starts out right, singing Schumann's "Beiden Grenadieren": "nach Frankreich zogen zwei Grenadier'n . . . ," stops and looks around)* One time I was singing, just like this, and one of the people in my office said: "You know, sir, you have a really loud voice." Then he thought for a minute and said: "loud . . . and ugly." *(Laughs and goes out)*

NÍNA: My father and my stepmother don't like my coming over here. They say you're all a bunch of bohemians. They're afraid I'll want to be an actress. But it's the lake that attracts me, as if I were a seagull. . . . My heart's overflowing with you. *(Looks around)*

KONSTANTÍN: We're alone.

NÍNA: I thought I heard someone over there. . . .

KONSTANTÍN: There's nobody there.

(They kiss.)

NÍNA: What kind of tree is that?

KONSTANTÍN: An elm.

NÍNA: Why's it so dark?

KONSTANTÍN: Because it's almost night! Things get dark at night! Don't go right back tonight, please. . . .

NÍNA: I have to.

KONSTANTÍN: What if I come with you? I'll stand in the garden all night long and stare at your window.

NÍNA: You can't; there's a watchman. Besides, Treasure isn't used to you—he'd bark.

KONSTANTÍN: I love you.

NÍNA: Shh . . .

KONSTANTÍN: (Hears steps) Who's that? That you, Yákov?

YÁKOV: (Behind the curtain) Yeah, it's us.

KONSTANTÍN: Get ready. Time to start. Is the moon rising?

YÁKOV: It sure is!

KONSTANTÍN: Is the firepot ready? And the sulfur? When the red eyes start to glow, there has to be a smell of sulfur. (To Nína) Go on, everything's ready. Are you nervous?

NÍNA: Oh, God, am I! I don't mean your mother—I'm not afraid of her—but Trigórin is here. I'm . . . I'm afraid to act in front of him. Ashamed too, I guess. He's such a famous writer. . . . Is he young?

KONSTANTÍN: Yes.

NÍNA: Those wonderful stories he writes!

KONSTANTÍN: (Coldly) I don't know. I never read them.

NÍNA: It's not easy, you know, acting in your play. There aren't any ordinary people in it.

KONSTANTÍN: Ordinary people! We have to show life not the way it is, or the way it should be, but the way it is in dreams!

NÍNA: But nothing happens in your play! It's all one long speech. And I think a play ought to have a love story. . . .

(They go behind the stage. Enter Paulína and Dorn.)

PAULÍNA: It's getting damp. Go back and put on your galoshes.

DORN: I'm hot.

PAULÍNA: You never take care of yourself! You're so pigheaded. You're a doctor, you should know the damp air is bad for you, but you just want to see me suffer. Yesterday you sat out on the terrace all night, and you did it on purpose.

DORN: (Sings from Prigózhy's song "The Heavy Cross") "Never say thy youth was wasted . . ."

PAULÍNA: You were so involved in your conversation with Irína, you never even noticed the cold. You find her attractive, don't you? Go on, admit it.

DORN: Look, I'm fifty-five years old!

PAULÍNA: Don't be silly. For men, that's not old. Anyway, you've kept yourself in shape. That's why women still like you.

DORN: What do you want me to do?

PAULÍNA: You fall at her feet, all of you, just because she's an actress. Every one of you!

DORN: *(Sings from Krásov's song "Stanzas")* "Once more, love, before you, enchanted I stand . . ." People love actresses. Of course they treat them differently . . . different, let's say, from a saleslady. That's just the way people are. They're always looking for an ideal image.

PAULÍNA: Women are always falling in love with you, hanging all over you. Is that what you call looking for an ideal image?

DORN: *(Shrugs his shoulders)* So what? I've had relationships with lots of women, and most of them were wonderful. But what attracted them most was the fact that I was a doctor. You remember, ten or fifteen years ago, I was the only decent obstetrician in the county. But I never took advantage of any of my patients.

PAULÍNA: *(Grabs for his hand)* Oh, my darling!

DORN: Shh. Here they come.

(Enter Arkádina arm in arm with Sórin, Trigórin, Shamráyev, Medvedénko, and Másha.)

SHAMRÁYEV: In Poltáva, about twenty-five years ago. She was wonderful! Ravishing! Brilliant acting! And that comic, Chádin, Pável Chádin? Do you remember him? Best Rasplúyev I ever saw; better than Sadóvsky, *madame*, I swear to God. Whatever became of him?

ARKÁDINA: How should I know? Why do you keep asking me about these old has-beens? *(Sits)*

SHAMRÁYEV: Pável Chádin! Ah, they don't make them like that anymore. The theater is in a decline, Irína Nikoláyevna! They were giants back then! Nothing left now but pygmies!

DORN: There aren't all that many geniuses nowadays, true, but I think acting in general has improved. In the smaller roles, I mean.

SHAMRÁYEV: No! There, I'm afraid, I cannot agree with you. But these are, after all, matters of taste. *De gustibus aut bene aut nihil.*

(Konstantín comes out from behind the stage.)

ARKÁDINA: *(To her son)* Dear boy, *when* are we going to start?

KONSTANTÍN: In just a minute. Please be patient.

ARKÁDINA: *(Recites from* Hamlet*)*
  "Oh, Hamlet, speak no more!
    Thou turn'st my eyes into my very soul,
    and there I see such black and grained spots
    as will not leave their tinct."

KONSTANTÍN: "Nay, but to live
    in the rank sweat of an enseamed bed,
    stewed in corruption, honeying and making love
    over the nasty sty—"

  (From behind the stage, the sound of a horn.)

Ladies and gentlemen, your attention, please! We are about to start!

  (Pause.)

I begin. *(Pounds with a stick and speaks in a loud voice)* Oh you ancient shadows, that float at night above this lake, wind us in your magic spell, make us sleep, and make us dream of what this place will be two hundred thousand years from now!

SÓRIN: In two hundred thousand years there'll be nothing left. Nothing!

KONSTANTÍN: Then let them show us that nothing.

ARKÁDINA: Let them, please! The magic spell is making us sleepy.

  (The curtain rises; we see the lake in the distance, the moon rising on the horizon, and its reflection glittering on the water. On a big rock sits Nína, dressed in white.)

NÍNA: Human beings, lions, eagles, quail . . . you horned deer, you wild geese, you spiders, and you wordless fish who swim beneath the wave . . . starfish, stars in heaven so distant the human eye cannot perceive them, all living things, all, all, all . . . all living things have ended their allotted rounds and are no more. . . . For more than a thousand centuries the earth has been lifeless, no single living creature yet remains. . . . And the weary moon in heaven lights her lamp in vain. The cranes in the meadows awake no more; their cries are silent; the flight of beetles in the linden woods is stilled. All is cold, cold, cold. All is empty, empty, empty. All is terror, terror, terror.

  (Pause.)

The bodies of all living beings have returned unto dust, and eternal matter has reduced them to stone, to water, to cloud. All the souls of the universe have been melded into one . . . and I am that universal soul! I contain them all—Alexander the Great, Caesar, Shakespeare, Napoleon, the lowliest worm in the garden. In me the spirit of humanity is distilled with the animal instinct. I remember it all, all, all! Every life that has ever lived lives once more within me, part of myself!

(In the background we see glowing points of light begin to move: will-o'-the-wisps.)

ARKÁDINA: *(Under her breath)* Is this supposed to be symbolic?

KONSTANTÍN: *(Imploring)* Mama, please!

NÍNA: I am alone. Once every hundred years I open my mouth to speak, and my voice resounds, mournful in this wasteland, and no one hears me. . . . Even you, pale fires . . . you cannot hear me. You are born before morning in the muddy swamp, you wander till dawn, without thought, without direction, without any shudder of life. For fear you may engender life, the eternal father of eternal matter, the Demon, changes you moment by moment, as he changes the rocks and the water; he makes your atoms dance unceasingly. In all the universe only I, pure soul, remain eternal and unchanged.

(Pause.)

I am like a prisoner thrown into a deep empty well; I have no sense of where I am or what awaits me. Yet I know that victory will at last be mine in the savage ceaseless struggle with the Demon, the source of all material impulses . . . and then matter and soul will join in beautiful harmony. But that moment will come slowly, after a long procession of centuries, when the moon, the bright star Sirius, the earth itself, have all returned to dust. And until that moment all is horror, horror. . . .

(Pause. From the lake come two burning red eyes.)

See! He approaches! My mighty enemy, the Demon! I see his terrible crimson eyes! I—

ARKÁDINA: Something smells. Is that part of the effect?

KONSTANTÍN: Yes.

ARKÁDINA: *(Laughs)* I can always recognize an effect!

KONSTANTÍN: Mama!

NÍNA: He mourns the absence of humanity—

PAULÍNA: *(To Dorn)* Put your hat back on! You're going to catch cold like that!

ARKÁDINA: The doctor wants to greet the Demon, the father of eternal matter!

KONSTANTÍN: *(An angry shout)* That's it! That's it! The play is over! Close the curtain!

ARKÁDINA: What are you getting mad for?

KONSTANTÍN: It's over! It's all over! Close the curtain! *(Stomps on the stage)* I said close the curtain!!

   (The curtain closes.)

   I'm very sorry. I forgot that only the chosen few can write plays—or act in them. I tried to break into the charmed circle, and see what happens! I . . . I just . . . *(Tries to say something, then waves his hand in disgust and leaves)*

ARKÁDINA: Now what's the matter with him?

SÓRIN: For God's sake, Irína, you can't talk to a young man like that! You've hurt his pride!

ARKÁDINA: What did I say?

SÓRIN: You insulted him!

ARKÁDINA: He told us himself this was going to be a joke, so that's the way I treated it! Like a joke!

SÓRIN: All the same—

ARKÁDINA: And now it turns out he's written a masterpiece! Can you believe this? He arranged all this, that foul smell, not as a joke, but as an attack upon me! He wants to teach us how to write and how to act. It's getting very boring! These constant attacks against me, these snide remarks . . . I don't care what you say, they'd drive anyone crazy! He's just a selfish, spoiled child!

SÓRIN: He only wanted to please you.

ARKÁDINA: Oh? Really? Did he ever think of what *I* might like to watch? No, he gives us some sort of Symbolist raving. I don't mind raving if it's part of the joke, but all this pretentious searching for new forms, for a new era in art! You want to know what I think? These aren't new forms: it's just old-fashioned nastiness.

TRIGÓRIN: Everyone writes the way he wants . . . the way he *can*.

ARKÁDINA: Fine. Let him write any way he wants. Any way he can. Just don't ask me to sit through it!

DORN: O mighty Jove, thou art angry—

ARKÁDINA: I'm not mighty Jove, I'm a woman. *(Lights a cigarette)* And I'm not angry; I'm just annoyed to think of a young man wasting his time like this. I didn't mean to insult him.

MEDVEDÉNKO: Also, you know, there's no scientific basis for separating soul from matter; I mean, the soul itself may be nothing but a collection of atoms. *(Brightly, to Trigórin)* You know what somebody ought to write a play about? Schoolteachers! And what a hard life we lead. I'd like to see that on the stage!

ARKÁDINA: Oh, let's talk about something else, shall we? What a marvelous evening! You hear that singing? *(Listens)* Absolutely marvelous!

PAULÍNA: It's coming from the other side of the lake.

(Pause.)

ARKÁDINA: *(To Trigórin)* Come sit here beside me. Ten or fifteen years ago, there was music and singing here by the lake almost every night. There were six big country houses on the lake then. I remember the laughter, the parties—people were always shooting off guns, all night long—and the love affairs, oh, the endless love affairs! And you know who was the handsome juvenile lead, the Don Juan of all six country houses? Our dear doctor here! *(Bows to Dorn)* He's still delightful, but then he was irresistible! *(Beat)* Oh, now my conscience is starting to bother me. Why did I have to be so rude to my poor boy? I'm all upset. *(Shouts)* Kóstya! Kóstya! My son!

MÁSHA: I'll go find him.

ARKÁDINA: Would you mind? Thank you, dear.

MÁSHA: Yoo-hoo! Konstantín! Konstantín! *(Goes out left)*

NÍNA: *(Comes out from behind the stage)* It doesn't look like we're going on, so I might as well come out. Hello! *(Exchanges kisses with Arkádina and Paulína)*

SÓRIN: Bravo! Bravo!

ARKÁDINA: Bravo! Bravo! We just adored you. With your looks and that marvelous voice, it's a sin to stay out here in the country. My dear, I *believe* in you! You simply must go on the stage!

NÍNA: Oh, that's my dream! *(Sighs)* But it'll never happen.

ARKÁDINA: Who knows? Here, let me introduce you: Borís Alexéyevich Trigórin.

NÍNA: Oh, I'm so honored! *(Embarrassed)* I read all your things. . . .

ARKÁDINA: *(Sits her down next to her)* Don't be embarrassed, my dear.

He may be famous, but he's very ordinary, really. See? He's embarrassed too.

DORN: I guess we should do something about the curtain. It looks a bit sinister hanging there like that.

SHAMRÁYEV: *(Shouts)* Yákov, my boy, raise that curtain!

(The curtain slowly rises.)

NÍNA: *(To Trigórin)* It was a strange play, wasn't it?

TRIGÓRIN: I'm afraid I didn't understand a thing. But it was interesting to watch. You were wonderful. And of course, the set was magnificent!

(Pause; they all look at the moonlit vista.)

I'll bet there are a lot of fish in that lake.

NÍNA: What? Oh, I suppose there must be. . . .

TRIGÓRIN: I love to fish. I can't think of a greater pleasure in the world than to sit on a dock, watching a float bob up and down.

NÍNA: Oh, but I'd think once you've known the thrill of creation, all other pleasures must pale by comparison.

ARKÁDINA: *(Laughs)* Don't say things like that to him! He hates it when people talk about art. He never knows what to say.

SHAMRÁYEV: I remember one time in Moscow, at the opera, the famous basso Silva sang a low C. Now, it so happened, that very evening, the bass from one of our local choirs was in the balcony, and all of a sudden—and I'm sure you can imagine our complete amazement—we heard him sing "Bravo, Silva!" *an entire octave lower!* Just like this: *(Sings in a low bass)* "Bravo, Silva!" The theater went absolutely wild!

(Pause.)

DORN: The angel of silence just flew past. . . .

NÍNA: I have to go. It's late.

ARKÁDINA: Why? Why so early? You must stay, we insist!

NÍNA: My father will be waiting up for me.

ARKÁDINA: Oh, that cruel man! Really! *(Kisses her)* Well, I suppose you must. I just hate to let you go.

NÍNA: If you only knew how I hate to leave!

ARKÁDINA: Wait, darling, we'll get someone to go back with you.

NÍNA: *(Terrified)* Oh, no, no, really, you mustn't!

SÓRIN: *(Pleading)* Oh, do stay awhile!

NÍNA: I'm afraid I can't.

SÓRIN: Just for an hour, that's all. Can't you . . . ?

NÍNA: *(Hesitates, with tears in her eyes)* I can't! I simply can't! *(Shakes hands and leaves)*

ARKÁDINA: She is the most unfortunate girl! They say her mother left her entire enormous fortune to her husband, nothing whatsoever to the girl, and now the father has remarried and made a will leaving it all to his second wife! It's simply a scandal.

DORN: It's true, the father's a monster.

SÓRIN: *(Rubs his chilly hands)* Let's go in, shall we? I'm going to catch my death in all this dampness. And my legs hurt.

ARKÁDINA: You're right, they're stiff as boards. Come on, you poor old dear. *(Takes his arm)*

SHAMRÁYEV: *(Offers his arm to his wife)* Madame?

SÓRIN: There's that dog barking again! *(To Shamráyev)* Ilyá Afanásyevich, have them tie him up, will you?

SHAMRÁYEV: Sorry, can't be done. Need him to guard the barn. I've got the barn full of millet. *(To Medvedénko, who goes out beside him)* Yes indeed, a whole octave lower. "Bravo, Silva!" And he wasn't even a trained singer; he was just from one of the local choirs.

MEDVEDÉNKO: How much do choir singers make, do you know?

(Everyone goes out, except Dorn.)

DORN: I don't know, maybe I'm crazy, but I really liked that play. . . . There was something to it. It was new, and different. . . .

(Enter Konstantín.)

KONSTANTÍN: They've all gone.

DORN: I'm here.

KONSTANTÍN: That Másha's been chasing me all over the place! I can't stand her.

DORN: Konstantín, I liked your play a lot, I really did. It was strange, yes, and of course we never heard the end, but it made a great impression on me. You're a very talented young man, you know. You have to keep on writing!

(Konstantín reaches for his hand, then impulsively throws his arms around him.)

Why, you're all upset! You've been crying. . . . What was it I wanted to say? Of course, you tackled a difficult subject, an abstract one. And you were right to. Every work of art has to express some great idea. True beauty is always a serious matter. *(Beat)* You're very pale; are you—

KONSTANTÍN: You really think I should keep on writing?

DORN: Of course. But you must deal only with serious, eternal topics. You know, I've led a . . . a varied life, lived it with taste, I like to think, and I've enjoyed it. But if I could experience, just for a moment, the excitement that must come with artistic creation . . .

KONSTANTÍN: Excuse me, but . . . where did Nína go?

DORN: And another thing. Everything you write has to have a clear, concise central idea. You have to be aware of what you're writing, otherwise you'll . . . you'll lose your way, and your talent will destroy you.

KONSTANTÍN: *(Impatiently)* Where's Nína?

DORN: She went home.

KONSTANTÍN: *(In despair)* What am I going to do? I've got to see her, I've just got to! I'm going after her. . . .

(Enter Másha.)

DORN: Calm down, my boy, calm down.

KONSTANTÍN: I don't care, I'm going. I *have* to!

MÁSHA: Konstantín, you should go back to the house. Your mother's looking for you. She's all upset.

KONSTANTÍN: Tell her I'm not here! Tell her I left! And will you all please leave me in peace! Just leave me alone! Stop following me around!

DORN: You mustn't talk like that, dear boy, you really mustn't.

KONSTANTÍN: *(Almost in tears)* Goodbye, Doctor. And thank you . . . *(Goes out)*

DORN: *(Sighs)* Ah, youth, youth.

MÁSHA: Whenever people can't think of anything better to say, they say "youth, youth." *(Takes a pinch of snuff)*

DORN: *(Takes the tobacco box from her and throws it into the bushes)* That's a disgusting habit!

(Pause.)

Somebody's playing the piano. I suppose we should go in.

MÁSHA: Wait a minute.

DORN: What's the matter?

MÁSHA: I wanted to talk to you. . . . I have to talk to somebody. . . . *(Upset)* I don't like my father. I like you better. I don't know why, but I feel close to you. Help me! Help me before I do something stupid, before I make a mess of everything.... I can't go on like this!

DORN: What's the matter? What can I do?

MÁSHA: I'm in such pain ... nobody knows how painful it is! *(Leans her head against his chest)* I'm in love with Konstantín.

DORN: You're so upset! You're all so upset! All this love ... It's that magic lake! *(Tenderly)* But what can I do to help, my child? Hm? What? What?

CURTAIN.

ACT TWO

The side lawn, laid out for croquet. Upstage right, the house, its broad veranda. The lake is visible off left, sparkling in the sun. Flower beds. It is noon, and hot. At the edge of the lawn, in the shade of an old linden tree, garden benches. Arkádina, Dorn, and Másha. Dorn holds an open book.

ARKÁDINA: *(To Másha)* Here. Stand up a minute.

(Both women stand.)

Over here, right next to me. You're ... what? Twenty-two? And I'm almost twice your age. Doctor, which one of us looks younger?

DORN: You do ... of course.

ARKÁDINA: There. You see? And why? Because I work all the time, I live life to the fullest, I'm constantly on the go. You do nothing; you just sit around here. You never *live.* I have a fixed rule: I never think about the future. I don't think about old age, I don't think about dying. Whatever happens happens.

MÁSHA: I always feel as if I'd been born ages and ages ago; I just drag myself from one day to the next, like the hem of my skirt. And there are days when I just don't feel like living. *(Sits down)* But that's all silly, isn't it? I should pull myself together, stop feeling like that.

DORN: *(Sings softly, from Gounod's* Faust*)* "Faites-lui mes aveux, portez mes voeux ..."

ARKÁDINA: You see, darling, I take care of my appearance. I am always tailored, always *fit.* Yes, that's the phrase. I'm always per-

fectly dressed, my hair is always done, everything *comme il faut.*
Do you think I'd ever leave the house—even out into the garden—in a housecoat or with my hair a mess? Never. That's why I
look so young. Nothing of the frump about *me*! I never let myself
go the way some women do. *(Puts her hands on her hips and parades
up and down the lawn)* You see how light on my feet I am? I could
play a girl of fifteen with no trouble at all.

DORN: Well . . . Should I keep on reading? *(Beat)* I suppose I should.
(Opens the book) Where did we leave off? The grain merchant
and the rats.

ARKÁDINA: The rats, right. Go on. *(Sits)* No, better yet, give me the
book. I'll read. It's my turn anyway. *(Takes the book and pages
through it until she finds the place)* The rats . . . Here we are.
(Reads) "But of course for people in fashionable society to get
involved with writers and try to make them part of their circle is
as dangerous as for a grain merchant to raise rats in his barn. But
they love to do it. So then, whenever a woman decides she wants
to make a conquest of a particular writer, she flatters him,
beguiles him with compliments, favors, entertainments. . . ."
Well, that may be true in France, but we don't do things that way
here. We're not so cynical. What usually happens here is, a
woman who tries to seduce a writer winds up head over heels in
love with him, thank you very much! Take myself and Trigórin,
for instance—

*(Enter Sórin, walking with a cane, arm in arm with Nína.
Medvedénko follows, pushing empty wheelchair.)*

SÓRIN: *(As if talking to a child)* Yes? Are we happy? Are we really,
really happy? Did our father and stepmother go 'way and leave us
by ourselves for three whole days? Are we happy?

NÍNA: *(Sits down next to Arkádina and kisses her)* Yes, we're happy!
And now I can be with you!

SÓRIN: *(Sits in the wheelchair)* Doesn't she look pretty today?

ARKÁDINA: Yes, very interesting . . . Her clothes are perfect. What a
smart girl! *(Kisses Nína)* But we mustn't overdo the compliments,
must we? Otherwise we'll spoil her. *(Beat)* Where's Borís?

NÍNA: Down at the dock, fishing.

ARKÁDINA: How *does* that man keep from getting bored? *(Prepares to
read again)*

NÍNA: What are you reading?

ARKÁDINA: Maupassant, darling. *Sur l'eau.* *(Reads a few lines to her-*

self) Oh, well, the rest is boring. Anyway, it's not true. *(Shuts the book)* I feel just awful about my son. What's going on with him—do you know? Why is he bored all the time? And why is he so distant? He spends whole days down by the lake. I almost never see him anymore.

MÁSHA: He's depressed. *(To Nína, a little too loudly)* Please! Recite something from his play, will you?

NÍNA: *(Shrugs her shoulders)* Why? It's so boring!

MÁSHA: *(With contained emotion)* You should see him whenever he recites something he wrote: his eyes burn, his face gets very pale and intense. He has such a beautiful, sad voice! You can tell he's a real poet.

> *(Beat. We are aware that Sórin is snoring loudly.)*

DORN: Nighty-night! Sleep tight!

ARKÁDINA: Petrúshka!

SÓRIN: Wha . . . ?

ARKÁDINA: You fell asleep.

SÓRIN: I did not.

> *(Pause.)*

ARKÁDINA: My dear, you haven't been taking your medicine! You simply must!

SÓRIN: I'd like to take my medicine, but the doctor here won't give me any.

DORN: You're sixty years old. Medicine won't help.

SÓRIN: But I want to go on living! Even at sixty!

DORN: *(Irritably)* Oh, all right! Go take a couple of aspirin!

ARKÁDINA: I think he ought to go to a spa somewhere. Go take the waters.

DORN: Fine. Why not? If he wants to go take the waters, let him. Or not. Whatever.

ARKÁDINA: How are we supposed to understand *that*?

DORN: What's there to understand? Seems clear enough to me.

> *(Pause.)*

MEDVEDÉNKO: What he really should do is stop smoking.

SÓRIN: Oh, don't be silly. There's nothing wrong with smoking.

DORN: He's not being silly; he's right. Smoking, drinking, they change your personality. You smoke a cigar or take a drink of vodka, and you're no longer Pyótr Nikoláyevich—you're Pyótr

Nikoláyevich plus something else, something that gives you a new identity, and you start thinking and behaving as if you were another individual entirely. You are no longer the real you.

SÓRIN: You're a fine one to talk! You've lived an interesting life. Me? I worked for twenty-eight years in a government office, and I haven't had a life, I haven't *experienced* it or anything. And I *want* to—you understand what I mean? You've been everywhere, done everything; it's easy for you to be philosophical: you don't care anymore. But I want to live! Which is why I drink sherry after dinner and smoke cigars. And everything. That's why.

DORN: Look, nobody said life was easy. But frankly, taking medicine at your age, complaining you wasted your youth ... well, excuse me, but I think *that*'s being silly.

MÁSHA: *(Gets up)* It must be almost lunchtime. *(Starts out slowly, dragging her foot slightly)* My foot's gone to sleep. . . . *(Goes out)*

DORN: She'll have a couple of vodkas before lunch.

SÓRIN: The poor child's never been happy.

DORN: That means nothing.

SÓRIN: You talk like a man who's had everything.

ARKÁDINA: Oh, what could be more boring than this divine country boredom! It's hot, it's quiet, nobody does a thing, we all just sit around and talk. . . . You know, my dears, I do love it here, but if I were working now—in a room in a hotel somewhere, memorizing my lines for a new play—that would be heaven!

NÍNA: *(Ecstatic)* Oh, yes! I know exactly what you mean!

SÓRIN: Well, of course! You're always better off in town. You've got your own office, nobody gets in to see you without an appointment, you've got a telephone ... and if you want to go someplace, you just call a cab. . . . Or something.

DORN: *(Sings)* "Faites-lui mes aveux, portez mes voeux ..."

(Enter Shamráyev; Paulína follows him.)

SHAMRÁYEV: Here they are! A beautiful day, eh? *(Kisses Arkádina's hand, then Nína's)* Glad to see you all looking so well. *(To Arkádina)* My wife tells me you and she are planning to go into town later today, that correct?

ARKÁDINA: That's what we were planning, yes.

SHAMRÁYEV: Ah, I see. Hmm. Well, now, dear *madame*, that's wonderful, only ... we're bringing in the rye today. All the men are busy; so are the horses. So exactly how were you planning to get there?

ARKÁDINA: How? How should I know! What do you mean, how?

SÓRIN: We have carriage horses—

SHAMRÁYEV: *(Angry)* Carriage horses? Yes, fine, we've got carriage horses, but what about harness? Where do you expect me to get harness for them? Hm? This is really incomprehensible! My dear *madame*, you'll have to excuse me. I am your greatest admirer, I'd give you ten years of my life, but I cannot give you any horses!

ARKÁDINA: This is ridiculous! And suppose I *have* to go to town?

SHAMRÁYEV: My dear *madame*, have you any idea what it takes to run a farm?

ARKÁDINA: *(Explodes)* Oh, for God's sake, it's always the same thing! Fine. If that's the way things are, I'm leaving! I'm going back to Moscow today. Have them go hire me some horses down in the village. Or I'll just *walk* to the station!

SHAMRÁYEV: *(Explodes)* Fine! Then I quit! Get yourselves another manager! *(Goes out)*

ARKÁDINA: Every summer, every summer, always the same thing! I come out here, and everybody insults me! I never want to set foot on this place again!

(Arkádina goes out left, toward the dock; after a moment we see her cross into the house. Trigórin follows her, carrying his fishing rods and basket.)

SÓRIN: *(Explodes)* This is outrageous! This is . . . damn it, this is . . . I have had enough of this! I mean, really! Go tell them to bring the carriage horses up here at once!

NÍNA: *(To Paulína)* But she's a famous actress! How could you? I just can't believe this! Why, anything she wants, anything her heart desires, is more important than this farm of yours!

PAULÍNA: *(In despair)* What can I do? Put yourself in my position! What can I do?

SÓRIN: *(To Nína)* Come on, we'll go talk to my sister. Come on, everybody. We'll all go persuade her to stay, won't we? *(Glancing in the direction of Shamráyev's exit)* That man is impossible! He's a tyrant!

NÍNA: *(Keeps him from getting up)* No, no, stay there, stay there. We'll push you.

(She and Medvedénko wheel Sórin off.)

Oh, this is just terrible. . . .

SÓRIN: Terrible! Yes, it is! Just terrible! *(Beat)* But he won't quit; you'll see; I'll talk him out of it.

(They leave. Dorn and Paulína remain.)

DORN: People are ridiculous. He should have thrown your husband out on his ear once and for all. Instead it'll end the way it always does—that old lady Pyótr Nikoláyevich and his sister will wind up *apologizing* to him. Wait and see!

PAULÍNA: He sent the carriage horses out to the field. And every day it's something else. If you only knew how upset he makes me! I get sick to my stomach, I really do—look, my hands are shaking. He's so vulgar! I can't stand him anymore, I really can't. *(Pleading)* Yevgény dear, my darling, please! Take me away from here! Let me come live with you. We're not getting any younger, but it's not too late. Let's stop lying, and pretending our lives are over....

(Pause.)

DORN: I'm fifty-five. That's a little late for a change of life.

PAULÍNA: I know why you want to be rid of me. It's because you've got lots of other women, don't you? I'm not the only one, am I? You can't have all of them move in with you, can you? I understand. Pardon me. I bore you, don't I?

(Nína appears by the house, picking flowers.)

DORN: No, you don't.

PAULÍNA: I'm dying of jealousy! And what do you care? You're a doctor—you see lots of women. I understand.

DORN: *(To Nína, who approaches)* What's going on in there?

NÍNA: Irína Nikoláyevna is crying, and Pyótr Nikoláyevich is having an asthma attack.

DORN: Come on. They're both going to need some aspirin.

NÍNA: *(Gives him the flowers)* Here. These are for you.

DORN: *Merci bien. (Goes toward the house)*

PAULÍNA: *(Follows him)* What lovely flowers! *(Under her breath, as they reach the veranda)* Give me those flowers! Come on, give them to me! *(Grabs the flowers, tears them to bits, and throws them away)*

(Exit Dorn and Paulína. Nína is alone.)

NÍNA: It's so strange, watching a great actress cry! And all over nothing! And even stranger to see a famous writer ... Everybody knows his work, he gets written about in all the papers, and all he wants to do is fish! And he was so proud of himself because he caught two little perch! I thought famous people would be serious and unapproachable, that they'd all hate publicity and hate being famous. But they cry and go fishing and play cards and laugh and get mad, just like the rest of us. . . .

(Enter Konstantín. He is hatless. He carries a rifle and a dead seagull.)

KONSTANTÍN: You all by yourself here?

NÍNA: Yes.

(Konstantín places the dead gull at her feet.)

NÍNA: What's this supposed to mean?

KONSTANTÍN: I've been a bad boy. I killed a seagull this morning. In your honor.

NÍNA: What's the matter with you? *(Picks up the seagull and looks at it)*

KONSTANTÍN: *(Beat)* I intend to shoot myself one of these days, just like this.

NÍNA: I don't recognize you anymore.

KONSTANTÍN: Sure. That's because I don't recognize you anymore either. You've changed. You look at me with that cold look; you're always on edge when I'm around.

NÍNA: Well, you've been trying to pick a fight with me for days now! You sulk, you talk and talk and I can't understand what you mean. You talk in symbols. Like this seagull—is this supposed to be a symbol too? Well, excuse me, but I don't quite get it. *(Sets the dead bird on the bench)* I must be too *ordinary* a person to understand what you mean.

KONSTANTÍN: It started that night my play was such a howling failure. Women never forgive failures. I burned it, every last page. I'm so unhappy, you don't even know! When you're cold to me like this, I can't believe it; it scares me: it's like I woke up one morning and the lake had disappeared right into the ground! *(Beat)* You said just now you were too ordinary to understand me. What's so hard to understand? Nobody liked my play, you think my ideas are stupid, you think I'm mediocre, you think I'm a failure, just like they all do. Oh, I understand that, I understand *you. (Kicks the ground)* I feel like somebody pounded a nail into my head! Goddamn it! *(Sees Trigórin, who enters reading a book)* Here comes the real talent! Behold, he enters! Just like Hamlet—

he was reading a book too. *(Makes fun of him)* "Words, words, words . . ." The sun rises, his rays barely touch you, and already you're smiling, your eyes are melting in the heat of his rays. Well, excuse me, I'll get out of your way. *(Runs out)*

TRIGÓRIN: *(Writes in his notebook)* . . . takes snuff, drinks . . . always wears black. The schoolteacher's in love with her—

NÍNA: Borís Alexéyich! Hello!

TRIGÓRIN: Oh. Hello! There's been an unexpected turn of events: I gather we'll be leaving today. And you and I haven't even gotten to know each other. Too bad. It's so rare that I meet interesting young girls your age, I forget what they're like. I can't remember anymore how people feel at eighteen or nineteen; that's why the young girls in my stories never ring quite right. I'd love to be in your shoes just for a moment, just to know what you're thinking and what kind of a person you are.

NÍNA: And I'd love to be in your shoes.

TRIGÓRIN: Why?

NÍNA: To see what it feels like to be a famous writer. What does fame feel like? How do you know when you're finally famous?

TRIGÓRIN: How? I don't know. I never think about it. *(Thinks for a minute)* Either you're exaggerating my fame, or there's no feeling involved. I don't feel anything.

NÍNA: What about when you read your name in the papers?

TRIGÓRIN: If they like you, it's fine; if they don't, you feel irritable for a couple of days.

NÍNA: What a wonderful life! You don't know how much I envy you! People's destinies are so different. Some people just drag along, unnoticed and boring—they're all alike, and they're all unhappy. Then there are others, like for instance you—you're one in a million! Your life turned out bright, interesting, full of meaning. You're happy—

TRIGÓRIN: I'm happy? *(Shrugs)* Hmm. You talk about fame, about happiness, about some sort of bright, interesting life, but those are just big words. They don't mean anything to me. Sorry. They're like gumdrops, which I never eat. You're very young . . . and very nice, but—

NÍNA: But you have such a beautiful life!

TRIGÓRIN: What's so wonderful about it? *(Looks at his watch)* It's time for me to get to work. Writing. I'm sorry, I really can't— *(Laughs)* You've stepped on my favorite sore toe—I think that's the expression—and I'm getting upset and a little angry. All right, let's talk, shall we? Let's talk about my bright, interesting life. Where shall we start? *(Thinks a bit)* Sometimes people get obsessive about things, ideas, like a man who spends all his time, let's say, thinking about the moon, staring at the moon. Well, I have a moon of my own. All I think about day and night is having to write. I have to write, I *have* to. I finish one story, and then I have to write another one, and then a third, and after that a fourth. I write without stopping, like an express train; it's the only way I know how. Now, I ask you, what's so beautiful and bright about that? It's a stupid life! Here I am talking to you, I'm all worked up, and still I can't forget for a minute that I've got a story to finish. I see a cloud, like that one, shaped like a piano. And all I can think is: I have to use that, one of my characters has to see a cloud shaped like a piano. I smell the heliotrope, I make a mental note: a sickly-sweet smell, a widow's color, use it to describe a summer evening. Every word you and I are saying right now, every sentence, I capture and lock up in the back of my brain. Because someday I can use them! When I finish working, I go out to the theater, or go fishing, to relax and get away from everything. Do you think I can? No, a great iron cannonball starts rolling around in my head, an idea for a new story, and I'm hooked, I can feel my desk reeling me in, and I have to go write and write. All the time! And I never get any rest. I feel like I'm devouring my own life. *(Beat)* Doesn't that sound crazy to you? You think my friends and family treat me as if I were sane? "What are you working on now?" they ask. It's always the same, and sometimes I think all the attention and the praise and the adoration is just delusion—they're deluding me into thinking I'm sane, and I'm really not, and someday they'll creep up behind me and drag me off to the crazy house. And when I was young, and could have been out enjoying myself, writing was sheer hell. A beginning writer, unless he's lucky, feels completely out of place—awkward, useless, nervous. He's obsessed with successful writers and people in the arts, he hangs around them, but nobody notices him. And he's afraid to look anyone in the eyes. He's like a compulsive gambler without any money! I never knew who my readers were, but I had this vision of them: hostile, unimpressed. I was afraid of the public, terrified of it, and whenever a new play of mine opened, I always thought the people with dark hair hated it and the ones with blond hair were bored by it. It's horrible!

NÍNA: Excuse me, but doesn't inspiration, the process of creation, give you some satisfaction, a few moments of sublime happiness?

TRIGÓRIN: No. *(Beat)* Oh, when I'm writing it's not bad, and doing the final editing, that's enjoyable. But once it's published I can't stand to read it, I can see how wrong it is, I realize I should never have written it, and I'm depressed and miserable. *(Laughs)* And then people read it and say: "Yes, very nice, he's quite talented, very nice, but he's no Tolstóy." Or they say: "Lovely story. But Turgénev's *Fathers and Sons* is better." And it'll never change; I'll go on being nice and talented, nice and talented, until the day they bury me, and my friends will stand around my grave and say: "Here lies Trigórin. He was a good writer, but Turgénev was better."

NÍNA: Excuse me, but I just don't understand any of that. I think success has spoiled you.

TRIGÓRIN: What success? I'm never satisfied with what I write. I hate being a writer. The worst is when I'm in a kind of trance and don't even know what I'm writing. . . . Look, I love this place—the lake, the trees, the sky; I feel very close to nature—it inspires me, gives me a real desire to write. But I'm not just a landscape painter, I'm also a citizen; I love my country and its people, and I feel that if I'm going to write, then I ought to write about them and their sufferings, their future, write about scientific advances and the rights of man, and so forth and so forth, and I do, and then people get angry with me and criticize me and attack me. I'm like a fox with a pack of hounds, and I see how science and life keep advancing and I keep falling behind, and finally I'm convinced the only things I *can* write are landscapes. Anything else and I'm a fake, a complete fake!

NÍNA: You've been working too hard; you've lost any sense of your own significance. You may not like yourself, but the rest of us love you! If I was a famous writer like you, I'd sacrifice my entire life for my readers, but I'd have the satisfaction of knowing I was the only image of happiness they had! And they would draw my chariot through the streets!

TRIGÓRIN: A chariot? What, like Agamemnon?

(They both smile.)

NÍNA: If I could have that, I'd put up with rejection, poverty, disappointment; I'd be willing to live in a garret and starve; maybe I wouldn't even like myself . . . just as long as I was famous! Really, spectacularly famous! *(Hides her face in her hands)* Ohh! I feel dizzy. . . .

ARKÁDINA'S VOICE: *(Calls from inside the house)* Borís! Borís Alexéyich!

TRIGÓRIN: They're calling me. Must be time to pack. And now I don't feel like leaving. *(Looks out at the lake)* God, how beautiful! Wonderful, isn't it?

NÍNA: You see that house on the opposite shore? The one with the garden?

TRIGÓRIN: Yes.

NÍNA: That's my mother's place. She's dead. I was born there. I've spent my whole life by this lake; I know every little island out there.

TRIGÓRIN: What a wonderful spot. *(Sees the dead seagull)* What's this?

NÍNA: A seagull. Konstantín shot it.

TRIGÓRIN: Such a beautiful bird. I really don't feel like leaving. *(Beat)* Why don't you persuade Irína Nikoláyevna to stay a little longer? *(Jots down something in his notebook)*

NÍNA: What are you writing?

TRIGÓRIN: Nothing, just making a note. *(Puts the notebook away)* Idea for a short story. The shore of a lake, and a young girl who's spent her whole life beside it, a girl like you ... She loves the lake the way a seagull does, and she's happy and free as a seagull. Then a man comes along, sees her, and ruins her life because he has nothing better to do. Destroys her like this seagull here.

(Pause. Arkádina appears at a window.)

ARKÁDINA: Borís, where are you?

TRIGÓRIN: Out here. *(Heads for the house, but stops and looks back at Nína. Then, to Arkádina)* What?

ARKÁDINA: We're staying.

(Trigórin goes into the house.)

NÍNA: *(Crosses downstage; pauses)* My dream!

CURTAIN.

ACT THREE

Sórin's dining room. Doors right and left. A sideboard. A medicine cabinet. In the middle of the room, a dining table. Suitcases and cartons; preparations for a departure. Trigórin sits at the table, having lunch. Másha stands next to the table.

MÁSHA: I'm telling you all this because you're a writer. Maybe you can use it. I swear to God, if he'd hurt himself seriously, I wouldn't have gone on living for another minute. But I'm very brave, you have to understand that. I made up my mind to tear love out of my heart, tear it out by the roots.

TRIGÓRIN: How are you going to do that?

MÁSHA: I'm getting married. I'm going to marry Medvedénko.

TRIGÓRIN: That schoolteacher?

MÁSHA: Yes.

TRIGÓRIN: I don't see what's your hurry.

MÁSHA: You love someone, it's hopeless, you wait years for something to happen ... *(Beat)* So I'm getting married. No love involved, just lots of responsibilities ... Make me forget the past. Besides, it's a change. You know. Shall we have another?

TRIGÓRIN: Haven't you had enough?

MÁSHA: Here we go. *(Pours them each another drink)* You don't have to look at me like that. Women drink a lot more than you think. Some of them are open about it, like me; most of them do it in secret. Oh, yes, they do. And it's always vodka or brandy. *(They clink glasses)* All the best! You're an easy man to get along with; I'm sorry you're leaving.

(They drink.)

TRIGÓRIN: I'm sorry I'm leaving too.

MÁSHA: Why don't you go ask her to stay?

TRIGÓRIN: She won't stay now. Her son's acting crazy. First he shoots himself, now he wants to fight a duel with me. What's the point? He sulks, he goes around whining about everything, wants to be a prophet of new forms.... There's plenty of room for all the forms you want—why fight about it?

MÁSHA: Well, he's jealous. Anyway, it's none of my business.

(Pause.)

(Yákov crosses from left to right, carrying a suitcase; enter Nína; she goes and stands by the window.)

My schoolteacher isn't all that smart, he's poor, but he's a good man, and he loves me very much. I feel sorry for him. And I feel sorry for his old mother. Well, I wish you all the best. Don't think too badly of me. *(Gives him a firm handshake)* I'm very grateful to you for being so nice to me. Send me your books, and be sure you autograph them. Only, please, don't write "Best wishes" or anything. Just write: "For Másha, who doesn't know where she came from or why she goes on living." Goodbye. *(Goes out)*

NÍNA: *(Makes a fist and holds out her hand to Trigórin)* Odd or even?

TRIGÓRIN: Even.

NÍNA: *(Sighs)* Wrong. All I had was one pebble in my hand. I was trying to guess if I'd be an actress or not. I wish someone would advise me.

TRIGÓRIN: Nobody can advise you about that.

(Pause.)

NÍNA: You're leaving; we probably won't see each other ever again. I want you to take this as a souvenir of me, a little medallion. I had your initials inscribed on it. And on the other side is the title of your book *Days and Nights*.

TRIGÓRIN: How sweet of you! *(Kisses the medallion)* What a lovely gift!

NÍNA: So you can think of me sometimes.

TRIGÓRIN: I will. I'll think of you the way you were that day last week . . . remember? The sun was shining, you were wearing a white dress, and we talked . . . and there was that white seagull lying on the garden bench.

NÍNA: *(Remembering)* Oh, yes, the seagull . . .

(Pause.)

They're coming; we mustn't talk anymore. Just give me two minutes before you go, please! Promise me! *(Goes out left)*

(Enter from right Arkádina, Sórin, dressed formally, and Yákov, who busies himself with the luggage.)

ARKÁDINA: Really, dear, don't you think you should stay home? You shouldn't go gadding around town, not with your rheumatism. *(To Trigórin)* Who was that who went out just now? Nína?

TRIGÓRIN: Yes.

ARKÁDINA: *Pardon.* Sorry if we interrupted something. *(Sits)* I think I've gotten everything packed. I'm exhausted.

TRIGÓRIN: *(Reading the medallion)* "*Days and Nights*, page one twenty-one, lines eleven and twelve."

YÁKOV: *(Clears the table)* Did you want me to pack your fishing rods?

TRIGÓRIN: Yes, I may still need them. You can give the books away.

YÁKOV: All right.

TRIGÓRIN: *(To himself)* Page one twenty-one, lines eleven and twelve. What is that? *(To Arkádina)* Do you have my books in the house anywhere?

ARKÁDINA: In my brother's study, the shelf in the corner.

TRIGÓRIN: Page one twenty-one . . . *(Goes out)*

ARKÁDINA: Really, Petrúsha, you should stay home.

SÓRIN: But you're going away. . . . It'll be so boring around here without you.

ARKÁDINA: What makes you think it'll be any better in town?

SÓRIN: It won't. But I still want to go. *(Laughs)* They're laying the cornerstone for a new city hall. Or something. I just want to get away from here for a few hours; this place makes me feel like a dead fish in a muddy pond. I told them to bring the horses at one o'clock. We can go together.

ARKÁDINA: *(Beat)* I don't know, I think you should stay here. You won't be bored. You have to take care of your health. Besides, I need you to take care of Konstantín. Keep an eye on him, will you? Help him out.

(Pause.)

Here I am leaving, and I don't even know why he shot himself. I think it was all about jealousy, which means the sooner I get Trigórin away from here the better.

SÓRIN: I don't know how to say this, but . . . well, there were other reasons. *You* understand: he's an intelligent young man, and here he is stuck out here in the country, miles from nowhere, no money, no job, no prospects. He has nothing to do. He's ashamed, afraid of what will happen to him if he keeps on doing nothing, like this. You know how much I love him, and he likes me, but still and all . . . I mean, really, he feels useless around here, he feels he's sponging off me. *You* understand: his pride is hurt. . . .

ARKÁDINA: He does nothing but cause me problems! *(Thinks)* Can't he just get an office job or something . . . ?

SÓRIN: *(Starts to whistle; then, hesitantly)* I think the best thing might be for you to . . . well, to give him some money. He really needs some decent clothing and whatever. Look at him: he's been wearing the same jacket for the last three years; he doesn't even have an overcoat . . . *(Laughs)* And if he could get out of here for a bit, that might help. Travel . . . It wouldn't cost too much.

ARKÁDINA: Now wait a minute. I suppose I could get him a new suit, but take a trip . . . no, I can't even afford the suit right now. *(Obstinately)* I don't have any money!

(Sórin laughs.)

I don't!

SÓRIN: *(Starts to whistle)* Right, right. Now don't get mad, dear, please. I believe you. You're a . . . a generous, unselfish woman.

ARKÁDINA: *(Practically in tears)* I don't have any money!

SÓRIN: I'd give him some myself, if I had any—*you* understand—but I don't. Not a cent. *(Laughs)* Shamráyev takes my entire pension check and spends it on crops and cows and hives of bees, and it all goes to waste. The bees die, the cows die, he never lets me use the horses . . .

ARKÁDINA: All right, I do have a little money, but I'm an actress! My clothes alone are enough to ruin me!

SÓRIN: You're a good woman. I . . . I respect you. You know I do. Yes . . . Something's wrong with me again. *(Staggers)* I'm getting dizzy. *(Holds on to the edge of the table)* I don't feel good. Or something. . . .

ARKÁDINA: *(Terrified)* Petrúsha! *(Trying to support him)* Petrúsha— oh, my God . . . *(Shouts)* Help! Somebody help!

(Enter Konstantín, with a bandage on his head, and Medvedénko.)

There's something wrong with him!

SÓRIN: I'm all right, I'm all right. *(Tries to smile, takes a drink of water)* It's over now. See? All gone!

KONSTANTÍN: *(To his mother)* Don't be frightened, Mama, it's not serious. He gets like this a lot. *(To Sórin)* Uncle, you should go lie down.

SÓRIN: Maybe for a bit, yes. But I'm still going to town. I'll go lie down for a bit, and then I'll go to town. *You* understand. *(Starts out, leaning on his cane)*

MEDVEDÉNKO: *(Takes him by the arm)* Do you know the famous rid- dle? What goes on four feet in the morning, on two feet at noon, on three feet in the evening—

SÓRIN: *(Laughs)* Sure! And flat on his back at night! Thank you, I can manage by myself!

MEDVEDÉNKO: Now, now, don't make such a fuss!

(Exit Medvedénko and Sórin.)

ARKÁDINA: He scared me half to death!

KONSTANTÍN: It's not good for him, living in the country. He gets bored. You know what, Mama? If you suddenly got generous and lent him a couple of thousand, he could live for a whole year in town.

ARKÁDINA: I don't have any money. I'm an actress, not a banker.

(Pause.)

KONSTANTÍN: Mama? Would you change my bandage for me? You're so good at it!

ARKÁDINA: *(Goes to the medicine cabinet, takes out the iodine and a fresh roll of gauze)* The doctor's late.

KONSTANTÍN: He said he'd come by ten, and it's already noon.

ARKÁDINA: Sit down. *(Takes the bandage off his head)* You look like you're wearing a turban! Last night, a delivery boy—in the kitchen—he asked what country you were from! Look, it's almost all healed. Nothing left but a scratch. *(Kisses him on the head)* Now, you won't go bang-bang again, will you, once I'm gone?

KONSTANTÍN: No, Mama. I was crazy with despair. I guess I lost control for a minute. I won't do it again. *(Kisses her hand)* You have magic hands. I remember one time a while back, you were still working at the State Theater—I was just a little kid—and there was a fight out in back of our building: someone beat up one of the tenants, the laundry lady. Remember? He knocked her unconscious. And you took care of her and got medicine for her and washed her kids in the bathtub. Don't you remember?

ARKÁDINA: No. *(Starts to put on the new bandage)*

KONSTANTÍN: There were two dancers living in the building. They used to stop by for coffee—

ARKÁDINA: I remember them.

KONSTANTÍN: They were both so religious!

(Pause.)

The last few days, I've loved you the way I did when I was little. Totally, tenderly. You're all I've got. Only there's that man—he always comes between us!

ARKÁDINA: You simply don't understand him, Kóstya. He's a very distinguished individual.

KONSTANTÍN: Maybe. Only he didn't act so distinguished when I tried to challenge him to a duel. He's leaving, running away!

ARKÁDINA: Don't talk nonsense. He's leaving because I'm taking him. I know you're not happy about our relationship, but you're an intelligent young man, and I have a right to expect you to respect my choice.

KONSTANTÍN: I do respect your choice, but you have to respect mine, and I choose to act toward that man the way I want. Some distinguished individual! Here we are almost quarreling over him, and he's out in the garden laughing at both of us, twisting Nína's mind, trying to convince her he's a genius.

ARKÁDINA: You love to annoy me, don't you? I respect that man, and I must ask you not to say nasty things about him in my presence.

KONSTANTÍN: Well, I don't respect him. You want me to treat him like a genius . . . well, excuse me. I can't lie. His writing makes me sick.

ARKÁDINA: That's just envy. People with no talent but lots of pretensions, all they know how to do is attack anyone with *real* talent. Why? Does it make you feel better?

KONSTANTÍN: *(Sarcastically)* Real talent! *(Angry)* I have more talent than all of you put together! *(Tears the bandage from his head)* You and those tired old friends of yours—you've taken over everything artistic; you think the only thing that's real and legitimate is your own work! Anybody different, you try to shut them up and get rid of them! I don't respect any of you! I don't respect you, and I don't respect him!

ARKÁDINA: You . . . Symbolist!

KONSTANTÍN: And you can just go back to your precious theater and act in those cheap, second-rate plays!

ARKÁDINA: I have never acted in anything second-rate! Get away from me! You wouldn't even know how to begin to write a *third*-rate play! You're from Kíev! You're from Kíev and you're middle class! You sponge!

KONSTANTÍN: Miser!

ARKÁDINA: You amateur!

(Konstantín sits down and starts to cry.)

You nobody! *(Walks up and down, upset)* Stop crying. There's no need to cry. . . . *(Starts to cry)* You mustn't. . . . *(Kisses his head, his forehead, his face)* Oh, my poor baby, I'm so sorry! Please, forgive me . . . I'm such an awful mother.

KONSTANTÍN: *(Embraces her)* If you only knew! I've got nothing, nothing left! She doesn't love me, and I can't write anymore. . . . All my hopes are gone. . . .

ARKÁDINA: You mustn't lose hope. Things will work out. I'm taking him away from here today—she'll be in love with you again. *(Wipes his tears)* There, that's enough. We're not mad at each other anymore, are we?

KONSTANTÍN: *(Kisses her hand)* No, Mama.

ARKÁDINA: *(Gently)* Go tell him you're not mad at him, won't you? You don't have to fight a duel. You don't, really . . . do you?

KONSTANTÍN: No. Only, Mama, please, don't make me go talk to him. I couldn't. It's just too painful. *(Enter Trigórin)* Here he comes. . . . I'll just go. *(Quickly puts the things back in the medicine cabinet)* The doctor can fix the bandage.

TRIGÓRIN: *(Paging through a book)* Page one twenty-one . . . lines eleven and twelve . . . Here it is. *(Reads)* "If you ever need my life, come take it."

(Konstantín picks up the bandage from the floor and goes out.)

ARKÁDINA: *(Looks at her watch)* The carriage will be here soon.

TRIGÓRIN: *(To himself)* "If you ever need my life, come take it."

ARKÁDINA: You're all packed, I hope?

TRIGÓRIN: *(Impatiently)* Yes, yes. *(Beat; to himself)* "If you ever need my life, come take it. . . ." *(To Arkádina)* Can't we stay another day?

(Arkádina shakes her head no.)

Please!

ARKÁDINA: My darling, I know why you want to stay. But you've got to get a grip on yourself. You're a little drunk. It's time to sober up.

TRIGÓRIN: No, I need *you* to be sober. You're a wise woman, you're a reasonable woman—I beg you, treat me as a true friend. *(Takes her hand)* You understand sacrifice . . . be my friend, let me go.

ARKÁDINA: *(With extreme emotion)* Are you that much in love?

TRIGÓRIN: She's calling me! This may be what I've always needed!

ARKÁDINA: The love of a country girl? How little you know yourself!

TRIGÓRIN: Sometimes people walk and talk, just like I'm talking to you, when they're really asleep and dreaming. I'm asleep and I'm dreaming of her, a sweet dream, a divine dream. . . . Let me go.

ARKÁDINA: *(Shaking)* No, no . . . I'm just an ordinary woman, Borís—you mustn't talk to me like this. Don't torment me. . . . I'm afraid!

TRIGÓRIN: You could be extraordinary if you wanted to! Love like this, young love, marvelous poetic love, a love that whirls you away to a land of dreams . . . it's the only thing on earth that can bring us happiness! I've never known a love like that! When I was young I never had the time—I was always trying to get myself published, make a living. And now it's happened! Young love has finally appeared in my life; it calls out to me. I can't just run away from it!

ARKÁDINA: *(Furious)* You're out of your mind!

TRIGÓRIN: If I am, then *let* me be!

ARKÁDINA: You're all against me today! You're trying to torment me! It's a conspiracy! *(Begins to cry)*

TRIGÓRIN: *(Slaps his head)* You don't understand! You don't want to understand!

ARKÁDINA: Am I so old and ugly you can discuss another woman in front of me like this? *(Embraces and kisses him)* Oh, you've lost your mind! My beautiful lover, my divine lover . . . You're the final page of my life story! *(Falls to her knees)* My joy, my pride, my happiness . . . *(Embraces his knees)* If you leave me, even for an hour, I won't survive it, I'll go out of my mind. My amazing lover, my magnificent lover, my conqueror—

TRIGÓRIN: Someone may come in. *(Helps her to her feet)*

ARKÁDINA: Let them! I'm not ashamed of my love for you. *(Kisses his hands)* My treasure, my foolish love, you want to destroy yourself, but *I* don't want you to, I won't let you. *(Laughs)* You're mine, you're mine. . . . This face is mine, these eyes are mine, your beautiful silken hair is mine—you're all mine! You're so talented, so smart, you're the greatest writer alive, you're the only hope of Russia. You have such truth, such simplicity, such freshness, such a vital sense of humor. One line, that's all it takes, and you have it all—you create living human beings! To read you is a triumphant experience! You think I'm exaggerating? Lying? Look into my eyes. . . . No, go on, look into them. Do I look like a liar? You know I'm the one person who knows how to appreciate you, the one person who'll tell you the truth. . . . My darling, my wonderful darling! You'll come with me, won't you? You won't ever leave me, will you?

TRIGÓRIN: I haven't got any willpower. I never have had. I'm a limp washrag, always do what I'm told. How can any woman be attracted to that? Go on, take me, take me away with you . . . but please, don't ever let me out of your sight.

ARKÁDINA: *(To herself)* He's mine again. *(Easily, as if nothing had hap-*

pened) Of course you can stay, if that's what you want. I'll go by myself; you can leave next week. There's no reason for you to hurry.

TRIGÓRIN: No, we'll leave together.

ARKÁDINA: Whatever you like. If you want to go together, we will.

(Pause.)

(Trigórin makes a note in his notebook.)

What are you writing?

TRIGÓRIN: I heard an interesting expression this morning. "Virgin woods." I can use it. *(Stretches)* So, we're off again. More trains, train stations, station restaurants, bad food, and talk, talk, talk . . .

(Enter Shamráyev.)

SHAMRÁYEV: The carriage is here, I regret to say. Time to go to the station, dear *madame*. The train gets in at five minutes after two. And I wonder, dear *madame*, if you wouldn't mind . . . Could you inquire about the actor Súzdaltsev? Is he still alive? Still working? We used to go out drinking together. I remember him in a play called *The Stagecoach Robbery*. Absolutely marvelous. And I remember one time, he was working at the State Theater in Yékaterinburg with Izmaílov, also a great actor. Don't hurry, dear *madame*, you still have a few minutes. And they were playing conspirators in some melodrama, and when they were suddenly discovered, he was supposed to say, "We're caught in a trap," and what he said was, "We're caught in a crap!" *(Guffaws)* In a crap!

(While he is speaking, Yákov fusses with the suitcases, the Maid brings Arkádina her hat, shawl, umbrella, gloves; they all help Arkádina to dress. The Cook appears in the door left, then enters hesitantly. Enter Paulína, then Sórin and Medvedénko.)

PAULÍNA: *(With a small basket)* Here are some plums for the trip. They're very sweet. You might want something to snack on.

ARKÁDINA: It's you who're sweet, Paulína.

PAULÍNA: Goodbye, dear. Excuse me if things weren't . . . you know. *(Starts to cry)*

ARKÁDINA: *(Hugs her)* Things were marvelous, simply marvelous. Now, now, you mustn't cry.

PAULÍNA: Our lives are almost over!

ARKÁDINA: I know, dear. But what can we do?

SÓRIN: *(In an overcoat with a shoulder cape, a hat, his walking stick)* Sister, it's time to go. You don't want to miss the train. Or something. I'll go out and get in the carriage. *(Goes out)*

MEDVEDÉNKO: I'll come see you off at the station. . . . It's all right, I'll walk. I'm a fast walker. *(Goes out)*

ARKÁDINA: Goodbye, my dears. We'll be back next summer, if we're all alive and well.

(The Maid, Yákov, and the Cook kiss her hand.)

Don't forget us, now. *(Gives the Cook a ruble)* Here's a ruble. That's for the three of you.

COOK: Many, many thanks, ma'am! Have a pleasant trip! We're very grateful!

YÁKOV: Good luck, now!

SHAMRÁYEV: Let's hope we hear from you one of these days! Goodbye, Borís Alexéyevich!

ARKÁDINA: Where's Konstantín? Tell him I'm leaving; we have to say goodbye. *(To Yákov)* I gave the cook a ruble. That's for the three of you.

(They all go out right. The stage is empty. Offstage, farewell sounds. The Maid runs back in after the basket of plums, then goes out. Trigórin returns.)

TRIGÓRIN: I forgot my walking stick. It must be out on the veranda.

(He heads for the door left, and runs into Nína.)

It's you! We're leaving. . . .

NÍNA: I knew we'd meet again. *(Nervous excitement)* Borís Alexéyevich, I've made up my mind! The die is cast: I'm going on the stage. I'm leaving tomorrow, I'm leaving my father, I'm leaving everything behind, I'm starting a new life. I'm leaving, just like you. I'm going to Moscow. We'll see each other there.

TRIGÓRIN: *(Looks around)* Stay at the Slavyánsky Bazaar Hotel. Let me know as soon as you get there. Molchánovka Street. I have to go. I'll be late.

(Pause.)

NÍNA: Just one minute more . . .

TRIGÓRIN: *(Softly)* You're so beautiful. . . . And I'm so happy to think we'll see each other again!

(She leans against his chest.)

To see your wonderful eyes, your tender, beautiful smile . . . this gentle face, this angelic purity . . . Oh, my darling . . .

(A long kiss.)

CURTAIN.

ACT FOUR

Two years later. A parlor in Sórin's house that Konstantín has converted into a study. Doors right and left, leading to the rest of the house. Upstage center, a pair of French doors that open onto the veranda. The usual collection of parlor furniture, plus a desk in the right corner. Beside the left door, a low divan with cushions; a bookshelf; books lying around on chairs and windowsills. Evening. One shaded lamp is lit. Semidarkness. We can hear the trees tossing outside and the wind howling in the chimneys. The night watchman makes his rounds, tapping his warning stick. Enter Medvedénko and Másha.

MÁSHA: *(Calls)* Konstantín! Konstantín! *(Looks around)* There's nobody here. The old man keeps asking where's Kóstya, where's Kóstya. He can't live without him.

MEDVEDÉNKO: He's afraid of being left alone. *(Listens)* What terrible weather! Two days of this . . . !

MÁSHA: *(Turns up the lamp)* There are waves on the lake. Big ones.

MEDVEDÉNKO: It's so dark out there. *(Beat)* Someone ought to tell them to take down that stage. It's bare and ugly, and the curtain keeps flapping in the wind. It's like a skeleton. Whenever I go past it at night, I think I hear someone crying.

MÁSHA: So what?

(Pause.)

MEDVEDÉNKO: Másha . . . ? Let's go home.

MÁSHA: *(Shakes her head no)* I'm staying here tonight.

MEDVEDÉNKO: *(Pleading)* Másha, please! Let's go! The baby must be getting hungry.

MÁSHA: So what? Matróna will feed him.

(Pause.)

MEDVEDÉNKO: I feel sorry for him. Three nights without his mother.

MÁSHA: You're getting boring. There was a time at least you talked, although I never knew what about. Now it's always the baby, the baby, the baby, let's go home. That's all I ever hear from you.

MEDVEDÉNKO: Come on, Másha, let's go.

MÁSHA: No. You go by yourself.

MEDVEDÉNKO: Your father won't let me have a horse.

MÁSHA: He will too. Just go ask him.

MEDVEDÉNKO: Well ... All right, I'll try. *(Beat)* You'll be home tomorrow?

MÁSHA: *(Takes a pinch of snuff)* I'll be home tomorrow. Just stop pestering me.

> *(Enter Konstantín and Paulína. Konstantín carries pillows and a quilt; Paulína carries bed linens. They set the bedclothes down on the divan, then Konstantín goes to his desk and sits.)*

What that for, Mama?

PAULÍNA: Pyótr Nikoláyich wants to sleep here tonight, in Kóstya's room.

MÁSHA: Here. Let me.

PAULÍNA: *(Sighs)* Old people are just like children. *(Crosses to the desk, leans on it, looks at something Konstantín has written)*

> *(Pause.)*

MEDVEDÉNKO: I guess I'll go now. Bye, Másha. *(Kisses her hand)* Goodbye, Mama. *(Tries to kiss Paulína's hand)*

PAULÍNA: *(Annoyed; pulls her hand away)* Please! Just go, if you're going!

MEDVEDÉNKO: Goodbye, Konstantín.

> *(Konstantín shakes his hand in silence; Medvedénko goes out.)*

PAULÍNA: *(Looking at Konstantín's writing)* I never thought you'd ever become a real writer, Kóstya. None of us did, really. And now you even get paid for what you write! Thank God! *(Runs her hand through Konstantín's hair)* And you've gotten so good-looking. . . . Kóstya, dear . . . can't you be a little nicer to my Másha?

MÁSHA: *(Making up the bed)* Don't bother him, Mama.

PAULÍNA: *(To Konstantín)* She's a wonderful girl. . . .

> *(Pause.)*

Women don't ask for much, Kóstya. . . . Just look at her once in a while . . . be nice. . . . It would mean so much. Believe me, I know.

(Konstantín gets up silently and leaves the room.)

MÁSHA: Now look. He's angry. Why did you have to go pestering him like that?

PAULÍNA: Because I feel so sorry for you, Másha.

MÁSHA: A lot of help you are!

PAULÍNA: My heart aches when I see you like this. I understand what you're feeling; it's all so obvious—

MÁSHA: It's all so stupid. Unrequited love is something you read about in novels. Doesn't mean a thing. If love invades your heart, you have to get rid of it. They've just offered my husband a job in another district. Once we move, I'll forget all this, rip it up by the roots.

(From two rooms away comes the sound of a piano, playing a melancholy waltz.)

PAULÍNA: That's Kóstya playing. He must be depressed.

MÁSHA: *(Waltzes quietly for a moment)* The main thing, Mama, is not to have to see him all the time. As soon as Semyón gets his new job, we'll move, and in a month I'll have forgotten him. None of this means a thing.

(Enter Medvedénko and Dorn from the door left, pushing Sórin in his wheelchair.)

MEDVEDÉNKO: I've got six mouths to feed at home. And flour costs seventy kopecks a pound.

DORN: Well, that's the way it goes.

MEDVEDÉNKO: No, I'm serious. But what do you care? You've got more money than you know what to do with.

DORN: *I've* got money? Look, I worked for thirty years without a break! I was always on call, night and day, never had a minute to myself, all I managed to save was two thousand, and I spent that last year on a trip to Italy. I don't have a cent left.

MÁSHA: *(To Medvedénko)* Haven't you gone yet?

MEDVEDÉNKO: *(Apologetically)* How can I? He won't give me a horse!

MÁSHA: *(Under her breath, bitterly)* I wish to God I'd never laid eyes on you!

(The wheelchair is positioned to the left of center. Paulína, Másha, and Dorn sit near it; Medvedénko, with a mournful expression, goes and sits in a corner.)

DORN: You really have changed things around, haven't you? You've made the parlor into a writer's study!

MÁSHA: Konstantín gets more work done here. And he can go out into the garden without disturbing anyone, whenever he wants to think.

(The sound of the watchman, tapping his warning stick.)

SÓRIN: Where's my sister?

DORN: She went to the station to meet Trigórin. She'll be back in a bit.

SÓRIN: If you decided to send for my sister, I must be in bad shape. *(Beat)* You see how he treats me? I'm in bad shape, but he won't give me any medicine.

DORN: What do you want? Aspirin? Bicarb? Cough syrup? Just tell me.

SÓRIN: Oh, here he goes again. Talk, talk, talk. I don't know how I put up with you. *(Nods his head toward the divan)* Is that for me?

PAULÍNA: Yes.

SÓRIN: Thank you.

DORN: *(Sings, from Shilovsky's serenade "The Tiger Cub")* "The bright moon sails the midnight sky . . ."

SÓRIN: I have a plot for Kóstya, for a short story. It has to be called "The Man Who Wanted." *"L'homme qui a voulu."* When I was young I wanted to become a writer, but I never did. I wanted to speak beautifully, but I never could. Just listen to me! *(Imitates himself)* "Or something, or something, or something . . . *you* understand." Whenever I had to make an oral report, I could never finish; I kept repeating myself until I was all in a sweat. I wanted to get married, but I never did. I wanted to live in town, and here I am, dying in the country. Or something.

DORN: You wanted to become a state councillor . . . and you did.

SÓRIN: *(Laughs)* I never wanted that. It just happened.

DORN: Having second thoughts about life at your age—seems a bit silly to me.

SÓRIN: You never let up, do you? Can't you understand? I want to live!

DORN: That's silly too. All life must end—that's a law of nature.

SÓRIN: You talk like a man who's been everywhere, done everything, so you don't care anymore. But you'll be afraid to die, just like me.

DORN: Fear of death is just an animal emotion. You have to get rid of it. The only people who fear death are those who believe in an afterlife, because they're afraid of being punished for their sins.

But *you* don't believe in an afterlife in the first place, and in the second place, what sins have you ever committed? You worked in a government office for twenty-five years, that's all.

SÓRIN: *(Laughs)* Twenty-eight.

(Enter Konstantín; he sits on a stool by Sórin's feet. Másha cannot take her eyes off him.)

DORN: We're keeping Konstantín from his work.

KONSTANTÍN: No, not at all.

(Pause.)

MEDVEDÉNKO: Doctor, may I ask you a question? Of all the cities you visited, which one did you find most pleasurable?

DORN: Genoa.

KONSTANTÍN: Why Genoa?

DORN: Because of the crowds in the streets. Evenings, when you left your hotel, the entire street was full of people. You drift along with the crowd, no destination in mind, just back and forth; it becomes a living thing, and you become part of it, spiritually as well as physically; you begin to believe that a universal world soul is possible ... like in your play, Konstantín, remember? "And I am the universal soul ..." That Zaréchny girl acted in it. Whatever happened to her, by the way? Where is she? How is she?

KONSTANTÍN: She's all right, as far as I know.

DORN: Someone told me she was ... how shall I say? Leading a rather irregular life. Do you know anything about it?

KONSTANTÍN: It's a long story, Doctor.

DORN: Then tell me the short version.

(Pause.)

KONSTANTÍN: She ran away from home and had an affair with Trigórin. Did you know that?

DORN: Yes, that I knew.

KONSTANTÍN: She had a baby. The baby died. Trigórin grew tired of her and went back to his former *involvement*, as you might have guessed. Of course, he never really left the former one, so he was cheating on them both. Typical. As far as I know, Nína's personal life is a complete disaster.

DORN: What about her career?

KONSTANTÍN: A bigger disaster. She started acting at a summer theater near Moscow, then she went out on a tour of the provinces. I used to follow her around in those days. She played leading roles, but she played them badly. Crude, no sensitivity, lots of screaming, very awkward gestures. There were moments when she was pretty good—usually when she was supposed to be suffering or doing a death scene. But moments only.

DORN: But she does have some talent?

KONSTANTÍN: Hard to say. Probably. I used to go watch her act, but she refused to see me. I knew how she must have felt, so I didn't insist.

(Pause.)

What else can I tell you? I finally came back here, and after a while she started writing to me. They were ... interesting letters: intelligent, full of feeling, no self-pity. But I could tell she was deeply unhappy. Every line she wrote was like a nerve stretched to the breaking point. And her mind seemed strange too; she used to sign her letters "The Seagull." Like the miller in Púshkin's play who keeps saying he's a raven, she kept writing, "I'm the seagull." Over and over. *(Beat)* She's here now, actually.

DORN: What do you mean, here?

KONSTANTÍN: Staying at the hotel in town. She's been there five days now. I wanted to go see her, and Másha actually did go, but she wouldn't see anybody. Semyón here swears he saw her late last night, walking in a field a couple of miles from here.

MEDVEDÉNKO: I *did* see her. She was walking toward town. I said hello and told her she should come to see us, and she said she would.

KONSTANTÍN: She won't.

(Pause.)

Her father and her stepmother won't have anything to do with her. They even hired guards to keep her away from the house. *(Goes to his desk; Dorn follows him)* How easy it is to make sense on paper, Doctor, and how hard it is in real life!

SÓRIN: She was an amazing girl.

DORN: Beg pardon?

SÓRIN: I said she was amazing, that girl. State Councillor Sórin was even a little bit in love with her once.

DORN: You old goat!

(We hear Shamráyev's loud laugh.)

PAULÍNA: That sounds like them; they're back from the station.

KONSTANTÍN: Yes, that's Mama's voice.

(Enter Arkádina and Trigórin; Shamráyev follows them.)

SHAMRÁYEV: *(As he enters)* We all keep getting older, more and more weather-beaten, but you, dear *madame*—you're still young! Full of life and elegance! And such amazing clothes!

ARKÁDINA: You're being boring. Besides, it's bad luck to say things like that.

TRIGÓRIN: *(To Sórin)* How are you? Not feeling too well? I'm sorry to hear it. *(Joyfully, as he sees Másha)* Másha!

MÁSHA: You remembered me! *(Shakes his hand)*

TRIGÓRIN: Did you get married?

MÁSHA: Oh, yes. A long time ago.

TRIGÓRIN: Are you happy? *(Shakes hands with Dorn and Medvedénko, then goes up to Konstantín. Hesitantly)* Your mother tells me you aren't mad at me anymore.

(Konstantín holds out his hand; they shake.)

ARKÁDINA: And see? Borís brought you the magazine with your new story in it.

KONSTANTÍN: *(Takes the magazine; to Trigórin)* Thank you. You're very kind.

(They all sit down.)

TRIGÓRIN: I bring you congratulations from your many admirers. There's a great deal of curiosity about you in Moscow and Petersburg; people are always asking me about you. They want to know what you're like, how old you are, even what color your hair is! For some reason or other, everybody thinks you're older than you are. And you publish under a pseudonym, so no one knows your real name. You're a mystery, just like the Man in the Iron Mask!

KONSTANTÍN: Will you be staying long?

TRIGÓRIN: No; I'm thinking of going back to Moscow tomorrow. I have to, actually. I have a deadline on a story I'm writing, and I promised an article for a magazine. Never changes, does it?

(While they talk, Arkádina and Paulína set up a card table in the middle of the room. Shamráyev lights candles, places chairs, and gets a lotto game from the cupboard.)

I'm not too lucky with the weather, am I? There's a wicked wind.

If it blows over by morning, I'm going down to the lake to do a little fishing. Oh, by the way, is that stage still out there? You remember? Where you did your play. I wanted to take a look at it; I'm writing a story about it, so I wanted to check the setting again.

MÁSHA: *(To Shamráyev)* Papa, will you please give my husband a horse? He has to go home!

SHAMRÁYEV: *(Mimicking her)* "Give him a horse, he has to go home." Look, the horses are just back from the station. They can't go right out again.

MÁSHA: But you've got other horses. *(Beat; Shamráyev doesn't answer)* Oh, what's the use of talking to you. . . .

MEDVEDÉNKO: I can walk back, Másha. Really, it's not—

PAULÍNA: *(Sighs)* Walk back? In weather like this? *(Sits down at the card table)* All right, ladies and gentlemen . . .

MEDVEDÉNKO: It's only four miles. . . . Goodbye . . . *(Kisses Másha's hand)* Goodbye, Mama . . .

(Paulína impatiently holds out her hand for him to kiss.)

I didn't mean to disturb you; it's because of the baby. . . . Goodbye, everybody. *(Goes out apologetically)*

SHAMRÁYEV: Don't worry, he'll make it. Who does he think he is? A general?

PAULÍNA: Come on, everybody. Dinner will be ready soon; we don't want to be late.

(Shamráyev, Másha, and Dorn sit down at the table.)

ARKÁDINA: *(To Trigórin)* Autumn nights like this, we play lotto. Come take a look; it's an old-fashioned lotto set. My mother used to play with us when we were children. Come sit down; we'll play a game while we're waiting for supper. *(Sits at the table, with Trigórin at her side)* It's a boring game, actually, but when you're as used to it as we are . . . *(She gives everyone three lotto cards)*

KONSTANTÍN: *(By his desk; he pages through the magazine)* He read his own story and didn't even cut the pages of mine. *(Sets the magazine down on the desk and heads for the door left; as he passes the table, he kisses his mother's head)*

ARKÁDINA: What about you, Kóstya?

KONSTANTÍN: Thanks, no; I don't feel like it. I'm going out for a walk. *(Goes out)*

ARKÁDINA: Everybody has to ante up. Ten kopecks. Doctor, can you ante for me?

DORN: Of course.

MÁSHA: Is everybody in? Then here we go. Twenty-two!

ARKÁDINA: Got it.

MÁSHA: Three!

DORN: Yes!

MÁSHA: Did you cover your three? Eight! Eighty-one! Ten!

SHAMRÁYEV: Don't go so fast.

ARKÁDINA: I was such a success in Hárkov, really! My head's still spinning!

MÁSHA: Thirty-four!

(From offstage, we hear Konstantín playing a melancholy waltz.)

ARKÁDINA: Some student group arranged the ovation. Three baskets of flowers and two wreaths, and this. Look. *(She unpins a brooch and lays it on the table)*

SHAMRÁYEV: Mm, that's quite something.

MÁSHA: Fifty!

DORN: Is that all?

ARKÁDINA: I had on an absolutely gorgeous dress. You can say what you want about me, but you have to admit I do know what to wear!

PAULÍNA: That's Kóstya playing. Poor boy, he's so depressed.

SHAMRÁYEV: The reviewers have not been kind to him.

MÁSHA: Seventy-seven!

ARKÁDINA: Then why does he read them?

TRIGÓRIN: He hasn't had much luck. Well, sometimes a writer just can't find his voice. He writes very strange stories, you know, very vague; sometimes it sounds like raving. He never writes about ordinary people.

MÁSHA: Eleven!

ARKÁDINA: *(Looking over at Sórin)* Petrúsha, aren't you bored over there?

(Pause.)

He's asleep.

DORN: State Councillor Sórin is asleep!

MÁSHA: Seven! Ninety!

TRIGÓRIN: If I lived out here in the country like this, you think I'd be a writer? I'd finally overcome my obsession and do nothing but fish.

MÁSHA: Twenty-eight!

TRIGÓRIN: Catch a perch or a pike—that's my idea of heaven.

DORN: Well, I believe in Konstantín. He's onto something. I know it! He thinks in images; his stories are very beautiful, bright; they move me very much. The problem is, though, they don't have any clear-cut point. They make a strong first impression, but then they just sort of trail off. And you can't get far on first impressions, can you? Irína Nikoláyevna, are you glad your son's a writer?

ARKÁDINA: You know, I still haven't read any of his things. There's just never enough time.

MÁSHA: Twenty-six!

(Enter Konstantín quietly; he goes to his desk.)

SHAMRÁYEV: *(To Trigórin)* By the way, we've got that thing of yours.

TRIGÓRIN: What thing?

SHAMRÁYEV: That seagull Konstantín shot one time—remember? You asked me to have it stuffed and mounted.

TRIGÓRIN: I did? *(Thinks)* I don't remember that.

MÁSHA: Sixty-six! One!

KONSTANTÍN: *(Opens one of the French doors, listens)* It's so dark out. I don't know why I feel so anxious.

ARKÁDINA: Kóstya, close the window; you're causing a draft.

(Konstantín closes the window.)

MÁSHA: Eighty-eight!

TRIGÓRIN: I win!

ARKÁDINA: *(Gaily)* Bravo! Bravo!

SHAMRÁYEV: Bravo!

ARKÁDINA: You wouldn't believe the luck this man has! Everywhere he goes! *(Stands)* Now let's all go have a bite to eat. Our celebrity hasn't eaten since breakfast. We can play some more after supper. *(To Konstantín)* Kóstya, that's enough writing! Come have something to eat.

KONSTANTÍN: No, thanks, Mama. I'm not hungry.

ARKÁDINA: Whatever you say, darling. *(Wakes Sórin)* Petrúsha, it's time to eat! *(Takes Shamráyev's arm and starts out)* Let me tell you about my reception in Hárkov. . . .

(Paulína blows out the candles, then she and Dorn wheel Sórin out. Everyone goes out left; only Konstantín remains, seated at his desk. He tries to write, then reads through something already written.)

KONSTANTÍN: I used to talk all the time about new forms, but now everything I write seems like a cliché. *(Reads)* "The poster on the fence announced ..." "Her pale face framed by dark hair ..." Announced ... framed ... That's so amateurish. *(Scratches out several lines)* I'll start with the hero waking up to the sound of the rain, get rid of all the rest. And the description of the moonlit night—it's too long and contrived. Trigórin has his technique all worked out; it's easy for him. "... the neck of a broken bottle gleaming on the dam, the dark shadows of the mill wheel ..." There's his moonlit night, all ready to go. And what have I got? "... a trembling light, the silent glimmer of the stars, the distant sounds of a piano, dying away in the perfumed stillness ..." Makes me sick!

(Pause.)

The more I write, the more I think it's not a matter of old forms and new forms: what's important is to write without thinking about forms at all. Just write and pour out whatever's in your heart.

(Someone knocks at the window near the desk.)

What's that? *(Goes and looks through the window)* It's so dark I can't see a thing. *(Opens the French doors, looks out at the garden, calls)* Who's there? *(Goes out; we hear his footsteps on the veranda)* Nína! Nína! *(In a moment he returns with Nína)* Nína!

(Nína leans her head on his chest and sobs softly.)

(Deeply moved) Nína! Nína! You! It's you! I knew you'd come, I knew it! All day long I've had this terrible sense of something wrong.... *(Takes off her hat and coat)* Oh, my darling, my wonderful darling, you've come back! Come on now, we're not going to cry!

NÍNA: There's someone here.

KONSTANTÍN: No there's not.

NÍNA: Lock the door; they may come in.

KONSTANTÍN: No one will come in.

NÍNA: I know your mother's here. Please, lock the door....

(Konstantín goes to the door right and locks it, then crosses to the door left.)

KONSTANTÍN: There's no lock on this one. I'll prop a chair against it.

(Pushes an armchair in front of the door) Don't be afraid; nobody's going to come in.

NÍNA: *(Stares at him intently)* Let me look at you. *(Beat; she looks around)* It's lovely here, nice and warm. . . . This used to be a parlor, didn't it? Have I changed a lot?

KONSTANTÍN: Yes. . . . You've gotten thinner; it makes your eyes look larger. Nína, do you know how strange this is, seeing you like this? Why didn't you want to see me? Why didn't you come see me before this? I know you've been here almost a week now. I've been going to stand under your window, like a beggar.

NÍNA: I was afraid you'd hate me. Every night I dreamed you were looking at me and you didn't recognize me. I wish you knew . . . Ever since I got here I've been coming out, just to walk around the lake. I walked by this house several times; I just couldn't bring myself to go in. Let's sit down.

(They sit.)

Let's sit and talk and talk. It's so nice here, so comfortable and warm. . . . Can you hear that wind? There's a passage in Turgénev . . . "Happy the man on such a night who has a roof of his own and a place by the fire . . ." I'm the seagull. . . . No, that's not right. *(Wipes her forehead)* What was I saying? Oh, yes, Turgénev. ". . . and may the Lord help all homeless wanderers." It doesn't matter. *(Sobs)*

KONSTANTÍN: Nína, don't cry, you're . . . Nína!

NÍNA: It doesn't matter; I feel better now. I haven't cried in two years. I came out here last night, late, to see if our theater was still standing. And there it was. And I cried for the first time in two years. It made me feel better, lighter somehow. See? I'm not crying anymore. *(Takes his hand)* So now you're a writer. You're a writer, and I'm an actress. We've both been sucked into the whirlpool. And that was such a happy life, back then. We were still children. I'd wake up in the morning and start singing. I was in love with you, I was in love with fame. . . . And now? I have to get up early tomorrow morning to catch the train to Yeléts, third class, with all the peasants, and in Yeléts I have to put up with the attentions of dirty-minded businessmen who claim to love art. What a horrible life!

TRIGÓRIN: What are you going to Yeléts for?

NÍNA: The theater there hired me for the winter season. It's time for me to go.

KONSTANTÍN: Nína, I cursed you, I hated you, I tore up your letters and photographs, but I realized every minute that my soul was tied to yours forever. I can't *not* love you, Nína, I just can't. Ever since you left, since I saw my first story in print, my life has been unbearable. My youth got snatched away, and I feel as if I've lived ninety years already. I call your name, I kiss the ground you walked on, everywhere I turn I see your face . . .

NÍNA: *(With dismay)* Why are you telling me all this? Why?

KONSTANTÍN: I'm all alone, no one loves me, I'm cold as an empty cave, and everything I write is dead. Stay here with me, Nína, please! Or let me come with you!

(Nína quickly takes up her coat and hat.)

Nína, where are you going? For God's sake, don't leave me! *(Watches her put on the coat and hat)*

(Pause.)

NÍNA: I've got a carriage waiting at the gate. Don't come with me; I want to go by myself. *(Almost in tears)* Can I have a drink of water?

KONSTANTÍN: *(Pours her a glass of water)* Where are you going now?

NÍNA: Back to town.

(Pause.)

Is your mother here?

KONSTANTÍN: Yes. My uncle took a turn for the worse on Thursday, so we sent a telegram asking her to come.

NÍNA: Why did you say you kissed the ground I walked on? You should have killed me instead. *(Leans on the table)* I'm so tired! I want to rest, I just want to rest! *(Raises her head)* I'm the seagull. . . . No, that's not it. I'm an actress. That's it.

(From the other room we hear Arkádina and Trigórin laughing. Nína listens for a minute, goes to the left door, and looks through the keyhole.)

He's here too. *(Crosses to Konstantín)* He is, isn't he? Well, never mind. He never believed in the theater, he laughed at all my dreams, and little by little I stopped believing in it too. And then all the emotional stress, the jealousy; I was always afraid for the baby. . . . I started getting petty, depressed, my acting was emptier and emptier. . . . I didn't know what to do with my hands, I didn't know how to hold myself onstage, I couldn't control my voice. You don't know what that's like, to realize you're a terrible actor. I'm the seagull.... No, that's not it.... Remember that seagull you shot? A man comes along, sees her, and destroys her life because he has nothing better to do ... subject for a short story. No, that's not it.... *(Rubs her forehead)* What was I saying? Oh, yes, the theater ... I'm not like that anymore. I'm a real actress now, I enjoy acting, I'm proud of it, the stage intoxicates me. When I'm up there I feel beautiful. And these days, being back here, walking for hours on end, thinking and thinking, I could feel my soul growing stronger day after day. And now I know, Kóstya, I understand, finally, that in our business—acting, writing, it makes no difference—the main thing isn't being famous, it's not the sound of applause, it's not what I dreamed it was. All it is is the strength to keep going, no matter what happens. You have to keep on believing. I believe, and it helps. And now when I think about my vocation, I'm not afraid of life.

KONSTANTÍN: I *don't* believe, and I don't know what my vocation is. You've found your way in life, you know where you're heading, but I just go on drifting through a chaos of images and dreams, I don't know what my work is good for, or who needs it.

NÍNA: *(Listens)* Shh ... I'd better go. Goodbye. When I become a great actress, come watch me act, won't you? Promise. It's late. *(Takes his hand)* I can barely stand. I'm so tired, I'm so hungry ...

KONSTANTÍN: Then stay. I'll get you something to eat.

NÍNA: No, no, I can't. No, don't come with me, I can go by myself; it's not far to where the carriage is.... So she brought him with her, didn't she? Oh, well, what difference does it make? When you see Trigórin, don't say anything about this.... I love him. I love him even more than before. Subject for a short story. I love him, I love him, I love him to despair. Things were so lovely back then, Kóstya, weren't they? Remember? We thought life was bright, shining, joyful, and our feelings were like delicate flowers. Remember? *(Recites)* "Human beings, lions, eagles, quail ... you horned deer, you wild geese, you spiders and you wordless fish who swim beneath the wave ... starfish, stars in heaven so distant the human eye cannot perceive them, all living things, all, all, all ... all living things have ended their allotted rounds and are no more.... For more than a thousand centuries the earth has been lifeless, no single living creature yet remains.... And the weary moon in heaven lights her lamp in vain. The cranes in the meadows awake no more, their cries are silent; the flight of beetles in the linden woods is stilled. . . ." *(Embraces Konstantín suddenly, then runs out through the French doors)*

KONSTANTÍN: *(Beat)* I hope nobody sees her in the garden and tells Mama. Mama would get upset.

(For the next two minutes he tears up all his manuscripts and throws them under the desk. Then he goes out through the door right.)

DORN: *(From outside the door left)* Strange. The door must be locked. *(Pushes his way in, puts the chair back where it belongs)* What is this, an obstacle course?

(Enter Arkádina, Paulína, Másha, Yákov carrying a tray with bottles, then Shamráyev and Trigórin.)

ARKÁDINA: Put the wine and the beer for Borís Alexéyich over here on the table. We'll play lotto and have a few drinks. Come on, everybody, sit down!

PAULÍNA: *(To Yákov)* And bring the tea. *(Lights the candles, then sits down at the card table)*

SHAMRÁYEV: *(Takes Trigórin over to a cupboard)* Here's what I was talking about before. *(Takes a stuffed seagull from the cupboard)* I did what you told me.

TRIGÓRIN: *(Looking at the seagull)* Funny, I don't remember. *(Thinks)* No, don't remember at all.

(From offstage left comes a gunshot; everyone jumps.)

ARKÁDINA: *(Frightened)* What was that?

DORN: Nothing. Probably a bottle in my medicine bag popped its cork. Don't let it worry you. *(Goes out right, and comes back after a half a minute)* Just like I thought. It was a bottle of ether. *(Starts singing)* "Once more, love, before you, enchanted I stand . . ."

ARKÁDINA: *(Sits down at the card table)* Oof! That scared me! It reminded me of when . . . *(Covers her face with her hands)* I thought for a minute I was going to faint.

DORN: *(To Trigórin, flipping through the pages of a magazine)* There was an article in here two months ago, a report from America. I wanted to ask you about it. . . . *(Puts his arm around Trigórin and leads him downstage)* It's a very interesting piece. . . . *(Lowers his voice)* Get Irína out of here somehow. Konstantín just shot himself.

CURTAIN.

THE SEAGULL: NOTES

Page 111. "Sórin's farm." What does Sórin's farm look like? Where are we exactly in Russia? What is the weather like? Chekhov gives us no precise indications, so the easiest way is to ask what experiences he had of life in the country. Late in 1891, Chekhov bought the five-hundred-acre farm of Melikhovo, about fifty miles south of Moscow, for thirteen thousand rubles. He moved there with his parents and brothers and sisters in March 1892.

The region around Melikhovo is rolling semi-open country with rivers, ponds, and marshy areas. There are many tall trees, generally larches, birches, oaks, lindens, and firs. The mean summer temperature is in the upper sixties, so it is reasonably cool outdoors at night. The mean winter temperature is seven degrees fahrenheit. Chekhov had elaborate plans for his estate. He built fish ponds (". . . near the house, so we can fish right out the window"), planted trees, and cared for his woodlands. He took his responsibilities as a farmer and landowner very seriously. He kept a few horses and cows and farmed the property extensively. The estate was a center of life for the Chekhov family and their friends; during the first summer, they built a croquet lawn, and the house saw a constant coming and going of visitors. We can assume Sórin's place is a smaller and less productive example of such a farm.

Page 113. Eleonora Duse (1859–1924), the Italian actress, was the model for an entire generation of world theatergoers. She would have been almost an exact contemporary of Arkádina. Duse toured Russia in 1891, when Arkádina might have seen her. She played the same kind of parts Arkádina plays, romantic and melodramatic heroines, Camille among them.

Camille, of course, is the play drawn by Alexandre Dumas *fils* from his celebrated novel *La Dame aux Camélias.* It was first produced in 1852 and has lasted in the repertory in one form or another for over a hundred years. Besides Duse, Sarah Bernhardt, Helena Modjeska, Ida Rubinstein, and Greta Garbo have played it, and Charles Ludlam of the Ridiculous Theatrical Company played it in drag.

The Fumes of Life, by Bóleslav Markévich, was a reworking of his scandalous roman à clef, *The Abyss.* Chekhov hated this kind of writing and promised his editor to write a parody of it.

Page 117. "And that comic, Pável Chádin." Pável Chádin seems invented, but he could hardly have been a better actor than Prov Mikhaílovich Sadóvsky, one of the most famous Russian actors of the nineteenth century and the progenitor of a famous theatrical family. He was famous for his portrayal of the miserly villain Rasplúyev in Sukhovó-Kobýlin's play *Krechínsky's Wedding.*

Page 117. Shamráyev's pompousness here trips over garbled quotations from Latin; he mixes up two commonplaces: *De gustibus non est disputandum* (There's no disputing about taste) and *De mortuis aut bene aut nihil* (If you can't speak well of the dead, say nothing). Both quotations are fairly apropos in a conversation about old actors.

Page 118. "Oh, Hamlet, speak no more!" In a play about playwrights and actors, the quotations from *Hamlet* do more than just give Arkádina a chance to show off. This reference to the closet scene in *Hamlet* prepares us for the scene with the bandage between Arkádina and Tréplev in Act Three, which is in its way a kind of parody of the closet scene.

Page 120. "I forgot that only the chosen few can write plays." Tréplev's protests against the theater his mother represents—the nineteenth-century romantic-realist-melodramatic tradition—are an echo of the arguments of Symbolist playwrights of the period. Tréplev's play is indeed an attempt at a Symbolist drama. It is rather overearnest and is in its way a gentle parody by Chekhov, but it is meant as a sympathetic picture of the new drama and ought not to be played farcically. Arkádina's comments on her son's play are the conservative actress's reaction to anything innovative, but it was not an opinion that Chekhov shared.

Page 122. "Bravo, Silva." Shamráyev's story about the famous basso Silva and the basso from the church choir is an old Russian chestnut, one that has been told many times about many bassos. That Shamráyev should try to pass it off again is a matter for an exasperated silence on the part of the whole company and prompts Dorn's ironic comment about the angel of silence.

Page 123. "With tears in her eyes." This stage direction (*skvoz slyozy:* literally, "through tears") is one that Chekhov uses over and over in his plays. On no account does it mean that Chekhov wants the actress in question to cry, or even necessarily to come near it. So many of them did, especially under Stanislávsky's often overwrought direction, that Chekhov wrote to Nemiróvich-Dánchenko, Stanislávsky's partner at the Moscow Art Theater: "I often use the phrase 'through tears' in my stage directions, but that indicates only a character's mood, not actual tears."

Page 126. "Maupassant, darling. *Sur l'eau.*" The similarities between Chekhov and Maupassant have been much overstated, although they were discussed in Chekhov's time and still are. Simon Karlinsky is accurate when he writes that "Maupassant's shallow despair and misanthropy are the very opposite of Chekhov's depth and compassion." Nevertheless, Chekhov makes several references to Maupassant in *The Seagull* and was definitely aware of Maupassant's ideas on the role of the artist in society. Here, however, in this passage from *Sur l'eau,* he gives a brilliant character indication for the actress who plays Arkádina. Her behavior to Trigórin, her shallowness, her almost cynical calculation, are accurately described in the passage that Arkádina, after reading it to herself, dismisses with: "Oh, well, the rest is boring. Anyway, it's not true." Here is how Maupassant's text continues: "Like drop upon drop of water, which will eventually pierce the hardest stone, praise falls word upon word into the susceptible heart of a writer. Then as soon as she sees him touched, weakened, softened by her constant flattery, she cuts him off; one by one she breaks whatever attachments he may have formed elsewhere, and little by little she gets him used to staying with her, to like staying with her, to yield up his mind to her. And to make sure that he stays with her, she takes care of him, arranges his successes, shows him off, makes a star of him, and before the entire world she gives him her marked respect, her unequaled admiration. And then, because he feels like an idol, he stays in the temple." No matter how real Arkádina's love or need for Trigórin may be, this passage is a cold preview of the scene between the two of them in Act Three.

Page 132. "What's so wonderful about it?" Trigórin's description in this speech of the way he writes seems clearly based on another passage from *Sur l'eau:* "A novelist . . . nibbles, steals, exploits everything he lays eyes on. You can never be at ease with him, never sure that someday he won't stick you flat on your back, stark naked, on the pages of a book. His eye is like a pump that sucks up everything, like the hand of an obsessive thief. Nothing escapes him: he gathers and collects without stopping; he collects movements, gestures, intentions, everything that happens in front of him; he gathers the smallest words, the smallest acts, the smallest things. He stores up from morning to night all kinds of observations, out of which he makes up stories that he sells."

Page 145. "Here's a ruble. That's for the three of you." The ruble Arkádina leaves for the three servants was worth a little more than an American dollar at the time. Even allowing for differences in purchasing power between now and then, it is a remarkably stingy tip.

Page 148. "The sound of a piano, playing a melancholy waltz." Tréplev has many of the stock characteristics of sensitive nineteenth-century heroes, including their penchant for expressing their emotions at the piano. Like Algernon Moncrieff in Oscar Wilde's *The Importance of Being Earnest,* he probably plays "not accurately, but with wonderful expression."

Page 153. "Autumn nights like this, we play lotto." Lotto is the ancestor of our bingo and is essentially played the same way. Each player has a card with three horizontal rows of nine spaces each. Four spaces in each row are blank, and the other five are marked with numbers up to ninety. Each player puts a certain sum in the bank, and one player acts as the banker, drawing small ivory markers from a bag. The banker calls out each number as it is drawn, and each player covers that number if it is on his card. When a player completes one covered row, he calls out "Lotto" and wins the money in the bank.

Page 157. "I'm the seagull. . . . No, that's not right." In addition to *Hamlet,* another play whose action parallels the plot of *The Seagull* is *The Water Nymph (Rusalka)* by Alexánder Sergéyevich Púshkin (1799–1837), Russia's foremost poet. Educated Russians would be as familiar with his work as we are with that of Shakespeare. *The Water Nymph* was written between 1829 and 1832, and was left unfinished. The reference here, however, is pertinent: Púshkin's play is about a young girl, a miller's daughter, who lives by the shore of a river and is seduced, made pregnant, and abandoned by a passing prince. In this scene between Tréplev and Nína, the line she repeats three times after she says she's the seagull ("No, that's not right") is a quotation from *The Water Nymph,* and some of her other lines in the scene are paraphrases from Púshkin's play.

Page 157. "There's a passage in Turgénev." Nína quotes from Turgénev's novel *Rúdin.* There is a certain similarity between Tréplev and Rúdin, at least in this scene. As with Tréplev, Rúdin's youthful projects and visions come to failure. The novel ends, like the play, with a rainstorm beating outside, with the words Nína quotes, and, within a few pages, in both novel and play, with the death of the hero.

A Reluctant Tragic Hero

(A Scene from Country Life)

A COMIC SKETCH IN ONE ACT

1889

CHARACTERS

Iván Ivánovich Tolkachóv, a family man

Alexéy Alexéyevich Muráshkin, his friend

The action takes place in St. Petersburg, in Muráshkin's apartment.

A room. Muráshkin alone. Enter Tolkachóv.

MURÁSHKIN: Iván Ivánich! Good to see you! What brings you here?

TOLKACHÓV: *(Breathing heavily)* Favor. Please! You're my friend, you have to . . . Favor. I'm in trouble, real trouble; I need your help. Can you lend me a gun? Please! Just till tomorrow. Be a friend. Do me a favor.

MURÁSHKIN: What do you need a gun for?

TOLKACHÓV: What do I need a gun for . . . ? Oh, boy. Oh boy oh boy oh boy. Give me a drink. Have to have something to drink. Fast. A glass of water, have to have water . . . See, I . . . Well, the fact is, I'm going to be spending the night out in the woods alone, way out in the woods, so I . . . You know. Just in case anything happens. So can you lend me a gun? Please! Do me a favor!

MURÁSHKIN: Iván Ivánich, you're not making any sense! What's all this woods business? You sound like Little Red Riding Hood. Are you in trouble? You're involved in something illegal, right? What's happened? What's the matter with you? You look sick.

TOLKACHÓV: Wait a minute. Give me a minute. I have to catch my breath. Oh, my God! I'm a wreck! My head, my whole body . . . I feel like a shish kebab. I can't stand it anymore. This is the end! Listen, don't ask questions, don't ask me for details—just be a real friend and give me a gun. Please!

MURÁSHKIN: Now that's enough! You're acting like a crybaby! Listen to yourself! A man like you, a married man, with a good steady job . . . You ought to be ashamed of yourself.

TOLKACHÓV: A married man! That's the whole problem! You know what it means, being a married man? It means I suffer. It means I am a pack animal, a garbage collector. I am a slave, a serf; I am a coward who sits quietly waiting for the next disaster and hasn't got the brains to blow his brains out. I am a fool and an idiot. Why am I still alive? *(Jumps to his feet)* Well? Tell me, why am I alive! Oh, what is the point of it all, this uninterrupted concatenation of mental and physical punishments? Hm? Look, I can understand sacrifice, I could suffer for ideas, or ideals, but to suffer for ladies' dresses and lightbulbs, no! A thousand times no! No, no, and no! This is the end! It's all over! I can't stand it anymore!

MURÁSHKIN: Stop shouting! The neighbors will hear.

TOLKACHÓV: Let the neighbors hear. I don't care! You won't give me a gun, someone else will, no problem, and then everything will be over and done with. At last. I've made up my mind, do you hear? I've made up my mind!

MURÁSHKIN: Stop that! You've just ripped off one of my buttons! Get a hold of yourself, man! Now! Now, just what's so bad about your life? I don't understand any of this.

TOLKACHÓV: What's so bad? You want to know what's so bad? All right, I'll tell you. I'll lay it all out for you in detail, in black and white, and then you'll know. And then maybe I'll feel better. Let's sit down, shall we? Good. Now. Just listen. (Beat) My God. I'm always so short of breath. Now. Suppose we consider, just for example, today. Take today. All right? Now. As you know, I go to the office by nine and I stay until four, taking care of business. Now, it is hot in the office, and it is stuffy, and there are flies all over the place, and it is, as you very well know, a bottomless and never-to-be-enlightened outpost of chaos. My secretary is on vacation, my assistant, Krápov, has gone off somewhere to get married, and what is laughingly referred to as "the staff" is preoccupied with the joys of summer: weekends in the country, the possibility of illicit love affairs, and probably, for all I know, amateur theatricals. They're always asleep, or exhausted, or hungover, and you can't get a lick of work out of them. I have a temporary replacement of a secretary who is deaf in one ear—the left ear—and hopelessly in love. The clients haven't got a brain in their heads; you can't get them to sit still: they run, they jump, they get mad, they shout. The whole thing is beyond bedlam. It leaves you screaming for help. It is a disaster area, it is a nest of vipers, it is a zoo for incurables. And the work! Well, it's the same thing over and over again: issue a certificate, write up a memo, issue a certificate, write up a memo. Monotonous. Like waves. Have you ever watched waves? Little ones? Very monotonous, waves. No variety. You know what I mean? Give me another drink of water. . . . So. Finally you leave the office. You are beaten into little bits. All you want is a drink and some dinner and a good night's sleep, but no! Because it dawns on you that it is summertime, and you have rented a place in the country for the summer, and that means you are an insignificant cog in the greater scheme of things, a niggling nothing, and now—do you follow me?—now you are about to flap around like a chicken with its head chopped off, because you have errands to run!

You see, we have a little custom out where we rent for the summer: if anybody is going into town, then any little sonofabitch whatsoever—and this is without even counting his own wife—has a perfectly natural, God-given right to give him a huge list of errands to run. My wife, for instance, wants me to go by the dress shop and tell them in no uncertain terms that the blouse is much too big . . . except the shoulders, which are much too small. Sónya wants me to return her slippers, and my sister-in-law needs two-thirds of a yard of crimson silk to match this sample here and six yards of braid. . . . No, wait a minute—I can read you the whole thing. *(Takes a list from his pocket and reads)* A globe for the lamp. One pound of smoked sausage. Cloves and cinnamon. Some castor oil for Mísha. Ten pounds of powdered sugar. Get the copper washtub and the sugar tongs from the house. Mothballs and bleach. Twenty bottles of beer. Smelling salts and a size eighty-two corset for Mademoiselle Chanceau. Oof! And bring out Mísha's galoshes and his fall jacket. *That* is my wife's list, and the family's. Now, *here*'s the list from all my dear friends and gentle neighbors, god-damn every one of them to hell. Tomorrow is Volódya Vlásin's birthday, so I'm supposed to buy him a bicycle. Colonel Víkhrin's wife is in what they call an interesting condition, so I have to go by the doctor's every other day and remind her to show up for the blessed event. And so on and so forth. I've got four different lists in my pocket and knots tied in my handkerchief for the rest of it. So there you are. Between the time you leave the office and the time your train leaves, you have to run all over town like a dog with its tongue in the mud, run run run run run, and curse the day you were born. The department store to the drugstore, the drugstore to the dress shop, the dress shop to the delicatessen, the delicatessen back to the drugstore. You're soaked in sweat, you keep dropping your money, the third stop you forget to pay and they carry on like you tried to rob them, the fourth stop a lady is wearing a long skirt and you step on it. . . . Oof! And what happens is, all this running around makes you crazy and turns you into a physical wreck, to the point where your bones crack all night long and you dream about crocodiles. So anyway, you finally get all your errands done, you've bought everything you're supposed to buy.

Now. Has it occurred to you that you may have a slight problem carting all this stuff out to the country with you? How, for example, do you pack a heavy copper washtub and a plunger and a lamp globe? And have you ever tried to make a single package out of twenty bottles of beer and a bicycle? You address the problem, you work at it like a Chinese puzzle, you try this way and that way, you wear out your ingenuity and your time trying to come up with something that will hold together, and of course something always falls out or rolls off at the last minute, no matter what you do, and when you get to the train station you have to stand there with your arms spread and your legs bowed, using your chin to hold on to a bundle held together with wire and tape and God knows what all. Finally the train arrives, and the crowd starts shoving and knocking your packages all over the place—you've got *your* things in *their* seats. They all start shouting, they get the conductor, they threaten to kick you off the train, and what can I do? I just stand there rolling my eyes, like a donkey with a stick in its mouth and a carrot up its ass.

So. Now comes the next round. I finally arrive at the cottage. And naturally what I'd like is what I'm entitled to: a couple of good stiff drinks and a little something to eat, and finally a little rest from the labors of the just. A little visit with Mr. Sandman! And I have a perfectly natural, God-given right to it, no? No! That's *not* what happens. What happens is, my wife has been waiting for this moment all day long. So you barely get started on your soup, and all of a sudden—wham, bam, thank you very much—wouldn't it be lovely to go out this evening, the drama group is putting on a show, or there's a dance at the club. . . . And that's that. You can protest and protest, and it doesn't mean a thing. You are a married man, and the words "married man" in the summertime mean a dumb beast of burden; you can load him down with anything you want, and nobody even mentions animal rights. So you go, and start losing your eyesight watching *The Duke's Decadent Daughter* or something with a short French name, and you clap your hands whenever your wife pokes you, and you sit there fading faster and faster until you start hoping an early emphysema will carry you off. Or suppose you go to the dance at the club. Then you have to work fast and try to round up enough suckers for your wife to dance with, and if you can't find enough suckers, you wind up dancing with her yourself. Dancing dance after dance with her! You get home from the show or the dance and it's after midnight and you're no longer a human being, you're a piece of dead meat. But at least you have attained your goal, the summit of your day is at hand, you proceed to divest yourself of your garments, and you get into bed. Unbelievable luxury! You close your eyes, and you are about to sleep. . . . Everything is suddenly wonderful and comfortable; it is positively poetry. The children aren't crying or fussing in the next room, your wife is still out, your conscience is clear, you cannot imagine anything better anywhere ever. You begin to drift off . . . you are falling asleep . . . And suddenly—suddenly you hear a tiny noise! Mosquitoes! *(Leaps to his feet)* Mosquitoes! Goddamn mosquitoes! Damn damn damn damn damn! Mosquitoes! *(Shakes his fist heavenward)* The ninth plague of Egypt! They bzzz and bzzz, and it is such a sorry sound, such a sad, depressing sound, you almost feel sorry for them, but since *you* are the poor sonofabitch they are biting, you begin to itch. Then you scratch. For a whole hour you scratch. Then you light a cigarette and blow smoke at them and you swat at them and you put your head under the covers, and nothing works. Finally you say the hell with it and you just lie back and let them destroy you: Eat me, you monsters, eat me! Finally you begin getting used to the mosquitoes. And then suddenly the tenth plague of Egypt strikes! Your wife has come home; she is in the living room, and she has brought along her tenors, and they begin rehearsing show tunes for their next show. You see, they spend their days sleeping, these tenors, and their nights rehearsing show tunes. And tenors, by Christ, are a torment beside which mosquitoes are positively benign. *(Sings)* "Never say thy youth was wasted . . ." Or this: "Once more, love, before you, enchanted I stand . . ." Oh, I tell you, tenors are mean and vicious. They attack the central nervous system, they pull your nerves shrieking from your body. . . . But I have discovered this little trick, you understand, and I use it against them, and it really seems to help. What I do is, I tap like this with my finger right here on my temple, right next to my ear. And I just go on tapping right here like this for the next four hours or so, until they all go away. . . . Water, please, water, I need a glass of water—I can't go on. . . .

Well, finally, there you are. It's morning, you haven't slept, and now you have to get up! And march on down to the station! And get on the train! And you run, because you're afraid you'll miss the train, and it is not a pleasant day; it is a miserable day! It's cold and rainy and you're freezing and the train is filthy! And then you get to town, and you go to the office, and the whole merry-go-round starts all over again. There. I've told you the whole thing, exactly as it happens. *That* is *life*. And that life, believe me, I can say in all seriousness, I would not wish on my worst enemy. It has made a wreck of me! I am ill, do you understand, physically ill! I suffer from shortness of breath. I have heartburn, my digestion is not functioning, my vision is blurred, and I am in constant fear of something. . . . You may not believe this, but I have become a psychopath. *(Glances quickly around him)* You understand this is strictly between you and me. I'm even thinking of going to see one of those doctors, you know, a psych . . . psychi . . . Psychic! No, no, I mean a psychiatrist. I can feel myself coming down with something, friend, and it's not going to be very pretty. You see, in these moments of aggravation, of stupefaction, when the mosquitoes are biting and the tenors are singing, I suddenly get this blur in my eyes, and what happens is, I leap up and run all over the house, screaming, "Blood! Blood, Iago, blood!" And the funny thing is, I really do get the urge to stick a knife into somebody or break a chair over their heads. So . . . you see what summertime can drive you to. And the worst of it is, nobody feels sorry for you, nobody knows how you feel, they all act as if it was perfectly normal. They even laugh. But I am a human being—you have to understand that— and *I want to live!* This isn't a comedy—it's a tragedy. Look, if you haven't got a gun you can lend me, at least tell me you know how I feel.

MURÁSHKIN: Believe me, I know how you feel.

TOLKACHÓV: I know. I can see that you know how I feel. *(Beat)* Goodbye. I've got to pick up the sardines and the sausage, and then there's the toothpaste, and then I catch my train.

MURÁSHKIN: Where exactly is it you're spending the summer?

TOLKACHÓV: At Rotten River.

MURÁSHKIN: *(Overjoyed)* No! Rotten River! I don't believe it! Do you happen to know Ólga Fineberg? She's spending the summer there too!

TOLKACHÓV: Do I know her? Of course I know her.

MURÁSHKIN: Oh, I can hardly believe this! What a surprise! What a coincidence! Listen, this is really wonderful of you—

TOLKACHÓV: What is?

MURÁSHKIN: You've got to do me a little favor. You won't mind—I know you're a friend! You will, won't you? Promise me you will!

TOLKACHÓV: Will what?

MURÁSHKIN: Be a friend! Oh, promise me you will! First of all, say hello to Ólga and tell her you saw me and that everything's fine, just fine, give her my best, and second of all, just take this one little thing with you when you go: she asked me to buy her a sewing machine, which of course I did, but of course there was no way to get it out to her, but now you can take it with you! And also there's this little cage with this little canary in it that has to go too, only you have to be very careful because the little door of the little cage is awfully loose and ... What's the matter? Why are you looking at me like that?

TOLKACHÓV: A sewing machine ... A little cage with a little canary ... A little birdie ... a little yellow birdie ...

MURÁSHKIN: Iván Ivánich, what's the matter with you? Why are you getting so red?

TOLKACHÓV: *(Stamps his foot)* Give me the goddamn machine! Give me the goddamn cage! Here! You want to ride me out there yourself? You want to play horsie? Go on, kick the horsie! Kill him! *(Makes two fists)* Blood! Blood, Iago, blood!

MURÁSHKIN: You're going crazy!

TOLKACHÓV: *(Jumps him)* Blood! Blood, Iago, blood!

MURÁSHKIN: *(Horrified)* He's gone crazy! *(Shouts)* Help! Help! Somebody help! Help!

TOLKACHÓV: *(Chases him around the room)* Blood! Blood, Iago, blood!

   CURTAIN.

THE WEDDING RECEPTION

A PLAY IN ONE ACT

1889

CHARACTERS

Yevdókim Zahárovich Zhigálov, a retired bureaucrat

Nastásya Timoféyevna, his wife

Dáshenka, their daughter

Epaminóndas Maxímovich Aplómbov, her fiancé

Fyódor Yakovlyóvich Revúnov-Karaúlov, chief petty officer, retired

Andréy Andréyevich Niúnin, an insurance salesman

Anna Martínovna Zmeyúkhina, a nurse's aide; wears a dark-red dress

Iván Mikháilovich Yatz, a telegraph operator

Harlámpy Spirodónovich Dímba, a Greek; owns a bakery

Dimítry Stepánovich Mozgovóy, a volunteer in the coast guard

The Master of Ceremonies

Wedding guests, waiters, etc.

The action takes place in a reception room in Andronov's restaurant.

A brightly lit hall. A long table set for a banquet. Waiters in tail-coats put finishing touches on the buffet. An offstage orchestra is playing the last section of a quadrille. Enter Zmeyúkhina, followed by Yatz, followed by the Master of Ceremonies.

ZMEYÚKHINA: No! No! No!

YATZ: *(Pursuing her)* Yes! Yes! Yes! Please! Say yes!

ZMEYÚKHINA: No! No! No!

MASTER OF CEREMONIES: *(Pursuing them)* Wait, wait, wait, you can't leave now—we're still dancing! What about the *grand rond? Grand rond, s'il vous play!*

(They exit. Enter Nastásya Timoféyevna and Aplómbov.)

NASTÁSYA TIMOFÉYEVNA: You ought to be in there dancing, instead of bothering me with all this talk.

APLÓMBOV: I am *not* interested in twisting my feet into knots like that Spanish dancer—what's his name—Spinoza. . . . No, I am a serious person. I take no pleasure in silly entertainments. But we are not talking about dancing here. Excuse me, *Maman*, but I simply don't understand your behavior. For instance. In addition to a certain number of domestic articles, your daughter's dowry was to include two lottery tickets with winning numbers. Well? Where are they?

NASTÁSYA TIMOFÉYEVNA: I have this splitting headache. . . . It happens every time the weather warms up like this. . . .

APLÓMBOV: Don't try to change the subject. I just found out you pawned those tickets! Now excuse me, *Maman*, but that is petty larceny! And I am not speaking out of sheer egoisticism, I don't need your tickets, but it's the principle of the thing. I refuse to let anyone put something over on me. I have been able to make your daughter happy, but unless I get those tickets, I swear she'll rue the day. I am a respectable man!

NASTÁSYA TIMOFÉYEVNA: *(Examining the table and counting places)* One, two, three, four, five . . .

WAITER: The cook wants to know what kind of sauce you want on the ice cream: rum, Madeira, or plain.

APLÓMBOV: Rum. And tell the manager there's not enough wine. Tell him to set out a few bottles of Haut-Sauternes. *(To Nastásya*

Timoféyevna) You also promised me you'd invite a general to the wedding luncheon. May I ask what's become of him?

NASTÁSYA TIMOFÉYEVNA: Now, dear, it's not my fault. . . .

APLÓMBOV: May I ask whose fault it is, then?

NASTÁSYA TIMOFÉYEVNA: Andréy Andréyich's. He came by yesterday and promised to bring a general to the reception, a real one. *(Sighs)* He probably couldn't find one; otherwise he'd be here. I feel bad about it: she's our only daughter, and we've spared no expense, and we certainly hoped to have a general. . . . But I'm afraid—

APLÓMBOV: And another thing. Everybody—and you especially, *Maman*—knows that before I proposed to her, that telegraph person Yatz wanted to marry her. So why did you have to invite him today? You must have known what an insult that would be!

NASTÁSYA TIMOFÉYEVNA: Oh, please! Epaminóndas Maxímich, you've barely been married two hours, and you haven't stopped tormenting me and Dáshenka with all this talk. What are you going to be like a year from now? Really! You're getting to be a bore!

APLÓMBOV: Can't stand to hear the truth, can you? Fine! Never mind! But please, just try to act respectable. That's all I want out of my in-laws—respectability.

(Through the room come pairs of dancers, finishing the grand rond. The Master of Ceremonies is in the lead with Dáshenka. The final pair is Yatz and Zmeyúkhina, who stay behind as the rest of the dancers exit.)

MASTER OF CEREMONIES: *(Shouts as he leads the dancers off)* Promenade! Promenade, messieurs, dames, promenade!

(Enter Zhigálov and Dímba; they head for the buffet.)

YATZ: *(To Zmeyúkhina)* Please! Please! You must!

ZMEYÚKHINA: Oh, you impetuous boy! I already told you, I'm not in voice today.

YATZ: Please! Please sing something! Just one note! Please! One single little note!

ZMEYÚKHINA: Oh, you! You'll wear me out! *(Sits and begins fanning herself)*

YATZ: Don't be so cruel! Such a heartless creature, and such a glorious voice! A voice like that, excuse my expressivity, you shouldn't be in the medical profession, you should be on the concert stage!

That final trill, that was divine! The one that went like this . . .
(Sings) "I loved you once . . ." Divine!

ZMEYÚKHINA: *(Sings)* "I loved you once, but will love come again . . ."
Is that the one you mean?

YATZ: Yes! Yes! That's the one! Divine!

ZMEYÚKHINA: No, I'm afraid I'm not in good voice today. Here, fan
me for a while, will you? It's so hot! *(To Aplómbov)* Epaminóndas
Maxímich, why are you looking so depressed? What's the matter?
It's your wedding day! Smile!

APLÓMBOV: Marriage is nothing to smile about! You have to pay constant attention to the smallest details.

ZMEYÚKHINA: Oh, you're so unromantic, all of you! I can't breathe
around you. I need a different atmosphere! Give me air! Give me
another atmosphere! *(Sings a few phrases)*

YATZ: Divine! Divine!

ZMEYÚKHINA: Fan me! Fan me, I feel faint! Faint! Why do I feel so
hot?

YATZ: Because you're all sweaty—

ZMEYÚKHINA: What a vulgar thing to say! Really! How dare you use
language like that!

YATZ: I'm sorry! I realize you're accustomed to high society, excuse
the expression, but I'm just—

ZMEYÚKHINA: Oh, leave me alone! I need poetry, something uplift-
ing. No, fan me, fan me, fan me. . . .

ZHIGÁLOV: *(To Dímba)* How about another? *(Pours drinks)* A man
can drink around the clock if he wants to, you know. The only
thing is, you can't neglect business. Never neglect business! Well,
special occasion, have a few drinks, why not? Here you go . . .
Bottoms up!

(They drink.)

Are there any tigers in Greece?

DÍMBA: Of course.

ZHIGÁLOV: What about lions?

DÍMBA: Lions too. Of course. In Greece is everyting, in Russia is notting. In Greece is my father, my uncle, my brothers. Here in Russia is notting.

ZHIGÁLOV: Hmm . . . What about whales? Do you have whales in
Greece?

DÍMBA: Of course. Greece have everyting.

NASTÁSYA TIMOFÉYEVNA: *(To Zhigálov)* Why are you drinking

already? It's time to get everybody to the table. And don't pick at the lobster—that's for the general. If he ever gets here, I mean . . .

ZHIGÁLOV: Lobsters! You have lobsters in Greece? I bet you don't have lobsters!

DÍMBA: Of course. In Greece everyting!

ZHIGÁLOV: Hmm . . . What about assistant professors? You have those?

ZMEYÚKHINA: I can just imagine the atmosphere you must have in Greece!

ZHIGÁLOV: A bunch of thieves too, probably. I mean, Greeks, right? They're like Gypsies or Armenians. They sell you a sponge, sell you a fish, and they're out to skin you alive. How about another?

NASTÁSYA TIMOFÉYEVNA: You've had enough! It's time we all sat down. It's already noon.

ZHIGÁLOV: Fine, let's get 'em to all sit down. *(Shouts)* Ladies and gentlemen, lunch! Time to eat! Please, everybody! Come sit down!

NASTÁSYA TIMOFÉYEVNA: This way, everybody! Please! Luncheon is served!

ZMEYÚKHINA: *(Takes her place at the table)* Poetry! I must have poetry! "But he, rebellious, seeks the storm, as if the storm could bring him peace!" Storms! I must have storms!

YATZ: *(Aside)* What a woman! I'm in love! Head over heels in love!

(The orchestra plays a march. Enter Dáshenka, Mozgovóy, wearing his uniform, Master of Ceremonies, male and female Guests. Hubbub; they all take places at the table. A brief pause.)

MOZGOVÓY: *(Stands)* Ladies and gentlemen! I have just one thing to say. . . . We have a lot of toasts and speeches to make today, so I propose we start right in. Ladies and gentlemen, here's to the happy couple!

(The orchestra plays a fanfare. Everybody shouts "Hurrah" and all clink glasses.)

MOZGOVÓY: Kiss the bride!

EVERYBODY: Kiss the bride! Kiss the bride!

(Aplómbov and Dáshenka kiss.)

YATZ: Fabulous! Fantastic! Excuse my expressivity, ladies and gentlemen, but I have to give credit where credit is due: this is magnificent, just magnificent! This room, the table, the flowers . . .

everything first class! Just fabulous! But there's one thing missing to make it a triumph! Electric light, if you'll excuse the expression! Every country in the world has electricity except us!

ZHIGÁLOV: *(Solemnly)* Electricity. Hmm ... The way I see it, electricity is a scam. They give you a few wires and expect you to call it a miracle. No, gentlemen, you want light, you want something more than a few wires—you want something substantial, something a man can get ahold of. You want fire! Flames! Fire is nature's light; nothing artificial about it!

YATZ: If you'd ever seen an electric battery, you'd change your mind.

ZHIGÁLOV: I have no desire to see an electric battery. It's all a scam. Just a way to squeeze what they can out of people's pockets. We all know what they're up to. . . . As for you, young man, instead of sticking up for a scam, you'd do better to have a drink! And pour a couple for the rest of us! That's the way!

APLÓMBOV: I couldn't agree more, Papa. Why all this talk about science? I have nothing against science, mind you, I can talk about science very scientifically if I have to, but this is not the time or place! *(To Dáshenka)* Is it, *chérie*?

DÁSHENKA: Some people are always trying to show off how educated they are and you can never understand what they're talking about!

NASTÁSYA TIMOFÉYEVNA: I've never had any education, thank God, and I've done very well, managed to marry off three daughters to decent husbands. *(To Yatz)* And if you think we're all so uneducated, why did you come to the wedding? You should have stayed home with your educated friends!

YATZ: Nastásya Timoféyevna, I have always had the greatest respect for you and your whole family, and about the electricity, believe me, I wasn't trying to show off. I merely wanted to propose a toast: I have always hoped for nothing more than a good husband for Dáshenka. And you know, Nastásya Timoféyevna, it's not easy to find a good man nowadays. Nowadays, most people marry for money—

APLÓMBOV: That's an insulting thing to say!

YATZ: *(Backs down)* I didn't mean to insult anybody. . . . Of course I'm not referring to present company. . . . I was just . . . I mean . . . I'm sorry! Everybody knows you married her for love, the dowry means nothing to you, it's a mere trifle—

NASTÁSYA TIMOFÉYEVNA: What do you mean, a trifle? You don't know what you're talking about! We gave him a thousand rubles cash, plus three fur coats and a complete set of furniture, all matching! Also a double bed! See if you can find a better deal on a dowry anywhere!

YATZ: I didn't mean … Furniture, of course, that's good, and the fur coats, but I was just … I was just trying to explain that I didn't mean to insult anybody.

NASTÁSYA TIMOFÉYEVNA: Well, don't! We're very fond of your family, and that's why we invited you to the wedding, and now you say all these awful things. And if you knew Epaminóndas Maxímich was marrying for money, why didn't you tell us sooner? *(Weepy)* My poor little girl! And I nursed her, I raised her, I used to sing her to sleep, she's more precious to me than diamonds or rubies—

APLÓMBOV: You mean you believe him? Thank you very much! *(To Yatz)* And as for you, Mr. Yatz, you may be a friend, but I will not allow you to say such insulting things in what is practically somebody's *home.* I must ask you to leave immediately!

YATZ: What did you say?

APLÓMBOV: And I can only wish you would behave with a little more respectability—as I do, for example. *I said,* I am asking you to leave immediately!

(The orchestra plays a fanfare.)

MALE GUESTS: *(To Aplómbov)* Stop this! That's enough! What's gotten into you? Sit down! Stop all this!

YATZ: I didn't mean … I mean … I really don't understand. Of course, I'll leave if that's what you want. But before I go, I want those five rubles I lent you last year, so you could buy—excuse my expressivity—a plaid vest. All right. One more drink, and then I'll go. Only first I want my money!

MALE GUESTS: That's enough! That's enough! Stop this! It's not worth making such a fuss!

MASTER OF CEREMONIES: *(Shouts)* To the parents of the bride! Yevdókim Zahárich and Nastásya Timoféyevna!

(Orchestra plays a fanfare. General hurrah.)

ZHIGÁLOV: *(Very emotional, bows to everyone)* Thank you! Thank you all! I'm grateful to all our dear friends here for coming today and sharing this happy occasion with us. I'm overcome with emotion—and I don't want anyone accusing me of being cheap! You're all wonderful people, and everything I have is yours!

Many, many thanks! *(Kisses Nastásya Timoféyevna)*

DÁSHENKA: Don't cry, Mama! I'm so happy!

APLÓMBOV: *Maman* is overcome with emotion at the thought of parting from her darling daughter. But I advise her not to forget our recent conversation.

YATZ: Don't cry, Nastásya Timoféyevna! Think: what are human tears? A petty psychological reaction, that's all.

ZHIGÁLOV: What about mushrooms? They have mushrooms in Greece?

DÍMBA: Of course. In Greece is everyting.

ZHIGÁLOV: I mean those big white ones, you know? You probably don't have those. . . .

DÍMBA: We have! Big white ones, yes. We have everyting!

MOZGOVÓY: Harlámpy Spirodónich, it's your turn to make a speech! Ladies and gentlemen, let him make a speech!

EVERYBODY: *(To Dímba)* Speech! Speech! Your turn! Speech!

DÍMBA: Spich? Spich? I'm not unnerstan. . . . What spich?

ZMEYÚKHINA: No, no, you can't refuse! It's your turn! Go on, stand up! Speech!

DÍMBA: *(Stands, embarrassed)* What I can say . . . Well, what's Russia and what's Greece? Okay, is Greek peoples in Greece and Russia peoples in Russia. Is also sailing across ocean *karavia*—how you say here?—boats. And on land is going railroads, all kinds. . . . We Greek peoples, you Russia peoples, that's all. . . . So, is my spich. Russia she's here, Greece she's over there.

(Enter Niúnin.)

NIÚNIN: *(Out of breath)* Ladies and gentlemen, just a minute! Stop! Hold the feast! Nastásya Timoféyevna, excuse me—can I have a word with you? Over here. *(Takes Nastásya Timoféyevna into a corner)* Listen . . . The general's coming! I finally found one! God, I had to look everywhere, but I found a real one, very impressive. Of course, he's old, maybe eighty . . . maybe even ninety . . .

NASTÁSYA TIMOFÉYEVNA: When will he get here?

NIÚNIN: He's on his way now. You'll be delighted—wait till you see. A perfect general! A real hero! And not some old infantry officer or artillery; he's a naval officer! Actually, he's a chief petty officer, but that's the naval equivalent of a major general. The same thing. Better, even!

NASTÁSYA TIMOFÉYEVNA: Now, Andréy, this isn't some kind of joke, is it?

NIÚNIN: A joke? Me? Of course not! Stop worrying!

NASTÁSYA TIMOFÉYEVNA: *(Sighs)* It's just that I don't want to spend a lot of money for nothing. . . .

NIÚNIN: Don't worry! He's a perfect general! Picture perfect! *(Raises his voice)* Anyway, I said: "Your Excellency, you mustn't forget your old friends! Nastásya Timoféyevna," I said, "is very annoyed with you!" *(Crosses to the table and sits down)* So then he says: "Excuse me, my boy, but how can I go to the wedding when I've never even met the bridegroom?" "Oh, Your Excellency," I said, "come on! Why be so formal? The groom," I said, "is a lovely young man, with a heart as big as all outdoors. And," I said, "this is not some half-pint pen pusher, Your Excellency; this man is a loan officer in a bank! Nowadays," I said, "even very respectable women work in banks." That convinced him! He slapped me on the back, offered me a Havana cigar, and said he'd be here. Please, ladies and gentlemen, don't start eating yet! Wait for the general!

APLÓMBOV: But when is he coming?

NIÚNIN: Right away! When I left him he was already putting on his galoshes. Please, wait, don't eat yet. . . .

APLÓMBOV: Then we should have them play a march. . . .

NIÚNIN: *(Shouts)* Hey! You musicians! Give us a march!

(The orchestra plays a march. Pause. Enter a waiter.)

WAITER: *(Announcing)* Mr. Revúnov-Karaúlov!

(Zhigálov, Nastásya Timoféyevna, and Niúnin rush toward the door. Enter Revúnov-Karaúlov.)

NASTÁSYA TIMOFÉYEVNA: *(Curtsies)* Welcome, Your Excellency! *So* good of you to come!

REVÚNOV: Well, yes! Lovely to be here!

ZHIGÁLOV: We are simple people, Your Excellency, nobody rich or famous here, just plain folks, but don't think we're trying to do this on the cheap! No, believe you me, we've spared no expense! Welcome to our wedding!

REVÚNOV: Yes, of course! Really lovely!

NIÚNIN: Allow me to introduce everybody, Your Excellency! The newlyweds, Epaminóndas Maxímich Aplómbov and his brand-new wife! Iván Mikháilich Yatz, works at the telegraph office! And a foreigner of the Greek persuasion, a pillar of our local baking industry, Harlámpy Spirodónich Dímba. Ósip Lukích

Babelmándevsky! And ... well, et cetera, et cetera; the rest are just small fry. Sit down, Your Excellency, please!

REVÚNOV: Yes, yes, of course. Excuse me, ladies and gentlemen, but I need a moment alone with young Andréy here. *(Takes Niúnin aside)* Look, I'm a little confused. Why do you keep calling me Your Excellency? I'm not a general! I'm only a chief petty officer; that's lower than a captain.

NIÚNIN: *(Talks right into his ear, as if he were deaf)* I know that, Fyódor Yakovlóvich, but just humor us! Let us call you Your Excellency, just for tonight! This family is ... well, patriarchal, let's say. They love titles and old-fashioned formality. . . .

REVÚNOV: Well, I suppose, if that's the case . . . All right. *(Goes to the table)* Lovely. Really lovely.

NASTÁSYA TIMOFÉYEVNA: Please sit down, Your Excellency! It's an honor to have you here! Eat something, Your Excellency! You'll have to excuse us; I imagine you're used to fancy food. But we're just plain folks, I'm afraid. . . .

REVÚNOV: *(He's hard of hearing)* What's that? Hmm ... Oh, yes. Lovely.

   (Pause.)

Yes ... Time was, we were all just plain folks, and everybody was happy. Now, I ... I'm a man of simple tastes myself. . . . Young Andréy here stopped by today, asked me to come to your wedding. How can I go? I said. I don't even know them! I'd feel out of place. . . . And he said, Oh, no, they're very simple people, patriarchal, he said, just like the good old days, they'd be overjoyed to have you. Well, I said, then I suppose it's all right. Matter of fact, I'm delighted. It's a bore here at home by myself, so if going to the wedding will make these good people happy, fine, let's go!

ZHIGÁLOV: You really mean that, Your Excellency? I respect that. I'm a simple man myself, but not cheap, no, no, and I'm proud to meet a man with the same attitudes as me! Eat something, Your Excellency!

APLÓMBOV: How long have you been retired, Your Excellency?

REVÚNOV: Excuse me? Oh, yes, right, I forgot. . . . Yes. . . . Well, shouldn't we drink to the happy couple before we eat? Here's to them!

EVERYBODY: To the happy couple! Kiss the bride! Kiss the bride!

   (Aplómbov and Dáshenka kiss.)

REVÚNOV: Hee hee hee . . . Yes, the happy couple!

(Pause.)

Yes. . . . Well, yes, time was, the good old days, we were all plain folks and we were all happy. Simple, but happy. I'm simple myself. Just love simplicity, in fact. I'm an old man now, retired thirty years ago . . . I'm seventy-two . . . yes. Of course, back then I had a fondness for the high life, but now . . . *(Sees Mozgovóy)* Yes. . . . Now, you, young man, you're a sailor. Am I right?

MOZGOVÓY: Yes, *sir!*

REVÚNOV: Aha! Well, yes . . . The navy! Always the toughest outfit. Hard work on board ship, right? Have to keep your wits about you, keep your eyes and ears open. Every little word aboard ship takes on an enormous significance. For example: Tops'ls in the for'ard shrouds! Fors'ls! Mains'ls! Skip me up a scuttle in the scuppers! What does all that mean? Hee hee hee . . . Sounds complicated, eh? But any ordinary sailor can tell you! Pretty clever, eh?

NIÚNIN: Here's a toast to His Excellency Fyódor Yakovlóvich Revúnov-Karaúlov!

(Orchestra plays a fanfare. Everybody shouts "Hurrah.")

YATZ: Now, you were quite . . . *expressive* just now, Your Excellency, about the hardships of the life on the bounding main. But do you think being a telegraph operator is easy? Nowadays, Your Excellency, everyone who works for the telegraph agency has to speak and write French and German! And the enormous skill it takes to send a message over the wires! Technical mastery, that's what you need! Here, listen, I'll show you. *(With his fork, he taps dots and dashes on the tabletop, imitating a telegraph operator at work)*

REVÚNOV: But what does it say?

YATZ: It says: "Thank you, Your Excellency, for coming to our wedding reception." You think that was too easy? Listen to this one! *(Taps again)*

REVÚNOV: Could you do that a little louder? I can't hear too well. . . .

YATZ: That one says: "Happy am I, madam, to be here in your arms at last."

REVÚNOV: Madam? Madam who? Well, yes. . . . *(Turns to Mozgovóy)* For example, now, you're under way in a stiff breeze, what do you need? Tops'l! Fo'c'sle! Mizzen royal! Frame out the gunnels on the larboard! Got to know your orders: All hands to the for'ard spar, set your jib and jimbo! All hands on deck! And up they go to get the mizzen t'gallant aloft, and you get all hands on deck! Batten down the bit board! Out with your lugs'ls and stays'ls! Main topmast stays'l!

MASTER OF CEREMONIES: Ladies and gentlemen, if I may have your attention—

REVÚNOV: *(Goes right on)* Yes indeed! And that's not all. Lots more! You have to know what they mean and shout 'em right. Up with the main brace bumpkin! Tighten the boom vang! It's easy when you know what that means. Haul on the sheets! You know what that means? Stays and braces! You know what that means?

NIÚNIN: *(To Revúnov)* Fyódor Yakovlóvich, our hostess wishes you'd talk about something else. It's getting a bit boring.

REVÚNOV: Boring? Boring who? *(To Mozgovóy)* All right now, young man! You're under way, under full sail, you're close-hauled on a starboard tack, and now you have to come about into the wind. So, you know what order to give? I'll tell you! All hands aloft, ready about, and haul as hard as you can! Hee hee hee . . .

NIÚNIN: Fyódor Yakovlóvich, please! That's enough! Eat something!

REVÚNOV: And as soon as you get 'em all up there, then what do you do? I'll tell you! All hands look sharp, ready about! God, that's living, eh? You shout out your orders, the crew jumps to like lightning, and you watch the sails take the wind! What a moment! I tell you, it gets you! Nothing like a first-rate crew! I tell you, it gets you right here! *(Slaps his chest, turns away, and begins coughing)*

MASTER OF CEREMONIES: *(Takes advantage of the pause)* And now, to celebrate this happy, so to speak, occasion, let us all join as one and raise our glasses in a toast to our dear—

REVÚNOV: Well, yes! And you have to know them all! For instance, mizzen, mizzen royal, mizzen royal stays'l, mizzen t'gallant, mizzen t'gallant stays'l—

MASTER OF CEREMONIES: *(Annoyed)* Can't somebody shut him up? We'll never get a chance to drink!

NASTÁSYA TIMOFÉYEVNA: We're simple people, Your Excellency, and I'm afraid we can't understand a word you're saying. Would you mind changing the subject? Please! Give us a break!

REVÚNOV: *(Can't hear a thing)* Thanks just the same, I've already eaten. Cake? Did you say cake? Oh, thanks, thanks . . . Yes, yes, good old cake, just like the good old days, I remember. . . . And that, young man, is happiness! Full sail, over the bounding main, not a care in the world, and then . . . and then . . . *(His voice begins to quiver)* You have to come about into the wind! Yes, into the teeth of the wind! There's not a seafaring man on the ocean who doesn't feel his heart leap up at the thought of that maneuver! You hear a shout: "All hands aloft, ready about"—and a spark of electricity fires up the entire crew! From the captain on down to the cabin boy, everyone ready for anything . . .

ZMEYÚKHINA: Boring! Boring!

(Loud chorus of boos, groans, etc.)

REVÚNOV: *(Can't hear a thing)* Thanks just the same, I've already eaten. *(Carried away by enthusiasm)* What a moment! All hands standing by! All eyes on the officer in charge! Fores'l and mains'l braces on the right, tops'l yard on the left, mizzens, all waiting for the captain's commands! And then it all happens in an instant! Fores'l sheets away, jib sheets away, helm astarboard! *(Leaps to his feet)* The ship turns into the wind, the sails began to flap, the commander shouts: "Braces, braces, look sharp!" And *he* looks sharp, doesn't take his eyes from the main tops'l, and finally he sees that sail begin to flap, and this is the tremendous moment now, and the command rolls like thunder from prow to stern: "Cast off main sheet, haul in the braces!" and everybody explodes into action. For a moment it's all bedlam, and then suddenly you're away again. The ship has come about! The maneuver is a complete success!

NASTÁSYA TIMOFÉYEVNA: General, you're being rude! At your age! You ought to be ashamed!

REVÚNOV: What? Oh, no, thank you, I've already eaten. . . .

NASTÁSYA TIMOFÉYEVNA: I *said*, at your age you ought to be ashamed, General! You're being rude!

NIÚNIN: *(Embarrassed)* Look, ladies and gentlemen . . . is this any time to make such a fuss? Really . . .

REVÚNOV: In the first place, I'm not a general. I'm a chief petty officer in the navy, and that's nowhere near a general. . . .

NASTÁSYA TIMOFÉYEVNA: Well, if you're not a general, what did you take our money for? We didn't pay you to come here and be rude to everybody!

REVÚNOV: *(Doesn't understand)* What money?

NASTÁSYA TIMOFÉYEVNA: You know what money! The money Andréy Andréyich paid you! *(To Niúnin)* And you should be ashamed of yourself too, Andréy! This is not the kind of officer I paid for!

NIÚNIN: Please, please! Let's change this subject! It isn't worth making all this fuss—

REVÚNOV: Paid for? Paid for? What does she mean?

APLÓMBOV: Excuse me, but ... didn't you get twenty-five rubles from Andréy Andréyich here?

REVÚNOV: What twenty-five rubles? *(Begins to understand)* This is disgraceful! Now I understand! What a cheap trick!

APLÓMBOV: Are you telling us you didn't get any money?

REVÚNOV: Of course I didn't get any money! Somebody get me out of here! *(Gets up from the table)* What a cheap, low-down trick! To make fun of an old man like this, a veteran member of the armed forces ... If any of you were respectable, I'd challenge you to a duel! But in this case ... *(Confused)* Waiter! Where's the door? Get me out of here! Waiter! What a mean trick! What a low-down trick! *(Goes out)*

NASTÁSYA TIMOFÉYEVNA: *(Beat)* Andréy, where's that twenty-five rubles?

NIÚNIN: This is no time to talk about money! Where's your sense of occasion? Everybody's trying to have a good time, and you want to argue about God knows what.... *(Shouts)* Here's to the bride and groom! Music! Let's have some music! Play us a march!

(The orchestra plays a march.)

Here's to the bride and groom!

ZMEYÚKHINA: I am simply suffocating! Atmosphere! I must have a different atmosphere!

YATZ: *(Ecstatic)* Isn't she magnificent? Isn't she divine?

(General uproar.)

MASTER OF CEREMONIES: *(Trying to be heard)* Ladies and gentlemen! On this so to speak happy occasion ...

CURTAIN.

THE FESTIVITIES

A COMIC SKETCH IN ONE ACT

1891

CHARACTERS

Andréy Andréyevich Shipúchin, manager of a savings and loan branch
office, a man in his forties; wears a monocle

Tatyána Alexéyevna, his wife, about twenty-five years old

Kuzmá Nikoláyevich Heérin, the office bookkeeper, an old man

Nastásya Fyódorovna Merchútkina, an old lady in a ratty overcoat

Bank depositors, tellers, etc.

The action takes place in the branch office of a savings and
loan association.

The manager's office. A door left leads into the bank. Two desks. The office is furnished with rather pretentious attempts at elegance: velvet chairs, a potted palm, statues, an Oriental rug, a telephone. It is noon. Heérin is alone; he wears felt bedroom slippers.

HEÉRIN: *(Yelling to someone beyond the door)* Somebody run down to the drugstore and get me a bottle of aspirin, large size, and bring me a glass of water! How many times do I have to tell you? *(Crosses to his desk)* I am one large ache from head to toe. I've been writing nonstop for the last four days and haven't had a wink of sleep. I sit here writing from morning to evening, and then I go home and write from evening to morning. *(Coughs)* And I'm burning up! Chills, fever, cough, pains in my legs; and my eyes . . . there's something wrong with my eyes. I must have conjunctions. *(Sits)* Our stuck-up friend the manager, that useless sonofabitch, is giving a talk at the festivities today, a talk on "Our Bank: Present and Future." Mr. Show-off. *(Writes)* Two . . . one . . . one . . . six . . . zero . . . seven . . . carry six . . . zero . . . one . . . six . . . He wants people to think he's such a big shot, but I'm the one who sits here and does all his work for him! He scribbles out a lot of highfalutin nonsense, but I'm the one who sits here day after day and checks his figures! Goddamn him to hell anyway. *(Scribbling his calculations)* I've had about all I can take! *(Writes)* That leaves one . . . three . . . seven . . . two . . . one . . . zero . . . He swore he'd reward me for my work. If the festivities come off without a hitch, and he manages to pull the wool over everybody's eyes, he swore I'd get a gold watch and a bonus of three hundred. . . . Well, we'll see. . . . *(Writes)* And if I'm doing all this work for nothing, then brother, watch out! I'm a mean man. Get me mad enough, and I won't stop at murder! I mean it!

(Offstage sound of voices and applause. Shipúchin's voice: "Thank you! Thank you! I'm really touched!" Enter Shipúchin. He wears a tailcoat and white tie. He carries a framed certificate they've just presented to him.)

SHIPÚCHIN: *(In the doorway, still talking to the group in the main room)* My dear colleagues, believe me, I will treasure till the day I die this memento of our happy days together! Till the day I die, ladies and gentlemen! And thank you all once again! *(Blows them a few kisses, then crosses to Heérin)* Kuzmá Nikoláyich! My dear, dear colleague!

(From time to time, as long as Shipúchin is onstage, assistants and tellers enter with forms for him to sign, then exit.)

HEÉRIN: Allow me to congratulate you, Andréy Andréyich, on this happy occasion, the fifteenth anniversary of our branch, and I hope and trust that—

SHIPÚCHIN: *(Shakes his hand warmly)* Thank you! Thank you so much! Well, this is a joyful day! *(Beat)* Oh, what the hell! Give me a hug! That'll be our part of the festivities!

(A rather formal embrace.)

Delighted! Absolutely delighted! I don't know how to thank you for all your devoted service! If I, as manager of this bank, have been able to accomplish *anything* useful, it's only because I can always rely on the devotion of my colleagues! *(Sighs)* Yes indeed, fifteen years! Fifteen years, or my name isn't Shipúchin! *(Brightly)* Now! How is my speech coming along? Almost ready?

HEÉRIN: Almost. I have about five pages to go.

SHIPÚCHIN: Perfect. So I can have it by three this afternoon?

HEÉRIN: As long as I'm not interrupted. There are only a few details left to work out.

SHIPÚCHIN: Marvelous. Marvelous, or my name isn't Shipúchin! The festivities begin at four o'clock. But look, let me have the first half now, will you? That way I can rehearse a little. Let me see.... *(Takes the speech)* I attach great importance to this speech. Enormous importance! This will be a sweeping statement of my professional credo, and I intend to dazzle them ... dazzle them, or my name isn't Shipúchin! *(Sits down and begins to read through the speech to himself)* Oh, God, I'm tired! Had a migraine last night, couldn't sleep, this morning I had to run around to all these meetings, and then back here, all this excitement, the cheering. I'm all wound up ... tired ...

HEÉRIN: *(Writes)* Two ... zero ... zero ... three ... nine ... two ... zero ... My mind's a blur of numbers.... Three ... one ... six ... four ... one ... five ... *(Scribbling his calculations)*

SHIPÚCHIN: Oh, by the way, there's one little thing. Your wife came by this morning; she says she wants to lodge a complaint against you again. Says last night you tried to attack her and her sister with a knife.... Now, really, Kuzmá Nikoláyich, what kind of behavior is that? Naughty naughty!

HEÉRIN: Andréy Andréyich, let me ask you, as part of the festivities, to show a little respect for my considerable efforts here and keep your nose out of my family affairs. Please!

SHIPÚCHIN: *(Sighs)* Really, Kuzmá Nikoláyich, you are impossible! Look at yourself—well brought up, respectable ... but when it comes to women, you act like Jack the Ripper. Really! I don't understand why you dislike them so much....

HEÉRIN: And I don't understand why you like them so much!

(Pause.)

SHIPÚCHIN: The employees just gave me this beautiful certificate, and the directors, so I'm told, intend to present me with a desk calendar and some kind of trophy.... *(Fiddles with his monocle)* Good, I say! Good, or my name isn't Shipúchin! These things aren't just petty trifles, you know. A bank's reputation requires a little pomp and circumstance! Of course ... well, you're like one of the family here, so I don't mind your knowing ... of course, I made up the certificate myself, and the silver trophy—I ordered that myself too.... And the gold frame for the certificate, that cost twenty-five rubles, but we couldn't do without it. Otherwise they'd accuse us of being cheap. *(Looks around)* Look at this office! All this fine furniture! People call me petty, you know, because I want the front doorknobs polished, because I want all our tellers in brand-new ties, and a uniformed doorman at the entrance.... Not true! No, sir! These are not petty concerns! If a man wants to live like a pig at home, why not? Lie around drunk all weekend, why not? He can—

HEÉRIN: Please, no invidious comparisons!

SHIPÚCHIN: I'm not comparing anything! Really, you are impossible. As I was saying: if you want to lie around at home acting lower class, doing whatever you feel like, that's your privilege. But this is a bank! Things here have to be larger than life! Every little detail here must convey an overwhelming impression. We want our clients to be overawed! *(Picks up a scrap of paper from the floor and flicks it into the wastebasket)* That is my great value to this bank: I augment its reputation. I improve the tone of the place enormously! Enormously, or my name isn't Shipúchin! *(Glances at Heérin)* Now look, my good friend, a delegation of the bank's directors will be arriving any moment now, and here you sit in your old bedroom slippers and that awful scarf. . . . And that ratty old jacket! What color do you call that? Couldn't you wear a tail-coat? Or at least a dress coat of some kind . . .

HEÉRIN: I'm more concerned with my health than with your directors. I've got a terrible fever and chills.

SHIPÚCHIN: *(Upset)* But you make such a sloppy impression! You're simply destroying the ambience I've tried to create here!

HEÉRIN: When your delegation gets here, I'll go hide. Where's the problem? *(Writes)* Seven . . . one . . . Seven . . . two . . . one . . . five . . . zero . . . I don't like sloppy impressions any more than you do. . . . Seven . . . two . . . nine . . . *(Scribbling his calculations)* I hate sloppy impressions! And I hope that you didn't decide to invite any of your women friends to the festivities today.

SHIPÚCHIN: Why not? Don't be ridiculous. . . .

HEÉRIN: I know you—you'll have the place full of them, just for the sake of your "ambience," but look: they'll spoil the entire event. With women, you've always got problems. Talk about sloppy impressions!

SHIPÚCHIN: I beg to differ. The presence of women has an elevating effect on any social gathering!

HEÉRIN: Sure . . . For instance, your wife . . . She seems like an educated woman, but last Monday she opened her mouth and put her foot right in it. It took me two days to get everything all smoothed over. Right in front of some clients, she asked me: "Is it true that my husband invested some of the bank's money in Dráshko-Práshko shares and then they went bankrupt? My husband is so worried about it!" Right in front of the clients! I don't know why you have to discuss bank business with her! One of these days her remarks will get you arrested!

SHIPÚCHIN: All right, all right, that's enough! You're depressing me! I'm trying to keep my mind on the festivities! Oh, but that reminds me . . . *(Looks at his watch)* My wife should be here shortly. I suppose I should have gone to the station to meet her, poor darling, but I had no time . . . and I was so tired. Actually, I suppose, I'm not all that glad to see her. I mean, I'm glad, but I wish she could have spent another couple of days at her mother's. She'll want me to spend the whole evening listening to her talk about her mother, and the fact is, some of the directors had proposed a little . . . bachelor outing this evening. . . . *(Giggles slightly, then groans)* Oh, now look. I'm making myself nervous. When I'm all worked up like this, the least little thing makes me want to burst into tears! And I can't, not today! Today I must be joyful! Joyful, or my name isn't Shepúchin!

(Enter Tatyána Alexéyevna. She wears a chic raincoat and carries a small overnight bag on a shoulder strap.)

SHIPÚCHIN: Oh, God. Speak of the devil.

TATYÁNA ALEXÉYEVNA: Darling! (Runs to her husband; a prolonged kiss)

SHIPÚCHIN: We were just talking about you! (Looks at his watch)

TATYÁNA ALEXÉYEVNA: (Breathlessly) Did you miss me? Was everything all right without me? I haven't even been home yet—I came right here from the station. I have so much to tell you, you can't imagine. I simply can't wait! No, no, I won't stay, I just dropped by for a minute. (To Heérin) Kuzmá Nikoláyich! Hello! (To Shipúchin) Is everything all right at home? No problems?

SHIPÚCHIN: No problems whatsoever. And you've lost a little weight over the past week; you look wonderful. . . . Well, how was your visit?

TATYÁNA ALEXÉYEVNA: Couldn't have been better. Mama and Kátya send their love. And Vasíly said to give you a kiss from him. (Kisses him) There! And Auntie sent you a jar of her homemade jam, and they're all mad at you for not writing. And Zína sends love and kisses too. (Kisses him) And oh! Wait till you hear what happened! I'm still terrified, thinking about it! Wait till you hear! (Beat) Darling, what's the matter? Aren't you glad to see me?

SHIPÚCHIN: Oh, I am, I am, of course I am! Sweetheart! (Kisses her)

(Heérin coughs with annoyance.)

TATYÁNA ALEXÉYEVNA: (Sighs) Poor Kátya! Poor dear Kátya! I feel so sorry for her!

SHIPÚCHIN: Now look, darling, we have our festivities all planned for this afternoon, the delegation from the directors' office will be here any minute now, and you're not really dressed. . . .

TATYÁNA ALEXÉYEVNA: Oh, of course! The festivities! I forgot! Congratulations, to both of you! What a wonderful occasion . . . That's right, the festivities . . . I just adore celebrations. And what about that wonderful certificate you had framed for the people who work here? Will they present it to you today?

(Heérin coughs with annoyance.)

SHIPÚCHIN: *(Embarrassed)* Darling, let's not talk about it now. . . . Really. You should go home and change.

TATYÁNA ALEXÉYEVNA: I will, I will; give me a moment. I've just *got* to tell you what happened to me! The *whole* story! Well. You remember you took me to the station when I left, and got me settled on the train, and I found a seat next to that fat lady, and I started to read—you know how I hate casual conversations with strangers in trains. So I sat through three stops, never said a word to anyone, just kept reading. Well, eventually it grew dark, and I began having the most depressing thoughts! And there was this young man sitting across from me, not too bad-looking, dark curly hair. . . . Well, we started talking . . . and then a sailor joined us, and some university student. . . . *(Laughs)* And I was naughty—I told them I wasn't married! And the attention that got me! We laughed and chatted away until almost midnight. The dark-haired young man told the *most* amusing anecdotes, and the sailor sang song after song. I nearly died laughing! And then the sailor . . . well, you know what sailors are like! When he found out my name was Tatyána, you know what he sang? He sang me that aria from *Eugene Onégin,* you know the one? Where he says he loves Tatyána? *(Sings, then bursts into gales of laughter)* Isn't that the most charming thing you've ever heard?

(Heérin coughs with annoyance.)

SHIPÚCHIN: Now, Tánya, we're disturbing Kuzmá Nikoláyich. You go on home, darling. We can talk about this later. . . .

TATYÁNA ALEXÉYEVNA: Oh, that's all right, that's all right, let him listen; this is *completely* fascinating! I'm almost done. Anyway, Seryózha came to the station to meet me, and then this other young man turned up, a tax auditor, I think . . . not bad-looking, but a little . . . a little *limp*, if you know what I mean; you can always tell by the eyes. Anyway, it turns out he knew Seryózha, so Seryózha introduced me, and the three of us went off together. . . . It was a *perfect* evening . . .

(From offstage: "No! Where do you think you're going? You can't go in there!" Enter Merchútkina.)

MERCHÚTKINA: *(In the doorway, waving them off)* Keep your hands to yourself! Is that any way to behave? I have to see your boss! *(Enters; to Shepúchin)* Your Excellency, sir! My name is Merchútkina, Nastásya Fyódorovna Merchútkina. My husband works for the county health department.

SHIPÚCHIN: What can I do for you?

MERCHÚTKINA: Well, Your Excellency, here's what happened. My husband was out sick for five months, and while he was home in bed, trying to recover, he got fired! Without any kind of reason! And then when I went to pick up his back salary—you're not going to believe this—they deducted twenty-four rubles and thirty-six kopecks. "What for?" I said. "Well," they said, "he borrowed the money from the credit union, and repayment was guaranteed." What do you mean? I said. He'd never borrow money without telling me! Just let him even try! Your Excellency, I'm a poor woman with no one to protect me. All I get from people is insults; nobody wants to help me out.

SHIPÚCHIN: Let me see. . . . *(Takes her petition and stands there reading it)*

TATYÁNA ALEXÉYEVNA: *(To Heérin)* Oh, but I have to start at the beginning. All of a sudden last week I got this letter from Mama; she wrote that my sister Kátya was going out with this man who wants to marry her, his name is Grendelévsky. Very good-looking young man, quite charming, but no job and not a cent to his name. And the worst thing is, Kátya is crazy about him. Mama was at her wit's end; she wanted me to come right away and try to change Kátya's mind.

HEÉRIN: *(Severely)* Please, you're interrupting my work! All this business about Mama and Kátya, I don't understand a word! And I have work to do.

TATYÁNA ALEXÉYEVNA: Well, I like that! Can't you pay attention when a lady is speaking to you? Why are you in such a bad mood today? *(Laughs)* You must be in love!

SHIPÚCHIN: Excuse me, I really don't understand . . . what is this all about?

TATYÁNA ALEXÉYEVNA: Are you? Yes, you are! You're in love! You're blushing!

SHIPÚCHIN: *(To Tatyána)* Tánya darling, wait for me outside, will you? I won't be a moment.

TATYÁNA ALEXÉYEVNA: Oh, all right. *(Goes out)*

SHIPÚCHIN: I don't understand any of this. I really think, madam, you've come to the wrong place. What you want has nothing to do with us. You'd better go see someone at the office where your husband worked.

MERCHÚTKINA: Your Excellency, I've been going to see them for the last six months, and they wouldn't even read my petition. I was out of my mind with worry, but then thank God for my brother-in-law: he told me to come see you. "You go see Shipúchin," he said. "He's an influential man, he can take care of anything." So here I am. Please, Your Excellency, you've got to help me!

SHIPÚCHIN: Mrs. Merchútkina, there is nothing we can do for you. Think: Your husband, so far as I can make out, worked for the health department, but this is a bank. We are a completely private commercial organization. Don't you understand that?

MERCHÚTKINA: If you need proof that my husband was sick, I've got a doctor's certificate. Here . . . See?

SHIPÚCHIN: *(Irritably)* Yes, I'm sure, I believe you, but I repeat, this has nothing to do with us!

(From offstage comes Tatyána's laugh, followed by much masculine laughter.)

SHIPÚCHIN: *(Glances at the door)* She's keeping them all from working out there! *(To Merchútkina)* This is quite out of the ordinary. A bit silly, really. Didn't your husband tell you where to go with the petition?

MERCHÚTKINA: He doesn't know anything more than I do, Your Excellency. All he says is: "Get out of here! It's none of your business!"

SHIPÚCHIN: Madam, let me say again: Your husband worked in the county health department, but this is a bank! We are not an official entity! We are an independent commercial institution!

MERCHÚTKINA: Yes, yes, yes, I know . . . I understand, Your Excellency. So in that case, Your Excellency, couldn't you just have them pay me, say, fifteen rubles? I don't need it all at once.

SHIPÚCHIN: *(Sighs with exasperation)* Ohh!

HEÉRIN: Andréy Andréyich, if this keeps on, I'll never be able to finish your speech!

SHIPÚCHIN: I understand, I understand. *(To Merchútkina)* This has really gone on long enough. Can't you understand that coming to us with this petition is . . . well, it's like taking a petition for divorce to a drugstore!

(A knock at the door. Tatyána's voice offstage: "Andréy! Can I come in?")

SHIPÚCHIN: *(Shouts)* No, darling. Just give me a minute; I'll be right out! *(To Merchútkina)* All right, they shortchanged you, but what am I supposed to do about it? Besides, madam, we are planning a few festivities here today, we're quite busy, and we're expecting some rather important people, so if you'll excuse me—

MERCHÚTKINA: Have a heart, Your Excellency! I'm all alone in the world. . . . I'm just a poor, weak woman, and I'm worn out. . . . I just can't do it anymore, I just can't! The landlord is suing us, I have to take care of my husband and do the housework, and now my brother-in-law is out of a job too!

SHIPÚCHIN: Mrs. Merchútkina, I really . . . Look, I'm very sorry, but I have no time to talk to you! You're giving me a headache with all this. . . . And you are keeping us from our appointed tasks, and we don't have all that much time! *(Sighs; aside)* What a mess, or my name isn't Shipúchin! *(To Heérin)* Kuzmá Nikoláyich, could you please explain to Mrs. Merchútkina here . . . Oh, I give up. *(Throws up his hands and goes out)*

HEÉRIN: *(Crosses to Merchútkina; severely)* Yes? What can I do for you?

MERCHÚTKINA: I'm just a poor, weak woman. . . . I know, you look at me and you think, Oh, she's strong as an ox, but you just take a good look: there's not a bone in my body that doesn't hurt! I can barely stand, I've lost my appetite. I couldn't even taste my coffee this morning.

HEÉRIN: I asked you, what can I do for you?

MERCHÚTKINA: Please, tell them to give me fifteen rubles! I can wait till next month for the rest.

HEÉRIN: But you've already been told quite clearly that this is a bank!

MERCHÚTKINA: Yes, yes . . . Do you need to see the doctor's certificate? I've got it right here. . . .

HEÉRIN: Are you out of your mind, or what?

MERCHÚTKINA: Look, dear, this is all perfectly legal, you know. I'm not asking for what doesn't belong to me.

HEÉRIN: And I repeat: Are you out of your mind? Damn it, madam, I haven't got time to waste talking to you. I'm busy! *(Points to the door)* Please! Just go!

MERCHÚTKINA: *(Astonished)* What about my money? When do I get it?

HEÉRIN: You are not merely out of your mind—you have obviously lost whatever mind you had! *(Taps a finger against his forehead)*

MERCHÚTKINA: *(Offended)* What do you mean? Well, I like that! Go knock on your own wife's head! My husband is a county official: you can't pull this kind of stuff on me!

HEÉRIN: *(Furious; between clenched teeth)* Get out of here!

MERCHÚTKINA: Oh, no, no, no . . . not on me!

HEÉRIN: *(Between clenched teeth)* If you don't get out of here this second, I'll call the doorman and have him throw you out! Out! *(Stamps his foot angrily)*

MERCHÚTKINA: Go on! You just try it! I'm not afraid of you! I've dealt with your kind before!

HEÉRIN: I swear to God, I have never in my entire life met anyone so . . . so *repellent*. Ohh! This is not helping my headache. *(Breathing heavily)* Listen, you old eyesore! I will say this one more time. If you don't get out of here right now, I will tear you into little pieces personally! I am a mean man! I can make you a cripple for life! I won't stop at murder!

MERCHÚTKINA: You just like to hear yourself bark! You don't scare me. I've dealt with your kind before!

HEÉRIN: *(In despair)* I can't take any more of this! She's making me sick! *(Crosses and sits at his desk)* If he wants this bank full of women, then I'm not going to finish this speech! I can't!

MERCHÚTKINA: All I want is what's legally mine! And look at you! Sitting around your office in bedroom slippers! Peasant! You ought to be ashamed of yourself!

(Enter Shipúchin and Tatyána Alexéyevna.)

TATYÁNA ALEXÉYEVNA: *(Following her husband)* . . . And the next night we went to the Berezhnítskys'. Kátya had on a light-blue silk with lace trimming, cut *very* low, and she wore her hair up, which suits her; I did it up myself. Oh, what a time we had! Dressing, doing our hair . . . And of course we looked absolutely ravishing!

SHIPÚCHIN: *(His migraine has started up again)* Yes, I'm sure . . . ravishing . . . They'll be here any minute. . . .

MERCHÚTKINA: Your Excellency!

SHIPÚCHIN: *(At the end of his tether)* Now what? What do you want?

MERCHÚTKINA: Your Excellency! *(Points at Heérin)* Do you know what he did, this . . . this . . . oh! He poked his forehead at me, like I was crazy. . . . You told him to help me, and instead he made fun of me, he said all these awful things! I'm just a poor, weak woman . . .

SHIPÚCHIN: Very well, madam, I will do what I can. . . . I'll see that something gets done . . . later, not *now!* For *now*, will you please get out? *(Aside)* My migraine's starting up again!

HEÉRIN: *(Crosses to Shipúchin, quietly)* Andréy Andréyich, call the doorman and have him throw her out on her ear! This can't go on!

SHIPÚCHIN: *(Terrified)* No, no! She'll raise a ruckus, and we'll have the whole neighborhood on our necks!

MERCHÚTKINA: Your Excellency!

HEÉRIN: *(Practically whining)* I have to finish your speech! And I can't, not like this!

MERCHÚTKINA: Your Excellency, when do I get my money? I need it right now!

SHIPÚCHIN: *(Aside, outraged)* What an *astonishingly* vulgar woman! *(To her, in a very controlled voice)* Madam, I have already explained to you that this is a bank. We are a commercial institution. We are not connected with any government program whatsoever.

MERCHÚTKINA: Please, Your Excellency, help me out! You're my only hope! Please! If the doctor's certificate isn't enough, I can get an affidavit from his office. Just tell them to give me my money!

SHIPÚCHIN: *(At his wit's end)* Ohh!

TATYÁNA ALEXÉYEVNA: My *dear* madam, you have just been informed that you are interfering in the business of this bank. Really! Is this any way to behave?

MERCHÚTKINA: Please, dear, help me out! There's no reason for them to get mad at me! I can barely eat anymore, and my coffee this morning had no taste whatsoever.

SHIPÚCHIN: *(Worn out, to Merchútkina)* How much did you say you needed?

MERCHÚTKINA: Twenty-four rubles and thirty-six kopecks.

SHIPÚCHIN: All right! *(Takes out his wallet, gives her money)* Here's twenty-five rubles. Just take them and get out!

(Heérin coughs with annoyance.)

MERCHÚTKINA: Oh, thank you, Your Excellency, thank you! I'm so grateful! *(Tucks the money away in her dress)*

TATYÁNA ALEXÉYEVNA: *(Sits down on the edge of her husband's chair)* Well, I suppose I should go home. . . . *(Looks at her watch)* Only I didn't finish my story! It'll only take me a minute, and then I'll go! You'll never *believe* what happened! So anyway, we went to the Berezhnítskys'; it was an enjoyable evening, nothing special . . . but of course Kátya's boyfriend Grendelévsky was there! Well, I had spent the day talking to Kátya, pleading with her, trying to get her to reconsider, and she did, and at the party that evening she broke off with Grendelévsky. Well, I thought, things couldn't have worked out better! I made Mama happy, I saved Kátya, and I thought: Good, now I can relax. And guess what happened? Just before dinner, Kátya and I went for a walk in the garden, and all of a sudden—*(bursts into tears)*—and all of a sudden we heard a shot. . . . Oh, I can't be unemotional about this! *(Sniffles into her handkerchief)* I really can't!

SHIPÚCHIN: *(Hopelessly)* Ohh!

TATYÁNA ALEXÉYEVNA: *(Weeps)* We ran to the gazebo, and there was poor Grendelévsky, lying there with a pistol in his hand. . . .

SHIPÚCHIN: All right, that's enough! I can't stand it! I can't stand it! *(To Merchútkina)* What do you want now?

MERCHÚTKINA: Your Excellency, couldn't you get my husband his job back?

SHIPÚCHIN: I can't stand any more of this! *(Weeps)* I can't, I can't! *(Gestures with both hands to Heérin, despairingly)* Get rid of her! For the love of God, get rid of her!

HEÉRIN: *(Crosses to Tatyána Alexéyevna)* You heard him! Out! Get out!

SHIPÚCHIN: Not her, the other one—that . . . that . . . horrible old . . . *(Points to Merchútkina)* That one!

HEÉRIN: *(Doesn't understand; to Tatyána Alexéyevna)* Out! Out! *(Stamps his foot)* Get out!

TATYÁNA ALEXÉYEVNA: What? Me? Are you mad?

SHIPÚCHIN: This is horrible! This is a disaster! Get her out of here! Get rid of her!

HEÉRIN: *(To Tatyána)* Out! Before I break your neck! I won't stop at murder!

TATYÁNA ALEXÉYEVNA: *(Runs from him; he chases her)* How dare you! You monster! Andréy! Help! Andréy! *(Circles the room)*

SHIPÚCHIN: *(Runs after them)* Stop! Please! For God's sake, don't make so much noise! Think of my career!

HEÉRIN: *(Chases Merchútkina)* Get out of here! Somebody get her! Catch her! Cut her throat!

SHIPÚCHIN: *(Screams)* Stop! Please! Please! Stop!

MERCHÚTKINA: *(Circles the room)* Oh, my God! My God! My God!

TATYÁNA ALEXÉYEVNA: *(Screams)* Save me! Save me! Oh, this is awful! Just awful! *(Climbs onto a chair, then collapses onto the sofa, moaning and groaning)*

HEÉRIN: *(Chases Merchútkina)* Catch her! Break her neck! Cut her throat!

MERCHÚTKINA: Oh, my God, I'm going to faint! Ohh! *(Falls senseless into Shipúchin's arms)*

(A knock at the door. A voice offstage announces: "The delegation from the board of directors!")

SHIPÚCHIN: Delegation . . . reputation . . . occupation . . .
HEÉRIN: *(Stamps his foot)* Out! Out before I cut you up into little pieces! *(Rolls up his sleeves)* Let me at her! I won't stop at murder!

(Enter the delegation: five men, all in tailcoats. One carries the desk calendar, another the silver trophy. Bank employees crowd in at the door behind them. Tatyána Alexéyevna is stretched out on the sofa, Merchútkina is in Shipúchin's arms. Both women whimper softly.)

A MEMBER OF THE DELEGATION: Dear Andréy Andréyich! As we cast a retrospective eye over the past of our financial institution and let our minds glide gratefully over the story of its constant growth and development, we are *most* gratified. True, in the early days, lack of available capital and a few frivolous investments, as well as a very confused idea of our corporate goals, led one inescapably to Hamlet's question, "To be or not to be," and of course there were always those who maintained we should shut the place down completely. . . . And then you came to take over our administration. Your knowledge, your energy, and your tact are the reasons for our extraordinary success and our remarkable expansion. The bank's reputation . . . *(Takes in the scene; coughs nervously)* The bank's reputation . . .
MERCHÚTKINA: *(Moans)* Oh! Ohh!
TATYÁNA ALEXÉYEVNA: *(Moans)* Water! Water!
MEMBER OF THE DELEGATION: Er, reputation . . . *(Coughs)* You have raised the bank's reputation to a point where we now feel able to compete with even the most renowned foreign establishments. . . .
SHIPÚCHIN: *(Babbling)* Delegation . . . reputation . . . occupation . . . "Oh, never say thy youth has flown . . ." "There was a little man, and he had a little house . . ."
MEMBER OF THE DELEGATION: *(Going bravely on)* So therefore, when we cast an objective glance at the present, we find ourselves eternally grateful to you, dear Andréy Andréyich. . . . *(His voice trails off)* So therefore we would like . . . we would like to . . .

(The delegation goes out in confused embarrassment.)

CURTAIN.

Uncle Vanya

SCENES FROM COUNTRY LIFE
IN FOUR ACTS

1896

CHARACTERS

Alexánder Serebriakóv, a retired professor

Yeléna, his wife, 27 years old

Sónya, his daughter by his first wife

Mrs. Voinítsky (María Vasílyevna), a widow, mother of the Professor's first wife

Iván Petróvich (Ványa), her son

Mikhaíl Lvóvich Ástrov, a doctor

Ilyá Ilých Telégin, an impoverished neighbor

Marína, the family's old nurse

A hired man

The action takes place on the Serebriakóv farm.

ACT ONE

The garden. Part of the veranda of the house is visible. Beneath an old poplar tree, a table set for tea. A bench, chairs. On the bench, a guitar. Beyond the table, a garden swing. It's past two in the afternoon on a muggy, overcast day. Marína, a slow-moving old woman, sits by the tea table, knitting a stocking. Ástrov walks back and forth.

MARÍNA: *(Pours him a cup of tea)* Here, dear. Have some tea.

ÁSTROV: *(Takes the cup reluctantly)* I don't feel like tea.

MARÍNA: How about a little drink?

ÁSTROV: No, I don't want to start drinking this early. Anyway, it's too hot. *(Pause)* Nanny, how long have we known each other?

MARÍNA: *(Thinks)* How long? Good heavens, let's see.... Well, you first moved to these parts ... when was it? Sónya's mother was still alive; you were coming over here at least two years before she died. So that would be—what?—eleven years. *(Thinks a bit)* Maybe more.

ÁSTROV: Have I changed a lot since then?

MARÍNA: Oh, my, yes; a lot. You used to be young and good-looking and now you're not. And of course now you drink.

ÁSTROV: Yeah, you're right. Ten years, and I'm a changed man. You want to know why? I work too hard, Nanny. I'm on my feet from morning to night, I never get any rest, I go to bed at night and I can't sleep: I just lie there waiting for an emergency call. I haven't had a day off the whole time you've known me. Of course I'm old! And I'm bored. Life is boring, it's stupid, it stinks ... it really gets to you after a while. And people are freaks, you know? You spend all your time with them, before you know it you're a freak yourself. Can't avoid it. *(Pulls at his long mustache)* And I let my mustache grow, see? Looks stupid, doesn't it? That's it, Nanny, I'm getting to be a freak. I'm not a complete idiot yet, thank God, I can still use my head, but my heart ... I don't have any feelings anymore. I don't want anything, I don't need anything, I don't love anybody— No, that's not right. I do love you. *(Kisses the top of her head)* I had a nanny just like you when I was a kid.

MARÍNA: How about a little something to eat?

ÁSTROV: No. A few weeks before Easter, I had to go out to Málitskoye; there was an outbreak of typhoid fever. Those backwoods shacks . . . the way those people are crammed in on top of one another; it was filthy! The stink, the smoke—they had livestock right in the same room with the sick people; pigs, even. I ran around all day trying to treat people, never stopped, didn't eat a thing, got home that night— and you think I got any rest? They brought in the signal man from the railroad yard, dumped him on my table, expected me to operate right then and there, and just as I was giving him anesthesia he goes and dies on me. And right then, just when I didn't need them, all my feelings came rushing back. I felt as if I'd killed him on purpose. I sat down and closed my eyes, just like this, and I thought: What are people going to say about all this a hundred years from now? We're supposed to be paving the way for them . . . you think they'll admire us for the way we live now, Nanny? They will not!

MARÍNA: Maybe people won't, but God will.

ÁSTROV: *(Beat)* You're right, Nanny. Thanks for saying that.

> *(Enter Ványa from the house. He has fallen asleep after lunch and looks rumpled. Sits on a bench, tries to fix his stylish tie.)*

VÁNYA: Yes, well . . .

> *(Pause.)*

Well . . .

ÁSTROV: Have a good nap?

VÁNYA: Oh, sure, wonderful. *(Yawns)* Ever since the Professor and his charming *spouse* have been with us, life around here is complete chaos. I don't sleep right, lunch and dinner I eat too much, I drink too much . . . not a very healthy way to live. Before, I never had a minute to myself, Sónya and I worked, we worked all the time. Now Sónya does all the work; I just eat, sleep, and drink. Awful, isn't it?

MARÍNA: Everything's gone haywire these days! The Professor doesn't get up till noon, the kettle's going all morning, breakfast ready for hours, and everybody has to wait for him. Before they came, we had dinner in the middle of the day like normal people; now we have to wait till after six. Then the Professor stays up all night, reading and writing, and all of a sudden it's two in the morning and he wants tea! So somebody has to get up and put the kettle on. It's haywire, that's what it is!

ÁSTROV: How long are they going to stay?

VÁNYA: *(Whistles)* Forever. The Professor has decided to settle amongst us.

MARÍNA: It's like right now. Tea's been sitting here for the last hour, and they're off taking a walk!

VÁNYA: Don't get upset. Here they come now.

> *(The sound of voices. From the garden come the Professor, Yeléna, Sónya, and Telégin.)*

PROFESSOR: Yes, lovely, lovely. Remarkable view.

TELÉGIN: Yessir, Your Excellency. Really remarkable.

SÓNYA: And tomorrow we can go visit the new forest, Papa. You want to?

VÁNYA: Tea's ready!

PROFESSOR: If you don't mind, I'll take tea in my study. Be good enough to have someone bring it up to me, will you? I still have a little work to do.

SÓNYA: I know you'll like the new forest. . . .

> *(Yeléna, Sónya, and the Professor go into the house. Telégin goes to the tea table and sits next to Marína.)*

VÁNYA: Hottest day of the year, and our famous intellectual has on an overcoat, gloves, and galoshes, and carries an umbrella.

ÁSTROV: He's just a careful man, that's all.

VÁNYA: And her! That amazing woman! Isn't she the most beautiful woman you've ever seen?

TELÉGIN: . . . just tramping through the underbrush, and all of a sudden I saw your table here, all set for tea, and I don't know, it was like a wave of happiness washed right over me. The weather's wonderful, our feathered friends are singing, we're all friends here—what more could a man ask? *(Takes a cup of tea)* Thank you! Very much obliged.

VÁNYA: *(Dreamily)* And those eyes . . . What a wonderful woman!

ÁSTROV: Oh, come on, Ványa, tell me something new.

VÁNYA: *(Vaguely)* What? There's nothing new to tell. Everything's old. I'm the same as I always was—no, I'm probably worse. I'm lazy, I can't get a thing done, I just go around grumbling and mumbling like an old fart. My magpie of a mother, my dear old *maman*? She's still babbling on about equal rights for women; she has one foot in the grave and the other on a stack of feminist pamphlets, still on the lookout for the millennium.

ÁSTROV: What about the Professor?

VÁNYA: The Professor does what he's always done. Sits in his study writing from morning to night. Scribble, scribble, scribble, eh? Pity the poor paper! What he ought to write is his autobiography. Now, there's a subject for you! A retired professor, a has-been, a moldy mackerel with a college degree. He has gout, rheumatism, migraines, his liver's swollen with jealousy and envy. And this poor fish now resides at his first wife's place in the country. Not that he wants to, mind you; he just can't afford to live in town anymore. He never shuts up about how unhappy he is, when the fact is he has the most amazing reasons to be happy. *(Irritably)* You can't imagine how happy he ought to be! His father was a poor country churchwarden or something, he got through school on scholarships, took all his graduate degrees, got to be a professor, started making people call him "Your Excellency," married a senator's daughter, and all the rest of it. But get this. Here's a man who for the last twenty-five years has been lecturing and writing about art, and he knows nothing whatsoever about art! For twenty-five years he's been regurgitating other people's ideas about realism, naturalism, all that bullshit. And now he's retired, and it turns out he's a complete fraud! He has no reputation whatsoever! For the last twenty-five years, all he's been doing is keeping some better man out of a job. And look at him: he walks around like he'd just stepped off Mount Olympus!

ÁSTROV: Sounds like you envy him.

VÁNYA: I do! I envy him! And his successes where women are concerned! Don Juan himself never had it so good! His first wife: my sister. So beautiful, so sweet, so innocent, so loving, so giving . . . she had more admirers than he had students, and she loved him! Loved him the way only an angel could love. His mother-in-law, my mother, worships the ground he walks on; to this day she treats him like the second coming. His second wife: beautiful, intelligent . . . well, you saw her just now. He was already an old man when she married him, and she gave up everything for him—her youth, her beauty, her freedom, her charm. For him! Why? What for?

ÁSTROV: Is she faithful to him?

VÁNYA: Yes, unfortunately.

ÁSTROV: Why unfortunately?

VÁNYA: Because her fidelity is false from beginning to end! It's all morality and no logic. Cheat on an old husband you can't stand—

what's immoral about that? Stifle your youth, your deepest feelings—now, *that*'s immoral!

TELÉGIN: *(Whiny voice)* Ványa, I don't like it when you talk like that,
really I don't. A person who cheats on a husband or wife is a
traitor. He might just as well betray his country!

VÁNYA: *(Annoyed)* Oh, for God's sake, Waffles, stop whining.

TELÉGIN: You don't understand, Ványa. My wife betrayed me. She
ran away with another man the day after our wedding. Because
she found me . . . facially repulsive. But I have never wavered in
my duty. I still love her, I am faithful to her, I help her out when I
can, and I support the children she had by the man she ran off
with. I have been deprived of happiness, true, but I still have my
pride. And what has she got? Her youth has flown, her beauty
has succumbed to relentless nature, and now her lover's dead.

> *(Enter Sónya and Yeléna; soon after them, Mrs. Voinítsky, with a
> book; she sits down and reads. When they pour her tea, she drinks it
> without looking up.)*

SÓNYA: *(To Marína, hurriedly)* Nanny, some of the local people are
here. Could you go see what they want and take care of it? I'll do
the tea. *(Sits down and begins to pour)*

> *(Marína goes out. Yeléna takes a cup of tea and goes to drink it in
> the garden swing.)*

ÁSTROV: *(To Yeléna)* I came to see your husband, you know. Your
message said he was very sick, rheumatism or something. . . . He
seems perfectly healthy to me.

YELÉNA: Last night he was miserable, he kept complaining about
pains in his legs; now today they're all gone—

ÁSTROV: And I nearly broke my neck getting here; it's over twenty
miles. Oh, well. It's not the first time. But you'll have to put me
up overnight, which means at least I'll get a good night's sleep.
Quantum satis.

SÓNYA: Oh, that's wonderful! It's always a special occasion, having
you stay over. Have you eaten?

ÁSTROV: No, I'm afraid not.

SÓNYA: Then you'll stay for dinner. Although nowadays we don't eat
until after six. *(Drinks)* The tea's cold!

TELÉGIN: There has indeed been a significant decline in the temperature of the teapot.

YELÉNA: That's all right, Iván Ivánich, we'll drink it cold.

TELÉGIN: I beg your pardon. It's not Iván Ivánich, it's Ilyá Ilých. Ilyá Ilých Telégin, that's my name. Some people call me Waffles—that's because of my acne, you know. His Excellency your husband, he knows my right name. I happen to be Sónya's godfather, and I live right here on the estate with you, and I also have dinner with you every day. As you may perhaps have noticed.

SÓNYA: Ilyá Ilých is our right-hand man. We couldn't do without him. *(Tenderly)* Here, Godfather. Have some more tea.

MRS. VOINÍTSKY: Oh!

SÓNYA: What's the matter, Grandmother?

MRS. VOINÍTSKY: I forgot to tell Alexánder ... oh, I must be losing my mind.... I got a letter today from Pável Alexeyévich in Hárkov. He sent me his new article.

ÁSTROV: Is it interesting?

MRS. VOINÍTSKY: Interesting, yes, but quite disturbing. He's now attacking the very principles he held sacred seven years ago! That's so typical nowadays, isn't it? People change opinions the way they change shirts. I call that disgraceful.

VÁNYA: There's nothing disgraceful about it, *Maman*. Just drink your tea.

MRS. VOINÍTSKY: Don't you interrupt me when I'm talking!

VÁNYA: But you've *been* talking. And so have I. Talking and talking for the last fifty years, and reading those damn review articles. Don't you think it's time to give it a rest?

MRS. VOINÍTSKY: You never want to listen to anything I say, do you? Excuse me, *Jean*, but in the last year you have changed so much I hardly recognize you. You used to be such a strong-minded young man, a brilliant personality—

VÁNYA: Oh, sure. A brilliant personality. Out here in the sticks, where nobody notices.

(Pause.)

I used to be "a brilliant personality." You don't have to rub it in! I'm forty-seven years old. Up until this last year I was just like you—I kept trying to fool myself with that intellectual gobbledygook of yours, so I wouldn't have to face reality. And I thought I was *doing* something. And now! If you only knew! I can't sleep nights, I'm so depressed, I'm so angry—all that time wasted, when I could have been doing everything I can't do now because I'm too old!

SÓNYA: Uncle Ványa, *please*.

MRS. VOINÍTSKY: You are making a mockery of all your former principles. They're not at fault; you are. Principles are a dead letter unless you act upon them, do something useful—which is something you have never done.

VÁNYA: Do something useful? Like your Herr Professor? We can't all be perpetual writing machines.

MRS. VOINÍTSKY: And exactly what is that supposed to mean?

SÓNYA: Grandmother! Uncle Ványa! Will you both please stop it?

VÁNYA: All right, I'll keep still. I'll keep still. I apologize.

(Pause.)

YELÉNA: The weather's lovely today. It's not too hot. . . .

(Pause.)

VÁNYA: Lovely weather for hanging yourself.

(Telégin strums the guitar; Marína comes from around the house, calling the chickens.)

MARÍNA: Here, chick, chick, chick . . .

SÓNYA: What did those people want, Nanny?

MARÍNA: Same old thing—that piece of empty field. Here, chick, chick, chick . . .

SÓNYA: What are you calling the chickens for?

MARÍNA: That speckle hen has gone off someplace with her chicks. And there's bound to be hawks around. *(Leaves)*

(Telégin plays a polka; they all listen in silence. Enter the Hired Man.)

HIRED MAN: Is the doctor here? *(To Ástrov)* Excuse me, Doctor, there's an emergency. They want you.

ÁSTROV: Where?

HIRED MAN: Down by the factory.

ÁSTROV: *(Resigned)* Thanks a lot. Well, that's that; I've got to go. *(Looks around for his cap)* Christ, wouldn't you know.

SÓNYA: Oh, that's too bad! But you can come back when you're finished and have dinner with us.

ÁSTROV: No, it'll be too late. Now, where . . . where the hell . . . *(To the Hired Man)* Listen, go inside, will you? Tell them I'd like a shot of vodka before I go.

(The Hired Man leaves.)

ÁSTROV: Where the hell ... *(Finds his cap)* Oh, here it is. You know, in one of Ostróvsky's plays, there's a character with a huge mustache and no talent. That's me. Well, everybody, time to say goodbye. *(To Yeléna)* If you'd like to come by for a visit sometime, you and Sónya here, I'd be delighted. Really. My place is small, seventy-five acres or so, but I've got a nursery, if that interests you, plants you won't find anywhere else around here. And then there's a state forest right next to my land. The forester's old, he's sick a lot, so I wind up taking care of the place.

YELÉNA: That's what they told me, that you were in love with a forest. It's important, I suppose, but doesn't it interfere with your real occupation? Being a doctor, I mean.

ÁSTROV: My real occupation? God only knows what that is.

YELÉNA: Is it interesting?

ÁSTROV: What, taking care of a forest? *(Beat)* Yes, it's interesting.

VÁNYA: *(Ironically)* Oh, yes, very interesting.

YELÉNA: *(To Ástrov)* You're still young, aren't you? You're—what?—thirty-six, maybe thirty-seven. *(Beat)* I doubt it's all that interesting. A forest? Just one tree after another. Sounds monotonous to me.

SÓNYA: No it's not—it's incredibly interesting! He plants new trees every year; he's already gotten a bronze medal and a certificate. And he's a leader in the campaign to preserve the old-growth forests. He says that trees are earth's most precious ornament, they teach us to recognize beauty! Forests help to temper a severe climate, and in regions with temperate climates, people spend less energy trying to combat nature, so the people themselves are kinder and gentler. And they're better-looking, and taller, and more at ease with their emotions; even their speech and their movements have a natural grace. Wherever there are trees, the arts and sciences flourish, and a positive attitude to life, and they treat women with respect—

VÁNYA: *(Laughs)* Bravo, bravo! That's a very lovely speech, dear, but it doesn't convince me. So ... *(to Ástrov)* please don't hate me if I go on cutting wood for the stove and timber to build a new barn.

ÁSTROV: You can burn turf in your stove and use bricks for your barn. Look, I'm not against cutting wood, but why destroy the forests?

VÁNYA: Why not? To listen to you, you'd think the only thing forests were good for is shade for picnics.

ÁSTROV: I never said that. But all our great woodlands are being leveled, millions of trees already gone, bird and animal habitats destroyed, rivers dammed up and polluted—and all for what? Because we're too lazy to look for other sources of energy! *(To Yeléna)* Don't you agree? You have to be a barbarian to burn all that beauty in your stove, to destroy something that can never be replaced. We were born with the ability to reason and the power to create and be fruitful, but until now all we've done is destroy whatever we see. The forests are disappearing one by one, the rivers are polluted, wildlife is becoming extinct, the climate is changing for the worse, every day the planet gets poorer and uglier. It's a disaster! *(To Ványa)* Oh, I know, you're giving me that ironic look again, you think I'm being ridiculous, and ... and well, maybe I am, but every time I drive by a stand of trees that I persuaded the owners to spare, or hear the breeze at night in young trees I planted myself, I realize that I *can* do something about the climate, and if a thousand years from now people are a little happier, then it's partly because of me. I ... I even ... *(Sees the Hired Man coming with a glass of vodka on a tray)* However ... *(Drinks)* I've got to go. I, ah, must have sounded like a freak just now. Nice to see you all. *(Goes toward the house)*

SÓNYA: *(Takes his arm and goes with him)* When will you be back?

ÁSTROV: I don't know.

SÓNYA: Will we have to wait another month?

(Ástrov and Sónya go into the house; Mrs. Voinítsky and Telégin remain at the table; Yeléna and Ványa stroll to the veranda.)

YELÉNA: Ványa, you're impossible. You never stop, do you? There was no need to quarrel with your mother like that. And calling Alexánder a perpetual writing machine! And you got into another argument with him at lunch. You're being very petty.

VÁNYA: It's because I don't like him! I hate him!

YELÉNA: Why do you hate him? He's no different from anybody else. He's no worse than you are.

VÁNYA: I wish you could see your face right now. Or see the indolent way you move. You're so ... so *detached.* You don't care about anything, do you? You just drift through life.

YELÉNA: Detached? Oh, yes. And bored. *(Beat)* Nobody likes my husband; they all pity me: oh, poor thing, stuck with an old man like that! But all this sympathy for me—oh, I know what's behind it. It's like Ástrov was saying just now: you destroy the forests without thinking, and pretty soon there won't be a tree left on the planet. You destroy human beings the same way, and pretty soon trust, and honesty, and the possibility of self-sacrifice, will vanish from the planet as well. *(Beat)* What is it about you men? You can't leave a woman alone until she belongs to you! Your doctor was right—there's a demon of destruction in every one of you. You don't spare the trees, nor the birds, nor the women, nor each other.

VÁNYA: I hate it when you get philosophical like this.

(Pause.)

YELÉNA: He has an interesting face, that doctor. Tired-looking. Always a bit on edge. Sónya likes him, I can tell. She's in love with him. I can understand why. He's been to visit three times now since I've been here, and I haven't once been nice to him, or even polite, but it's only because I'm so shy. He must think I'm terrible. *(Beat)* You know why we're such good friends, Ványa, you and I? Because we're both boring, disagreeable people. Don't look at me like that. I don't like it.

VÁNYA: How else can I look at you? I love you. You're my life, my happiness, my youth! I know there's no chance of us ever ... being together—zero—but I don't care; all I want is to see you, hear your voice—

YELÉNA: Be quiet, someone may hear you!

(They start into the house.)

VÁNYA: Just let me talk to you, tell you how much I love you—that's all I need, that's enough to make me completely happy.

YELÉNA: You really are aggravating. . . .

(They go into the house. Telégin strums the guitar and plays a polka; Mrs. Voinítsky makes a note in the margin of the book she's reading.)

CURTAIN.

ACT TWO

The dining room. Night. We hear the night watchman outside the house, tapping his warning stick as he makes his rounds. The Pro-

*fessor sits in an armchair before an open window, dozing. Yeléna
sits near him, also dozing.*

PROFESSOR: *(Waking)* Who's that? Sónya, is that you?

YELÉNA: It's me.

PROFESSOR: Oh, it's you, Léna. *(Beat)* I can't stand this pain!

YELÉNA: Your blanket's on the floor. *(Picks it up and tucks it around
his legs)* I'll shut the window, Alexánder.

PROFESSOR: No, don't; it's stifling. I must have dozed off. I was
dreaming my left leg didn't belong to me, and then this terrible
pain woke me up. It isn't the gout this time; it has to be rheumatism. What time is it?

YELÉNA: Almost twelve-thirty.

   (Pause.)

PROFESSOR: Look in the library tomorrow, will you, and see if we
have a copy of Bátiushkov's poems. I think we do.

YELÉNA: What?

PROFESSOR: I said, see if we have Bátiushkov. We used to, I remember. Why am I having such a hard time breathing?

YELÉNA: You're tired. This is the second night you haven't slept.

PROFESSOR: They say Turgénev's gout eventually gave him a heart
condition. I think that's what's happening to me too. Damn old
age! God, how I hate it! I got old, and now I'm repulsive. I
repulse myself, and all the rest of you too, probably.

YELÉNA: You talk as if the rest of us are to blame for your getting old.

PROFESSOR: You more than any of them. You *really* think I'm repulsive. *(Yeléna moves away from him and sits in another chair)* And
you're right. I'm not stupid, I understand things. You're young,
you're beautiful, you've got your health, you want to live, and I'm
an old man with one foot in the grave. Right? You think I don't
understand that? It's ridiculous of me to be still alive. Well, just
wait. You'll all be rid of me soon enough.

YELÉNA: For God's sake, will you please stop it? I'm worn out.

PROFESSOR: I wear everybody out: that's what it's come to, hasn't it? I
bore everybody, I make you all miserable, while I sit here enjoying my retirement. Oh, yes, of course!

YELÉNA: Be quiet! You're driving me crazy!

PROFESSOR: Yes, of course! I drive everybody crazy.

YELÉNA: *(Almost in tears)* I can't stand any more of this. What do you
want from me? Just tell me!

PROFESSOR: Nothing.

YELÉNA: Then just be quiet. *Please.*

PROFESSOR: It's very strange, isn't it. Ványa starts talking, or that old idiot his mother: fine, wonderful, everybody pays attention; but I say one word, and you all start feeling miserable. Even my voice is repulsive. All right, I agree! I'm repulsive, I'm an egotist, I'm a tyrant, but don't I have the right to a little ego in my old age? Haven't I earned it? I ask you, don't I have the right to a little peace and quiet, and a little respect from the rest of you?

YELÉNA: Nobody's denying you your rights.

> *(A shutter flaps in the breeze.)*

The wind's come up; I'd better shut the window. *(Closes the window)* It's going to rain. No one is trying to deny you your rights.

> *(Pause. Outside, the watchman makes his rounds; he taps his warning stick and sings a song.)*

PROFESSOR: I have devoted my entire life to scholarship. I had my own office, my lecture hall, I had colleagues who treated me with respect—and now, suddenly, it's all gone. I sit here in this graveyard, surrounded by stupid people saying stupid things. But I'm still alive! I still want to be famous and successful, I want all the excitement I used to feel! This place—it's like a prison. I sit here dreaming about the past, I have to watch other people succeed, I'm terrified of dying—and I can't do it anymore! I don't have the strength! And now you all hate me because I'm old!

YELÉNA: Just be patient. Five or six years and I'll be old too.

> *(Enter Sónya.)*

SÓNYA: Papa, you had us send for Doctor Ástrov, and when he gets here you refuse to see him. That's very rude. You got him out in the middle of the night for no reason.

PROFESSOR: I don't want anything to do with your Ástrov! He knows as much about medicine as I do about astronomy.

SÓNYA: You cannot expect the entire medical faculty to come take care of your gout!

PROFESSOR: The man's a fool, and I refuse to talk to him!

SÓNYA: Fine. Whatever you say. *(Sits)* I don't care.

PROFESSOR: What time is it?

YELÉNA: One o'clock.

PROFESSOR: I can't breathe. . . . Sónya, give me my drops, there on that table.

SÓNYA: Here. *(Gives him the drops)*

PROFESSOR: *(Irritably)* Not these; the other ones! I can't even ask you to do the simplest thing—

SÓNYA: Will you stop making scenes? Please. Maybe some people enjoy it; I don't. I hate it. Anyway, I don't have time for all this. I have to get up early in the morning. We're cutting hay.

(Enter Ványa in a bathrobe. He carries a candle.)

VÁNYA: There's going to be a storm. *(Lightning and thunder)* See, what did I tell you! *Hélène*, Sónya, go to bed. I'm the relief nurse.

PROFESSOR: *(In fright)* No! No, please, don't leave me alone with him! Please! He'll talk my head off!

VÁNYA: They've got to get some rest! This is the second night they've had to sit up with you!

PROFESSOR: Fine, let them go rest, only you go too. Do me that favor. For the sake of our former friendship, don't argue, just go. We can discuss this later.

VÁNYA: *(Angry laugh)* Former . . . our former friendship . . .

SÓNYA: Stop it, Uncle Ványa.

PROFESSOR: My dear, don't leave me alone with him. He'll talk my head off!

VÁNYA: This is getting comical.

(Enter Marína with a candle.)

SÓNYA: You go to bed, Nanny. It's very late.

MARÍNA: The table still hasn't been cleared. How do you expect me to go to bed?

PROFESSOR: None of you can sleep—you're all worn out, aren't you? I'm the only one around here who's enjoying himself.

MARÍNA: *(Tenderly, as she crosses to the Professor)* Oh . . . you're feeling poorly, are you, dear? Oh, I know how it is; my own legs give me trouble too. *(Adjusts his blanket)* Been troubling you for a long time, too. I remember your first wife, Sónya's mother, she wouldn't sleep nights either; used to kill her to see you like this. She loved you very much. . . . *(Pause)* But nobody takes care of us old people, do they? *(Kisses the Professor's shoulder)* Let's go, dear, time to go to bed. Come on, my angel, I'll make you some chamomile tea, get you something to warm your legs . . . say a little prayer for you. . . .

PROFESSOR: *(Touched)* Thank you, Marína. Yes, let's go. . . .

MARÍNA: My own legs give me trouble too, oh! Such trouble! *(Helps the Professor to his feet; Sónya comes to help her)* Yes, your first wife used to cry and cry, she felt so sorry. . . . And Sónya was just a little thing then, weren't you, dear, couldn't even talk yet. Come on, come on, dear. . . .

(Professor, Sónya, and Marína go out.)

YELÉNA: He was driving me to distraction. I haven't got the strength left to stand.

VÁNYA: He drives you to distraction; I drive myself to distraction. This is the third night in a row I haven't slept.

YELÉNA: There's something terribly wrong going on in this house. Your mother pays no attention to anything except her precious pamphlets and the Professor. The Professor is always irritable; he doesn't trust me, he's afraid of you. Sónya gets mad at her father, she gets mad at me; she hasn't spoken a word to me for the last two weeks. You hate my husband, and you insult your own mother. I'm upset; I must have started crying twenty times today. . . . No, no, something's terribly wrong here.

VÁNYA: Please! Let's not start getting philosophical.

YELÉNA: Ványa, you're an educated man, you're intelligent. You know perfectly well it's not crime and criminals that are destroying the world; it's petty little emotions like envy, all these silly squabbles that end up with good people hating one another. You ought to try to make peace, not always be quarreling with everyone.

VÁNYA: First tell me how to make peace with myself. Oh, my darling—*(Reaches for her hand)*

YELÉNA: Stop that! *(Takes away her hand)* Just go away, will you?

VÁNYA: It's going to rain soon. The whole world will cool off, everything in nature will breathe easy. Except me. I haunt this house like a lost soul; it makes me crazy, the thought that I've thrown away my life and I'll never get it back. My past is gone, wasted on stupidity, and the present is so pointless it's grotesque. And that's it, that's my life, and that's my love, and what can I do about it? My feeling for you is hopeless, like a ray of sunlight falling into a black hole. I'm dying.

YELÉNA: Whenever you talk to me about love, I simply freeze up, I don't know what to say. Forgive me. There's nothing I can say. *(Starts to leave)* Good night.

VÁNYA: *(Tries to stop her)* And if you only knew the pain I feel, knowing there's another soul in this house dying right alongside me. You. What are you waiting for? What are all these damn-fool notions that keep holding you back? Why can't you understand me? Why?

YELÉNA: Ványa, you're drunk!

VÁNYA: All right, maybe I am, maybe I am.

YELÉNA: Where's the doctor?

VÁNYA: Inside. He's spending the night. Maybe I am. May be. May be anything.

YELÉNA: Why did you have to start drinking today? What's the point?

VÁNYA: So I can feel for a few minutes like I have a real life ... And don't try and stop me, *Hélène*!

YELÉNA: You never used to drink like this. You never used to talk like this either. Go to bed. You're beginning to bore me.

VÁNYA: *(Grabs at her hand again)* My darling ... you wonderful woman ...

YELÉNA: Leave me alone! You're disgusting! *(Goes out)*

VÁNYA: *(Alone)* She's gone.

   (Pause.)

I first met her ten years ago, at my poor sister's. She was seventeen then, and I was thirty-seven. Why didn't I fall in love with her right away and ask her to marry me? It would have been so easy! And she'd be my wife right now ... yes. The storm would wake us both up, and she'd be scared, and I'd put my arms around her and I'd whisper, "Don't be afraid, I'm right here." Oh, that would be wonderful, and then I'd even— Oh, God, my mind's a mess. *(Beat)* Why am I so old? Why can't she understand me? All her rhetoric, her trivial morality, all that stupid talk about envy destroying the world—I hate all that.

   (Pause.)

I let them make a fool of me! I used to worship that Professor, that gout-ridden nonentity; I worked like a dog for him! Sónya and I squeezed every last drop out of this property, we worked and worked, we sold vegetable oil and beans and farmer cheese, we starved ourselves and scrimped and saved money until it added up to thousands, and we sent it all to him. And I was so proud of him and his studies; I lived and breathed for him! Everything he wrote was a work of genius to me. Oh, God, and now? It turns out he's a complete unknown, the stuff he wrote is all academic drivel, hot air! And I'm a fool! I see it all now—I've been made a complete fool!

(Enter Ástrov. His jacket is unbuttoned, vest and tie are off; he's been drinking. Telégin follows him with the guitar.)

ÁSTROV: Go on, play!

TELÉGIN: But everybody's asleep!

ÁSTROV: I said play!

(Telégin plays softly.)

ÁSTROV: *(To Ványa)* You're all alone. What happened to the ladies? *(Stretches out his arms and begins to sing and dance)*
"Hódi, háta, hódi, páych,
hozyáinu nigdeh láych . . ."
The storm woke me up. Well, we can certainly use a little rain. What time is it?

VÁNYA: Who the hell cares.

ÁSTROV: I somehow had the idea I heard Yeléna's voice.

VÁNYA: She just left.

ÁSTROV: She's quite a woman. *(Looks at the medicines on the table)* Medicine! Look at all the little bottles! Moscow, Hárkov, Túla . . . he's been boring the whole country with his gout. You think he's sick, or is he just pretending?

VÁNYA: He's sick.

(Pause.)

ÁSTROV: What are you so down about? Feeling sorry for your poor Professor, s'that it?

VÁNYA: Leave me alone.

ÁSTROV: Oh, I get it! You're in love with the Professor's lady!

VÁNYA: She is my friend!

ÁSTROV: Already?

VÁNYA: What do you mean, already?

ÁSTROV: A woman becomes a man's friend in three steps: first acquaintance, then lover, then friend.

VÁNYA: That is a vulgar thing to say.

ÁSTROV: What? Oh, yeah, probably is. I've gotten vulgar, haven't you noticed? Look, I'm drunk too. Usually I only get drunk like this once a month. But when I do, I get crude and vulgar and carry on like a sonofabitch. And I let nothing stand in my way! I take on the most complicated operations, and I do them perfectly; I draw up vast plans for the future; I no longer feel like a freak; I'm convinced I am the bearer of blessings for humanity—enormous blessings for humanity! When I'm drunk, I have my own personal vision of the universe, and the rest of you, kiddies, the rest of you . . . you're nothing but insignificant little bugs. Microbes. *(To Telégin)* Go on, Waffles, play!

TELÉGIN: Look, you know I'd be more than happy to, but everyone in the house is asleep!

ÁSTROV: I said play! *(Telégin plays quietly)* Time for a drink. Come on, there's still some brandy left. And as soon as it gets light, we'll go to my place. Shall we *gow? (Laughs)* I've got an assistant, he never says "go," he pronounces it "gow." Shall we *gow? (Sees Sónya at the door)* Oh, excuse me—I . . . I forgot my tie. *(Goes out quickly)*

> *(Telégin follows him out.)*

SÓNYA: Uncle Ványa, why did you and the doctor have to get drunk again? You're behaving like a pair of teenagers! He does it all the time now, but why do you have to join in? At your age!

VÁNYA: Age has nothing to do with it. When you don't have a real life, you make do with dreams. It's better than nothing.

SÓNYA: The hay's cut, it's been raining for days, it's all rotting in the field, and you talk about dreams. You've completely given up running this place! I have to do everything myself, and I just can't anymore, I'm worn out. *(Startled)* Uncle Ványa, you're crying!

VÁNYA: I am not—what do you mean? Don't be silly. . . . *(Beat)* You looked like your poor dead mother just now. Darling . . . *(Kisses her hands and face yearningly)* My sister . . . My darling sister . . . where is she now? If only she knew! If only she knew!

SÓNYA: Knew what? If only she knew what, Uncle?

VÁNYA: So painful . . . it's awful. Nothing . . . Later, I'll . . . S'all right, it's nothing. . . . I'm going to bed. *(Goes out)*

SÓNYA: *(Goes to the other door and calls)* Mikhaíl Lvóvich? Are you asleep? Can you come here a moment, please?

ÁSTROV: *(Off)* Just a minute! *(Pause; he comes in; he has on his vest and tie)* What can I do for you?

SÓNYA: Look. Go ahead and drink, if that's what you want. Only please, I beg of you, don't let Uncle Ványa get drunk. It's very bad for him.

ÁSTROV: Good. We won't drink anymore.

(Pause.)

I'm going home now. The die is cast. By the time I get hitched up, it'll be light.

SÓNYA: It's still raining. Wait till morning.

ÁSTROV: No, the storm's over; this is just the tail end of it. I'm going. And please don't ever ask me to come see your father again. I tell him he has gout, he wants to call it rheumatism. I tell him to lie down, he sits up. Today he wouldn't even speak to me.

SÓNYA: It's just that he's spoiled. *(Opens the sideboard)* Would you like something to eat?

ÁSTROV: I would, yes. Please.

SÓNYA: I love eating in the middle of the night. I think there's something here in the sideboard. He used to be very successful with women, they tell me. All that admiration spoiled him. Here, have some cheese.

(They both stand at the sideboard and eat.)

ÁSTROV: I haven't eaten anything all day; all I did was drink. Your father's a hard man. *(Takes a bottle of vodka from the sideboard)* You mind? *(Drinks a glass of vodka)* We're all alone here; we can be honest with each other. You know, I couldn't survive a single month in this house; I'd suffocate. All your father can think about is his gout and his books; your Uncle Ványa's constantly depressed; then there's your grandmother, and of course your stepmother—

SÓNYA: What about my stepmother?

ÁSTROV: Well . . . well, the way I see it, we human beings are meant to lead harmonious lives. Our bodies, our minds, our souls, even our clothes—they're all meant to be in harmony. Now, she's beautiful, no denying that, but . . . all she does is eat, sleep, go for long walks, charm everybody she meets—and that's it. She has nothing to do; other people do her work for her. Aren't I right? She's bored. And a boring life can't be an honest one.

(Pause.)

Well, maybe I'm being too hard on her. I don't like my life either. Neither does your Uncle Ványa. We're getting to be a couple of old farts, the two of us.

SÓNYA: You really don't like life?

ÁSTROV: I do, I love life—in general. But our life, this stupid clodhopping life we lead around here—I can't stand it. I hate it with every fiber of my being. And my own personal life ... hell, it's a complete mess. You know how it is sometimes: you're out in the woods at night and you see a light in the distance, and all of a sudden you forget how tired you are, you forget the darkness and the branches that scratch your face. I work all the time—you know that—harder than anyone around here, but nothing ever works out for me. I can't see any light in the distance. *(Beat)* Sometimes I can't stand it. But I don't expect anything for myself anymore. I don't like people. I don't love anybody. Haven't for a long time.

SÓNYA: You don't love anybody?

ÁSTROV: I don't love anybody. Oh, I have a warm feeling for your nanny—she reminds me of my own. But the people around here, they're all alike: no education, they live in filth. And I don't get on with intellectuals. They wear me out. Everyone we know, all these nice people we know, their ideas are petty, their feelings are petty, they can't see beyond the ends of their noses. They're just plain stupid! And the ones with a little brains and energy, they're all eaten up with analysis and self-doubt. They piss and moan, they hate everything and everybody, they look a person up and down, and bang! they label him. "Psychopath!" Or "Windbag!" And when they don't know what label to stick on *me*, they call me a crank. I love trees, that makes me a crank. I don't eat meat, that makes me a crank. Nobody can be spontaneous anymore. You have a clean, honest love for nature or for your fellow human beings, you can't talk about it. You just can't. *(Starts to pour another drink)*

SÓNYA: *(Stops him)* No, please, don't drink anymore.

ÁSTROV: Why not?

SÓNYA: It's so wrong for you! You're a sensitive person, you have a kind voice, and more than that, you're ... you're a beautiful human being, more than anybody I know. Why do you want to waste your time drinking? Don't do it, please. You always talk about how people don't create, they just destroy what God has given them. Then why are you destroying yourself? Why? You mustn't, you just mustn't, please!

ÁSTROV: *(Holds out his hand to her)* All right, I won't drink anymore.

SÓNYA: Promise me?

ÁSTROV: I promise.

SÓNYA: *(Takes his hand eagerly)* Oh, thank you!

ÁSTROV: *Basta!* I've sobered up. You see? I'm completely sober, and

I'll stay this way for the rest of my life. *(Looks at his watch)* Now, what was I saying? It's too late for me, my life is over, I'm old, I'm all worked out, I've gotten vulgar, my feelings are gone, I don't think I could have a relationship with another human being, I can't love anybody anymore. The only thing that still moves me is beauty. I'm enthralled by it. I think if your Yeléna wanted to, she could turn my head overnight. But that's not love, that's not a relationship. *(Covers his eyes with his hands and shudders)*

SÓNYA: What's the matter?

ÁSTROV: Oh, nothing. I—just before Easter I had a patient die on me. Right on the operating table.

SÓNYA: You've got to forget about that!

(Pause.)

Tell me something, Mikhaíl Lvóvich . . . Suppose I had a friend or a younger sister, and you found out that she . . . well, let's say she loved you. How would you react?

ÁSTROV: *(Shrugs)* I don't know. I probably wouldn't. I guess I'd try to explain to her I couldn't love her. *(Beat)* Well, if I'm going home, I'd better get going, otherwise we'll be here till morning. Good night, sweetheart. *(Pats her shoulder)* I'll go out this way, through the living room, otherwise your Uncle Ványa will want me to dance. *(Leaves)*

SÓNYA: *(Alone)* He didn't say anything. . . . I still don't know what he thinks or feels about me, so why do I feel so happy? *(Laughs happily)* I told him he was sensitive, that he had a gentle voice. . . . I hope that was a proper thing to say. . . . When I said that about having a younger sister, he didn't understand. *(Clasps her hands together)* Oh, why aren't I beautiful? It's awful, just awful, being so plain, and I am, I'm ugly, I know I am, I know I am! Last Sunday coming out of church, I heard two ladies talking about me, and one of them said, "She's such a good girl, such a sweet disposition; it's too bad she's so plain." Plain . . .

(Enter Yeléna; she goes to a window and opens it.)

YELÉNA: The storm is over. Feel how fresh the air is!

(Pause.)

Where's the doctor?

SÓNYA: He left.

(Pause.)

YELÉNA: *Sophie* . . .

SÓNYA: What?

YELÉNA: How long are you going to stay mad at me? We haven't done anything to hurt each other; it doesn't make sense, being angry like this. Let's stop it, shall we?

SÓNYA: Oh, I've wanted to. . . . *(Hugs Yeléna)* I'm tired of being angry all the time.

YELÉNA: Oh, I'm so glad!

(Both women are genuinely moved.)

SÓNYA: Is Papa asleep?

YELÉNA: No; he's sitting up in the living room. It's been weeks now that you and I haven't been speaking—God only knows why. *(Notices the sideboard is open)* What's all this?

SÓNYA: I fixed the doctor something to eat.

YELÉNA: There's some wine left. Let's drink to friendship—you want to?

SÓNYA: All right, let's.

YELÉNA: Out of the same glass. *(Pours a glass of wine)* That's the best way. Friends?

SÓNYA: Friends.

(They drink and kiss.)

SÓNYA: I've wanted to make up for a long time, but I was ashamed, I don't know why. . . . *(Starts to cry)*

YELÉNA: What are you crying for?

SÓNYA: I don't know . . . it's just me.

YELÉNA: There, there . . . *(Begins crying herself)* You silly, now you've gotten me started.

(Pause.)

You were mad at me because you thought I took advantage of your father when I married him. I swear to you, Sónya, I married him out of love. Won't you believe me? I was dazzled by him; he was so famous and so intelligent. It wasn't real love, it was all a fantasy, but at the time I thought it was real. And I'm not sorry I married him. But ever since the wedding you've been looking at me with those intelligent, accusing eyes of yours.

SÓNYA: Oh, don't. Friends, friends—remember?

YELÉNA: You mustn't look at people like that. It's not really like you. If you can't trust people, what's the point of living?

(Pause.)

SÓNYA: Tell me something truly, as a friend. . . . Are you happy?

YELÉNA: No.

SÓNYA: I knew you weren't. Let me ask another question. Be honest, now. . . . Wouldn't you rather have a younger husband?

YELÉNA: What a child you are! Of course I would. *(Laughs)* Well, go on—ask me something else.

SÓNYA: Do you like the doctor?

YELÉNA: Yes, very much.

SÓNYA: I must seem stupid, don't I? He just left, and I can still hear his voice and his footsteps, and I look at the darkened window and I think I see his face—no, let me finish. Only I really can't say it out loud; I'm too embarrassed. Come on up to my room; we can talk there. Do you think I'm being stupid? Do you? *(Beat)* Talk to me about him.

YELÉNA: What should I say?

SÓNYA: He's so smart, he knows about everything, he takes care of people, he plants trees—

YELÉNA: Oh, it's more than just caretaking and tree planting. Don't you understand, darling? That man has genius! Do you know what genius means? It means daring, a free-ranging mind, a sense of vision. To plant a tree and be able to imagine that tree a hundred years from now—that means to imagine the future happiness of humanity! People like that are very rare; they deserve to be loved. Yes, he drinks; yes, he's messy and vulgar; but what's so wrong with that? These days you can't expect a man of genius to be neat and orderly. Think of the life that doctor leads! The miserable roads, the cold, the rain and snow, huge distances he has to travel; these people out here, they're all backward and filthy. A man who struggles with all that day in, day out, you can't expect him to reach his forties and still be sober. *(Kisses her)* With all my heart, I want you to be happy. You deserve to be. *(Stands)* Me? I'm boring, I'm trivial. When I play the piano, when I'm home with my husband, in all my relationships, it's always the same. I'm a trivial person. It's the truth. When I think about it, Sónya, I have to face it. I'm a very, very unhappy woman! *(Begins to pace agitatedly)* There is no happiness for me anywhere; no, none. Why are you laughing?

SÓNYA: *(Laughs, hides her face)* Because I am happy—I'm so happy!

YELÉNA: I feel like playing the piano now, I really do.

SÓNYA: Then go play something. *(Kisses her)* I can't go to sleep now. Please, play something.

YELÉNA: All right, I will! *(Beat)* But your father's still awake. When he's feeling like this, music drives him crazy. Go ask him. If he doesn't mind, I will. Go on.

SÓNYA: I'll be right back. *(Goes out)*

(Outside, the watchman's tapping is heard.)

YELÉNA: I've been without music for such a long time. All I want to do now is play and weep, weep like a lost soul. *(At the window)* Is that you, Yefím?

WATCHMAN: *(Off)* Yes, ma'am, it's me.

YELÉNA: Don't make so much noise; the Professor isn't feeling well.

WATCHMAN: *(Off)* All right; I was just going home. *(Whistles to his dog)* Here, boy! Come on, boy! Come on!

(Sónya appears in the doorway.)

SÓNYA: He said no.

CURTAIN.

ACT THREE

The living room. Three doors: right, left, and center. It is early afternoon. Ványa and Sónya are seated; Yeléna paces slowly, preoccupied.

VÁNYA: Our Herr Professor has expressed a burning desire to see us all here in the living room. At exactly one o'clock. *(Looks at his watch)* It's a quarter to. He must be going to inform the world of something.

YELÉNA: It's probably just business—

VÁNYA: He doesn't *have* a business. All he does is write rubbish and sit around bitching.

SÓNYA: *(Reproachfully)* Uncle!

VÁNYA: All right, all right, I'm sorry. *(Gesturing toward Yeléna)* Just look at her, will you? Practically staggering with inertia. Charming, don't you think? Really charming!

YELÉNA: Talk, talk, talk—that's all you do all day long. I'm sick of it. *(Dispirited)* If I don't find something to do, I'll die of boredom. I don't even know what.

SÓNYA: *(With a shrug)* There's plenty to do. You just have to want to do it.

YELÉNA: Like *what?*

SÓNYA: Help out around the place, or go teach school, or go be a nurse. Isn't that enough? Before you and Papa came, Uncle Ványa and I used to take the flour to market ourselves.

YELÉNA: I don't know how to do those things. Besides, I'm not interested. Going out to teach the poor, nursing them, all those high moral ideals—that only exists in books. What do you expect me to do, run out and teach, just like that?

SÓNYA: Frankly, I don't understand how you can *not* do something. You'd get used to it after a while. *(Hugs Yeléna)* Don't be bored, darling; it's contagious. *(Laughs)* You get bored and fretful, and we all catch it from you. Look at Uncle Ványa: he doesn't do a thing anymore except follow you around; he's like your shadow. I drop whatever I'm supposed to be doing to come sit with you and talk. And the doctor used to come visit once a month, if that, and I always had to persuade him; now he's here every day. He's forgotten all about his trees and ignores his practice. You've put a spell on us all, that's what it is.

VÁNYA: *(To Yeléna)* Oh, now, don't be depressed! *(Playfully)* My darling, my heart's delight, use your imagination! You've got mermaid's blood in your veins, so be a mermaid! Let yourself go at least once in your life, fall head over heels in love with a merman, dive in with a big splash, and leave the Herr Professor and the rest of us standing on the shore, helplessly waving our arms!

YELÉNA: *(Angrily)* Just leave me alone, all of you! What a cruel thing to say! *(Starts to leave)*

VÁNYA: *(Stops her)* Wait, wait, darling, I'm sorry. Forgive me. *(Kisses her hand)* Peace.

YELÉNA: You'd try the patience of a saint!

VÁNYA: You're absolutely right, and I'll bring you a peace token, I promise, a bouquet of roses. I picked them for you this morning . . . autumn roses. So beautiful, and so sad . . . *(Goes out)*

SÓNYA: Autumn roses. So beautiful, and so sad . . .

(Both women look out the window.)

YELÉNA: It's September already. How will we ever make it through the winter, all of us cooped up like this!

(Pause.)

Where's the doctor?

SÓNYA: In Uncle Ványa's room. He's writing something. *(Beat)* I'm glad Uncle Ványa left; there's something I need to talk to you about.

YELÉNA: What?

SÓNYA: What? *(Hugs Yeléna desperately)* Oh . . .

YELÉNA: Now, now, come on . . . *(Strokes her hair)* Now, now . . .

SÓNYA: I'm ugly.

YELÉNA: You have beautiful hair—

SÓNYA: No I don't! *(Turns to look at herself in the mirror)* That's what people always say to an ugly woman; they say: "Oh, you have beautiful eyes. Oh, you have beautiful hair." I've been in love with him for six years now; I love him more than my own mother. All I can hear is the sound of his voice, feel the touch of his hands. I keep watching the door, I always think it's him coming. And now look, I keep coming to you so I can talk about him. He's here every day now, but he never looks at me, he doesn't even see me. . . . It hurts so much! And it's all so hopeless, it's completely hopeless! *(Despairingly)* Oh, my God, I don't know where I'll get the strength. . . . I lie in bed all night long, just praying. . . . And I have no shame anymore—I hang around talking to him, I keep looking him right in the eyes. . . . I just can't help myself anymore! Yesterday I told Uncle Ványa I was in love with him. . . . And the servants know, they all know.

YELÉNA: And does he know?

SÓNYA: No. He pays no attention to me.

YELÉNA: *(Bemused)* He's a strange man. . . . You know what? If you want me to, I'll speak to him. I'll be very discreet, I won't say anything directly.

(Pause.)

After all, it's time you knew for sure one way or the other. . . . Will you let me?

(Sónya nods her head yes.)

Good. Either he loves you or he doesn't. It won't be hard to find out. Don't be embarrassed, darling, and don't worry: I'll question him so carefully he won't even notice. All we have to do is find out, yes or no.

(Pause.)

And if it's no, then he has to stop coming here. Am I right?

(Sónya nods her head yes.)

It'll be easier if you don't see him. We shouldn't put it off, either; I'll speak to him right away. He said he wanted to show me some charts or something. Go tell him I'd like to see him now.

SÓNYA: *(Extremely nervous)* You promise to tell me the truth? What he says, I mean.

YELÉNA: Of course. I think the truth, whatever it may be, is never as terrible as not knowing. Trust me, darling.

SÓNYA: I do, I do. . . . I'll go tell him you want to see his charts. *(Starts to leave, then stops by the door)* No, not knowing is better. At least then there's still some hope. . . .

YELÉNA: What?

SÓNYA: Nothing. *(Goes out)*

YELÉNA: *(Alone)* It's awful, seeing someone else in pain and not being able to help. *(Musingly)* He doesn't love her, that's obvious. But why shouldn't he marry her? She's not good-looking, but for a country doctor, at his age, she'd make a good wife. She's smart, goodhearted, innocent. . . . No, that's wrong; that won't work. . . .

(Pause.)

Poor girl. I know just how she feels. The despair and boredom around here, these gray smudges of people: they're so petty; all they know how to do is eat, sleep, and drink—and then he shows up. And he's different from all the rest—good-looking, intelligent, fascinating, like the new moon on a dark night. . . . It would be so easy to let yourself go and give in to the charm of a man like that. . . . I think I'm even a little attracted to him myself. I must be: I don't feel bored when he's around, and whenever I think about him I smile . . . look at me. *(Beat)* Our Uncle Ványa says I have mermaid blood in my veins. "Let yourself go at least once in your life." Well, maybe I should. . . . Just open the cage and fly away, forget about all of you . . . your dull faces, your boring talk. No . . . no, I'm a coward; I haven't got the energy. Besides, my conscience bothers me. He's here every day now and I know why, and I feel so guilty. I want to beg Sónya to forgive me, I want to cry—

ÁSTROV: *(Enters with a large chart)* Well, hello! *(Beat)* You wanted to take a look at my artwork?

YELÉNA: Last night you promised to show me what you were working on. Is this a good time?

ÁSTROV: Absolutely. *(Unrolls a large chart on the card table, starts to fasten it with thumbtacks)* Where is it you're from, again?

YELÉNA: *(Gives him a hand)* Saint Petersburg.

ÁSTROV: You went to school there?

YELÉNA: Yes, to the conservatory.

ÁSTROV: So this stuff probably won't interest you.

YELÉNA: Why not? I don't know much about life out here in the country, but I read a lot, and—

ÁSTROV: I have my own workplace here, a desk in Ványa's room. Whenever I get completely fed up with things, I head over here and spend a couple of hours fooling around with these. . . . Ványa and Sónya sit there doing the accounts; I sit in my corner drawing away. I feel relaxed and at home, and there's always a cricket chirping somewhere. But it's a pleasure I don't allow myself too often . . . maybe once a month. *(Points to the chart)* Now. You see here, this is a map of the region the way it was fifty years ago. These green areas, the light green and the dark green, represent woodlands. Over half the entire area is forested. Where you see the red crosshatching, those areas were teeming with elk and wild goats. . . . See, what I've done is indicate both flora and fauna. And on this lake here there used to be swans, geese, ducks. "A powerful lotta birds"—that's what the old people used to say— darkened the sky out there as far as the eye could see. And there weren't any towns or villages, not many inhabitants, a few settlements, cabins, hunting camps, one or two water mills. . . . Lots of horses and cattle—that's the areas shaded in light blue. For instance, see how the blue in this area is very heavy? There used to be whole herds there; every settler had at least three horses.

(Pause.)

Now look over here. This is the way it was twenty-five years ago. And already less than a third of the woodland area is left. The elk are still there, but the goats are gone. Both the green and the blue areas are shaded lighter. The same over here—you see how it goes? And now let's look at the third diagram: here's the region the way it is today. There're still some green areas, but just patches, none of them connected. The elk are gone, and the swans, and the wood birds. And the settlements, the cabins, the camps, the water mills, all gone. In other words, a history of gradual deforestation, and then, inevitably, the collapse of the environment. And you can tell in about ten or fifteen years it'll be total. Well, all right, you say, that's only natural, that's progress. Right; I agree; I could understand if in place of the trees we destroyed we had *something*. If there were communities, jobs, schools, then people might be better off, right, but none of that happened! We still have the same swamps, the same mosquitoes, the same poverty, the same diseases—typhoid, diphtheria. . . . What we're seeing here is the result of an uncontrolled struggle for survival. A man is freezing, hungry, sick, trying to save what's left of his life, trying to take care of his children, so what does he do? He lets instinct take over; he grabs whatever he thinks will feed him and keep him warm, he destroys everything around him without a thought for the future. It's almost all gone already, and there's nothing to replace it. *(Suddenly cool)* But none of this interests you, does it? I can tell.

YELÉNA: It's just that I understand so little of these problems—

ÁSTROV: There's nothing to understand; they just don't interest you.

YELÉNA: *(Beat)* I'll be honest with you: I haven't really been concentrating. I'm sorry. The thing is, there's a little matter that . . . I'd like to have a little talk with you, and I'm a bit embarrassed; I don't quite know where to begin.

ÁSTROV: A little talk about what?

YELÉNA: It's nothing serious, but . . . Why don't we sit down?

    (They sit.)

It concerns a certain young person. I hope we can talk like friends now, honestly, without beating around the bush. Can we?

ÁSTROV: Of course.

YELÉNA: It's about my stepdaughter. About Sónya. Do you like her?

ÁSTROV: Yes; I'm very fond of her.

YELÉNA: Do you find her . . . attractive? As a woman, I mean?

ÁSTROV: *(After a hesitation)* No.

YELÉNA: Haven't you noticed how she feels about you?

ÁSTROV: No. What do you mean?

YELÉNA: *(Takes his hand)* No, you don't love her, do you? I can tell by your eyes. But she loves you. And she suffers because of it. You've got to understand what that means . . . and promise not to come here anymore.

ÁSTROV: *(Stands)* Well, I'm a little old for her. I . . . Look, I haven't got time to . . . *(Shrugs)* So what do you expect me to do . . . ? *(Embarrassed)*

YELÉNA: God, this is unpleasant, having to talk like this! Well, at least now things are clear. I feel as if I'd gotten a huge weight off my shoulders. Can we forget we ever had this talk? And . . . and you should leave right away. You're an intelligent man; you understand how it is. . . . *(Beat)* All this is making me blush. . . .

ÁSTROV: If you'd mentioned this a few months ago, I might have felt different—about her, I mean—but now . . . *(Shrugs his shoulders)* Of course, if she's suffering, well . . . *(Beat)* There's just one thing I'd like to know: why did *you* want to have this little talk? *(Looks at her, points his finger)* You're really clever, aren't you?

YELÉNA: What do you mean?

ÁSTROV: *(Laughs)* Really clever. All right, so Sónya's suffering; it's possible, let's assume she is, but why were you so eager to find out how I felt about her? *(Stops her from interrupting, and continues with intensity)* No, please, don't look so surprised. You know exactly why I come over here every day. And you know exactly who I come to see, too. Oh, no, sweetheart, don't give me one of those looks. I'm not some dumb kid—

YELÉNA: *(Bewildered)* I don't know what you mean.

ÁSTROV: You're a real little weasel, aren't you? You've got sharp claws under your soft fur. And you need some fresh meat. I've been coming over here for the last month—I dropped everything to come sniffing around after you—and you love it, don't you? You really love it. All right, here I am! I'm yours—you knew that without any little talks. *(Holds out his arms)* I give in. Come on, take me! Sink your claws into me!

YELÉNA: Have you lost your mind?

ÁSTROV: *(A wicked grin)* And you said you were so shy—

YELÉNA: You think I'm that cheap? How insulting! I'm not like that! *(Tries to go)*

ÁSTROV: *(Steps in front of her to stop her)* All right, all right, I'll leave, I won't come around here anymore if that's the way you want it. . . . *(Grabs her hands, looks around)* But we've got to get together! Where—come on, tell me where? And when? Come on, tell me fast; someone may see us here. *(Passionately)* You witch, you sexy little witch . . . Come on, give me a kiss, just one. . . . Let me kiss your hair, smell the perfume in your hair—

YELÉNA: I swear to God—

ÁSTROV: You don't have to swear. You don't have to say anything. God, you're beautiful! I love your hands. . . . *(Kisses her hands)*

YELÉNA: That's enough, please! Will you please just go away? *(Pulls back her hands)* You don't know what you're saying—

ÁSTROV: Then *you* say something—come on, tell me where you'll meet me tomorrow. *(Grabs her around the waist)* We have to do it—you can't get away from me now!

> *(He kisses her; at that moment Ványa appears in the doorway, carrying a big bouquet of roses.)*

YELÉNA: *(Not noticing Ványa)* Have some respect for my feelings. . . . Leave me alone. . . . *(Gives in for a moment and leans her head on Ástrov's chest; then tries to pull away)* No!

ÁSTROV: *(Holding her by the waist)* Come to my place tomorrow. Around two. All right? Right? Will you come?

YELÉNA: *(Sees Ványa)* Let me go! *(Breaks free and crosses to the window; she is extremely embarrassed)* This is horrible.

VÁNYA: *(Puts the bouquet down on a chair; he is upset, wipes his face and neck with his handkerchief)* S'all right. I . . . I . . . it's all right.

ÁSTROV: *(Resentful)* Sure. Terrific weather we're having, isn't it, Ványa? Looked like rain this morning, but now, see? The sun's out. Oh, we're going to have a wonderful autumn, believe me. *(Rolls up his chart)* Too bad the days are getting shorter. *(Goes out)*

YELÉNA: *(Crosses immediately to Ványa)* You have got to arrange things, do whatever you have to, and get me and my husband out of here! Today, you understand!

VÁNYA: *(Still wiping his face)* What? Oh, yes, yes, of course . . . *Hélène*, I saw everything, I heard everything—

YELÉNA: *(Irritably)* Did you hear what I said? Today! We have to leave today!

> *(Enter the Professor, Sónya, Telégin, and Marína.)*

TELÉGIN: I'm not feeling too well myself, Your Excellency, as a matter of fact. Been a bit sick these last two days. Headachy, you know, and—

PROFESSOR: Where is everybody? I hate this house, it's like a labyrinth; twenty-six enormous rooms, people always wandering off, you can never find anyone. *(Rings a bell)* Please tell María Vasílyevna we're waiting for her. And tell my wife as well.

YELÉNA: I'm right here.

PROFESSOR: Then will you please sit down, all of you?

SÓNYA: *(Crosses to Yélena, anxiously)* What did he say?

YELÉNA: I'll tell you later.

SÓNYA: You're shaking, you're all upset.... *(Looks at her face intently)* I understand. He said he won't be coming here anymore. Didn't he?

(Pause.)

Didn't he?

(Yélena nods her head yes.)

PROFESSOR: *(To Telégin)* I can put up with being sick, I get through it one way or the other. What I cannot stand is the chaotic way things get done in the country! I always have the feeling I've landed on another planet. Sit down, please, all of you. Sónya!

(Sónya doesn't hear him; she stands to one side, downcast.)

Sónya!

(Pause.)

Is she even listening to me? . . . You sit down too, Nanny.

(Marína sits and begins knitting her stocking.)

Let me ask you all, ladies and gentlemen, to tune your ears to a pitch of attention. *(Laughs)*

VÁNYA: *(Upset)* You don't need me, do you? I was just leaving.

PROFESSOR: No, no, stay; we need you most of all.

VÁNYA: Me? What exactly is it you need from me?

PROFESSOR: I—what are you getting so mad for?

(Pause.)

Believe me, if I have offended you in any way, I beg your pardon.

VÁNYA: Oh, please, don't use that tone with me! Let's just get down to business. What do you want?

(Enter Mrs. Voinítsky.)

PROFESSOR: Ah, here's *Maman*. Well. Let me begin.

(Pause.)

I have summoned you, ladies and gentlemen, to tell you that an inspector general is on his way to pay us a visit. *(Beat)* All right, then, all joking aside. This is a serious business anyway. I have gathered you all, ladies and gentlemen, to ask your advice and your help, and I trust in your kindness, as I always have. I, of course, am a scholar, a man of letters; I have always been a stranger to practical matters. I rely on those with more experience than myself, I always have, and so I turn now to you, Ványa, to you, Ilyá Ilých, to you, *Maman* ... *(Beat) Manet omnes una nox*— we all know that, don't we, that we are in the hands of God, I mean. I am an old man, a sick man, and I find this an appropriate time to concern myself with my family's welfare, to take stock of my financial situation. I don't mean myself, of course—my life is over, after all—but I have a young wife and an unmarried daughter.

(Pause.)

There is no way I can go on like this, living in the country. We are simply *not* country people. But of course we cannot afford to live in town on the income we get from this property. And if we were to do something like, say, sell the timber rights ... well, that is a onetime transaction; it could never be repeated. So we have to find something that will guarantee us a more or less regular fixed income. Now, I have thought of something that I think will serve our purposes, and I would like to explain it to you all now and ask your opinions. I won't go into the details, just give you the general outline. The average return on the property here is about two percent per year. I propose we sell it. We can then invest the proceeds in managed funds, which will bring us in at least four to five percent, and I rather imagine there will be a few thousand extra, which would enable us to purchase a small vacation home in Finland.

VÁNYA: Wait a minute. I think my hearing is beginning to go. Would you repeat what you just said?

PROFESSOR: That we invest the proceeds in managed funds, and with the extra money buy a summer place in Finland.

VÁNYA: No, no, not Finland, you said something before that.

PROFESSOR: I propose that we sell this place.

VÁNYA: That was it. Sell this place. That's ... oh, that's a brilliant idea. That's just wonderful.... And where do you suggest I go live? And my old mother? And Sónya?

PROFESSOR: We don't have to decide everything right away. We can work out the details later on.

VÁNYA: Wait a minute. I seem to be losing whatever mind I may have had. I seem to remember—correct me if I'm wrong—that "this place" belongs to Sónya. My father bought it as a dowry for my sister. Of course, I may be naive, I may be thinking of Turkish law or something, but I thought Sónya inherited the property when her mother died.

PROFESSOR: Of course the place belongs to Sónya! Who said it didn't? I certainly wouldn't sell it without Sónya's permission. Besides, what I am proposing is precisely for Sónya's benefit.

VÁNYA: This is absolutely unbelievable, absolutely unbelievable! Either I've lost my mind, or else—

MRS. VOINÍTSKY: *Jean,* don't always contradict Alexánder. He knows better than we do.

VÁNYA: Oh, I need a drink! Give me some ... give me some water.... *(Drinks a glass of water)* Go on, say whatever you want, go on, go on, go on!

PROFESSOR: I don't understand why you seem so upset. I don't claim that my proposal is an ideal solution. If you all think I'm being ridiculous, fine, I won't insist.

   (Pause.)

TELÉGIN: *(Embarrassed)* I have a great deal of admiration for scholarship, Your Excellency ... and you know I have a family connection as well. My brother's wife's brother has an M.A. You may have—

VÁNYA: Not now, Waffles, please! You can talk about that later. *(To the Professor)* Wait a minute—why don't you ask him? We bought the property from his uncle.

PROFESSOR: Ask him what? What are you talking about?

VÁNYA: We bought this property back then for ninety-five thousand. My father paid seventy thousand, and that left a balance of twenty-five thousand. Now listen: we never could have bought this place if I hadn't agreed to give up my own inheritance, which I did because I loved my sister. Plus I have worked like a dog for the last ten years in order to pay off the balance—

PROFESSOR: I'm sorry I ever brought this matter up.

VÁNYA: —and the only reason we own it free and clear is because of my personal efforts. And now that I'm old, you want to throw me out on my—

PROFESSOR: I don't understand any of this! What exactly is it you are trying to say?

VÁNYA: I have been running this place for the last twenty-five years, slaving away. I sent you all the money we made, like the good and faithful servant, and in that whole time you never once thanked me! And the whole time you paid me—what?—five hundred a year: what kind of money was that? You never even once offered me a raise!

PROFESSOR: How was I supposed to know? Look, Ványa, I am not a businessman; I know nothing about these matters. Why didn't you just give yourself a raise?

VÁNYA: Why didn't I just steal, you mean? You must all think I'm a fool because I didn't just steal! I should have; I wouldn't be broke right now!

MRS. VOINÍTSKY: *(Sternly)* Jean!

TELÉGIN: *(Upset)* Ványa, Ványa dear, don't . . . don't talk like that. You've got me so upset I'm shaking. You mustn't fight with your own family. *(Hugs him)* You really mustn't.

VÁNYA: For twenty-five years I have shut myself up here in the country, me and this mother of mine, and all we ever thought about was you. We talked about you all day long, about your work; we were so proud of you, we worshiped you, we wasted our evenings reading your books and articles—and what trash they turned out to be!

TELÉGIN: Don't, Ványa, you mustn't, you really mustn't. I can't—

VÁNYA: We thought you were some kind of higher being! We memorized your scholarly articles! And now it's all clear! You write about art? You don't know a goddamn thing about art! I was so proud of everything you wrote, and now I can see it wasn't worth shit! You've cheated us all!

PROFESSOR: Will some of you please calm him down! I've had enough of this! I'm leaving.

YELÉNA: Iván Petróvich, I demand that you stop this! Right now! You hear me?

VÁNYA: I will not stop this! *(Prevents the Professor from leaving)* You stay right there: I'm not finished! You've destroyed the best years of my life! Thanks to you, I've never even *had* a life! You are my mortal enemy!

TELÉGIN: I can't, I just can't . . . I'm leaving. . . . *(Completely distraught, he goes out)*

PROFESSOR: What do you want from me? And how dare you take that tone with me! You . . . you mediocrity! The place is yours? Fine, take it; I don't want anything to do with it!

YELÉNA: Get me out of this hellhole right this minute! *(Screams)* I can't take any more of this!

VÁNYA: My life is ruined! I had talent, I was smart, I had energy. . . .
If I'd had a normal life, I could have been another Schopenhauer,
another Dostoevsky! Oh, I don't even know what I'm saying—
I'm going crazy. . . . Oh, Mama, Mama, I'm in despair! Mama!

MRS. VOINÍTSKY: *(Sternly)* You do what Alexánder tells you!

SÓNYA: *(Falls to her knees and puts her head in Marína's lap)* Oh,
Nanny! Nanny!

VÁNYA: Mama! What am I supposed to do? *(Beat)* No, don't say anything—I already know. I know what I'm supposed to do. *(To the
Professor)* You're going to remember me for a long time! *(Goes
out the middle door)*

(Mrs. Voinítsky goes after him.)

PROFESSOR: Will someone please tell me what this is all about? And
keep that madman away from me! I refuse to live in the same
house with him! He has got to move into the village, or out to the
barn—I don't care, but I absolutely refuse to spend another night
under the same roof with him!

YELÉNA: *(To the Professor)* We're leaving here today. We've got to
start packing this very minute!

PROFESSOR: That mediocre little man!

SÓNYA: *(Turns to her father, still on her knees; extremely upset, almost in
tears)* Papa, you have to understand: we're both so unhappy,
Uncle Ványa and I! *(Choking back her despair)* You have to understand. You remember, when you were younger, how Uncle
Ványa and Grandmother used to sit up nights translating books
for you, copying your papers . . . night after night! And Uncle
Ványa and I worked round the clock; we saved everything we
could and sent it all to you! We never spent anything on ourselves. Oh, I'm saying this all wrong, I know, all wrong, but
you've got to understand how we feel, Papa! You've got to understand!

YELÉNA: *(Upset, to her husband)* Alexánder, for the love of God, go
talk to him, will you? Make it up to him . . . I beg you.

PROFESSOR: Very well, I'll go talk to him, I'll see what I can do. I
have nothing against him, and I am not in the least angry, but you
must admit, his behavior is absolutely outrageous! All right, I'll
go talk to him. *(Goes out the middle door)*

YELÉNA: *(Following him)* Be nice to him, explain things. Just calm
him down . . . try to calm him down.

SÓNYA: *(Hugging Marína)* Nanny! Oh, Nanny!

MARÍNA: It's all right, love, it's all right. They're like geese—they cackle for a while, and then they stop . . . then they stop.

SÓNYA: Nanny!

MARÍNA: *(Strokes Sónya's hair)* You're shivering like you were freezing! You poor dear. Just remember, God is good. . . . A little chamomile tea, or some raspberry tea—that'll fix you up. *(Looks at the middle door, forcefully)* Go on, you geese, you git! You leave us in peace!

> *(From offstage a shot is heard. Yeléna screams. Sónya shivers.)*

Now what are they up to!

PROFESSOR: *(Runs on, shaking with terror)* Stop him! Stop him! He's out of his mind!

> *(In the doorway, Yeléna struggles with Ványa, who has a gun. She tries to get it away from him.)*

YELÉNA: Give me that! Give it to me, I told you!

VÁNYA: Let go of me, *Hélène!* Let go of me! *(Breaks loose and comes into the room, looking for the Professor)* Where is he? There he is! *(Fires the gun at him)* Bang!

> *(Pause.)*

Missed! I missed again! *(Furiously)* Damn it, damn it, goddamn it! *(Throws down the gun and falls into a chair)*

> *(The Professor is in shock; Yeléna leans against the wall, practically fainting.)*

YELÉNA: Take me away from here—please, please, let me go. I can't stay here another minute—I can't. . . .

VÁNYA: *(In despair)* What am I doing? Oh, what am I doing?

SÓNYA: *(Softly)* Nanny! Nanny!

CURTAIN.

ACT FOUR

Ványa's room, which also serves as the estate office. A bed in one corner. By the window, a large table with ledgers and various business papers spread out, a scale, shelves, pigeonholes, etc. A smaller table for Ástrov, with drawing tools, a paint box, and a file. A bird-

*cage with a starling. A large map of Africa hangs on the wall,
clearly of no use to anybody. An enormous sofa, covered in oilcloth.
Left, a door leading to the rest of the house; right, a door leading to
the outside entryway. Beside the right door there's a mat, so people
don't track mud into the room. Autumn weather. Quiet. Telégin
and Marína sit facing each other, winding knitting wool.*

TELÉGIN: You'd better hurry it up, Marína; it's almost time to say
goodbye. They've already sent for the carriage.

MARÍNA: *(Trying to wind faster)* I'm almost done.

TELÉGIN: They're moving to Hárkov. Going to live there.

MARÍNA: It's about time.

TELÉGIN: They really got a scare, you know. Yeléna Andréyevna
said, "I will not stay a moment longer in this house. We're going,
and we're going right away. We can live in Hárkov for a while,
see how we like it, then we can send for our things." Just think,
leaving without even taking their things. It's fate, that's what it is.
They just weren't fated to live here. Or maybe it's . . . predestina-
tion.

MARÍNA: It's about time, too. All that yelling back there a while ago,
and shooting off a gun. They ought to be ashamed of themselves!

TELÉGIN: True. It was a scene worthy of an old master.

MARÍNA: I never saw the likes!

   (Pause.)

Maybe now we can go back and live the way we always did.
Breakfast at eight, dinner at one, a little supper in the evening—
do things right, lead a good Christian life again. *(Sighs)* I haven't
had a decent dish of dumplings in months.

TELÉGIN: True, it's been ages since we had dumplings. *(Beat)* Ages.
(Beat) You know, this morning I was on my way through the village, and one of the shopkeepers yelled at me. He called me a
freeloader. It made me feel just awful.

MARÍNA: Don't you pay him any mind, dear. We all freeload off of
God. Besides, you work; you and Ványa and Sónya and me, we're
all busy all the time. *(Beat)* Where *is* Sónya?

TELÉGIN: Outside. Everybody went with the doctor to find Ványa.
They were afraid he might lay violent hands on himself.

MARÍNA: Where's his gun?

TELÉGIN: *(Whispers)* I hid it! In the cellar!

MARÍNA: *(A snort of derision)* Sinners, the whole lot of us.

(Ványa and Ástrov come in from outside.)

VÁNYA: Leave me alone. *(To Marína and Telégin)* Go away, will you? Just leave me alone for a while! You're all watching me, and I can't stand it!

TELÉGIN: Of course, Ványa, right away. *(Tiptoes out)*

MARÍNA: Here go the geese again! *(Picks up her yarn and leaves)*

VÁNYA: Leave me alone!

ÁSTROV: I'd be happy to, nothing would give me greater pleasure, but I won't go, I repeat, I will not go until you give back what you took.

VÁNYA: I didn't take anything.

ÁSTROV: I'm serious, Ványa. Give it back. I have to go.

VÁNYA: I told you, I didn't take anything!

(Both men sit down.)

ÁSTROV: Really? Look, I'm giving you just a minute longer, then I use force. We'll tie you up and search you. I mean that in all seriousness.

VÁNYA: Do whatever you want.

(Pause.)

God, how stupid can you get! I shot twice and missed him both times! I'll never forgive myself.

ÁSTROV: You felt like shooting somebody, you should have put a bullet in your own head.

VÁNYA: *(With a shrug)* Funny, isn't it? I try to kill someone, nobody calls the police, nobody tries to arrest me. Which means you all think I'm crazy. *(A mean laugh)* I'm crazy? What about someone who pretends to be a professor so we won't find out he's a stupid, sadistic no-talent? What about someone who marries an old man and then proceeds to cheat on him in front of everybody? I saw you! I saw you—I saw you kissing her!

ÁSTROV: You're right, I was, I was kissing her! So what? Go to hell, will you! *(Gives him the finger)*

VÁNYA: *(Looks toward the door)* What's really crazy is a world like this one, that lets you all exist!

ÁSTROV: Look, you're being really stupid.

VÁNYA: What do you expect? I'm crazy, right? I'm out of my mind, I have the right to say stupid things.

ÁSTROV: Oh, come off it, Ványa, will you? You're not crazy; you're just the comic relief around here. You're a freak, you know that? *(Beat)* I used to think freaks were sick, but I've changed my mind. Now I think being a freak is the normal human condition. I think you're completely normal.

VÁNYA: *(Covers his face with his hands)* I'm so ashamed! It's like a knife, the shame I feel, worse than any pain! *(Anguished)* I can't stand it! *(Lays his head on the table)* What am I going to do? What am I going to do?

ÁSTROV: You're going to do nothing.

VÁNYA: You've got to give me something to . . . Oh, my God . . . I'm forty-seven; suppose I live to be sixty—that means thirteen more years! It's too much! What am I supposed to do for the next thirteen years? Oh, can't you understand? *(Makes a compulsive grab for Ástrov's hand)* Can't you understand how I feel? All I want is a different life! I want to wake up some morning, some bright, quiet morning, and find that the past has vanished like smoke. *(Cries)* All I want is a new life. Tell me how to find one . . . where should I look . . . ?

ÁSTROV: *(Irritated)* Will you listen to yourself? There is no new life! None for you, none for me. For us, it's hopeless.

VÁNYA: It is?

ÁSTROV: It is. I know it is.

VÁNYA: You've got to give me something. *(Feels his chest)* Something in here is burning me up!

ÁSTROV: *(Shouting angrily)* Stop it! Just stop it! *(Calms down)* Maybe a couple of hundred years from now people will realize how stupid we were, what a mess we made of our lives. . . . Maybe by then they'll even know how to be happy. But you and me . . . the only thing we have to look forward to is a little peace and quiet when we're finally in our graves. *(Sighs)* Oh, Ványa, Ványa . . . In this whole neighborhood there are only two sensitive, intelligent people, and that's you and me. But this sordid, narrow-minded life has sucked us dry, the filth has gotten to us, and now we're just as rotten as the rest of them. *(With sudden energy)* Anyway, stop trying to change the subject. Give back what you took.

VÁNYA: I told you, I didn't take anything.

ÁSTROV: You took a bottle of morphine from my bag.

(Pause.)

Listen, if you're so determined to kill yourself, just go off in the woods and shoot yourself. But give me back the morphine! Oth-

erwise people will think I gave it to you, there'll be an inquest . . .
and if there is, I'm the one who has to do the autopsy! You think
I'm going to enjoy that?

(Enter Sónya.)

VÁNYA: Go away. Just leave me alone.

ÁSTROV: *(To Sónya)* Sónya, your uncle took a bottle of morphine out
of my bag and he won't give it back. Tell him . . . tell him he's
being stupid. I can't waste any more time. I have to go.

SÓNYA: Uncle Ványa, did you take the morphine?

(Pause.)

ÁSTROV: He took it. I know he did.

SÓNYA: Give it back. Why do you want to scare us like that? *(Gently)*
Uncle Ványa, give it back. I'm just as unhappy as you are, but I
won't give in to despair. I have to accept things the way they are. I
have to go on living until I die. You've got to do the same.

(Pause.)

Give it back! *(Kisses his hand)* Dear Uncle Ványa, give it back!
(Weeps) You don't want to hurt us, I know you don't, I know
you'll give it back. We have to go on living, Uncle Ványa!

VÁNYA: *(Takes the bottle out of his desk drawer and gives it to Ástrov)*
Here, take it. *(To Sónya)* But we have to get back to work, right
away, we have to keep busy, otherwise I . . . otherwise I can't . . .

SÓNYA: We will. We'll work. As soon as they leave, we'll get back to
work. *(Nervously shuffling papers on the desk)* We've let everything
slide, haven't we?

ÁSTROV: *(Puts the bottle in his bag and closes it)* There. Now I can get
started.

YELÉNA: *(Enters)* Iván Petróvich. Here you are. We're leaving right
away. Go talk to Alexánder, will you? He has something he
wants to say to you.

SÓNYA: Do it, Uncle Ványa. *(Takes his arm)* I'll come with you. I
want you and Papa to be friends again. You've got to.

(Sónya and Ványa go out.)

YELÉNA: I'm leaving. *(Holds out her hand)* Goodbye.

ÁSTROV: Already?

YELÉNA: The carriage is here.

ÁSTROV: Goodbye, then.

YELÉNA: You promised me earlier you'd stop coming here.

ÁSTROV: I haven't forgotten. I'm leaving right now.

(Pause.)

ÁSTROV: Are you still frightened? *(Takes her hand)* Was it all so terrible?

YELÉNA: Yes.

ÁSTROV: Then why not stay? Hm? And come see me tomorrow.

YELÉNA: No. I've made up my mind. That's why I can look you in the eye like this, because I've made up my mind to go. There's just one thing I'd like to ask. Will you try to believe I'm really a good person? I want you to respect me.

ÁSTROV: Oh, come on! *(An impatient shrug)* Why not stay? Look, your life is empty, you have no goals; you must realize that. You've never had a chance to use your mind, and sooner or later you're going to give in to your feelings. You can't avoid it. And instead of Hárkov, wouldn't it be better to do it out here in the bosom of nature? Why not? That'd make a kind of poetry out of it. Beautiful fall weather, lots of trees, rickety old country houses, just like a Turgénev novel . . .

YELÉNA: What a funny man you are. You make me angry, but still . . . You're completely original. I intend to remember you with pleasure. *(Beat)* We'll never see each other again, so why hide anything? I was attracted to you . . . a little. So let's shake hands and part friends, shall we? And please don't hate me.

ÁSTROV: *(Shakes her hand)* Yes, you should definitely go. *(Beat)* You probably are a good person, but there's something strange about you, about your entire existence. You and your husband show up here one day, we're all busy working away at our little jobs, we get things done, and all of a sudden we have to drop everything and spend all our time taking care of you and your husband's gout. You and your husband—the pair of you, you do nothing, and you infect us all. *(Beat)* I fell hard for you, you know that. I haven't done a thing for over a month, and there are a lot of sick people out there, and the goddamn cattle are eating up my seedlings. . . . Wherever you and your husband go, you destroy whatever you find, don't you? I'm joking, of course, but still . . . *(Beat)* It's funny too: if you did stay, I know what would happen. Complete and utter disaster. I'd never survive it, and you . . . it might not be too much fun for you either. All right, you're leaving, just go. *Finita la commedia.*

YELÉNA: *(Takes a pencil from his table and pockets it)* I'm taking this pencil with me. As a souvenir.

ÁSTROV: Funny, isn't it? We got to know each other so well, and now all of a sudden we'll never see each other again. That's the way it goes, I guess. There's no one around, no Uncle Ványa with his bunch of flowers, so let me . . . I want to kiss you goodbye. All right? *(Kisses her cheek)* There. That was nice.

YELÉNA: I wish you all the best. *(Looks around)* At least once in my life . . . Why not? *(Embraces him violently; then they both move away from each other)* Time to go.

ÁSTROV: Then go! The carriage is here; just get in it and go!

(Enter the Professor, Uncle Ványa, Mrs. Voinítsky with a book in her hand, Telégin, and Sónya.)

PROFESSOR: *(To Ványa)* No point in going over the past. After everything that's happened, after what I have learned in these last few hours, I could write volumes for posterity about the way we ought to be living our lives. I accept your apology gladly, and I ask you to accept mine. Goodbye. *(Embraces Ványa)*

VÁNYA: We'll send you exactly what we used to, the very same amount. Everything will be the way it was before.

(Yeléna embraces Sónya.)

PROFESSOR: *(Kisses Mrs. Voinítsky's hand)* Maman . . .

MRS. VOINÍTSKY: *(Kisses him)* Now, Alexánder, you have them take another photo and send me a copy. You know how much you mean to me.

TELÉGIN: Goodbye, Your Excellency! Don't forget us all out here!

PROFESSOR: *(Kisses Sónya)* Goodbye . . . Goodbye, everybody! *(Shakes Ástrov's hand)* I've enjoyed getting to know you, actually. I respect your ideas, your enthusiasm, your passion—but, if you will allow an old man one parting observation: You must all get down to work! Do something useful! You simply must! *(Bows to the group)* Well, I wish you all the best of luck! *(Goes out)*

(Mrs. Voinítsky and Sónya follow him out.)

VÁNYA: *(Kisses Yeléna's hand with intensity)* Goodbye . . . Forgive me . . . We'll never see each other again.

YELÉNA: *(Touched)* Goodbye, my darling. *(Kisses him on the head and goes out)*

ÁSTROV: *(To Telégin)* Waffles, go ask them to bring my wagon around too, will you?

TELÉGIN: I'd be happy to. *(Goes out)*

(Ástrov and Ványa are alone.)

ÁSTROV: *(Clears his paints from the table and puts them in a suitcase)* You're not going to go see them off?

VÁNYA: I can't. It's too painful. Just let them go.... I've got to get busy with something right away. Work! We've got to get to work! *(Begins looking through papers on his desk)*

(Pause. The sound of the departing carriage.)

ÁSTROV: There they go. The Professor must be breathing easier now. Wild horses couldn't drag him back here again.

MARÍNA: *(Enters)* They're gone. *(Sits down in an armchair and starts knitting her stocking)*

SÓNYA: *(Enters)* They're gone. *(Wipes her eyes)* I hope everything works out for them. *(To Ványa)* Well, Uncle Ványa, we should get back to work.

VÁNYA: Right. Work, work ...

SÓNYA: It's been a long time since we sat here together. *(Lights the lamp on the table)* Oh, there's no more ink.... *(Takes the inkwell to a cupboard and fills it with ink)* I'm sad, actually, now that they're gone.

MRS. VOINÍTSKY: *(Enters slowly)* They're gone. *(Sits down and is soon engrossed in her reading)*

SÓNYA: *(Sits down at the table and begins leafing through one of the ledgers)* We've got to do the bills, Uncle Ványa. They're all in a muddle. A new batch just came today. Here. You take care of this account, I'll do the other one....

VÁNYA: *(Writes)* "In account with ..."

(Both write in silence.)

MARÍNA: *(Yawns)* Oh, time for me to go beddy-bye....

ÁSTROV: It's so quiet. Your pens scratching away, the cricket chirping. How warm and comfortable it all is.... I hate to leave.

(The sound of a carriage.)

That must be mine. Well. Time to say goodbye to you. All of you. My dear friends. And say goodbye to my little table ... and then I'm off! *(Puts his charts into his briefcase)*

MARÍNA: What are you in such a rush for? Why don't you stay awhile?

ÁSTROV: I can't.

VÁNYA: *(Writes)* "With a balance of two seventy-five . . ."

(Enter the Hired Man.)

HIRED MAN: Mikhaíl Lvóvich, your wagon's ready.

ÁSTROV: Good, so am I. *(Gives him his bag, suitcase, and briefcase)* Here, take these out for me, will you? Watch out you don't crush the briefcase.

HIRED MAN: Right. *(Goes out)*

ÁSTROV: Well . . . *(Starts to say goodbye)*

SÓNYA: When will we see you again?

ÁSTROV: Probably not before next summer. I'm tied up all winter. . . . Of course, if anything happens, you need me, just let me know— I'll be here right away. *(Takes her hand)* Thanks for your kindness, your hospitality . . . well, for everything. *(Crosses to Marína and kisses her on the head)* Goodbye, dear.

MARÍNA: Don't you want some tea before you go?

ÁSTROV: No, thanks, Nanny.

MARÍNA: How about a little drink?

ÁSTROV: *(Hesitates)* Well, I wouldn't mind. . . .

(Marína goes out. Pause.)

I think my lead horse is lame. I noticed it yesterday, when they took him down to drink.

VÁNYA: He probably needs reshoeing.

ÁSTROV: I'll have to stop by the blacksmith on my way home. Can't be helped. *(Crosses to the map of Africa and looks at it)* It must be hot in Africa right now. Really hot.

VÁNYA: Probably . . .

MARÍNA: *(Returns with a tray with a glass of vodka and a piece of bread)* Here you go, dear.

(Ástrov drinks the vodka.)

You should always have a bite to eat with it.

ÁSTROV: No, thanks; I take it straight now. *(Beat)* So! I wish you all the best! *(To Marína)* You stay here, Nanny. No need to come out with me. *(Goes out)*

(Sónya takes a candle and goes out with him; Marína sits in her armchair.)

VÁNYA: *(Writes)* "February second, corn oil, twenty gallons ... February sixteenth, another twenty gallons ... Buckwheat ..."

(Pause. The sound of the departing carriage.)

MARÍNA: He's gone.

(Pause.)

SÓNYA: *(Comes in, sets down the candle on the table)* He's gone.
VÁNYA: *(Adding up his totals)* Fifteen ... twenty-five ...

(Sónya sits down and starts writing.)

MARÍNA: *(Yawns)* Oh, Lord help us all. ...

(Telégin enters on tiptoe; he sits by the door and quietly begins to tune his guitar.)

VÁNYA: *(Strokes Sónya's hair)* I'm so unhappy, dear! If you only knew how unhappy I am!
SÓNYA: I know. But we have to go on living.

(Pause.)

You and I, Uncle Ványa, we have to go on living. The days will be slow, and the nights will be long, but we'll take whatever fate sends us. We'll spend the rest of our lives doing other people's work for them, we won't know a minute's rest, and then, when our time comes, we'll die. And when we're dead, we'll say that our lives were full of pain, that we wept and suffered, and God will have pity on us, and then, Uncle, dear Uncle Ványa, we'll see a brand-new life, all shining and beautiful, we'll be happy, and we'll look back on the pain we feel right now and we'll smile ... and then we'll rest. I believe that, Uncle. I believe that with all my heart and soul. *(Kneels down by Ványa and puts her head in his hands; wearily)* Then we'll rest.

(Telégin plays softly.)

We'll rest! We'll hear the angels singing, we'll see the diamonds of heaven, and all our earthly woes will vanish in a flood of compassion that overwhelms the world! And then everything will be calm, quiet, gentle as a loving hand. *(Wipes away his tears with her handkerchief)* Poor Uncle Ványa, you're crying. ... *(Almost in tears herself)* I know how unhappy your life has been, but wait a while, just a little while, Uncle Ványa, and you and I will rest. *(Embraces him)* We will, I know we will.

(We hear the night watchman outside the house, tapping his stick as he makes his rounds. Telégin continues to play quietly; Mrs. Voinítsky makes a note in the margin; Marína knits her stocking.)

We'll rest. I know we will.

THE CURTAIN FALLS SLOWLY.

UNCLE VANYA: NOTES

Page 213. *"Quantum satis."* In Latin medical prescriptions, the phrase means roughly "as much as is needed."

Pages 216–17. Ástrov's passionate speech here about ecology and his illustrated lecture to Yeléna in Act Three are reflections of the author's own concerns. Chekhov planted hundreds of trees on his farm at Melikhovo. Concern for the destruction of the natural environment forms an important subtext to his last three plays. In *Uncle Ványa*, it is crucial to the dynamic of the piece. In *Three Sisters,* when Natásha is left in possession of the house, the first thing she intends to do is cut down all the trees in the Prózorovs' garden. And in *The Cherry Orchard*, of course, the destruction of the cherry trees is a central theme. It says much for Chekhov's vision that Ástrov's speeches about ecology are as pertinent today as they were a hundred years ago.

Page 218. The watchman tapping his warning stick is one of Chekhov's favorite sound effects; he uses it several times here in *Uncle Ványa* and also in Act Four of *The Seagull*. Chekhov was very precise in his indications for sound effects; his directions for music and sound are essential to the import he intends for a scene. Stanislavsky, enamored of everything theatrical, adored sound effects and used them impressively. He overused them, in Chekhov's view: the playwright was very dissatisfied during rehearsals for *The Seagull* when Stanislavsky added more sounds than were specified in the script. Chekhov's sounds are often very abstract, like the snapping string in *The Cherry Orchard* or, as here, the tapping of the watchman's warning. What is intended in such instances is not a reference to some element of the real world but the creation onstage of a rhythm, almost a musical one, for the scene. The tapping sound, made by a hand-held wooden device with a large clapper, is hollow, rather like a gavel on wood, probably in a pattern of two strokes in two seconds, then a pause of five or six seconds, then a repetition. It is an empty, autumnal sound.

Page 219. Konstantín Bátiushkov (1787–1855) was a contemporary of Pushkin and a poet of grace and charm. His mellifluous verse was praised by Pushkin: "It sounds as sweetly as if it were written in Italian. What a miracle worker that Bátiushkov is!"

Page 221. Here and throughout the play, characters often address each other by the French versions of their names: *Jean* for Ványa, *Hélène* for Yeléna, *Sophie* for Sónya. The habit was not necessarily affectation but a reflection of cultured Russian society's common knowledge of French.

Page 224. *"Hódi háta . . ."* Astrov sings and dances a folk song; the words mean: "Farmhouse, dance, and fire, dance, / the master has nowhere to lay his head." I could find no music for the song.

Page 230. Yeléna's description of Ástrov's life as a country doctor, and Ástrov's own description in Act One, parallel Chekhov's own experience as a country doctor. In a letter to his friend Suvorin he writes: "Of all the Serpukhov doctors, I am the most pitiful; my carriage and horses are mangy, I don't know the roads, I can't see anything at night, I have no money, I tire very quickly . . ."

Page 240. *"Manet omnes una nox."* The quotation, from Horace's Ode 28, Book One, means: "A single night awaits us all."

Page 240. A vacation home in Finland. The Finnish coast is only a short distance from Saint Petersburg, and it was a popular summer resort for Russians. Finland was part of the Russian Empire at the time.

Page 249. *"Finita la commedia."* "The comedy is over," in Italian. Chekhov uses the same phrase in *Platónov.*

Page 252. Alcoholism was endemic in Russia in Chekhov's time and remains so to this day. Chekhov saw plenty of the disasters caused by alcohol in his rounds as a country doctor, and he was instrumental in setting up a clinic for alcoholics. Drinking forms a substantial subtext for his plays. Each of the major plays with the exception of *The Cherry Orchard* has an alcoholic character: Lébedev in *Ivánov*, Másha in *The Seagull*, Ástrov and Ványa in *Uncle Ványa*, and Chebutýkin in *Three Sisters.*

Russians tend to drink ritualistically, making constant toasts to each other—and to anything they can think of. "Drink" almost always means vodka. Russians drink it neat, but the cultural imperative is that it must be followed by a bite of something to eat. The fact that Ástrov rejects the bread Marína brings him confirms his alcoholic status.

THREE SISTERS

A DRAMA IN FOUR ACTS

1900

CHARACTERS

Andréy Prózorov

Ólga ⎫
Másha ⎬ his sisters
Irína ⎭

Natásha, his fiancée, later his wife

Kulýgin, Másha's husband, a high-school teacher

Vershínin, colonel, battery commander

Baron Túzenbach, first lieutenant

Solyóny, captain

Chebutýkin, army doctor

Fedótik, second lieutenant

Róhde, second lieutenant

Ferapónt, janitor at the County Council, an old man

Anfísa, the Prózorovs' eighty-year-old nurse

ACT ONE

The Prózorov house. A big living room, separated by columns from a dining room in the rear. It is noon; the weather is sunny and bright. In the dining room, the table is being set for lunch.

Ólga wears a dark-blue high-school teacher's dress; she stands or walks about, correcting blue books. Másha wears a black dress; she is seated reading, with her hat on her lap. Irína wears a white dress; she stands lost in thought.

ÓLGA: It's a year ago today that Father died, May fifth, on your birthday, Irína. It was very cold, and it snowed. I never thought I'd live through it. You fainted, and you were lying there as if you were dead too. But now it's a year later, and it doesn't bother us to talk about it; you're wearing a white dress and you look lovely.

(The clock strikes noon.)

And the clock struck that morning just the same way. *(Pause)* I remember when they carried Father's coffin out, there was a band playing; it was a military funeral, and at the cemetery they fired rifles over the grave. He was a general, a brigade commander. I thought there should have been more people, but it was raining, raining hard, and then it started to snow.

IRÍNA: I don't want to think about it.

(Baron Túzenbach, Chebutýkin, and Solyóny appear in the dining room.)

ÓLGA: Today it's warm enough to leave the windows wide open, even though the birch trees haven't put out any leaves yet. Father got his command eleven years ago, and we left Moscow and came here. It was the beginning of May then too; I remember exactly: Moscow was already full of flowers, it was warm, and there was sunshine everywhere. That was eleven years ago, and I remember it all exactly, just as if we'd only left Moscow yesterday. Oh, my! This morning I woke up and realized it was springtime: everything was so bright, I felt such a wave of happiness inside me, and I wanted so much to go back home.

CHEBUTÝKIN: The hell you say!

TÚZENBACH: You're right, it's all a lot of nonsense.

(Másha looks up absently and whistles under her breath.)

ÓLGA: Másha, don't whistle like that! Really! *(Pause)* I spend the whole day at school, and then I do extra tutoring in the evenings, and my head aches all the time; and I get so depressed sometimes, it's as if I'd gotten old all of a sudden. Four years at that high school, and every day I feel as if a little more life and strength was slipping away from me. There's only one thing that keeps me going—

IRÍNA: Moscow! Going back to Moscow! Selling this house and everything and going back to Moscow . . .

ÓLGA: Yes. Going back to Moscow, as soon as we can.

(Chebutýkin and Túzenbach laugh.)

IRÍNA: Brother of course will be a scientist; he certainly can't go on living here. Only there *is* a problem about poor Másha. . . .

ÓLGA: Másha can come spend the summers with us, every year.

(Másha whistles under her breath.)

IRÍNA: Well, I hope everything will work out. *(Looks out the window)* The weather is wonderful today. I don't know why I feel so good! This morning I remembered it was my birthday, and all of a sudden I felt wonderful; I thought about when I was little, when Mama was alive—I kept thinking the most wonderful things!

ÓLGA: You do look lovely today—you seem really beautiful. And Másha is beautiful too. Andréy would be better-looking, but he's gotten awfully heavy; it doesn't look good on him. And I've gotten old. I've lost far too much weight; I'm sure it's all because of the girls at the high school—they keep making me so angry. But today is Sunday, I can stay home, my head doesn't ache, and I feel much younger than I did yesterday. Well, that's all right, it's God's will, but sometimes I think if I'd gotten married and could stay home all day long, that would be better somehow. *(Pause)* I would have loved my husband.

TÚZENBACH: *(To Solyóny)* Nothing you say makes any sense! I can't take it anymore. *(Comes into the living room)* I forgot to tell you. Our new commanding officer is coming to pay you a visit today. Colonel Vershínin. *(Sits down at the piano)*

ÓLGA: Really? We'd be delighted.

IRÍNA: Is he old?

TÚZENBACH: No, not at all. Maybe forty, forty-five at the most. *(Starts to play quietly)* He seems very nice. Definitely not stupid. He just talks a lot.

IRÍNA: Is he interesting?

TÚZENBACH: I suppose so. Only he has a wife, a mother-in-law, and two little girls. And it's his second marriage. Everywhere he goes he tells people he has a wife and two little girls. Wait and see, he'll tell you too. His wife is a little crazy. She wears her hair in braids like a schoolgirl, she uses very highfalutin language, talks philosophy, and spends a lot of time trying to kill herself—mostly in order to annoy her husband, so far as I can tell. I would have left a woman like that long ago, but he just hangs on and complains about her.

(Solyóny comes into the living room with Chebutýkin.)

SOLYÓNY: I can only lift fifty pounds with one arm, but with two arms I can lift a hundred and fifty pounds, even more. What do I conclude from that? That two men are not just twice as strong as one, but three times as strong, or even more . . .

CHEBUTÝKIN: *(Reading his newspaper as he walks)* "To prevent falling hair: two ounces of naphtha in half a bottle of alcohol. Shake and use daily. . . ." *(Writes in a little notebook)* Well, let's just make a little note of that! *(To Solyóny)* All right now, as I was saying, you take a cork, stick it in the bottle, then you get a little glass pipe and stick it through the cork. Then you take a pinch of ordinary, everyday baking soda . . .

IRÍNA: Iván Románich! Dear Iván Románich!

CHEBUTÝKIN: What is it, child, what is it, dearest?

IRÍNA: Tell me why I feel so happy today! I feel as if I had sails flying in the wind, and the sky over me was bright blue and full of white birds. . . . Why is that? Do you know why?

CHEBUTÝKIN: *(Kissing both her hands tenderly)* You're my little white bird. . . .

IRÍNA: When I got up this morning, everything in the world was suddenly clear, and I realized I knew how to live. Dear Iván Románich! I do know, everything. Man must work, work in the sweat of his brow. No matter who he is, that's the whole point of his life. And all his happiness. How wonderful it must be to get up at dawn and pave streets, or be a shepherd, or a schoolteacher who teaches children, or work on a railroad. My Lord, not even a man, a horse or something, as long as you work—anything's better than waking up at noon and having breakfast in bed and then taking two hours to dress. What an awful life that is! I want to work the way I want cold drinks in hot weather. And if I don't do that from now on, get up and go to work, then don't you ever have anything more to do with me, Iván Románich.

CHEBUTÝKIN: *(Tenderly)* I won't, I promise. . . .

ÓLGA: Father trained us all to get up at seven o'clock. Now Irína wakes up at seven and lies in bed for hours and thinks about things. And with such a serious face! *(Laughs)*

IRÍNA: You always treat me like a little girl! You think it's funny when I'm serious, but I'm twenty years old!

TÚZENBACH: My God, I really understand that desire to work! I've never worked a day in my life. I was born in Petersburg, where it's cold and boring, and no one in my family has ever worked, or even had to worry. I remember whenever I got home from military school there was always a servant to take my boots off. I was a real little monster to them, but my mother just smiled and let me do whatever I wanted. She never understood when other people objected to the way I behaved. They tried to protect me from hardship, but I don't think they quite managed. And now the time has come, there's a storm gathering, a wild, elemental storm, it's coming, it's almost over our heads! And it will clean out our society, get rid of laziness and indifference, and this prejudice against working and this lousy rotten boredom. I intend to work, and in twenty-five or thirty years we will all work! All of us!

CHEBUTÝKIN: Not me.

TÚZENBACH: You don't count.

SOLYÓNY: In twenty-five years you won't be around, thank God. I give you a couple of years more; then you either die of a stroke, angel, or I shoot your head off. *(Takes out a little bottle of cologne and rubs some on his hands)*

CHEBUTÝKIN: *(Laughing)* I never have done anything, ever. Once I graduated, I never did another lick of work, I never read a single book. All I read are newspapers. *(Takes another newspaper out of his pocket)* For instance, I read in the papers, let's say, about a writer named Dobrolyúbov, so I know he exists, but God only knows what he wrote; I don't.

(Somebody knocks on the floor from below.)

Somebody wants me downstairs; I must have a visitor. I'll be right back. . . . Just give me a minute or so. . . . *(Hurries out, combing his beard)*

IRÍNA: I think he's dreamed up another surprise.

TÚZENBACH: You're right. Did you see the look on his face as he went out? You are about to receive a birthday present.

IRÍNA: That's so embarrassing.

ÓLGA: It really is terrible. He's always overdoing things.

MÁSHA: "Beside the sea there stands a tree, and on that tree a golden chain . . . and on that tree a golden chain . . ." *(Stands and hums quietly)*

ÓLGA: You're not very cheerful today, Másha.

(Másha keeps humming and puts on her hat.)

Where are you going?

MÁSHA: Home.

IRÍNA: That's rude.

TÚZENBACH: . . . Leaving a birthday party!

MÁSHA: It's all right, I'll be back later on. Goodbye, darling. *(Kisses Irína)* I want you to be well and happy. When Father was alive we used to have thirty or forty officers at our birthday parties—it was noisy and fun. Today there's only a man and a half and it's dull as a desert. I'm leaving. I'm in a kind of depressed mood today. I don't feel well—don't mind what I say. *(Laughs, almost in tears)* We'll have a talk later on, but goodbye for now, dear. I'm going for a walk.

IRÍNA: *(Upset)* But what's the matter . . . ?

ÓLGA: *(Tearfully)* I know what you mean, Másha.

SOLYÓNY: When a man talks philosophy you get philosophy, or at least sophistry, but when a woman talks philosophy, or two women, all you get is wee, wee, wee, wee, all the way home.

MÁSHA: And exactly what is that supposed to mean?

SOLYÓNY: Nothing. "Said the dog to the flea, don't jump on me."

MÁSHA: *(To Ólga, angrily)* Oh, stop crying!

(Enter Anfísa, and Ferapónt with a birthday cake.)

ANFÍSA: Come on in. Come on, come on, it's all right—your feet are clean. *(To Irína)* It's a birthday cake. A present from Protopópov over at the council office.

IRÍNA: Thank you. *(Takes the cake)* Tell him thank you.

FERAPÓNT: What?

IRÍNA: *(Louder)* Tell him thank you.
ÓLGA: Nana, give him something to eat. Ferapónt, go on, she'll give you something to eat.
FERAPÓNT: What?
ANFÍSA: Come on, old man, come on, come on.

(She goes out with Ferapónt.)

MÁSHA: I don't like that Protopópov, or whatever his name is. You shouldn't have invited him.
IRÍNA: I didn't.
MÁSHA: Good.

(Chebutýkin comes in; he is followed by an orderly carrying a huge silver tea service. There is a general reaction of surprise and embarrassment.)

ÓLGA: *(Making a gesture of exasperation)* A silver service! How awful! *(Goes into the dining room)*
IRÍNA: Iván Románich, how could you?
TÚZENBACH: *(Laughing)* What did I tell you!
MÁSHA: Iván Románich, you really are disgraceful!
CHEBUTÝKIN: My dears, my little girls, you are all I have, you are dearer to me than anything else in the world. I'm sixty years old, I'm an old man, a lonely, broken-down old man. The only decent thing left in me is my love for you; if it weren't for you, I wouldn't have gone on living. *(To Irína)* Darling, I ... my sweet little girl, I've known you since the day you were born ... I carried you when you were a baby ... I was in love with your sainted mother ...
IRÍNA: But why such expensive presents?
CHEBUTÝKIN: *(Almost in tears; angrily)* Expensive presents! Well, that's just ... *(To the orderly)* Take it away. *(Mimicking her)* Expensive presents!

(Anfísa enters from the hall.)

ANFÍSA: There's a colonel just arrived, dears. Never laid eyes on him before. He's already got his coat off and everything. Rinie dear, you be nice to him. Mind your manners now. *(Leaving)* And it's long past lunchtime already.... Oh, Lord ...
TÚZENBACH: It's probably Vershínin.

(Enter Vershínin.)

Lieutenant Colonel Vershínin!

VERSHÍNIN: *(To Másha and Irína)* How do you do? I'm delighted to be here at last, delighted, believe me. Well, well! How you've grown!

IRÍNA: Won't you sit down. . . . It's very nice of you to come.

VERSHÍNIN: *(Happily)* I'm delighted, really delighted! But there's three of you, isn't there? I remember three sisters, three little girls. . . . I don't recall your faces, but I remember perfectly: your father, Colonel Prózorov, had three little girls. I saw you with my own eyes. Well, well, how time does fly!

TÚZENBACH: Alexánder Ignátych is from Moscow.

IRÍNA: Moscow! You're from Moscow?

VERSHÍNIN: Yes indeed. Your father was a battery commander in Moscow, and I was an officer in his command. *(To Másha)* Now, your face I think I remember. . . .

MÁSHA: Funny, I don't remember yours.

IRÍNA: Ólga! Ólga! *(Shouting into the dining room)* Ólga, come here!

(Ólga comes into the living room.)

Colonel Vershínin is from Moscow.

VERSHÍNIN: You must be Ólga Sergéyevna, the oldest. And you are María. . . . And you are Irína, the youngest—

ÓLGA: You're from Moscow?

VERSHÍNIN: Yes. I went to school in Moscow and began my service career there. Served there quite a while, in fact, and I've finally gotten my own command—here, as you see. I don't remember you individually; all I remember is that there were three of you. Three sisters. I remember your father very well; when I close my eyes I can see him as if it were yesterday. I used to spend a lot of time at your house in Moscow. . . .

ÓLGA: I thought I remembered everybody, but . . .

VERSHÍNIN: Perhaps you remember my full name—Alexánder Ignátych. . . .

IRÍNA: Alexánder Ignátych, you're from Moscow. . . . What a surprise!

ÓLGA: We're moving back there, you know.

IRÍNA: We expect to be there by autumn. It's our hometown, we were born there. . . . On Old Basmány Street . . .

(They both laugh delightedly.)

MÁSHA: We never expected to see anyone from Moscow here. *(Excited)* Now I remember! Ólga, remember—they used to tell us about "the lovesick major"? You were a lieutenant then, and you were in love with someone, and they used to tease you about being a major. . . .

VERSHÍNIN: *(Laughing)* Yes, yes, that's right. The lovesick major, yes . . .

MÁSHA: You didn't have a mustache then. . . . Oh, you've gotten old. . . . *(Almost in tears)* You've gotten so old!

VERSHÍNIN: Yes, when they called me the lovesick major, I was young and I was in love. Now I'm not.

ÓLGA: But you really don't look so bad. I mean, you've gotten old, but you're not really . . . old.

VERSHÍNIN: Well, I'm almost forty-four. *(Beat)* How long has it been since you left Moscow?

IRÍNA: Eleven years. Másha, what's the matter? Don't cry—you're so silly. *(Almost in tears)* You'll make me start.

MÁSHA: I'm all right. What street did you live on?

VERSHÍNIN: On Old Basmány Street.

ÓLGA: So did we. . . .

VERSHÍNIN: Then for a while I lived on Nemétsky Street. I used to walk from there to the barracks. You have to cross a big bridge to get there; the water makes a noise underneath you. If you're lonely, it makes you feel awful. *(Pause)* But the river you've got here is wonderful! Wide, strong . . .

ÓLGA: Yes, but it gets cold here. It's cold, and there are mosquitoes. . . .

VERSHÍNIN: Oh, come now, this is a very good climate, very healthy, very Russian. The woods, the river . . . And you've got birch trees. Wonderful, uncomplicated birch trees. They're my favorite tree. Life here must be very good. But it's funny, the nearest railroad station is eighteen miles away. And nobody seems to know why.

SOLYÓNY: Well, I know why.

(Everybody looks at him.)

Because if the station were close it wouldn't be far away, and if it's far away then it can't be close.

(An awkward silence.)

TÚZENBACH: Very funny, Vassíly Vassílich.

ÓLGA: Oh, now I remember you. I really do.

VERSHÍNIN: I knew your mother.

CHEBUTÝKIN: She was a wonderful woman, God rest her.

IRÍNA: Mama is buried in Moscow.

ÓLGA: In Nóvo-Dévichy Cemetery.

MÁSHA: It's funny: I'm beginning to forget what she looked like. The same thing will happen to us. No one will remember us.

VERSHÍNIN: True. No one will remember us. That's fate; there's nothing you can do about it. Things that seem important to us, serious and significant things . . . the time will come when they'll all be forgotten—or they won't seem so important anymore. *(Pause)* And the interesting thing is, there's no way we can guess what will be considered important and serious, and what will be considered petty and silly. Remember the discoveries of Copernicus or, let's say, Columbus—how they seemed silly and unnecessary at first, while a lot of nonsense was propounded as eternal truth? So in time perhaps this life of ours, the one we're so proud of, will seem strange, stupid, messy, perhaps even sinful. . . .

TÚZENBACH: But who knows? They may also think of the life we lead as a high point and remember it with respect. Today we have no torture, no capital punishment, no invasions, but there's still so much suffering. . . .

SOLYÓNY: Wee, wee, wee . . . The baron doesn't live on food like the rest of us; he just lives on philosophy!

TÚZENBACH: Vassíly Vassílich, will you leave me alone, for God's sake? *(Changes his seat)* It's not funny anymore.

SOLYÓNY: *(In a high voice)* Wee, wee, wee, wee, wee . . .

TÚZENBACH: *(To Vershínin)* . . . and the suffering observable everywhere today would seem to indicate that society has already attained a certain moral elevation. . . .

VERSHÍNIN: Yes, yes, of course.

CHEBUTÝKIN: You just said, Baron, that people in the future will think of our life as a high point, but people nowadays are still pretty low. *(Stands up)* Look how low I am. But of course you make me feel better by calling my life a high point.

(A violin is played offstage.)

MÁSHA: That's our brother Andréy playing.

IRÍNA: He's the family intellectual. He'll probably be a scientist. Papa was in the service, but his son has decided on a scientific career.

MÁSHA: That's what Papa wanted him to do.

ÓLGA: We were teasing him today. He seems to be a little bit in love.

IRÍNA: With one of the local girls. I imagine she'll be here for lunch.

MÁSHA: But her clothes! It's not just that they're ugly, or out of style; they're absolutely pitiful. She'll wear a funny yellow skirt with some awful fringe, and a red blouse. And those little pink cheeks, always scrubbed clean, clean, clean! Andréy can't be in love—I don't believe it. He does have *some* taste, after all. He's just teasing us, that's all; he's acting silly. I heard someone saying yesterday she's supposed to marry Protopópov, the chairman of the County Council, and I certainly hope she does. *(Goes to the side door)* Andréy, come here a minute! Just for a minute, dear.

(Andréy enters.)

ÓLGA: This is my brother, Andréy Sergéyich.

VERSHÍNIN: Vershínin.

ANDRÉY: How do you do? *(Wipes his perspiring face)* You're the new battery commander?

ÓLGA: Can you believe it, Colonel Vershínin is from Moscow.

ANDRÉY: Are you? Well, congratulations; now my sisters won't let you alone.

VERSHÍNIN: I think I've already managed to bore your sisters.

IRÍNA: Look at this picture frame Andréy gave me for a present. *(Shows him the frame)* He made it himself.

VERSHÍNIN: *(Looking at the frame and not knowing what to say)* Yes, well, it certainly is . . .

IRÍNA: And this other frame over on the piano—he made that too.

(Andréy makes a deprecating gesture and starts off.)

ÓLGA: Andréy's our intellectual and he plays the violin and he can carve almost anything in wood. He's our genius. Andréy, don't go! He's always doing that; he wants to be alone. Come on back!

(Másha and Irína take his arms and lead him back, laughing.)

MÁSHA: Come on, come on!

ANDRÉY: Please, don't . . .

MÁSHA: He's so funny! We all used to call Alexánder Ignátych the lovesick major, and he never got mad.

VERSHÍNIN: Never!

MÁSHA: I've got a name for you: the lovesick violinist!

IRÍNA: Or the lovesick scientist!

ÓLGA: He's in love! Andréy's in love!

IRÍNA: *(Applauding)* Bravo, bravo! Encore! Andréy's in love!

CHEBUTÝKIN: *(Going up behind Andréy and grabbing him around the waist)* "It's love that makes the world go round . . . !" *(Laughs; still has his newspaper)*

ANDRÉY: Will you all please stop it. *(Wipes his face)* I couldn't sleep all night, and I feel sort of funny today—a little upset, I guess. I sat up reading until four and then I got into bed, but I just lay there. I kept thinking about things, and all of a sudden the sun came up and the bedroom was full of light. .... As long as I'm going to be here through the summer, I want to translate this book from the English—

VERSHÍNIN: You read English?

ANDRÉY: Yes. My father, God rest him, educated us with a vengeance. It's funny—and I guess it's sort of silly too—but you know, after he died I started putting on weight, and in just a year I've gotten kind of heavy. It's almost as if my body were letting itself go after all that education. My father made sure that my sisters and I knew French, German, and English, and Irína even knows Italian. But a lot of good it does us!

MÁSHA: What's the point of knowing three languages in a town like this? It's a useless luxury. No, not even a luxury; it's an unnecessary appendage, like a sixth finger. We know a lot that's unnecessary.

VERSHÍNIN: Well! *(Laughs)* You know a lot that's unnecessary! I don't think there exists—I don't think there *could* exist—a town so dull and boring that it didn't have a real need for intelligent, educated people. All right, let's agree that this town is backward and vulgar, and let's suppose now that out of all its thousands of inhabitants there are only three people like you. Of course you won't be able to overcome the unenlightened mass that surrounds you; little by little you'll disappear into this crowd of thousands, life will swallow you up. But you won't simply disappear; you will have some influence. And after you've gone there will be six more, let's say, like you, then twelve, and so on, until finally people like you will be in the majority. In two or three hundred years, life on earth will be unimaginably beautiful, astonishing. Man needs a life like that, and if we don't have it yet we must wait for it, dream of it, prepare for it, and that's the reason we must be able to see and know more than our fathers and grandfathers. *(Laughs)* And you complain that you know a lot that's unnecessary!

MÁSHA: *(Taking off her hat)* I'm staying for lunch.

IRÍNA: *(Sighing)* You know, you really ought to write all that down. ...

(Andréy has left unnoticed by now.)

TÚZENBACH: You say life on earth will eventually be beautiful and wonderful. That's true. But in order for us to have a share in all that, even at this point, we have to get ready for it, we have to work. . . .

VERSHÍNIN: Yes. *(Gets up)* What a lot of flowers you've got! *(Looks around)* And a beautiful house. I envy you. All my life I've lived in dumpy apartments with two chairs and a sofa, and the stove always smokes. And the one thing I've always wanted was a lot of flowers like this. . . . *(Rubs his hands)* Oh, my! Well . . .

TÚZENBACH: Yes, we have to *work*. Oh, I know you're all thinking: Listen to the German getting sentimental again, but I'm really Russian, honestly I am; I don't even speak German. And my father was baptized in the Russian church.

(Pause.)

VERSHÍNIN: *(Walking around)* Sometimes I think what it would be like to start life all over again, and do it deliberately. The life we'd already lived would be a kind of rough draft, and the new one would be a clean copy! And I think each of us would try not to repeat the same mistakes, at least try to arrange a new environment, find a room like this to live in, with flowers in it and lots of light! I have a wife and two little girls, and my wife is not a well woman, and what with one thing and another, if I could start life over again, believe me, I certainly wouldn't get married.

(Enter Kulýgin.)

KULÝGIN: *(Going up to Irína)* Dearest sister, allow me to congratulate you on this happy occasion and to convey to you my heartfelt wishes for good health and whatever else a girl of your age may desire—properly desire, that is. And allow me to present you with this little book as a small token of my esteem. *(Gives her a book)* It's a history of the first fifty years of our local high school. I wrote it myself. A mere trifle, written in an idle hour, but I want you to be sure to read it anyway. Ladies and gentlemen, good afternoon! *(To Vershínin)* Kulýgin. I teach at the local high school. *(To Irína)* This little book contains the names of all those who have graduated from our high school over the last fifty years. *Feci quod potui, faciant meliora potentes. (Kisses Másha)*

IRÍNA: But you gave me the same book as a present last Easter.

KULÝGIN: *(Laughing)* No! Well, then, give it back. Or better yet, give it to the colonel. Here, Colonel. Read it sometime when you have nothing better to do.

VERSHÍNIN: Thank you. *(Gets ready to go)* I'm really delighted we've gotten to know each other again. . . .

ÓLGA: Are you leaving? Oh, don't!

IRÍNA: You must stay and have lunch. Please.

ÓLGA: Do, really; please!

VERSHÍNIN: *(Bowing)* I seem to have intruded on a birthday party. Excuse me, I didn't know. I should have congratulated you. . . .

(He goes into the dining room with Ólga.)

KULÝGIN: Today is Sunday, ladies and gentlemen, a day of rest. Let us all seek rest, each according to his age and status. These rugs should be rolled up and stored for the summer, in mothballs or naphtha. . . . The Romans were a healthy race, they knew how to work, they also knew how to rest. They had a *mens sana in corpore sano.* They lived their lives according to the proper forms. Our headmaster always says the main thing in life is form. When things lose their form, they lose their identity—and in our daily lives it is precisely the same. *(Puts his arm around Másha's waist and laughs)* Másha loves me. My wife loves me. And the window drapes should be stored with the rugs. . . . I'm very happy today, in an excellent frame of mind. Másha, we're going to the headmaster's this afternoon at four. There's an outing for the teachers and their families.

MÁSHA: I'm not going.

KULÂGIN: *(Hurt)* Másha dearest, why not?

MÁSHA: I'll tell you later. . . . *(Angrily)* All right, all right, I'll go, only please just leave me alone. . . . *(Moves away from him)*

KULÝGIN: And he's invited us all back to spend the evening at his place. Despite his precarious health, that man does his best to be sociable. Astonishing personality. A remarkable man, really extraordinary. Yesterday at the faculty meeting he turned to me and said, "I'm tired, Fyódor Ilých. Tired." *(Looks at the clock, then at his own watch)* Your clock is seven minutes fast. Tired. That's what he said.

(A violin is heard offstage.)

ÓLGA: Ladies and gentlemen, lunch is served! And the birthday cake!

KULÝGIN: Ólga dearest! Ólga dearest! Yesterday I worked from early morning until eleven at night; I was tired. And today I feel very happy. *(Goes to the dinner table)* Dearest . . .

CHEBUTÝKIN: *(Folding his newspaper, putting it in his pocket, and combing his beard)* Birthday cake? Wonderful!

MÁSHA: *(To Chebutýkin, severely)* Now you listen to me: I don't want to see you drinking today! Understand? It's very bad for you.

CHEBUTÝKIN: Oh, whoa, whoa, whoa, whoa. Now wait just a minute. I gave it up. I haven't been drunk in two years, for God's sake. Anyway, what difference does it make?

MÁSHA: Never mind; just don't drink, that's all. *(Angrily, but so that her husband can't hear her)* Another goddamn boring evening at the headmaster's!

TÚZENBACH: If I were you, I just wouldn't go. It's very simple. Why not?

CHEBUTÝKIN: Don't go, sweetheart. . . .

MÁSHA: Oh, fine, don't go, as easy as that. . . . What a miserable goddamn life! *(Goes into the dining room)*

CHEBUTÝKIN: *(Going with her)* Now, now . . .

SOLYÓNY: *(Crossing to the dining room)* Wee, wee, wee, wee . . .

TÚZENBACH: That'll do, Vassíly Vassílich! Let it alone.

SOLYÓNY: Wee, wee, wee, wee . . .

KULÝGIN: *(Happily)* Your health, Colonel! I am a pedagogue by profession, but here I'm just one of the family, Másha's husband. She's a wonderful woman, a wonderful woman. . . .

VERSHÍNIN: I'll have a little of this dark vodka. . . . *(Drinks)* Your health! *(To Ólga)* I feel very much at home here. . . .

(Only Irína and Túzenbach are left in the living room.)

IRÍNA: Másha really feels awful today. She was only eighteen when she married him, and she thought he was very intelligent. Not anymore. He's a nice man, but he's not very intelligent.

ÓLGA: *(Impatiently)* Andréy, come on! We're all waiting for you!

ANDRÉY: I'm coming. *(Enters and crosses to the table)*

TÚZENBACH: What are you thinking about?

IRÍNA: Oh, nothing. I don't like that Solyóny. I'm afraid of him. He says the stupidest things. . . .

TÚZENBACH: He's strange. I feel sorry for him. He makes me mad sometimes, but mostly I just feel sorry for him. I think he's really very shy. When there's just the two of us, he's good company and quite intelligent, but whenever he's in a group he gets crude and vulgar, he always tries to start a fight. Don't go yet;

let them all get settled first. Let me spend some time with you, just the two of us. What are you thinking about? *(Pause)* You're twenty years old, I'm not thirty yet. Think how much time we've got ahead of us, days and days, all of them full of my love for you. . . .

IRÍNA: Nikolái Lvóvich, don't talk to me about love. . . .

TÚZENBACH: *(Not listening)* I have such a desire to live, Irína, and to work and fight for something, and my love for you makes that desire even stronger. You're so beautiful, you make life seem just as beautiful! *(Beat)* What are you thinking about?

IRÍNA: You say life is so beautiful. But suppose it isn't? Look at us. Three sisters. Our life hasn't been so beautiful; it's choking us up like a lawn full of weeds. There, now I'm starting to cry. I really don't mean to. . . . *(Wipes her eyes and smiles)* We have to work, we really do. The reason we're unhappy and think life is so awful is because we don't know what it means to work. We come from families who thought they never had to work. . . .

(Enter Natásha; she wears a pink dress with a green belt.)

NATÁSHA: They're already eating. . . . I guess I'm late. . . . *(Stops briefly in front of the mirror and fixes herself up)* Well, at least my hair's okay. *(Seeing Irína)* Irína Sergéyevna, happy birthday! Congratulations, honey! *(Gives her a hug and several effusive kisses)* You've got so many guests, I feel sort of embarrassed. . . . Hello, Baron, how are *you*?

ÓLGA: *(Coming into the living room)* Well, if it isn't Natálya Ivánovna. How *are* you, my sweet?

(They exchange kisses.)

NATÁSHA: You've got such a big party I really feel awfully embarrassed. . . .

ÓLGA: Now, now, none of that, it's all just friends. . . . *(Lowers her voice, a bit shocked)* A green belt! Darling, that just isn't done!

NATÁSHA: Why? Is it bad luck or something?

ÓLGA: No . . . it just doesn't look right with that dress . . . well, it looks a bit odd, that's all.

NATÁSHA: *(In a whiny voice)* But why? It isn't really *so* green—I mean, it's more, you know, green*ish*. . . .

(She follows Ólga into the dining room. Everyone is now at the table; the living room is empty.)

KULÝGIN: Irína dearest, here's hoping you find a suitable fiancé. It's about time you got married.

CHEBUTÝKIN: Here's hoping Natálya Ivánovna finds herself a boyfriend too.

KULÝGIN: Natálya Ivánovna already has a boyfriend.

MÁSHA: *(Banging her plate with a fork)* I'll have another little glass of that wine. Well, we only live once, by God, and sometimes you win, sometimes you lose.

KULÝGIN: You get an F-minus in conduct.

VERSHÍNIN: This vodka is delicious. What gives it that special taste?

SOLYÓNY: Cockroach juice.

IRÍNA: *(Crybaby voice) Oh!* That's dis*gust*ing!

ÓLGA: We're having roast turkey and apple pie for dinner tonight. Thank God, I've got the whole day off, and the evening too. . . . I hope you'll all be able to come for dinner.

VERSHÍNIN: I hope you'll let me come too.

IRÍNA: Of course.

NATÁSHA: They're very informal around here.

CHEBUTÝKIN: "It's love that makes the world go round . . . " *(Laughs)*

ANDRÉY: *(Angry)* Will you all please stop it! Aren't you tired of it yet?

(Fedótik and Róhde enter with a big basket of flowers.)

FEDÓTIK: Oh, they're already having lunch.

RÓHDE: *(In a deep, loud voice, with exaggerated r's)* Lunch? Yes, it's true, they are already having lunch!

FEDÓTIK: Wait a minute! *(Takes a picture)* There! Now one more . . . everybody hold still! *(Takes another picture)* There! Now you can all move!

(They take the basket of flowers and go into the dining room, where everyone greets them noisily.)

RÓHDE: *(In a loud voice)* Happy birthday and best wishes! The very best! The weather is just wonderful today, really beautiful. I took some of the high-school boys out for a walk this morning. . . . I'm the gymnastics coach at the high school.

FEDÓTIK: That's all right, Irína Sergéyevna, you don't have to hold still, it's all right! *(Takes a picture)* You look very interesting today. *(Takes a top out of his pocket)* Oh, I forgot. A present for you, a top. It makes an amazing sound. . . .

IRÍNA: Oh, it's divine!

MÁSHA: "Beside the sea there stands a tree, and on that tree a golden chain ... and on that chain an educated cat goes around and around and around ..." *(Tearfully)* Why do I keep saying that? I can't get it out of my head....

KULÝGIN: There are thirteen of us at the table!

RÓHDE: *(In a loud voice)* Surely, ladies and gentlemen, you are above such silly superstitions?

(Laughter.)

KULÝGIN: If there are thirteen at table, that means two of them are in love. Iván Románich, I certainly hope nobody's in love with *you*....

(Laughter.)

CHEBUTÝKIN: Oh, not me; I'm just an old boozer. But look at Natálya Ivánovna: what do you suppose she's got to blush about?

(Everybody laughs loudly; Natásha gets up and runs into the living room. Andréy follows her.)

ANDRÉY: It's all right, don't pay any attention to them! Wait.... Don't go, please....

NATÁSHA: I'm so embarrassed. I just don't know what's the matter with me; they just make fun of me all the time. I know it's not polite to leave the table like that, but I just couldn't stand it, I really couldn't.... *(Hides her face in her hands)*

ANDRÉY: Oh, darling, please, please don't get upset. They're only joking, honestly they are; they all mean well. Darling, they're all nice people; they love me and they love you too. Come on over here by the window—they can't see us over here.... *(Looks around)*

NATÁSHA: It's just that I'm not used to these social occasions....

ANDRÉY: Oh, you're so young, so young and beautiful! Darling, oh, darling, don't get upset. Believe me, believe me ... I feel so good. I feel so full of love and I'm so proud. ... Oh, they can't see us! Don't worry, they can't see us. I don't know how I fell in love with you, or when, or why—I just don't understand any of it. Darling, you're so sweet and so ordinary. ... I want you to marry me! I love you, I love you. ... I've never loved anybody before....

(They kiss. Two officers enter, see them kissing, and stop in amazement.)

CURTAIN.

ACT TWO

The same set as Act One. Eight o'clock at night. Somewhere at a distance, someone in the street is playing an accordion. The room is dark.

Enter Natásha in a housecoat, carrying a candle. She crosses to the door to Andréy's room and stops.

NATÁSHA: Andy, what you doing? You reading? That's okay. I just wanted to . . . *(Goes to another door, opens it, looks in, closes it)* The lamps aren't lit. . . .

ANDRÉY: *(Coming in with a book in his hand)* What's the matter, Natásha?

NATÁSHA: I was just looking to see if the lamps were lit. Tonight's carnival; the maid's all in a tizzy. You got to keep your eyes on them so nothing happens. Last night after midnight I was going through the dining room and there was this candle burning. I never could find out who did it. *(Puts down the candle)* What time is it?

ANDRÉY: *(Looking at the clock)* Quarter after eight.

NATÁSHA: And Ólga and Irína are still out. Haven't come home yet. They just work and work, poor dears. Ólga at the Board of Education, Irína at the telegraph office . . . *(Sighs)* This morning I told your sister, I said you take care of yourself Irína, you hear me, honey? She never listens. Did you say quarter after eight? I'm worried about Bóbik; I think maybe he's a little sick. Why is he so cold? Yesterday he had a fever, and today he's cold all over. . . . I get so worried!

ANDRÉY: He's all right, Natásha. The baby's all right.

NATÁSHA: Well, all the same I better start him on a different diet. I'm just worried. And they said the carnival people are supposed to come tonight. I just don't think they better, Andy.

ANDRÉY: Look, I don't know. They *were* invited.

NATÁSHA: This morning the baby woke up and looked at me, and all of a sudden he smiled and I just know he recognized me. Hello, Bóbik, I said, hello, darlin'. And he laughed. Babies know exactly what's going on, Andy, they really do. . . . So I guess I'll just tell them not to let the carnival people in when they come.

ANDRÉY: *(Hesitantly)* Well, whatever my sisters say. It's their house; it's up to them.

NATÁSHA: It's theirs too; I'll tell them too. They're so sweet. *(Gets up to go)* I told them to get you some yogurt for supper. Doctor says you shouldn't eat anything except yogurt, otherwise you're not ever going to lose weight. *(Stops)* Bóbik's cold. I'm worried he's going to catch cold in that room of his, he could, you know? We should move him into another room until the warm weather comes. For instance, Irína's room is just right for a baby's room; it's dry and gets the sun all day long. We should tell her, and she can move in with Ólga until then. . . . She's never here during the daytime anyway; she just spends the night here. . . . *(Pause)* Andy, how come you never talk to me?

ANDRÉY: Nothing; I was just thinking. . . . What is there to say?

NATÁSHA: Yeah. . . . There was something else I wanted to tell you. . . . Oh, yes. Ferapónt from the council is here; he says he has to talk to you.

ANDRÉY: *(Yawning)* Tell him to come in.

(Natásha goes out. Andréy sits by the candle she has left and reads his book. Ferapónt comes in. He is wearing an old tattered over-coat with the collar turned up and his scarf tied over his ears.)

Hello, old man. What's up?

FERAPÓNT: Chairman sent over a book and some papers. Here. *(Gives him a book and a packet)*

ANDRÉY: Thanks. That's fine. Why did you come by so late? It's already after eight.

FERAPÓNT: What?

ANDRÉY: *(Louder)* I said, you came by late. It's already after eight.

FERAPÓNT: That's right. I came by a while ago, it was still light. Wouldn't let me in. Said you were busy. That's what they said. Well, that's fine: if he's busy he's busy. I'm not in no hurry. *(Thinks Andréy asked him something)* What?

ANDRÉY: Nothing. *(Looks through the book)* Tomorrow's Friday, there's no meeting, but I'll go in anyway . . . get something done. It's a bore around here. . . . *(Pause)* How funny life is! Today I had nothing to do, I was bored, I picked up this book—my old lecture notes from the university—and I started to laugh. . . . My God, I'm the secretary of the County Council, the same council that Pro-topópov is chairman of; I'm the secretary, and the highest honor I can hope for is to become a full member! Me, a member of the local County Council, and every night I dream I'm a professor at the University of Moscow, a famous scientist, the pride of Russia!

FERAPÓNT: I dunno. . . . Can't hear too well.

ANDRÉY: If you could hear, I wouldn't be telling you all this. I have to talk to someone. My wife doesn't understand me; I'm afraid of my sisters, I don't know why. . . . I'm always afraid they'll laugh at me, make me feel ashamed. . . . I don't drink, I don't like bars, but I'd love to be in Moscow right now, sitting at a table at Téstov's or the Grand Moscow.

FERAPÓNT: Now, in Moscow, there's a fella over to the office the other day, he says there was this bunch of men in Moscow, businessmen, he says, and they were eatin' pancakes. Now, this one fella, he ate forty of 'em, he up and died. Or maybe it was fifty. Can't remember.

ANDRÉY: In Moscow you can sit in a restaurant full of people, and nobody knows you and you don't know anybody, but still you don't feel like a stranger. In this town you know everybody and everybody knows you, but you're always a stranger. . . . A stranger, and alone.

FERAPÓNT: What? *(Pause)* This same fella, he was tellin' us—coulda been lyin', I dunno—he was sayin' they got a rope in Moscow, hangs all across town, one side to the other.

ANDRÉY: What's it for?

FERAPÓNT: I dunno. This fella was tellin' us.

ANDRÉY: He made it up. *(Reads the book)* Were you ever in Moscow?

FERAPÓNT: Nope. Things just didn't work out that way. *(Pause)* Mind if I go?

ANDRÉY: Sure. Take care of yourself.

(Ferapónt goes out.)

Take care of yourself. Come over tomorrow, will you, and pick up these papers . . . wait a minute— *(Pause)* He's gone.

(The doorbell rings.)

That's it, work. . . .

(He stretches and goes slowly to his room. Offstage a nurse sings a lullaby to the baby. Enter Másha and Vershínin. While they talk, the maid lights the lamps and candles in the room.)

MÁSHA: I don't know. *(Pause)* I don't know. Of course, habit can be very strong. For example, after Father died it took us a long time to get used to the fact that we didn't have orderlies anymore. But I think I'm being fair about it, even allowing for habit. Maybe it's different in other places, but in this town the most respectable, the best brought up, and the best educated people are in the military.

VERSHÍNIN: I'm really thirsty. I'd love a cup of tea.

MÁSHA: *(Looking at the clock)* It ought to be ready in a minute. I got married when I was eighteen, and I was afraid of my husband because he was a teacher, and I was barely out of school. I used to think he was terribly wise, intelligent, and important. Now I've changed my mind. Unfortunately.

VERSHÍNIN: Yes. Well . . .

MÁSHA: Oh, I don't mean my husband. I've gotten used to him. But most of the people in this town are so vulgar, so unpleasant, so stupid. Vulgarity upsets me, it wounds me; I get physically sick when I see someone who lacks finesse, who lacks kindness and gentleness. When I have to spend time with my husband's colleagues from the high school, it makes me sick.

VERSHÍNIN: Well . . . I don't see that much difference, though, between military and civilians—in this town at least. They both seem uninteresting. They're all alike! Listen to any one of the locals who claim to be sensitive or intelligent—civilian or military. His wife depresses him, his house depresses him, everything he owns depresses him. We are all supposed to be such highly developed abstract thinkers, but why are our lives so depressing? Why?

MÁSHA: Why?

VERSHÍNIN: Why does his wife depress him? And his children? And why do they get depressed by him?

MÁSHA: You're a bit depressed yourself today.

VERSHÍNIN: Maybe. I didn't have any lunch. I haven't eaten a thing since this morning. My daughter wasn't feeling well, and whenever something is the matter with my two little girls I always get very upset; it kills me to think of the mother they've got. God, you should have seen her this morning! What a fool she is! We started fighting at seven this morning, and at nine I slammed the door and left. *(Pause)* I never talk about these things. It's funny, you're the only one I complain to about it. . . . *(Kisses her hand)* Don't be angry with me. You're absolutely all I've got.

   (Pause.)

MÁSHA: Listen to the noise in the chimney. Right before Father died, the wind made a noise in the chimney. Just like that.

VERSHÍNIN: Are you superstitious?

MÁSHA: Yes.

VERSHÍNIN: That's strange. *(Kisses her hand)* You're a strange, wonderful woman. Strange and wonderful. I can see your eyes shining in the dark.

MÁSHA: *(Moving to another chair)* There's more light over here.

VERSHÍNIN: I love you, I love you, I love your eyes, the way you move, I dream about you. . . . You strange, wonderful woman!

MÁSHA: *(Laughing quietly)* When you talk to me that way it makes me laugh somehow—even though it terrifies me. Don't say it again, please. . . . *(Half to herself)* No, go on, say it; what difference does it make? *(Makes an exasperated gesture)* It doesn't make any difference. Someone's coming; talk about something else. . . .

(Irína and Túzenbach enter through the dining room.)

TÚZENBACH: I have a triple family name—Baron Túzenbach-Króne-Áltschauer—but I'm Russian just like you; I was baptized in the Russian church. There's very little German left in me, except for patience—stubbornness, I guess it seems to you. I walk you home every night.

IRÍNA: I'm so tired.

TÚZENBACH: And every evening I'll show up at the telegraph office and walk you home, I promise, for the next ten or twenty years, until you chase me away. . . . *(Notices Másha and Vershínin, delightedly)* Oh, it's you! Hello!

IRÍNA: Home at last. *(To Másha)* A lady came in tonight to send a telegram to her brother in Sarátov—her son died today—and she couldn't remember the address. So she sent it without one, just to Sarátov. She was crying. And I was rude to her, for no reason. "I'm in a hurry," I said. It was such a stupid thing to do. Are the carnival people coming tonight?

MÁSHA: Yes.

IRÍNA: *(Sitting down in an armchair)* I've got to get some rest. I'm worn out.

TÚZENBACH: *(With a smile)* Whenever you get off work you look so little, so helpless. . . .

(Pause.)

IRÍNA: I'm tired. I hate the telegraph office. I hate it.

MÁSHA: You've lost weight. *(Whistles softly)* It makes you look younger; your face is like a boy's.

TÚZENBACH: That's because of the way she wears her hair.

IRÍNA: I've got to find another job; this one is all wrong for me. Whatever it was I wanted or was dreaming of, this is definitely not it. It's work, but there's no poetry in it, no meaning in it. . . .

(A knock on the floor from below.)

The doctor's knocking. *(To Túzenbach)* You knock, dear, will you? I haven't got the strength—I'm worn out. . . .

(Túzenbach knocks on the floor.)

He'll be right up. Listen, we have got to do something. Last night the doctor and Andréy were playing cards at the club, and they lost again. Somebody said Andréy lost two hundred rubles.

MÁSHA: *(Apathetic)* What can we do about it now?

IRÍNA: Two weeks ago he lost, in December he lost. I wish he'd hurry up and lose everything, then maybe we could get out of town. Oh, my God, I dream about Moscow night after night; sometimes I think I'm going absolutely crazy. *(Laughs)* We're moving in June, so that leaves . . . February, March, April, May . . . almost half a year!

MÁSHA: The main thing is not to let Natásha find out he's lost all that money.

IRÍNA: I don't think she even cares.

(Chebutýkin enters, combing his beard. He has just gotten up from a nap after dinner. He sits down at the dining room table and takes a newspaper out of his pocket.)

MÁSHA: Here he comes. Has he paid his rent?

IRÍNA: *(Laughing)* No. Not for the last eight months. I guess he forgot.

MÁSHA: Look at him sit there!

(Everybody laughs; pause.)

IRÍNA: Why are you so quiet, Alexánder Ignátych?

VERSHÍNIN: I don't know. I want some tea! My kingdom for a cup of tea! I haven't eaten a thing since this morning. . . .

CHEBUTÝKIN: Irina Sergéyevna!

IRÍNA: What do you want?

CHEBUTÝKIN: Please come here. *Venez ici.*

(Irína crosses and sits down at the table.)

I can't do without you.

(Irína lays out a game of solitaire.)

VERSHÍNIN: Now what? If we're not going to have tea, let's talk.

TÚZENBACH: All right, let's. What about?

VERSHÍNIN: What about? Let's make up things. For instance, let's talk about what life will be like after we're gone, say in two hundred or three hundred years.

TÚZENBACH: Well, after we're gone, people will travel around in flying machines, they'll wear different-style jackets, maybe they'll discover a sixth sense and expand our perceptions, but life won't change. It will still be hard and happy and mysterious. Three hundred years from now, people will still go around complaining, "Oh, life is so hard," and they will still be afraid to die, the same as they are now.

VERSHÍNIN: *(Thinking a bit)* No! How can I make myself clear? I believe that everything in the world will change, little by little; it's already changing right before our eyes. In two or three hundred years . . . well, in a thousand, maybe—the number of years isn't so important—a new and a happier life will begin. Of course, we'll never see it, but we are working toward it right now. We work for it, we suffer for it, we create it, in fact. And that's the whole point of our existence. That's what happiness is, I think.

(Másha laughs softly.)

TÚZENBACH: What are you laughing about?

MÁSHA: I don't know. I started laughing this morning, and I've been laughing all day long.

VERSHÍNIN: I graduated from the same school you did, even though I never went to the academy. I read a lot, but I'm not very good at choosing books; sometimes I think I'm reading all the wrong things. Still, the longer I live, the more I want to know. My hair is turning gray, I'm almost an old man, and I know so little—so little! But all the same, I think I do know the most important thing. The only real thing. And I want to convince you of it too. That happiness doesn't exist as yet, it will never exist for us, and that's all right, that's as it should be. . . . Our task is only to work and work; happiness is reserved for our descendants. *(Pause)* It's not for me. It's for my distant descendants.

(Fedótik and Róhde appear in the dining room; they sit down and hum softly. Fedótik strums a guitar.)

TÚZENBACH: According to you, we can't even dream of happiness! But what if I'm happy already?

VERSHÍNIN: You're not.

TÚZENBACH: *(Making a deprecating gesture and laughing)* Obviously we are on opposite sides of the fence. Now, how am I going to convince you?

(Másha laughs softly. He shakes a finger at her.)

Go ahead and laugh! *(To Vershínin)* Not just in two or three hundred years, but even in a million years, life will still be the same as it's always been. It doesn't change, it always stays the same, it has its own laws, which are none of your business, or at least you'll never find out what they are. Birds that migrate—cranes, for instance—just fly and fly, and no matter what thoughts they may be thinking, great thoughts or small thoughts, they keep on flying without knowing where or why. They fly, and they will always fly, no matter what great philosophers may arise among them; they can talk philosophy if they want, but they can never stop flying. . . .

MÁSHA: But there has to be some meaning in it. . . .

TÚZENBACH: Meaning? Look out the window: it's snowing. Is there any meaning in that?

(Pause.)

MÁSHA: I think a person has to believe in something, or has to look for something to believe in, otherwise his life is empty, empty. . . . Just to live and not to know why the cranes fly, why children are born, why there are stars in the sky . . . Either you know the reason why you're alive, or nothing makes any difference.

(Pause.)

VERSHÍNIN: Still, it's too bad youth doesn't last. . . .

MÁSHA: You know what Gógol said: Ladies and gentlemen, life is a bore!

TÚZENBACH: And I say: Ladies and gentlemen, arguing is a bore! With you anyway . . .

CHEBUTÝKIN: *(Reading from the newspaper)* Balzac was married in Berdíchev.

(Irína hums to herself.)

Let's just make a little note of that one. *(Writes)* Balzac was married in Berdíchev. *(Goes back to his paper)*

IRÍNA: *(Laying out another game of solitaire, thoughtfully)* Balzac was married in Berdíchev.

TÚZENBACH: Well, the die is cast. María Sergéyevna, did you know I'm resigning from the military?

MÁSHA: So I heard. I don't know what's so wonderful about it. I hate civilians.

TÚZENBACH: What difference does it make? *(Gets up)* I'm not very good-looking—what kind of military man is that? Anyway, it doesn't make any difference, really it doesn't. . . . I'm going to work. At least once in my life I'm going to work so hard I'll come home at night and fall into bed all worn out and go right to sleep. *(Goes into the dining room)* Working people must sleep very well.

FEDÓTIK: *(To Irína)* I was down on Moscow Street today and I bought these for you at Pýzhikov's. Crayons. And a little knife . . .

IRÍNA: You always treat me like a little girl, but I *am* grown up, you know. . . . *(With delight, as she takes the crayons and the knife)* Oh, they're divine!

FEDÓTIK: And I got a knife for myself too. . . . Look. Here's one blade, and another one, and another one, and this is for cleaning your ears, and this is a pair of scissors, and this is for cleaning your nails . . .

RÓHDE: *(Loud voice)* Doctor, how old are you?

CHEBUTÝKIN: Me? Thirty-two.

(Laughter.)

FEDÓTIK: Here . . . do you want me to show you another way to play solitaire?

(He lays out the game. They bring in things for tea. Anfísa busies herself with the tea; soon Natásha comes in and busies herself at the table as well. Solyóny comes in, says hello to people, and sits down at the table.)

VERSHÍNIN: Listen to that wind!

MÁSHA: Yes; winter's a bore. I can't even remember what summer is like.

IRÍNA: Look, the solitaire is coming out. That means we'll get to Moscow.

FEDÓTIK: No it isn't. See, you've got an eight on a two of spades. *(Laughs)* That means you won't get to Moscow.

CHEBUTÝKIN: *(Reading the newspaper)* Tsítsikar. An epidemic of smallpox has broken out there.

ANFÍSA: *(To Másha)* Másha dear, tea's ready.

MÁSHA: Bring mine here, Nana. I can't budge!

IRÍNA: Nana!

ANFÍSA: *Coming!*

NATÁSHA: *(To Solyóny)* Little babies understand everything you say. "Hi, Bóbik," I said. "Hello, darlin'." And you should have *seen* the way he looked at me. Oh, I know what you think—I'm just his mother—but it's more than that, believe you me. He's an extraordinary child.

SOLYÓNY: If that child were mine, I would have sautéed him in butter and eaten him long ago. *(Takes his tea into the living room and sits in a far corner)*

NATÁSHA: *(Making a gesture of exasperation)* Oh, that man is so crude and vulgar!

MÁSHA: How wonderful it must be not to know whether it's winter or summer. I think if I lived in Moscow I wouldn't care what the weather was.

VERSHÍNIN: The other day I was reading the diary of that French politician, the one who went to prison because of the Panama scandal. It was so moving the way he described the birds he could see from his prison window, birds he never even noticed when he was a government official. Of course, now that he's out of prison he probably doesn't notice them anymore. It's the same with you: once you're actually living in Moscow you won't notice it anymore either. We're never happy, we can never be happy. We only *want* to be happy.

TÚZENBACH: *(Taking a box from the table)* What happened to the candy?

IRÍNA: Solyóny ate it.

TÚZENBACH: He ate it *all?*

ANFÍSA: *(Handing Vershínin a cup of tea)* Somebody brought a note for you, dear.

VERSHÍNIN: For me? *(Takes it)* It's from my daughter. *(Reads it)* Oh, God, wouldn't you know. . . . Excuse me, María Sergéyevna, I have to go. I'll just slip out quietly. I can't stay for tea. *(Stands up, upset)* It's the same old story. . . .

MÁSHA: What's the matter? Can't you tell me?

VERSHÍNIN: *(Quietly)* My wife has taken too many pills again. I have to go. I'll go out this way. It's all very unpleasant. *(Kisses Másha's hand)* My dearest, you wonderful woman . . . I'll just go out quietly. . . . *(Leaves)*

ANFÍSA: Now, where's he going? I just gave him his tea! Really, I never saw the likes. . . .

MÁSHA: *(Flaring up)* Go away! You just stand there bothering me all the time. . . . *(Goes with her teacup to the table)* I'm sick and tired of that old woman. . . .

ANFÍSA: Now what's gotten into her? My Lord!

ANDRÉY'S VOICE: Anfísa!

ANFÍSA: *(Mimicking him)* "Anfísa!" He just sits there. . . . *(Goes out)*

MÁSHA: *(At the dining room table, angrily)* Give me some room to sit down! *(Shoves the cards to one side)* You've got cards all over the place. Drink your tea!

IRÍNA: Másha, you're being mean.

MÁSHA: Well, if I am, don't talk to me! Just leave me alone.

CHEBUTÝKIN: *(Laughing)* Leave her alone, leave her alone . . .

MÁSHA: And you! You're sixty years old, and all you do is talk a lot of goddamn nonsense, just like some kid!

NATÁSHA: *(Sighing)* Másha dear, why do you always use language like that! You have a very attractive personality, and I'm sure you could make a real nice impression on social occasions, I'll tell you quite frankly, if it weren't for those vulgar words of yours. *Je vous prie, pardonnez-moi, Marie, mais vous avez des manières un peu grossières.*

TÚZENBACH: *(Choking back a laugh)* Give me . . . oh, give me . . . there . . . I think there's some cognac . . .

NATÁSHA: *Il paraît que mon Bobik déjà ne dort pas*—he woke up. He hasn't been feeling well all day. I'll just go take a look. Excuse me. . . . *(Goes out)*

IRÍNA: Where did Alexánder Ignátych go?

MÁSHA: Home. There's something going on with his wife again.

TÚZENBACH: *(Going up to Solyóny with the decanter of cognac in his hands)* You're always sitting off by yourself, thinking about something—only nobody ever knows what. Listen, let's be friends. Have a drink.

> *(They drink.)*

I've got to play the piano tonight; all night, probably—just silly stuff. Well, that's all right.

SOLYÓNY: What do you mean, be friends? Who said we were enemies?

TÚZENBACH: You always make me feel as if something had gone wrong between us. You're kind of strange, you must admit. . . .

SOLYÓNY: *(Reciting)* "I am strange, we all are strange! Forget thy wrath, Aléko!"

TÚZENBACH: Aléko? Who's Aléko?

(Pause.)

SOLYÓNY: Whenever I'm alone with someone, I feel all right, just ordinary, but when I'm in a group I feel depressed and shy, and I . . . I say a lot of stupid things. But still, I'm more honest and open than a lot of other people. A lot of others. And I can prove it.

TÚZENBACH: I know I get mad at you a lot—you're always trying to pick a fight with me whenever we're out anywhere—but I still like you anyway. What the hell. I feel like getting drunk tonight. Let's have a drink!

SOLYÓNY: Let's have a drink.

(They drink.)

I don't have anything against you, Baron. But I have the soul of Lérmontov. *(Quietly)* I even look a little like Lérmontov. . . . At least that's what people say. . . . *(Takes out his bottle of cologne and rubs some on his hands)*

TÚZENBACH: I'm resigning from the service. *Basta!* I've been thinking about it for five years, and I finally decided to do it. I'm going to go to work.

SOLYÓNY: *(Reciting)* "Forget thy wrath, Aléko! Forget thy dreams . . ."

(While they talk, Andréy comes in with his book and sits near a lamp.)

TÚZENBACH: I'm going to work.

CHEBUTÝKIN: *(Going into the living room with Irína)* And it was a real Caucasian dinner, too: we had onion soup and a meat dish called *chekhartmá.*

SOLYÓNY: *Cheremshá* isn't meat; it's a kind of onion.

CHEBUTÝKIN: No, no, angel. *Chekhartmá* isn't an onion; it's a meat dish, made with lamb.

SOLYÓNY: And I'm telling you *cheremshá* is an onion.

CHEBUTÝKIN: And I'm telling you *chekhartmá* is a meat dish.

SOLYÓNY: And I'm telling you *cheremshá* is an onion.

CHEBUTÝKIN: What am I arguing with you for? You were never in the Caucasus and you've never eaten *chekhartmá!*

SOLYÓNY: I've never eaten *cheremshá* because I can't stand it. It tastes worse than garlic!

ANDRÉY: *(Imploring)* That's enough! Will you two please stop it?

TÚZENBACH: When are the carnival people coming?

IRÍNA: They should be here now; they promised to come around nine.

TÚZENBACH: *(Hugging Andréy and singing)* "Akh, vy séni, móyi séni, séni nóvye moyí . . ."
ANDRÉY: *(Dancing and singing)* "Séni nóvye, klenóvye . . ."
CHEBUTÝKIN: *(Dancing)* "Reshóchatye!"

(Laughter.)

TÚZENBACH: Goddamn it, let's have a drink. Andy, let's drink to being friends. And I'll go with you, Andy, to the university in Moscow.
SOLYÓNY: Which one? There are two universities in Moscow.
ANDRÉY: There's only one university in Moscow.
SOLYÓNY: And I'm telling you there are two.
ANDRÉY: I don't care if there are three. The more the merrier.
SOLYÓNY: There are two universities in Moscow!

(Booing and hissing.)

There are two universities in Moscow: the old university and the new university. And if it bothers you all to listen to me, if my words offend you, I don't have to say anything. I can even leave the room. . . . *(Goes out)*
TÚZENBACH: Bravo, bravo! *(Laughs)* All right, ladies and gentlemen, here we go! I am about to play! That Solyóny is a clown. . . . *(Sits down at the piano, plays a waltz)*
MÁSHA: *(Waltzing by herself)* The baron is drunk, the baron is drunk, the baron is drunk!

(Enter Natásha.)

NATÁSHA: *(To Chebutýkin)* Iván Románich!

(She whispers something to Chebutýkin, then goes out quietly. Chebutýkin taps Túzenbach on the shoulder and whispers something; he stops playing.)

IRÍNA: What's the matter?
CHEBUTÝKIN: It's time for us to go. Good night now.
TÚZENBACH: Good night. It's time to go.
IRÍNA: Excuse me—but what about the carnival people?
ANDRÉY: *(Embarrassed)* They're not coming. Well, you see, dear, Natásha says that Bóbik isn't feeling well, and so . . . Look, I don't know—what difference does it make?
IRÍNA: *(Shrugging her shoulders)* Bóbik isn't feeling well!
MÁSHA: Well, sometimes you win, sometimes you lose. If they kick

us out, then I guess we go. *(To Irína)* Bóbik isn't sick, she is! In the head! *(Points a finger at her head)* That cheap little . . .

(Andréy goes into his own room, Chebutýkin follows him. In the dining room, everyone is saying goodbye.)

FEDÓTIK: What a shame! I was really counting on spending the evening, but if the baby is sick, of course . . . I'll bring him a little present tomorrow. . . .

RÓHDE: *(Loudly)* Today I took a long nap after dinner on purpose, because I thought we'd be up all night dancing. It's not even ten o'clock yet!

MÁSHA: Let's go out in front of the house; we can talk there. Let's think of someplace else to go.

(We hear: "Goodbye!" "Good night!" Túzenbach's happy laugh. Everybody leaves. Anfísa and the maid clear the table and turn out the lamps. The nurse is singing somewhere. Andréy, in an overcoat and hat, and Chebutýkin enter quietly.)

CHEBUTÝKIN: I never managed to get married because life just went by like a flash, and also because I was crazy in love with your mother and she was already married. . . .

ANDRÉY: Nobody should get married. It's boring.

CHEBUTÝKIN: Maybe so, but loneliness is worse. No matter how you rationalize it, my boy, loneliness is an awful business. Although when you get right down to it, actually—what difference does it make?

ANDRÉY: Come on, let's go.

CHEBUTÝKIN: What are you in such a rush for? We'll make it.

ANDRÉY: I'm afraid my wife might stop me.

CHEBUTÝKIN: Oh.

ANDRÉY: Tonight I'm not going to play cards; I'm just going to sit and watch. I don't feel very well. What are you supposed to do for pains in your chest, Iván Románich?

CHEBUTÝKIN: Don't ask me. I don't know, my boy; I can't remember.

ANDRÉY: Let's go out the back way.

(They leave. The doorbell rings, then again. Voices and laughter.)

IRÍNA: *(Entering)* Who is that?

ANFÍSA: *(In a whisper)* The carnival people!

(The doorbell.)

IRÍNA: Tell them there's nobody home, Nana. And say we're sorry.

(Anfísa leaves. Irína wanders about the room, thinking; she is upset. Enter Solyóny.)

SOLYÓNY: *(Bewildered)* There's no one here. . . . Where did everybody go?

IRÍNA: They went home.

SOLYÓNY: That's funny. Are you alone?

IRÍNA: Yes. *(Pause)* Good night.

SOLYÓNY: I behaved badly before. I lost control; it was tactless. But you're not like the others, you're different: you are pure and distant, you understand the truth. . . . You're the only one who can understand me, the only one. I love you . . . I love you deeply, endlessly. . . .

IRÍNA: Good night! Please go.

SOLYÓNY: I can't live without you. *(Goes up to her)* You're divine! What happiness! You have wonderful eyes, brilliant, disturbing eyes. I've never seen a woman with eyes like yours before. . . .

IRÍNA: *(Coldly)* Stop it, Vassíly Vassílich!

SOLYÓNY: This is the first time I've ever talked about my love for you. *(Puts his hand on his forehead)* Well, maybe it doesn't make any difference. I can't force you to be nice to me, I know that. . . . But no happy rivals . . . None. I swear by all that's holy, any rivals, I will kill them.

(Natásha crosses the room with a candle.)

NATÁSHA: *(Glancing in at one door, then another, and passing the door to her husband's room)* Andréy . . . Oh, let him read. *(Sees Solyóny)* Oh! Excuse me, Vassíly Vassílich, I didn't know you were here; I'm not dressed. . . .

SOLYÓNY: What difference does that make? Good night. *(Leaves)*

NATÁSHA: Irína, you're all worn out, you poor thing! *(Kisses Irína)* You shouldn't stay up so late.

IRÍNA: Is Bóbik asleep?

NATÁSHA: Yes. But not very well. By the way, I wanted to tell you before, but you weren't here or I never had time. I think Bóbik's room is too cold and damp—where he is now, I mean. And your room is exactly right for a baby's room. You just move in with Ólga for a while, dear, that's a good girl.

IRÍNA: *(Not understanding)* What?

(The sound of sleigh bells outside.)

NATÁSHA: You and Ólga will have one room, and Bóbik goes in your room. Just for a while. He's such a darlin'. This morning I said to him, "Bóbik," I said, "you're mine! All mine!" And he just looked at me with those big eyes of his.

(*The doorbell rings.*)

That must be Ólga. She's so late!

(*The maid comes in and whispers something in Natásha's ear.*)

Protopópov? What a crazy man! Protopópov is outside; he wants me to go for a sleigh ride with him. (*Laughs*) Men are so funny. . . . Well, maybe just a little one, fifteen minutes or so . . . (*To the maid*) Tell him I'll be right out.

(*The doorbell.*)

Now who is it? Well, *that* must be Ólga.

(*She leaves. The maid hurries out; Irína sits thinking. Enter Kulýgin, Ólga, and behind them Vershínin.*)

KULÝGIN: Now how do you like that. And they said they were having a party.

VERSHÍNIN: That's funny. I only left about a half hour ago, and they were waiting for the carnival people.

IRÍNA: Everybody left.

KULÝGIN: Did Másha leave? Where did she go? And why is Protopópov waiting outside? Who's he waiting for?

IRÍNA: Oh, stop bothering me! I'm worn out!

KULÝGIN: Well, Miss High-and-Mighty!

ÓLGA: The meeting just ended. I'm in agony. Our headmistress is sick and I have to substitute for her. And my head, my head is aching so. . . . (*Sits down*) Andréy lost two hundred rubles playing cards last night. . . . The whole town is talking about it. . . .

KULÝGIN: Yes, even I got tired at that meeting. (*Sits down*)

VERSHÍNIN: My wife tried to kill herself again, but she was just trying to throw a scare into me. She's out of danger now, and I feel better. But I suppose that means we should go. Well, I wish you all a very good night. Fyódor Ilâch, let's go out somewhere! I really can't go home right now—what do you say?

KULÝGIN: I'm tired; I can't. (*Stands*) I'm tired. Did my wife go home?

IRÍNA: Probably.

KULÝGIN: *(Kisses Irína's hand)* Goodbye. Tomorrow and the day after are holidays. Have a pleasant rest! *(Goes)* I would dearly love a cup of tea. I'd been counting on spending an evening with entertaining company. . . . Well. . . . *O, fallacem hominum spem!* Accusative of exclamation.

VERSHÍNIN: All right, I'll go by myself.

(He leaves with Kulýgin, whistling.)

ÓLGA: My head aches so. Andréy lost . . . the whole town is talking. . . . I'm going to bed. *(Starts off)* I've got the day off tomorrow. . . . Oh, God, how pleasant! Tomorrow off, and the day after too . . . But my head aches so. *(Leaves)*

IRÍNA: They've all gone. There's no one left.

(Out in the street, someone is playing an accordion. The nurse sings. Natásha crosses the room in a fur coat and hat; the maid follows her.)

NATÁSHA: I'll be back in half an hour. I'm only going for a little ride. *(Leaves)*

IRÍNA: *(Alone, longing)* I want to go to Moscow! Moscow! Moscow!

CURTAIN.

ACT THREE

Ólga and Irína's room. Beds right and left, behind screens. It is after two in the morning. Fire alarms are heard in the distance; they have been going for some time, and it's obvious that no one in the house has been to bed yet. Másha lies on the sofa, dressed in black as usual.

Enter Ólga and Anfísa.

ANFÍSA: They're sitting downstairs in the hallway right now. . . . I told them to come on up. "Come on up," I said. "You can't just sit there like that." And they're crying their eyes out. "We don't know what happened to Papa," they said. "Maybe he got burned up." Can you believe it? And there's some more people out in the yard; they don't hardly have any clothes on, either. . . .

ÓLGA: *(Taking a dress out of the closet)* Nana, take that gray one . . . and that one too . . . and the blouse too . . . and take this skirt, Nana. . . . What a terrible thing, my God! The whole of Kirsánov Street must have burned. . . . Take this one . . . and this. *(Piles dresses on Anfísa's arms)* The poor Vershínins got an awful scare; their house nearly burned down. They can spend the night with us; we can't just let them go home. And poor Fedótik lost everything; his place burned to the ground. . . .

ANFÍSA: Ólga dear, you better get Ferapónt. I'll never manage all this myself.

ÓLGA: Who's down there? Ferapónt, come up here, will you?

(Outside the windows, the sky is red from the fire; fire engines are heard going by the house.)

ÓLGA: What a nightmare all this is. And how tired of it all I am.

(Enter Ferapónt.)

Here . . . take this stuff, take it downstairs. The Kolotílin girls are in the hallway; give it to them—wait, give them this too.

FERAPÓNT: All right. Moscow burned down too, long time ago. Them Frenchies sure got a surprise.

ÓLGA: Go on, go on, get out. . . .

FERAPÓNT: All right, I'm goin'. . . .

ÓLGA: Nana dear, give it all away. We don't need any of it, Nana; give it all away. . . . I'm so tired I can hardly stand. . . . We can't let the Vershínins go home. The girls can sleep in the living room, the colonel can stay with the baron, Fedótik can stay with the baron too, or maybe someplace downstairs. The doctor is drunk again—dead drunk, wouldn't you know it—so we can't put anyone in with him. And Vershínin's wife can go in the living room too.

ANFÍSA: *(Breaking with fatigue)* Ólga dear, Ólyushka, don't send me away, please! Please don't!

ÓLGA: Don't talk nonsense, Nana. Nobody's going to send you away.

ANFÍSA: *(Leaning against Ólga)* My little girl, my little darling, I do what I can, I work all the time. . . . I know I'm not what I used to be, everybody says send her away, but where am I supposed to go? Where? I'm old, I'm old, I'm old . . .

ÓLGA: Nana, why don't you sit down. . . . Poor love, you're worn out! *(Helps her sit down)* You just rest, darling. You're so pale!

(Natásha enters.)

NATÁSHA: They're saying we better get a group together to organize aid for the people who got burned out. It's a lovely idea, don't you think? We should help out the poor anyway; that's one of your responsibilities if you're rich. Bóbik and little Sophie are fast asleep; they're sleeping as if nothing in the world were going on. And we've got so many people; everywhere you look, the house is full of them. There's some kind of flu going around; I'm scared the children will catch it.

ÓLGA: *(Not listening to her)* You really can't see the fire from this room; it's quieter here.

NATÁSHA: Yes. . . . I must be a mess. *(Looks in the mirror)* Who said I was putting on weight? It's not true! Not a bit! And Másha's asleep; she must be worn out, poor thing. . . . *(To Anfísa, coldly)* Don't you dare sit down when I'm around! Get up! And get out of here!

(Anfísa goes out; pause.)

Why you keep that old woman around I will never understand.

ÓLGA: *(Stunned)* Excuse me, I don't understand either. . . .

NATÁSHA: You just spoil her! She doesn't do a thing! She's a peasant, she should be living on a farm. I like things nice and neat around the house, I don't want things sloppy! *(Pats Ólga's cheek)* Poor sweet thing, you're tired! Our headmistress is all tired out! When my little Sophie grows up and starts high school, I'll have to start being scared of you.

ÓLGA: I'm not going to be headmistress.

NATÁSHA: Yes you are, Ólga. It's all settled.

ÓLGA: I refuse. I can't, I just don't have the strength for it. *(Takes a drink of water)* You were so rude to Nana just now. . . . Forgive me, I'm in no condition for scenes like that. . . . I'm even a little faint. . . .

NATÁSHA: *(Upset)* I'm sorry, Ólga, I'm sorry. I didn't mean to upset you.

(Másha gets up, takes her pillow, and leaves, angrily.)

ÓLGA: Dear, you have got to understand. We may have been brought up rather differently; still, I . . . I can't bear scenes like that. I get depressed when I see someone treated like that; I get physically *sick*. . . . Really, I . . . my strength just goes. . . .

NATÁSHA: I'm sorry, I'm really sorry. . . . *(Kisses her)*

ÓLGA: The least little vulgarity, an indelicate expression, and I get terribly upset. . . .

NATÁSHA: I know I say things I shouldn't, dear, I know, but you have to agree she could go live on a farm.

ÓLGA: But she's been with us for thirty years!

NATÁSHA: But she can't do any work anymore! Either I don't understand you or you don't want to understand me. She *cannot work*; she just sits around or she sleeps.

ÓLGA: Then let her sleep.

NATÁSHA: *(Astonished)* What do you mean, let her sleep? She's a servant, isn't she? *(Almost crying)* I just don't understand you, Ólga. I have two nurses for the children, we have a maid and a cook. . . . What do we need that old woman for? What for?

(Fire alarms in the distance.)

ÓLGA: I think I've aged ten years tonight.

NATÁSHA: We've got to come to some agreement, Ólga. Once and for all. You're at the high school, I'm at home. Your job is teaching, mine is running this house. And if I tell you something about the servants, then I know what I'm talking about. I know what *I am talk-ing a-bout*! And I don't want to see that stupid old woman around here tomorrow! *(Stamps her foot)* And don't you dare argue with me! Don't you dare! *(Calms down a little)* Really, if you don't move down to the basement apartment, we are always going to be fighting like this. It's terrible.

(Enter Kulýgin.)

KULÝGIN: Where's Másha? We should have gone home long ago. They say the fire's dying down. *(Yawns and stretches)* They only lost one block, but it was so windy, at first they thought the whole town would burn down. *(Sits down)* I'm tired. Ólga dearest . . . I sometimes think if I hadn't married Másha I would have married you, Ólga. You're a wonderful woman. . . . I'm so tired. *(Listens for a bit)*

ÓLGA: What's the matter?

KULÝGIN: The doctor's been drinking, wouldn't you know. He's extremely drunk. Wouldn't you know! *(Gets up)* I think he's coming up here. . . . Do you hear him? Yes, here he comes. . . . *(Laughs)* What a character, really. . . . I'm going to hide. *(Goes behind a screen in the corner)* The old joker.

ÓLGA: He hasn't had a drop in two years, and all of a sudden he starts in again. . . .

(Ólga goes upstage with Natásha. Chebutýkin enters; he walks

straight as if he were sober, crosses the room, stops, looks around, goes over to the washstand, and starts to wash his hands.)

CHEBUTÝKIN: *(Sullen)* The hell with 'em all ... the hell with 'em. They think I'm a doctor and I know how to cure people, but I don't know anything. I forgot everything I knew, I don't remember a thing. Not a thing.

(Ólga and Natásha go out; he doesn't notice.)

The hell with 'em. Last Wednesday I went out to Zásyp to take care of a sick woman. She died, and it's my fault she died. My fault ... Maybe I knew something twenty-five years ago, but now I can't remember a thing. My head is empty, and so is my heart. Maybe I'm not even human. . . . Maybe I don't even exist . . . maybe it's all my imagination. *(Starts to cry)* Oh, I wish I didn't exist! *(Stops crying. Sullen, as before)* What the hell ... Two days ago I went to the club, they were all talking about Shakespeare and Voltaire; I never read 'em, but I pretended like I did. So did all the rest of 'em. They all pretended. Made me sick! I kept thinking about that woman who died on Wednesday, I kept thinking about everything, and I got feeling ugly and twisted and mean. . . . So I went out and got drunk.

(Irína, Vershínin, and Túzenbach enter; Túzenbach has on brand-new civilian clothes, very stylish.)

IRÍNA: Come in and sit down. Nobody will bother us here.

VERSHÍNIN: If it weren't for the troops, the whole town would have burned! Terrific, every one of them! *(Rubs his hands with satisfaction)* Good boys! Just terrific!

KULÝGIN: *(Coming out from behind the screen)* Does anybody know what time it is?

TÚZENBACH: It's already after three. It's getting light.

IRÍNA: Everybody's just sitting around downstairs; nobody wants to leave. Even that Solyóny of yours is down there.... *(To Chebutýkin)* Doctor, you ought to go to bed.

CHEBUTÝKIN: S'all right. Thanks a lot. *(Combs his beard)*

KULÝGIN: *(Laughing)* You've been at the bottle, Iván Románich. *(Slaps him on the back)* Congratulations! *In vino veritas,* the ancients used to say.

TÚZENBACH: They've been after me to organize a benefit concert for the people who were burned out.

IRÍNA: Here? Who could you get?

TÚZENBACH: We could do it if we really wanted to. María Sergéyevna, for instance. She plays the piano beautifully.

KULÝGIN: Beautifully!

IRÍNA: She forgot how long ago. She hasn't played in three years ... maybe four.

TÚZENBACH: Nobody in this town understands music, not a single soul, but I do, and I tell you she has talent.

KULÝGIN: You're right, Baron. I love Másha a great deal. She's a splendid woman.

TÚZENBACH: Can you imagine what it must be like to play so beautifully and to realize that there is no one, no one, who understands you!

KULÝGIN: (Sighing) Yes. ... But would it be proper for her to perform in public? (Pause) Of course, I really know nothing about it. It might be perfectly all right. But you have to remember that our headmaster has rather particular views. He's a fine man, a very fine man, very intelligent. ... I suppose it's not really his business, but still—if you want, I could probably have a talk with him.

(Chebutýkin picks up a porcelain clock and examines it.)

VERSHÍNIN: I'm a mess. I got terribly dirty at the fire. (Pause) I heard a rumor the other day, something about our brigade being transferred. Maybe to Poland, maybe to the Chinese border; nobody knows.

TÚZENBACH: That's what I heard too. Well, that will empty out the town.

IRÍNA: And we're leaving too!

(Chebutýkin drops the clock, and it smashes to pieces.)

CHEBUTÝKIN: Smash!

(Pause; everyone is distressed and upset.)

KULÝGIN: (Picking up the pieces) Iván Románich, Iván Románich, such an expensive clock, and you broke it! You get an F-minus in conduct!

IRÍNA: That was Mama's clock.

CHEBUTÝKIN: Maybe. Mama's. All right, so it was Mama's. Maybe I didn't even break it. Maybe it just looks like it's broken. Maybe we don't even exist; maybe it just looks like it. I don't know anything, and nobody else knows anything either. (At the door) What

are you all looking at? Natásha's having a little affair with Protopópov, but you can't see that. You just sit there, and you can't
see that Natásha is having a little affair with Protopópov. *(Sings)*
"Don't you like this little fig I'm giving you . . ." *(Leaves)*

VERSHÍNIN: Well . . . *(Laughs)* This is all really very strange, isn't it?
(Pause) When the fire started, I ran right home; as soon as I got
there, I realized our house was safe and sound, but my two little
girls were standing in the doorway. All they had on was their
underwear, their mother was gone, there were people running
everywhere, horses, dogs barking, and on those little girls' faces
was a look of horror, fear, anxiety, I don't know what all—it
wrung my heart to see them like that. My God, I thought, what
will those little girls have to go through during their lifetime! I
picked them up and brought them here, but all I could think of
was what they would have to go through before they die.

(Fire sirens; pause.)

And when I got here, I found their mother—angry, screaming.

(Másha enters, carrying her pillow; she sits down on the sofa.)

And when my little girls were standing there in their underwear,
with no shoes on, and the street was all red from the fire, and the
noise was terrible, I thought: This is the way things used to happen years ago—a surprise enemy attack, arson and looting . . .
And yet of course there's really an enormous difference between
then and now, isn't there? And after a little time goes by, say two
or three hundred years, people will look back on our life with
horror, or they'll laugh, and the things we do today will seem
strange and complicated and impractical. And oh, what a life
that will be then! *(Laughs)* Excuse me, I'm talking too much
again; it's just the mood I'm in. *(Pause)* You're all asleep. Well,
I'll keep talking anyway. What a life that will be! Just think:
right now there are only three people like you in this town;
another generation and there will be more, and then more and
more, and a time will come when the whole world will have
changed because of you, and everyone will live like you do, and
finally even you will become part of the past, and people will be
born who are better than you. . . . *(Laughs)* I'm in the strangest
mood today. I feel an urge to live, to do something wild! *(Sings)*
"*Lyubví vse vósrasty pokórny, yeyó porývy blagotvórny* . . ."
(Laughs)

MÁSHA: *Tram-tam-tam* . . .
VERSHÍNIN: *Tram-tam* . . .
MÁSHA: *Tra-ra-ra?*
VERSHÍNIN: *Tra-ta-ta. (Laughs)*

> *(Enter Fedótik.)*

FEDÓTIK: *(Dancing)* It's all burned up! Everything's gone! It's all burned up!

> *(Laughter.)*

IRÍNA: What's so funny about it? Is everything burned?
FEDÓTIK: Everything. It's all gone. The guitar burned and the camera burned and all my letters burned. . . . And I bought a little notebook for you, and that burned too. . . .

> *(Enter Solyóny.)*

IRÍNA: No, please, Vassíly Vassílich, go away! You can't come in here!
SOLYÓNY: How come the baron can and I can't?
VERSHÍNIN: We should all go, in fact. How's the fire?
SOLYÓNY: They said it's stopped. Now, I find that extremely funny, that the baron can come in here and I can't. *(Takes out his cologne bottle and rubs some on his hands)*
VERSHÍNIN: *Tram-tam-tam.*
MÁSHA: *Tram-tam.*
VERSHÍNIN: *(Laughing; to Solyóny)* Let's go downstairs.
SOLYÓNY: Very well. We'll just make a little note of this. *(Looking at Túzenbach)* Wee, wee, wee, wee . . .

> *(He goes out with Vershínin and Fedótik.)*

IRÍNA: That Solyóny has gotten the place all smelly. . . . *(Surprised)* The baron's asleep! Baron! Baron!
TÚZENBACH: *(Opening his eyes)* I was tireder than I thought. . . . A brick factory . . . Actually, it's not a dream: I'll be starting work soon at a brick factory. I've already had an interview with them. *(To Irína, tenderly)* You're so pale and beautiful . . . you're fascinating . . . your paleness lights up the dark. . . . You're sad, you're unhappy with life—oh, come away with me, let's go off and work together!
MÁSHA: Nikolái Lvóvich, will you please get out?
TÚZENBACH: *(Laughing)* Are you here? I didn't see you. *(Kisses*

Irína's hand) Goodbye, I'm going. . . . When I look at you now, Irína, I remember a while back, on your birthday, how alive you were, laughing and talking about going to work. . . . What a happy life I dreamed of then—and where is it? *(Kisses her hand)* You have tears in your eyes. Go to bed; it's already daylight; it's morning. . . . Oh, if only I could sacrifice my life for you!

MÁSHA: Nikolái Lvóvich, get out! Really, you are the limit. . . .

TÚZENBACH: I'm going. *(Leaves)*

MÁSHA: *(Lying down)* Are you asleep, Fyódor?

KULÝGIN: What?

MÁSHA: You should go home.

KULÝGIN: Másha dearest, my sweet Másha . . .

IRÍNA: She's worn out, Fyódor. Let her get some rest.

KULÝGIN: I'm going right now. . . . My dear wife, my wonderful wife . . . I love you, my only—

MÁSHA: *(Angrily)* Amo, amas, amat, amamus, amatis, amant.

KULÝGIN: *(Laughing)* Isn't she astonishing! I've been married to you for seven years, and it seems like only yesterday. No, truly, you're astonishing. And I'm happy. I'm a happy, happy man!

MÁSHA: And I'm bored. I am bored, bored, bored! *(Straightens up and speaks, sitting there)* There's one thing I can't get out of my head; it feels like someone nailed it there. I mean Andréy—he took out a mortgage on this house, and his wife got all the money, and this house isn't just his, it belongs to the four of us! He must know that, if he's got any decency left.

KULÝGIN: Why bring it up, Másha? It doesn't affect you. Andréy owes money all over town; I feel sorry for him.

MÁSHA: I don't care, it's still revolting. *(Lies down)*

KULÝGIN: You and I are not poor. I work, I teach at the high school, I give private lessons in my spare time. . . . I'm a plain, honest man. *Omnia mea mecum porto,* as they say.

MÁSHA: I don't want anything, but the injustice of it revolts me. *(Pause)* Go on home, Fyódor.

KULÝGIN: *(Kissing her)* You're tired, you take a little rest; I'll wait downstairs for you. Get some sleep. . . . *(Crosses to the door)* I'm a happy, happy man. *(Goes out)*

IRÍNA: Andréy has gotten so petty, so slow, and so old, living with that woman. He used to want to be a scientist, and yesterday he was bragging that he'd finally become a member of the County Council. He's a member, and Protopópov is the chairman. . . . The whole town is talking and laughing, and he's the only one who doesn't know anything, doesn't see anything. Tonight everybody went to see the fire, but not him. He just sits in his room and pays no attention to anything; he just plays his violin. *(On edge)* Oh, it's awful, it's awful, awful! *(Cries)* I can't stand it. I can't stand it anymore! I can't, I can't!

(Ólga enters and goes to straighten up her dressing table. Irína sobs loudly.)

Throw me out, please, get rid of me! I can't stand it anymore!

ÓLGA: *(Frightened)* What's the matter? Darling, what's the matter?

IRÍNA: *(Sobbing)* Where is it? Where did it all go? Oh, my God, my God! I've forgotten everything; my head is all mixed up. . . . I can't remember the Italian word for window, or ceiling. . . . I keep forgetting things; every day I forget more and more, and life goes by and it won't ever come back and we're never going to Moscow, never, never. I can see it all now—we're never going to get there. . . . *(Trying to control herself)* Oh, I'm so unhappy. . . . I can't work anymore, I won't work anymore. I'm sick of it, I've had enough! I worked at the telegraph office, and now I work at the municipal building, and I despise it, I hate everything I have to do there. . . . I'm almost twenty-four, I've been working all this time, and my brain has shriveled up; I've lost my looks, I've gotten old, and nothing, nothing! There's no satisfaction in any of it, and the time passes and you realize you'll never have the beautiful life you dreamed of; you just keep digging yourself deeper and deeper into a hole. . . . I'm in despair, I am really in despair! And I don't understand why I'm still alive. I should have killed myself long ago.

ÓLGA: Don't cry, my little girl, don't cry. . . . It tears me apart.

IRÍNA: I'm not crying, I'm not. . . . It's all right. . . . There, see, I'm not crying anymore. It's all right, it's all right!

ÓLGA: Dearest, let me talk to you, as your sister, as a friend. If you want my advice, marry the baron.

(Irína weeps quietly.)

After all, you respect him, you value his friendship. . . . I know he's not very good-looking, but he's a good man, an honest man. . . . People don't marry for love; they marry because they're supposed to. At least I think they do. I would have married without love. It wouldn't have made any difference who it was, as long as he was an honest man. I'd even marry an old man. . . .

IRÍNA: I kept waiting for us to move to Moscow. I knew I'd meet my true love there; I used to dream about him. But you see it was all a lot of nonsense. . . .

ÓLGA: *(Hugging her sister)* Oh, darling, I know, I know. When the baron resigned from the service and first came to see us in his civilian clothes, he was so plain-looking I started to cry. . . . And he asked me what I was crying about, and what could I tell him? But if God brings the two of you together, I would be very happy. You see, things are very different from what you thought, very different.

(Natásha enters with a candle in her hand. She walks silently across the room in a straight line from right to left.)

MÁSHA: *(Sitting)* You'd think she started the fire herself.

ÓLGA: Másha, you are so silly. You are the silliest person in this family! . . . I'm sorry; excuse me.

(Pause.)

MÁSHA: My dear sisters, I want to confess something. I want to bare my soul. I want to confess something to you, and then I never want to say another word about it ever again. I want to tell you everything right now. *(Quietly)* It's my secret, but you should know it anyway . . . I can't keep it to myself anymore. *(Pause)* I'm in love, I'm in love . . . I love that man, the one you saw just now. . . . Well, that's it: I love Vershínin.

ÓLGA: *(Going behind the screen to her bed)* Stop that; I'm not going to listen.

MÁSHA: What can I do! *(Puts her hands to her head)* At first I thought he was strange, then I started feeling sorry for him . . . then I fell in love with him: in love with his voice, with the things he says, with all his problems, with his two little girls . . .

ÓLGA: *(Behind the screen)* I'm not listening. I don't care what you're saying; I'm not listening.

MÁSHA: Oh, Ólga, you're the silly one. I'm in love! It's fate, I guess— I mean it's just my luck. And he loves me. . . . It's all so funny. Don't you think so? Doesn't it strike you funny? *(Takes Irína's hand, draws her close)* Oh, my darling, we'll get through life somehow, no matter what happens to us. . . . When you read about these things in books, it all seems terribly silly and predictable, but when you fall in love yourself, you realize nobody knows anything about it, everyone has to figure it out for herself. My dear sisters, there. I've told you. Now I will never say another word about it. The rest is silence.

(Enter Andréy, then Ferapónt.)

ANDRÉY: What is it you want? I don't understand. . . .

FERAPÓNT: *(At the door, impatient)* Andréy Sergéyich, I already told you ten times.

ANDRÉY: In the first place, when you speak to me, you call me Sir and not Andréy Sergéyich.

FERAPÓNT: Sir. The firemen want to know can they go through the yard to get to the river; they can't keep goin' around and around like they been.

ANDRÉY: All right! Tell them all right.

(Ferapónt leaves.)

What a bore. Where's Ólga?

(Ólga motions from behind the screen.)

I came to ask you for a key to the cupboard. I lost mine. I know you've got that little one.

(Ólga gives him a key in silence. Irína goes behind her screen; pause.)

What a terrible fire! It seems to be dying down. That damn Ferapónt made me so mad, I didn't know how silly I sounded. . . . "Sir . . ." *(Pause)* Why don't you say anything, Ólga? *(Pause)* Look, it's time you stopped this nonsense, all this sulking for no reason. You and Másha are here, Irína's here, fine—let's get this out in the open once and for all. What is it you all have against me? Huh?

ÓLGA: Not now, Andréy. We can talk tomorrow. *(Shaking)* What an awful night!

ANDRÉY: *(Terribly embarrassed)* Don't get upset. I just want to know very calmly what it is you all have against me. Just tell me.

(Vershínin's voice: "Tram-tam-tam.")

MÁSHA: *(Standing; loudly)* Tra-ta-ta! *(To Ólga)* Goodbye, Ólga, God bless you. *(Goes behind the screen and kisses Irína)* Sleep well. Goodbye, Andréy. Leave them alone; they're exhausted. We can talk tomorrow. *(Leaves)*

ÓLGA: Please, Andréy. Let it go until tomorrow. . . . *(Goes behind her screen)* It's time to go to bed.

ANDRÉY: No, I'm going to say what I came for, and then I'll go. Right this minute. In the first place, you've got something against my wife, Natásha, and I've noticed it since the day I got married. Natásha is a lovely person, honest and straightforward and well brought up. In my opinion. I love my wife and I respect her, you understand? I respect her and I want to make sure the rest of you respect her too. I repeat, she is a lovely person, and all your remarks and attitudes—well, excuse me, but you're just being stuck-up. . . . *(Pause)* In the second place, you all seem mad at me because I'm not a scientist or a professor or something. But I have an occupation: I'm a member of the County Council, and I consider that just as honorable and just as important as an intellectual career. I'm a member of the County Council and I'm proud of it, if you want to know. . . . *(Pause)* In the third place—I still have something more to say—I mortgaged this house, and I didn't get your permission. It's my fault and I'm sorry and I ask you to forgive me. I had to do it because I owed a lot of money—thirty-five thousand. I don't gamble anymore, I gave it up, but the main thing is you're all girls, you get a military pension, and I don't! I don't have any income at all. . . .

  (Pause.)

KULÝGIN: *(At the door)* Isn't Másha here? *(Nervously)* Where is she? That's funny. . . . *(Leaves)*

ANDRÉY: You're not listening. Natásha is a fine, honest woman. *(Walks up and down in silence, then stops)* When I got married, I thought that we'd all live happily together . . . happily. . . . But oh, my God . . . *(Starts to cry)* Oh, my dear sisters, my darling sisters, don't believe me, don't believe me. . . . *(Leaves)*

KULÝGIN: *(At the door, nervously)* Where's Másha? Isn't she here? This is very disturbing.

  (He leaves. Sirens. The stage is empty.)

IRÍNA: Ólga! Somebody's knocking.

ÓLGA: It's the doctor. He's drunk.

IRÍNA: What an awful night! *(Pause)* Ólga . . . *(Glances from behind the screen)* Did you hear the news? The brigade is leaving. They're being transferred someplace far away.

ÓLGA: That's just a rumor.

IRÍNA: We'll be left here all alone. . . . Ólga!

ÓLGA: What?

IRÍNA: Ólga dear, I do respect the baron, I do, he's a wonderful man, I will marry him, I promise, only please let's go to Moscow! I beg you, please! There's no place in the world like Moscow! Let's go, Ólga! Please!

CURTAIN.

ACT FOUR

The old garden of the Prózorov house. A long walk lined with fir trees, leading to the river. Across the river is a forest. At the right is the porch of the house; a table with a bottle and glasses. They have just been drinking champagne. It is noon. People occasionally walk through the garden toward the river. A group of five soldiers crosses in a hurry.

Chebutýkin is in good spirits; he remains so for the duration of the act. He sits in a chair in the garden, waiting for someone to send for him; he wears a cap and carries a stick. Irína, Kulýgin, wearing a decoration and with his mustache shaved off, and Túzenbach stand on the porch, saying goodbye to Fedótik and Róhde, who are coming down the steps; both officers are in field uniform.

TÚZENBACH: *(Hugging Fedótik)* You're a good friend; we had good times together. *(Hugs Róhde)* Once more . . . Goodbye, Róhde!

IRÍNA: Till we meet again!

FEDÓTIK: No; this time it's goodbye forever. We'll never see each other again!

KULÝGIN: Who knows? *(Wipes his eyes and smiles)* Even I'm starting to cry.

IRÍNA: We may meet again sometime.

FEDÓTIK: What, in ten or fifteen years? But we won't hardly recognize each other, and we'll be very nervous and embarrassed. *(Takes a picture)* Hold it! Just one more time.

RÓHDE: *(Hugging Túzenbach)* No, we'll never see each other again. . . . *(Kisses Irína's hand)* Thank you for everything; thank you so much!

FEDÓTIK: *(Vexed)* Oh, just hold it a minute!

TÚZENBACH: I hope we do meet again. But you be sure and write us; don't forget.

RÓHDE: *(Looking around the garden)* Goodbye, trees! *(Shouts)* Hey! Hey! *(Pause)* Goodbye, echo!

KULÝGIN: Who knows? Maybe if you're lucky you'll get married there in Poland.... You get a Polish wife, they kiss you all the time and call you *Kokhány. (Laughs)*

FEDÓTIK: *(Looking at his watch)* We've got less than an hour. Solyóny's the only one from our battery going on the barge; the rest of us go with the men. There are three batteries going today and three more tomorrow—and after that peace and quiet will settle down upon the place once again.

TÚZENBACH: As well as god-awful boredom.

RÓHDE: Where's María Sergéyevna?

KULÝGIN: Másha's somewhere out here in the garden.

FEDÓTIK: I've got to say goodbye to her.

RÓHDE: Goodbye. I'd better go, otherwise I'll start crying. *(Hugs Túzenbach and Kulýgin, and kisses Irína's hand)* We had such a wonderful time here....

FEDÓTIK: *(To Kulýgin)* Here's a little souvenir: a little book with a little pencil attached.... We'll go this way, down by the river....

(They go off through the trees, looking around as they go.)

RÓHDE: *(Shouting)* Hey! Hey! Hey-ay!

KULÝGIN: *(Shouting)* Goodbye!

(In the garden, Fedótik and Róhde meet Másha and say goodbye; she goes off with them.)

IRÍNA: They're gone.... *(Sits down on the lowest step)*

CHEBUTÝKIN: They forgot to say goodbye to me.

IRÍNA: Why didn't you say goodbye to them?

CHEBUTÝKIN: I must have forgot. Anyway, I'll see them two days from now; I'm leaving tomorrow. Hmm ... only one day left. But next year I retire, and then I'll come back here and spend the rest of my days with you. Just one more year, and I get my pension.... *(Puts one newspaper in his pocket and takes out another)* I'll come back here and reform my life. I'll be so reserved, so re ... so respectable—a real model of retirement.

IRÍNA: You certainly ought to reform your life, my dear. Anything would help.

CHEBUTÝKIN: You're right. I think so too. *(Sings softly)* Ta-ra-ra boom-de-ay, it's gonna rain today ...

KULÝGIN: Iván Románich, you're unreformable! Unreformable!

CHEBUTÝKIN: Maybe I should take lessons from you. Then I'd do better, eh?

IRÍNA: Fyódor shaved his mustache off. I can't bear it.

KULÝGIN: So?

CHEBUTÝKIN: I could tell you what your face looks like now, but I won't.

KULÝGIN: What do you mean? It's perfectly normal, a *modus vivendi.* Our headmaster shaved his mustache, so when I was promoted I shaved mine. Nobody likes it, but that makes no difference to me whatsoever. I'm quite happy. With a mustache or without a mustache, I am still a happy man.

(*He sits down. Upstage, Andréy wheels a baby carriage.*)

IRÍNA: Iván Románich dear, I'm really worried. What happened yesterday on the boulevard?

CHEBUTÝKIN: What happened? Nothing. Just a lot of nonsense. *(Reads his paper)* What difference does it make?

KULÝGIN: What *I* heard was, Solyóny and the baron met on the boulevard near the theater ...

TÚZENBACH: Please! That's enough, for God's sake ...

(*Makes a gesture of impatience and goes into the house.*)

KULÝGIN: ... near the theater, and Solyóny started teasing the baron, and he couldn't take it anymore and said something insulting ...

CHEBUTÝKIN: I don't know anything about it. It's all a lot of nonsense.

KULÝGIN: ... and they say that Solyóny is in love with Irína and that's why he can't stand the baron. Well, it's understandable. Irína's a wonderful girl. She's very much like my Másha, both very thoughtful. Only your personality is easier, Irína. Of course, Másha has a very good personality too. I love her, I really do.

(*From the garden backstage: Hey! Hey! Yoo-hoo!*)

IRÍNA: *(Shivering)* Everything scares me today. *(Pause)* I'm all ready to leave; I just have to finish packing after lunch. The baron and I are getting married tomorrow, and then we go away to the brick factory, and the day after, I start teaching, and that's when our new life begins. God, I hope it all works out! When I passed the exams for my teaching certificate, I practically cried.... *(Pause)* The cart is coming to pick up my things....

KULÝGIN: Well, I suppose you're doing the right thing, but somehow it doesn't seem all that serious to me. It's just a lot of ideas, not much practice. Anyway, I wish you all the best, sincerely I do.

CHEBUTÝKIN: *(Tenderly)* My dear, my little darling ... You've all gone so far ahead of me, I'll never catch up. I'll stay right here, left behind like a migrating bird that's too old to fly. You fly, sweetheart, you fly! *(Pause)* Fyódor Ilých, you should never have shaved off your mustache.

KULÝGIN: That's enough out of you. *(Sighs)* Well, the troops are leaving today, and then everything will be back the way it used to be. Whatever people say, Másha is a wonderful woman, an honest woman. I love her and thank God for her. People turn out differently.... There's a clerk in the local tax office, Kózyrev his name is; we went to high school together. He never graduated because he couldn't understand the *ut consecutivum* construction. He's terribly poor, not well at all, and whenever I see him I say, "Hello there, *ut consecutivum!*" "Yes," he says *"ut consecutivum,* that's right," and then he coughs. I've been lucky all my life. I'm happy, I've even got a certificate of merit, and now I teach the *ut consecutivum* to others. Of course, I'm intelligent, more intelligent than most, but that won't necessarily make you happy....

(Inside the house, someone is playing "The Maiden's Prayer.")

IRÍNA: And after tomorrow evening I won't ever have to hear her play that "Maiden's Prayer" again; I'll never see Protopópov again.... *(Pause)* Protopópov is sitting right there in the living room; he even showed up today....

KULÝGIN: Has the headmistress gotten home yet?

(In the distance, Másha walks slowly in the garden.)

IRÍNA: No. We sent for her. If you only knew how hard it's been for me, living here alone without Ólga, now that she has an apartment near the high school. She's headmistress and she's busy all day long, and I'm here by myself; I have nothing to do, I'm bored, and I hate that room I'm in.... I made up my mind: if I can't go to Moscow, then that's the way it has to be; it's fate. There's nothing you can do about it.... Nikolái Lvóvich proposed to me, and I accepted. He's a good man; it's amazing how good he is. And all of a sudden I felt happy, less depressed, and I felt like working again. Only last night something happened—nobody will tell me what, but I feel uneasy about it....

CHEBUTÝKIN: Nothing happened. Just a lot of nonsense.

NATÁSHA: *(At the window)* The headmistress is here!

KULÝGIN: Here's the headmistress. Let's go.

> *(He and Irína go into the house.)*

CHEBUTÝKIN: *(Reading his paper and singing softly)* Ta-ra-ra boom-de-ay, it's gonna rain today . . .

> *(Másha comes up; in the distance, Andréy wheels the baby carriage.)*

MÁSHA: He sits there, he just sits and sits. . . .

CHEBUTÝKIN: So what?

MÁSHA: *(Sitting down)* Nothing. *(Pause)* Did you love my mother?

CHEBUTÝKIN: Very much.

MÁSHA: Did she love you?

CHEBUTÝKIN: *(After a pause)* That I can't remember.

MÁSHA: Where's my man? That's the way our old cook, Martha, used to talk about her policeman: "My man." Where's my man?

CHEBUTÝKIN: He's not here yet.

MÁSHA: When you only get your happiness in bits and pieces and then lose it anyway, like me, you begin to get bitter about it. You don't care what you say anymore. *(Touches her breast)* I'm full of anger inside.

> *(Looks at Andréy, who pushes the baby carriage toward them.)*

Look at our little brother, Andréy: all his hopes are gone. A thousand people raise a bell, they spend all kinds of money and effort, and all of a sudden it falls and goes smash. All of a sudden. Nobody's fault. Just like Andréy.

ANDRÉY: I wish they'd quiet down in there. What a racket.

CHEBUTÝKIN: Won't be long now. *(Takes out his watch; he winds it, and it strikes)* I've got an old-fashioned watch; it strikes. The first and second and fifth batteries all leave exactly at one. *(Pause)* And I leave tomorrow.

ANDRÉY: For good?

CHEBUTÝKIN: I don't know. Maybe I'll come back next year. Who the hell knows? . . . And what difference does it make?

> *(Somewhere in the distance, street musicians are playing a harp and a violin.)*

ANDRÉY: The town's almost empty. It seems to be falling asleep. . . . *(Pause)* What happened by the theater yesterday? Everybody's talking about it, and I don't know a thing.

CHEBUTÝKIN: Nothing. It's all a lot of nonsense. Solyóny started teasing the baron, and he lost his temper and insulted Solyóny, and the way it wound up, Solyóny had to challenge him to a duel. *(Looks at his watch)* It ought to be about time now ... twelve-thirty in the state forest across the river—you can see it from here. Bang-bang. *(Laughs)* Solyóny thinks he's Lérmontov; he even writes poetry. I think he carries the joke too far. This is his third duel.

MÁSHA: Whose third duel?

CHEBUTÝKIN: Solyóny's.

MÁSHA: What about the baron?

CHEBUTÝKIN: What about the baron?

(Pause.)

MÁSHA: I'm all confused. All the same, I don't think you should let him. He might hurt the baron, or even kill him.

CHEBUTÝKIN: The baron's a good man, but one baron more, one baron less—what difference does it make? Let 'em fight! It doesn't make any difference.

(Someone shouts in the distance: Yoo-hoo! Hey! Hey!)

That's him. That's Skvortsóv calling. He's the second. He's waiting for me.

ANDRÉY: In my opinion, dueling, or even being the doctor at one, is immoral.

CHEBUTÝKIN: It only looks that way. There's nothing here, we're not here, we don't even exist, it just looks like it. What difference does anything make?

MÁSHA: You just talk, talk, all day long.... *(Walks)* You live in a climate like this, where it always seems to be about to snow, and still you go on talking. *(Stops)* I won't go into that house; I can't.... Tell me when Vershínin gets here.... *(Walks toward the trees)* The birds are migrating already. *(Looks up)* Swans. Or maybe they're geese. You happy things ... *(Walks off)*

ANDRÉY: Our house is emptying out. The officers are going away, you're going away, Irína's getting married. I'll be here all by myself.

CHEBUTÝKIN: What about your wife?

(Ferapónt enters with some papers.)

ANDRÉY: My wife? My wife is ... my wife. She's honest, she's respectable ... well, she's a good woman, but somewhere deep down inside her there's something blind and vicious and mean, some kind of animal. Whatever it is, she's not really a human being. I'm telling you this as a friend; you're the only person I could ever say this to. I love Natásha, you know that, but sometimes she disgusts me so much I get sick to my stomach, and I can't understand what it was ... why I love her. Or why I used to.

CHEBUTÝKIN: *(Standing)* My boy, I'm leaving tomorrow, we may never see each other again, so let me give you a little advice, all right? Put on your hat, pick up your stick, and get out of here. Don't look back. And the farther away you get, the better.

(Solyóny, with two officers, crosses the garden upstage; when he sees Chebutýkin he crosses toward him. The officers continue on.)

SOLYÓNY: Doctor. Time to go. It's already twelve-thirty. *(Greets Andréy)*

CHEBUTÝKIN: I'm coming. I'm sick and tired of you people, every one of you. *(To Andréy)* If anybody wants me, Andréy, tell them I'll be right back. . . . *(Sighs)* You people . . .

SOLYÓNY: "Said the dog to the flea, don't jump on me." *(Begins to walk off with him)* What's the matter with you, old man?

CHEBUTÝKIN: Leave me alone!

SOLYÓNY: Not feeling well?

CHEBUTÝKIN: You go to hell!

SOLYÓNY: No need to get upset; I'm just going to have a little fun with him. All I want to do is wing him like a woodcock. *(Takes out his cologne bottle and rubs some on his hands)* That makes a whole bottle today, and they still smell. My hands smell like a corpse. *(Pause)* Right. . . . How does Lérmontov's poem go? "But every rebel seeks a storm, as if a storm will bring him peace . . . "

CHEBUTÝKIN: Yeah, sure. "Said the dog to the flea, don't jump on me."

(He exits with Solyóny. Shouts in the distance: Yoo-hoo! Hey! Hey!)

FERAPÓNT: Papers to sign . . .

ANDRÉY: *(Irritated)* Leave me alone! For God's sake leave me alone! *(Pushes the baby carriage)*

FERAPÓNT: You got papers, you gotta get 'em signed.

(He goes off after Andréy. Enter Irína, and Túzenbach wearing a straw hat. Kulýgin crosses the garden, shouting, "Másha! Yoohoo!")

TÚZENBACH: He must be the only man in town who's glad the soldiers are going.

IRÍNA: You're probably right. *(Pause)* Our town is emptying out.

TÚZENBACH: Listen, dear, I'll be back in a few minutes.

IRÍNA: Where are you going?

TÚZENBACH: I have to go and . . . I promised them I'd see them off.

IRÍNA: That's not true. Nikolái, why are you acting so funny today? *(Pause)* What happened yesterday by the theater?

TÚZENBACH: *(An impatient gesture)* I'll be back in an hour. *(Kisses her hand)* My beloved . . . *(Looks directly at her)* I have loved you for five years, and I still can't get used to the fact; you seem more and more beautiful to me. You have such wonderful hair! Such eyes! Tomorrow I'll take you away from here, we'll work, we'll be rich, my dreams will all come true. You'll be happy. There's just one thing wrong: you don't love me.

IRÍNA: I can't. I'll be your wife, I'll . . . I'll do what I'm supposed to do, I'll be faithful, but I don't love you. I'm sorry. *(Cries)* I've never been in love. I used to dream about love, I used to dream about it all the time, but now my soul is like a piano that's been locked up and the key's lost. *(Pause)* You look so upset.

TÚZENBACH: I didn't get much sleep last night. I've never been frightened in my life. I've never been afraid of anything, yet now I can't sleep—I'm tormented by the thought of that lost key. Say something. *(Pause)* Say something to me. . . .

IRÍNA: What? It's so quiet here; these old trees just stand in the silence. *(Leans her head on his breast)*

TÚZENBACH: Say something to me. . . .

IRÍNA: What do you want me to say? What?

TÚZENBACH: Anything . . .

IRÍNA: Oh, stop it! Stop it!

(Pause.)

TÚZENBACH: It's funny how the stupidest little things in life can seem so important, all of a sudden and for no reason. Oh, let's not talk about it! I feel happy. It's almost as if I were seeing these trees for the first time in my life; they all seem to be looking at me and waiting for something. What beautiful trees they are! And how beautiful the life around them ought to be.

(Shouts in the distance: Yoo-hoo! Hey! Hey!)

I must go; I'll be late. This tree is dead, but it still moves in the wind with the others. I feel like that: if I die, I mean, I'll still be part of life somehow.... Goodbye, my darling. *(Kisses her hand)* Those papers you gave me are on my desk, under the calendar.

IRÍNA: I'm coming with you.

TÚZENBACH: *(Worried)* No, no! *(Walks off quickly, but stops near the trees)* Irína!

IRÍNA: What?

TÚZENBACH: *(Not knowing what to say)* I didn't have any coffee this morning. Ask them to fix me some, will you?

> *(Walks off quickly. Irína stands thinking for a moment, then wanders into the garden and sits in a swing. Andréy comes in with the baby carriage, followed by Ferapónt.)*

FERAPÓNT: Andréy Sergéyich, they're not my papers. They're official papers. I didn't write them.

ANDRÉY: Oh, whatever happened to the past, when I was young and happy and intelligent, when I dreamed wonderful dreams and thought great thoughts, when my life and my future were shining with hope? What happened to it? We barely begin to live, and all of a sudden we're old and boring and lazy and useless and unhappy. This town has a hundred thousand people in it, and not one of them has ever amounted to a thing. Each one is just like all the others: they eat, drink, sleep, and then they die ... more of them are born, and they eat, drink, and sleep too, and then because they're bored they gossip, they drink, they gamble, they sue each other, the wives cheat on the husbands and the husbands lie, they pretend they don't see anything or hear anything, and the children end up just as aimless and dead as their parents.... *(Angrily, to Ferapónt)* What do you want?

FERAPÓNT: What? Papers! Gotta get 'em signed.

ANDRÉY: I'm sick and tired of you.

FERAPÓNT: Doorman over to the government office was saying ... says this winter in Petersburg it got down to two hundred below, he says.

ANDRÉY: The present is awful, but when I think of the future, I feel better; in the distance a light begins to break, I can see freedom; my children and I will be free from laziness, from drinking too much, from eating too much every Sunday, from too many naps after dinner, from living like insects . . .

FERAPÓNT: Two thousand people froze, he says. Says people was scared. Or maybe it was Moscow. Can't remember.

ANDRÉY: *(Full of tenderness)* My dear sisters, my wonderful sisters! *(Almost crying)* Másha, dear Másha . . .

NATÁSHA: *(Yelling at the window)* Who's making all that noise out there? That you, Andy? You'll wake up little Sophie. *Il ne faut pas faire du bruit, la Sophie est dormée déjà. Vous êtes un ours. (Gets angry)* You want to talk, give the baby carriage to somebody else! Ferapónt, you take that carriage away from him!

FERAPÓNT: Yes, ma'am. *(Takes the carriage)*

ANDRÉY: *(Embarrassed)* I'll be quiet.

NATÁSHA: *(Inside, to the baby)* Bóbik! Naughty Bóbik! Silly Bóbik!

ANDRÉY: All right, I'll look through them and sign what I have to, and you can take them back to the office.

(He goes into the house, looking through the papers, and Ferapónt wheels the carriage.)

NATÁSHA: *(Inside)* Bóbik, how do you say Mama? Oh, sweet thing! And who's that? That's Auntie Ólga! Say Hello, Auntie Ólga!

(Street musicians, a man and a girl, come into the yard. They play a violin and a harp. Vershínin, Ólga, and Anfísa come out on the porch and listen for a while. Irína comes up.)

ÓLGA: Our yard is like a parade ground; people are always coming and going. Nana, give the musicians some money.

ANFÍSA: *(Giving them some money)* God bless you, dears.

(The musicians bow and exit.)

Poor people. *(To Irína)* Rinie, hello! Oh, my dear, what a life, what a life! We're at the high school, Ólga and me, in one of the faculty apartments. The Lord is taking care of my old age. I never lived so good, ever. It's a big apartment, rent-free, and I've got a room and a bed of my own! All rent-free! And when I say my prayers and go to sleep at night . . . My Lord! I'm the happiest woman in the world!

VERSHÍNIN: *(Looking at his watch)* Ólga Sergéyevna, we're leaving right away. I have to go. *(Pause)* I wish you all the best, the very best. . . . Where's María Sergéyevna?

IRÍNA: She's in the garden somewhere. I'll go find her.

VERSHÍNIN: Please. I have to hurry.

ANFÍSA: I'll go look too. *(Shouts)* Másha! Yoo-hoo!

(She and Irína go off into the garden, calling.)

VERSHÍNIN: Well, everything comes to an end. Now it's time to say goodbye. *(Looks at his watch)* The town gave us a sort of farewell lunch, champagne, the mayor made a speech, and I ate and listened, but my heart was here, I kept thinking of you. *(Looks around the garden)* I'm going to miss this place.

ÓLGA: Do you think we'll ever see each other again?

VERSHÍNIN: Probably not. *(Pause)* My wife and my two little girls will stay on another month or so; if they need any help, do you think you could . . . ?

ÓLGA: Yes, yes. Of course. Don't worry. *(Pause)* Tomorrow there won't be a single military man left in town; it will all be a memory. And of course for us it will be the beginning of a new life. . . . *(Pause)* Things never work out the way we want them to. I didn't want to be headmistress, but here I am. Headmistress. And of course I'll never get to Moscow. . . .

VERSHÍNIN: Well . . . Thank you for everything. Forgive me if things were . . . I talked a lot—too much, I know. Forgive me for that too, and don't think badly of me.

ÓLGA: *(Wiping her eyes)* Why doesn't that Másha hurry up . . . ?

VERSHÍNIN: What else can I tell you by way of farewell? Shall we talk a little more? *(Laughs)* Life isn't easy. Sometimes it must seem stupid and hopeless, but we have to remember that it is getting constantly brighter and better, and I don't think the time is far off when it will be completely bright. *(Looks at his watch)* I've really got to go. Mankind is passionately seeking something, and eventually we'll find it. I just hope we find it soon. *(Pause)* We must find a way to join love of work to love of higher things, mustn't we? *(Looks at his watch)* Well, now I must go. . . .

ÓLGA: Here she comes.

(Enter Másha.)

VERSHÍNIN: I came to say goodbye. . . .

(Ólga moves a little distance away, in order not to hinder their leave-taking.)

MÁSHA: *(Looking him in the face)* Goodbye . . .

(A prolonged kiss.)

ÓLGA: Now, now, that's enough. . . .

(Másha sobs violently.)

VERSHÍNIN: Write me . . . don't forget. Let me go—I've got to go. . . . Ólga Sergéyevna, take her—I've got to go. . . . I'm late. *(Shaken, kisses Ólga's hand, embraces Másha once again, and goes away quickly)*

ÓLGA: Now, now, Másha! Stop, dear . . .

(Enter Kulýgin.)

KULÝGIN: *(Embarrassed)* It's all right, let her cry, it's all right. . . . Másha dearest, my sweet Másha . . . You're my wife, and I'm happy, no matter what happened. . . . I'm not complaining; I haven't a single reproach to make to you—Ólga is my witness. . . . Let's start life over again just the way it was before. I'll never say a single word about this, never. . . .

MÁSHA: *(Holding back her sobs)* "Beside the sea there stands a tree, and on that tree a golden chain . . . a golden chain. . . ." I'm going crazy. . . . "Beside the sea . . . a golden chain."

ÓLGA: Calm down, Másha, calm down. Give her a drink of water.

MÁSHA: I won't cry anymore.

KULÝGIN: She's not going to cry anymore . . . that's good.

(A muffled shot is heard in the distance.)

MÁSHA: "Beside the sea there stands a tree, and on that tree a golden chain . . . an educated cat . . . a golden tree. . . ." I'm all confused. *(Takes a drink of water)* My life is a disaster. . . . I don't need anything anymore. . . . I'm all right now. . . . What difference does it make? What does that mean, "beside the sea . . ."? Why can't I get it out of my head? I'm all confused.

(Irína comes in.)

ÓLGA: Calm down, Másha. That's a good girl. . . . Let's go lie down.

MÁSHA: *(Angrily)* I won't go in there. *(Sobs, but stops immediately)* I'm not going into that house. . . .

IRÍNA: Let's just sit here for a moment; we don't have to say anything. I'm going away tomorrow, remember.

(Pause.)

KULÝGIN: Yesterday I took this away from one of the boys at school. *(Takes out a fake beard and mustache and puts it on)* It looks just like the German teacher. *(Laughs)* Doesn't it? Those boys are so funny.

MÁSHA: It really does look like your German.

ÓLGA: *(Laughing)* It really does.

(Másha cries.)

IRÍNA: Don't, Másha!

KULÝGIN: Exactly like him.

(Enter Natásha.)

NATÁSHA: *(To the maid, inside the house)* What? Little Sophie is in there with Protopópov, so tell Andréy to take care of Bóbik. Such a fuss, having children! *(To Irína)* You're going away tomorrow, Irína, what a shame. Why don't you stay a few days longer?

(She sees Kulýgin and screams; he laughs and takes off the fake beard.)

Oh, you.... You gave me a scare! *(To Irína)* I've gotten used to having you around, you know that; it won't be easy seeing you go. I'm having them move Andréy into your room ... *and* his violin; he can screech away in there! And little Sophie gets his room. She's just the sweetest thing! Such a darlin' little baby; this morning she looked right at me with those big eyes of hers and said: "Mama!"

KULÝGIN: She is a charming child, I must say.

NATÁSHA: That means tomorrow I'll be here all by myself. *(Takes a deep breath)* First thing I'm going to do is have them cut down all these old trees, especially that dead one. It's so ugly and scary, especially after dark. *(To Irína)* Sweetie, that belt doesn't do a thing for you. Not a thing. You need something more stylish, something with a little color in it.... And then I'm going to have them plant lots and lots of flowers, all over the place, so it'll smell nice and pretty.... *(Angrily)* Who left this fork out here? *(Goes into the house, calling to the maid)* I want to know who left this fork out here! Do you hear me? Shut up when I'm talking to you!

KULÝGIN: She does get mad.

(Music plays, a march; everyone listens.)

ÓLGA: They're going away.

(Enter Chebutýkin.)

MÁSHA: Our men. They're going away. Well ... I hope they have a pleasant trip. *(To her husband)* Let's go home. Where's my hat and my coat?

KULÝGIN: I took them inside.... I'll get them right away. *(Goes into the house)*

ÓLGA: Yes, time to go. Now we can all go home.

CHEBUTÝKIN: Ólga Sergéyevna!

ÓLGA: What? *(Pause)* What?

CHEBUTÝKIN: Nothing, it's just ... I don't know how to tell you.... *(Whispers in her ear)*

ÓLGA: *(Horrified)* It's not true!

CHEBUTÝKIN: Yes, it is. What a mess. I'm all upset, I'm all worn out. I don't want to talk about it anymore.... *(Annoyed)* Anyway, what difference does it make?

MÁSHA: What happened?

ÓLGA: *(Hugging Irína)* What a horrible day! Darling, I don't know how to tell you....

IRÍNA: What? What is it? For God's sake, tell me! *(Cries)*

CHEBUTÝKIN: The baron was killed in the duel.

IRÍNA: I knew it, I knew it....

CHEBUTÝKIN: *(Sitting on a bench upstage)* I'm all worn out.... *(Takes a newspaper out of his pocket)* Let 'em cry. *(Sings softly)* Ta-ra-ra boom-de-ay, it's gonna rain today ... What difference does it make?

(The three sisters stand close to one another.)

MÁSHA: Oh, listen to the music! They're going away. One of them has already gone away for good. We're alone, and now we have to start our lives all over again ... we have to go on living....

IRÍNA: Someday everyone will know what this was all about, all this suffering—it won't be a mystery anymore—but until then we have to go on living ... and working, just keep on working. I'll go away tomorrow, by myself. I'll teach school and devote my whole life to people who need it ... who may need it. It's autumn; winter will come, the snow will fall, and I will go on working and working.

ÓLGA: The music sounds so happy, so positive, it makes you want to live. Oh, dear God. The day will come when we'll go away forever too. People will forget all about us, they'll forget what we looked like and what our voices sounded like and how many of us there were, but our suffering will turn to joy for the people who live after us, their lives will be happy and peaceful, and they'll remember us kindly and bless us. My dears, my dear sisters, life isn't over yet. We'll go on living. The music sounds so happy, so joyful, it almost seems as if a minute more, and we'd know why we live, why we suffer. If only we knew. If only we knew!

(The music grows softer and softer; Kulýgin, happy, smiling, brings out Másha's hat and coat; Andréy wheels another baby carriage, with Bóbik.)

CHEBUTÝKIN: *(Singing softly)* Ta-ra-ra boom-de-ay, it's gonna rain today . . . *(Reads his newspaper)* What difference does it make? What difference does it make?

ÓLGA: If only we knew! If only we knew!

CURTAIN.

THREE SISTERS: NOTES

Page 259. Irína's birthday. The Russians traditionally celebrated a name day, the feast of the saint a person is named after. A name-day party is the social equivalent of our birthday party.

Page 262. "A writer named Dobrolyúbov." Nikolái Dobrolyúbov (1836–1861) was the chief literary critic of the influential journal *Sovreménnik (The Contemporary)*. He was read by all progressive thinkers. That Chebutýkin doesn't know what he wrote is a good indication of the doctor's shallowness.

Page 263. "Beside the sea . . ." Here and throughout the play, Másha quotes the first two lines from *Ruslan and Liudmilla*, a well-known fairy-tale poem by Alexander Pushkin (1799–1837), Russia's most famous poet. On page 274, when the sound of the spinning top makes Másha repeat the lines, I have added the next two lines of the poem, since they explain why the first two stick in her head. Pushkin's poems have always been widely known and memorized, and most educated Russians, hearing the first two lines, would automatically supply the two that follow. The educated cat, going around in circles on a chain, is clearly Másha's image of herself.

Page 263. "Said the dog to the flea, don't jump on me." Solyóny quotes here from a fable by Ivan Krylov. Literally, the lines are: "He didn't catch his breath before the bear jumped on him." They rhyme, and the main point here is the rhyme and the appositeness of the sneering retort to Másha. The image of the bear is incidental, although I have heard long discussions of this quote at rehearsals, where the savage Russian bear was taken as a vast symbol for Solyóny and Russian society. But Chekhov had used this quote before; a character in a story goes around spouting these lines, and about him Chekhov notes: "He had an irritating habit; in the middle of a conversation he would pronounce loudly some phrase or other that had nothing to do with what he was talking about." Chekhov is concerned here with a speech characteristic, not with symbols.

Page 264. "A silver service! How awful!" A Russian tea service consists of an urn designed to keep water hot, called a samovar, a teapot that is kept warm on its top, and perhaps a tray. So much "Russianness" is attached to samovars in America that we often miss Chekhov's point: this is the kind of elaborate present offered at bridal showers or silver wedding anniversaries, and it seems especially inappropriate for the doctor to offer it to a young girl. A fancy American silver tea service—tray, teapot, sugar, and creamer—would probably make the point clear for an American audience and save the prop people the job of tracking down a samovar.

Page 266. "In Nóvo-Dévichy Cemetery." Nóvo-Dévichy is a famous cemetery in Moscow. Chekhov himself is now buried there.

Page 270. *"Feci quod potui, faciant meliora potentes."* Kulýgin teaches Latin and quotes it whenever he can. This phrase means: "I have done my best; let others do better if they can." *"Mens sana in corpore sano"* means: "A healthy mind in a healthy body."

Page 276. "Tonight's carnival." Mardi gras, just before the beginning of Lent, was celebrated in old Russia as elsewhere with parties and costume parades.

Page 283. "You know what Gogol said." The line is from a Gogol short story with a long name, "The Tale of How Iván Ivánovich Had a Fight with Iván Nikofórovich."

Page 283. "Balzac was married in Berdíchev." Balzac did, in fact, get married in what was then part of the Russian Empire.

Page 285. "The Panama scandal." Baihot, the French minister of public works, was sent to prison in 1893 for accepting a bribe from a group of developers who hoped to build a canal in Panama. On his release, in 1898, he published his diary under the title "Notes from a Prison Cell."

Page 286. *"Je vous prie . . ."* Natásha says, in rather stilted French, "I beg of you, excuse me, Másha, but your manners are a little unrefined." In her next speech she goes on to say, in even worse French, "It seems my Bobik no longer sleeps."

Page 286. "I am strange, we all are strange! Forget thy wrath, Aléko!" Solyóny quotes correctly from Alexánder Griboyédev's play *Woe from Wit,* then makes a garbled reference to Aléko, the hero of Pushkin's poem "Gypsies."

Page 287. "I have the soul of Lérmontov." The poet Mikhaíl Lérmontov (1814–1841) was the great Russian example of the Byronic hero and met his early death in a duel. While this remark might foreshadow the duel in Act Four, it's important to recall Chekhov's remark about these lines: "Solyóny thinks he looks like Lérmontov, but of course he doesn't. It's all in his head."

Page 287. "A meat dish called *chekhartmá*. . . .*Cheremshá* . . . a kind of onion."
Both Solyóny and Chebutýkin are correct in their use of these Georgian
words. *Chekhartmá* is a meat dish, and *cheremshá* is a kind of onion.
Page 288. "*Akh, vy séni.* . . ." This is a well-known Russian folk song. The
words mean literally: "Oh, my little front porch, my new front porch of
maple wood and latticework . . ." but they're no more significant than
"Polly wolly doodle all the day" is in English.
Here's the tune and a phonetic rendering of the words:

AKH, VEE SAY-NEE, MY-EE SAY-NEE, SAY-NEE NO-VEE-YEH MY-EE, SAY-NEE

NO-VEE-YEH, KLEH-NO-VEE-YEH, 'REH-   SHAW-CHA-TEE - YEH

Page 292. "*O, fallacem hominum spem!*" means: "Oh, mistaken hope of men!"
Page 297. "*In vino veritas*" means: "There is truth in wine."
Page 298. "Don't you like this little fig . . ." The doctor sings this line, but the
actor will have to make up his own tune. One of the actors at the Moscow
Art Theater wrote to Chekhov asking him about this line. Chekhov
answered: "Chebutýkin should sing only the words 'Don't you like this little fig I'm giving you.' They're from an operetta I heard a while ago at the
Hermitage Theater, I can't remember the name. . . . He shouldn't sing any
more than that, otherwise he'll spoil his exit."
Page 299. "*Lyubví vse vósrasty pokórny, yeyó porývy blagotvórny* . . ." Vershínin
sings two lines from Tchaikovsky's opera *Eugene Onegin*. They mean literally: "Love is appropriate to any age, its delights are beneficent." They are
from the famous aria sung by Prince Gremin in Act Three; any complete
recording of the opera has it, and it is often included in basso recitals.
Here's a transliteration:
"Lyub-*vee* syeh *voz*-ras-tee pa-*kor*-nee, yeh-*yaw* pa-*ree*-vee bla-got-*vor*-nee . . ."
Page 299. "*Tram-tam-tam* . . ." Ólga Knipper, who first played Másha, wrote
Chekhov to ask what these lines mean. He wrote back: "Vershínin pronounces the words *tram-tam-tam* as a kind of question and you as a kind of
answer, and this seems to you such an original joke that you say your *tram-
tam* with a laugh . . . you should say *tram-tam* and start to laugh, but not
out loud, just a little, almost to yourself."
Page 300. "*Omnia mea mecum porto*" means "All I own is what I carry with me."
Page 308. "I won't ever have to hear her play that 'Maiden's Prayer' again."
Natásha is playing a nineteenth-century parlor favorite: "*La Prière d'une
Vierge*" by Baranowski.

Page 311. "But every rebel seeks a storm . . ." Solyóny recites (he misquotes slightly, as usual) from Lérmontov's famous poem "The Sail."

Page 314. "*Il ne faut pas faire du bruit, la Sophie est dormée déjà. Vous êtes un ours.*" Again, in Natásha's bad French: "Stop making noise, Sophie is asleep already. You sound like a bear."

The Dangers of Tobacco

A MONOLOGUE IN ONE ACT

1902

CHARACTERS

Iván Ivánovich Nyúkhin, the husband of a wife who runs a music and boarding school for young ladies

The stage represents a lecture hall in a small-town social club.
Nyúkhin makes an impressive entrance. He has long side-whiskers
but no mustache and is dressed in an old, worn tailcoat. He crosses
to the lectern, bows, and adjusts his vest.

NYÚKHIN: Ladies and—so to speak—gentlemen. *(Scratches his whiskers)* Someone suggested to my wife that it might be nice if I gave some sort of lecture here today, open to the general public, with the proceeds to go to charity. That's fine with me. A lecture? Why not? Really, what do I care? Of course, you understand I am not a professor, I am devoid of academic degrees, but nonetheless, for almost thirty years now, and at considerable risk to my health and whatever, mind you, I have been working on problems of a scientific nature, pondering them, and occasionally I even write scholarly articles, if you can believe that ... what I mean is, not exactly scholarly but—if you'll excuse the expression—sort of scholarly. As a matter of fact, I have written a very interesting article entitled "The Problem with Insects." My daughters liked it a lot, especially the part about the bedbugs. I read it to them. Of course, then I tore it up. You can write about bedbugs all you want, you know, but the only thing that will get rid of them is boric acid. And we even had them in the piano.

As the subject of my lecture today I have chosen—I think I may put it that way—the harmful effects which can be observed in human beings as a direct result of indulgence in tobacco. I myself smoke, but my wife told me I should speak today about the dangers of tobacco, so of course there's nothing more to say, is there? Dangers? Why not? What do I care? You on the other hand, ladies and gentlemen, will, I hope, devote your serious attention to what I am about to say, otherwise I really don't think we'll get anywhere. If there is anyone here who has qualms about a dry scientific lecture, anyone who doesn't like the idea, feel perfectly free not to listen, or leave if you want. *(Adjusts his vest)* Let me make a special point of reminding any physicians who may be present that my lecture contains many useful observations for them, since tobacco, aside from its harmful effects, is also used in medicine. For instance, a fly placed in a container of tobacco will die, usually from nervous convulsions.

Tobacco is, so to speak, a plant. . . . Whenever I give a lecture, my right eye twitches a little. Sorry. Please don't pay any attention; it's just nerves. I am a very nervous man, generally speaking, and my eye began twitching in 1889, on September 13, actually: that was the day my wife gave birth to Barbara—that's our fourth daughter. All my daughters were born on the thirteenth. Nonetheless *(Looks at his watch)*, since our time is short, I think we had better stick to the subject of our lecture. I should point out, however, that my wife runs a music school and a private boarding school—that is, not exactly what you'd call a school but something . . . sort of like a school. Now, just between you and me, my wife likes to complain about never having enough of anything, but the fact is she has managed to put, so to speak, a little something aside, maybe forty or fifty thousand. Of course, I don't have a penny to my name, not one. . . . But what's the point of talking about it?

At the boarding school, I am in charge of the housekeeping department. I make all the purchases, take care of the help, do the accounts, manufacture the students' notebooks, keep the bedbugs under control, walk my wife's dog, catch the mice. . . . Last night one of my duties was to issue a premeasured amount of flour and butter to the cook, since the schedule called for pancakes for breakfast. Now, to make a long story short, today, when the pancakes were ready, my wife sent word down to the kitchen that three of our boarders would not be eating pancakes, since they had swollen glands. The result of this of course was that we had a few extra pancakes, and what exactly were we supposed to do with them? Well, at first my wife told us to put them in one of the storage closets, and then she thought it over; she thought it over and she said, "Oh, go ahead and eat them yourself, you old bag of bones." That's what she calls me when she's in a bad mood: bag of bones, or sometimes snake in the grass, or sometimes Satan. Now, I ask you, do I look like Satan? And she's always in a bad mood. Well, I didn't just eat those pancakes; I gobbled them down without even chewing, because I'm always very hungry. Yesterday, for instance, she wouldn't let me have any dinner. You're just an old bag of bones, she said; what's the use of feeding you?

However *(Looks at his watch)*, we seem to be gossiping, and I think we've gotten a little off the topic. Let us continue. Although I'm sure you'd all rather be listening to some music—some show tunes or an aria ... *(Sings)* "Our eyes shall never waver in the heat of the battle ..." I can't remember exactly what that's from.... Oh, by the way, I forgot to tell you that at my wife's music school I am not only in charge of the housework but I also teach all the courses in mathematics, physics, chemistry, geography, history, solfeggio, literature, and so on. We also offer dance, voice, and drawing lessons: my wife charges extra for them, although I am the dancing and voice instructor as well. Our school of music is located on Mutt Street, number thirteen Mutt Street. That's probably why my life is such a failure, living as I do at number thirteen. And all my daughters were born on the thirteenth, and our house has thirteen windows....

Well, what's the point of talking about it? If you'd like to discuss any of this with my wife, you can stop by the school anytime; a school catalog is available from the man at the door for thirty cents a copy. *(Takes a few brochures from his pocket)* Or you can get them from me if you'd like! Thirty cents a copy. Would anybody care for one? *(Pause)* No? Twenty cents a copy? *(Pause)* Too bad. That's right, number thirteen Mutt Street. I'm afraid I haven't been much of a success at anything; I've gotten old and stupid. And here I am, giving a lecture. I look perfectly happy up here, but what I'd really like to do is start screaming at the top of my lungs or run away someplace where nobody could ever find me. And there's nobody I can complain to; there are times when I even feel like crying.... You say, Well, there's always your daughters.... What daughters? I try to talk to them, they only laugh at me. My wife has seven daughters. No, excuse me, I think it's six.... *(Brightens)* No, seven! Anna, the oldest, she's twenty-seven, and the youngest is seventeen.

Ladies and gentlemen! *(Looks around)* I am not happy. I have grown into a half-wit, a non-wit, but essentially what you see before you is a very happy father. Essentially that's the way it's supposed to be, and I certainly wouldn't want anything different. If only you knew! I have lived with my wife for thirty-three years, and I can say that those were the best years of my life ... well, not exactly the best, you know, but ... so to speak. They have passed, to make a long story short, in one happy twinkling of an eye, and frankly I don't give a good goddamn anymore. *(Looks around)* Anyway, I don't think she's here yet—yes, she is *not here*—so I can say whatever I feel like.... I'm really afraid. She terrifies me whenever she looks at me. And here's another thing: all my daughters are unmarried; they've been unmarried for a long time, which is probably because they're bashful but also because men never get the chance to meet them. My wife won't give parties, she never invites anyone to dinner, she's so cheap; she's a hateful, stuck-up old shrew, and that's why no one ever comes to see us, but . . . now, this is confidential, just between you and me *(Goes to the edge of the platform)* . . . you can meet my wife's daughters on all major holidays at their aunt Natalie's—she's the one with rheumatism, who always wears a yellow dress with little black dots that makes her look as if she had cockroaches crawling all over her. She always serves something to eat, and if my wife's not around, you can also . . . *(Gestures taking a drink)* Of course, I have to point out to you that it only takes one little shot to get me drunk, which makes me feel good inside, but at the same time I get so sad I can't even tell you: I start thinking about when I was young, for some reason, and for some reason it makes me want to run away. If only you knew how it makes me want to run away! *(With intensity)* Run away! Just dump everything and run and never look back. Where? I don't care where! Just run away from this cheap, vulgar, filthy life that has turned me into a pathetic old wreck, a pathetic old half-wit, run away from that stupid, petty, evil, evil miser of a woman I'm married to, run away from a wife who's tormented me for thirty-three years, from the music lessons and the kitchen and my wife having all the money, and from all the ugly, mean things I have to live with . . . until I get to some-place far away, and then I'll stop in a field somewhere and stand there like a tree or a fence post, like a scarecrow, and stare up at the enormous sky, stand there all night just looking at the moon, the quiet, shining moon, and forget it all . . . oh, if only I could for-get it all! If only I could get out of this ugly old tailcoat I got mar-ried in thirty-three years ago *(Tears off the coat and throws it to the floor),* the one I give lectures in where the proceeds go to charity. Take that! *(Stomps on the coat)* And that! I know, I'm old, I'm poor, I'm pathetic, just like this vest—the back is all worn and falling apart. *(Turns to show his back)* But I don't need a thing! I'm better than all this, and I'm an honest man, I used to be young, I was smart, I went to the university, I had dreams, I wanted to be a decent human being. . . . Now I don't want anything! The only thing I need is peace and quiet . . . just a little peace and quiet!

(Looks into the wings and quickly puts the coat back on) How-ever, my wife is now waiting in the wings. She's here. She's wait-

ing for me. *(Looks at his watch)* Well, I see my time is about up. . . . If she asks, would you mind saying that the lecture . . . I'd be very grateful if you wouldn't mind saying that the old bag of bones—me, I mean—behaved . . . with dignity. *(Looks toward the wings and coughs)* She's watching.

(Raises his voice) As a consequence of which—the fact, I mean, that tobacco contains a powerful toxic agent, as I have just described—we see that smoking is by no means advisable, and I hope, so to speak, that my lecture here today on the dangers of tobacco will produce a beneficial effect. That's all I have to say. *Dixi et animam levavi. (Bows grandly and exits)*

CURTAIN.

The Cherry Orchard

A COMEDY IN FOUR ACTS

1903

CHARACTERS

Liubóv Ranyévskaya, who owns the estate

Ánya, her daughter, 17 years old

Várya, her adopted daughter, 24 years old

Leoníd Gáyev, Liubóv's brother

Yermolái Lopákhin, a businessman

Pétya Trofímov, a graduate student

Borís Semyónov-Píshchik, who owns land in the neighborhood

Carlotta, the governess

Semyón Yepikhódov, an accountant

Dunyásha, the maid

Firs, the butler, 87 years old

Yásha, the valet

A homeless man

The stationmaster

The postmaster

Guests, servants

The action takes place on Ranyévskaya's estate.

ACT ONE

A room they still call the nursery. A side door leads to Ánya's room. Almost dawn; the sun is about to rise. It's May; the cherry orchard is already in bloom, but there's a chill in the air. The windows are shut. Enter Dunyásha with a lamp, and Lopákhin with a book in his hand.

LOPÁKHIN: The train's finally in, thank God. What time is it?

DUNYÁSHA: Almost two. *(She blows out the lamp)* It's getting light.

LOPÁKHIN: How late is the train this time? Must be at least two hours. *(He yawns and stretches)* That was dumb. I came over on purpose just to meet them at the station, and then I fell asleep. Sat right here and fell asleep. Too bad. You should have woke me up.

DUNYÁSHA: I thought you already left. *(She listens)* Listen, that must be them.

LOPÁKHIN: *(He listens)* No, they still have the luggage to get, and all that. *(Pause)* She's been away five years now; no telling how she's changed. She was always a good person. Very gentle, never caused a fuss. I remember one time when I was a kid, fifteen or so, they had my old man working in the store down by the village, and he hit me, hard, right in the face; my nose started to bleed. And we had to come up here to make a delivery or something; he was still drunk. And Liubóv Andréyevna—she wasn't much older than I was, kind of thin—she brought me inside the house, right into the nursery here, and washed the blood off my face for me. "Don't cry," she told me. "Don't cry, poor boy; you'll live long enough to get married." *(Pause)* Poor boy ... Well, my father was poor, but take a look at me now, all dressed up, brand-new suit and tan shoes. Silk purse out of a sow's ear, I guess ... I'm rich now, got lots of money, but when you think about it, I guess I'm still a poor boy from the country. *(He flips the pages of the book)* I tried reading this book, couldn't figure out a word it said. Put me to sleep.

(Pause.)

DUNYÁSHA: The dogs were barking all night long; they know their mistress is coming home.

LOPÁKHIN: Don't be silly.

DUNYÁSHA: I'm so excited I'm shaking. I may faint.

LOPÁKHIN: You're getting too full of yourself, Dunyásha. Look at you, all dressed up like that, and that hairdo. You watch out for that. You got to remember who you are.

(*Enter Yepikhódov with a bunch of flowers; he wears a jacket and tie and brightly polished boots, which squeak loudly. As he comes in, he drops the flowers.*)

YEPIKHÓDOV: (*Picking up the flowers*) Here. The gardener sent these over; he said put them on the dining room table. (*He gives the flowers to Dunyásha*)

LOPÁKHIN: And bring me a beer.

DUNYÁSHA: Right away. (*She goes out*)

YEPIKHÓDOV: It's freezing this morning—it must be in the thirties— and the cherry blossoms are out already. I cannot abide the climate here. (*He sighs*) I never have abided it, ever. (*Beat*) Yermolái Alexéyich, would you examinate something for me, please? Day before yesterday I bought myself a new pair of boots, and listen to them squeak, will you? I just cannot endear it. Do you know anything I can put on them?

LOPÁKHIN: Will you shut up? You drive me crazy.

YEPIKHÓDOV: Every day something awful happens to me. It's like a habit. But I don't complain. I just try to keep smiling.

(*Enter Dunyásha; she brings Lopákhin a beer.*)

YEPIKHÓDOV: I'm going. (*He bumps into a chair, which falls over*) You see? (*He seems proud of it*) You see what I was referring about? Excuse my expressivity, but what a concurrence. It's almost uncanny, isn't it? (*He leaves*)

DUNYÁSHA: You know what? That Yepikhódov proposed to me!

LOPÁKHIN: Oh?

DUNYÁSHA: I just don't know what to think. He's kind of nice. . . . He's a real quiet boy, but then he opens his mouth, and you can't ever understand what he's talking about. I mean, it sounds nice, but it just doesn't make any sense. I do like him, though. Kind of. And he's crazy about me. It's funny, you know, every day something awful happens to him. People around here call him Double Trouble.

LOPÁKHIN: (*He listens*) That must be them.

DUNYÁSHA: It's them! Oh, I don't know what's the matter with me! I feel so funny; I'm cold all over.

LOPÁKHIN: It really is them this time. Let's go; we should be there at the door. You think she'll recognize me? It's been five years.

DUNYÁSHA: *(Excited)* Oh, my God! I'm going to faint! I think I'm going to faint!

(The sound of two carriages outside the house. Lopákhin and Dunyásha hurry out. The stage is empty. The sound outside gets louder. Firs, leaning heavily on his cane, crosses the room, heading for the door; he wears an old-fashioned butler's livery and a top hat; he says something to himself, but you can't make out the words. The offstage noise and bustle increases. A voice: "Here we are . . . this way." Enter Liubóv Andréyevna, Ánya, and Carlotta, dressed in traveling clothes. Várya wears an overcoat, and a kerchief on her head. Gáyev, Semyónov-Píshchik, Lopákhin, Dunyásha with a bundle and an umbrella, Servants with the luggage—all pass across the stage.)

ÁNYA: Here we are. Oh, Mama, do you remember this room?

LIUBÓV ANDRÉYEVNA: The nursery!

VÁRYA: It's freezing; my hands are like ice. We kept your room exactly as you left it, Mama. The white and lavender one.

LIUBÓV ANDRÉYEVNA: The nursery! Oh, this house, this beautiful house! I slept in this room when I was a child. . . . *(She weeps)* And I feel like a child again! *(She hugs Gáyev, Várya, then Gáyev again)* And Várya hasn't changed at all—still looks like a nun! And Dunyásha dear! Of course I remember you! *(She hugs Dunyásha)*

GÁYEV: The train was two hours late. What kind of efficiency is that? Eh?

CARLOTTA: And my dog loves nuts.

SEMYÓNOV-PÍSHCHIK: Really! I don't believe it!

(Everyone leaves, except Ánya and Dunyásha.)

DUNYÁSHA: We've been up all night, waiting. . . . *(She takes Ánya's coat and hat)*

ÁNYA: I've been up for four nights now. . . . I didn't sleep the whole trip. And now I'm freezing.

DUNYÁSHA: When you went away it was still winter, it was snowing, and now look! Oh, sweetie, you're back! *(She laughs and hugs Ánya)* I've been up all night, waiting to see you. Sweetheart, I just can't wait—I've got to tell you what happened. I can't wait another minute!

ÁNYA: *(Wearily)* Now what?

DUNYÁSHA: Yepikhódov proposed the day after Easter! He wants to marry me!

ÁNYA: That's all you ever think about. . . . *(She fixes her hair)* I lost all my hairpins. . . .

DUNYÁSHA: I just don't know what to do about him. He really, really loves me!

ÁNYA: *(Looking through the door to her room)* My own room, just as if I'd never left. I'm back home! Tomorrow I'll get up and go for a walk in the orchard. I just wish I could get some sleep. I didn't sleep the whole trip, I was so worried.

DUNYÁSHA: Pétya's here. He got here day before yesterday.

ÁNYA: *(Joyfully)* Pétya!

DUNYÁSHA: He's staying out in the barn. Said he didn't want to bother anybody. *(She looks at her watch)* He told me to get him up, but Várya said not to. You let him sleep, she said.

(Enter Várya. She has a big bunch of keys attached to her belt.)

VÁRYA: Dunyásha, go get the coffee. Mama wants her coffee.

DUNYÁSHA: Oh, I forgot! *(She goes out)*

VÁRYA: You're back. Thank God! You're home again! *(She embraces Ánya)* My angel is home again! My beautiful darling!

ÁNYA: You won't believe what I've been through!

VÁRYA: I can imagine.

ÁNYA: I left just before Easter; it was cold. Carlotta never shut up the whole trip; she kept doing those silly tricks of hers. I don't know why you had to stick me with her.

VÁRYA: Darling, you couldn't go all that way by yourself! You're only seventeen!

ÁNYA: We got to Paris, it was cold and snowy, and my French is just awful! Mama was living in this fifth-floor apartment, we had to walk up, we get there and there's all these French people, some old priest reading some book, and it was crowded, and everybody was smoking these awful cigarettes—and I felt so sorry for Mama, I just threw my arms around her and couldn't let go. And she was so glad to see me, she cried—

VÁRYA: *(Almost crying)* I know, I know . . .

ÁNYA: And she sold the villa in Mentón, and the money was already gone, all of it! And I spent everything you gave me for the trip; I haven't got a thing left. And Mama still doesn't understand! We have dinner at the train station, and she orders the most expensive things on the menu, and then she tips the waiters a ruble each! And Carlotta does the same! And Yásha expects the same treatment—he's just awful. You know, Yásha, that flunky of Mama's—he came back with us.

VÁRYA: I saw him, the lazy good-for-nothing.

ÁNYA: So what happened? Did you get the interest paid?

VÁRYA: With what?

ÁNYA: Oh, my God, my God . . .

VÁRYA: The place goes up for sale in August.

ÁNYA: Oh, my God.

(Lopákhin sticks his head in the doorway and makes a mooing sound, then goes away.)

VÁRYA: Oh, that man! I'd like to— *(She shakes her fist)*

ÁNYA: *(She hugs her)* Várya, did he propose yet? *(Várya shakes her head no)* But you know he loves you! Why don't the two of you just sit down and be honest with each other? What are you waiting for?

VÁRYA: I don't think anything will ever come of it. He's always so busy, he never has time for me. He just isn't interested! It's hard for me when I see him, but I don't care anymore. Everybody talks about us getting married, people even congratulate me, but there's nothing. . . . I mean, it's all just a dream. *(A change of tone)* Oh, you've got a new pin, a little bee. . . .

ÁNYA: *(With a sigh)* I know. Mama bought it for me. *(She goes into her room and starts to giggle, like a little girl)* You know what? In Paris I went for a ride in a balloon!

VÁRYA: Oh, darling, you're back! My angel is home again!

(Dunyásha comes in, carrying a tray with coffee things, and begins setting them out on the table. Várya stands at the doorway and talks to Ánya in the other room.)

You know, dear, I spend the livelong day trying to keep this house going, and all I do is dream. I want to see you married off to somebody rich, then I can rest easy. And I think then I'll go away by myself, maybe live in a convent, or just go traveling: Kiev, Moscow . . . spend all my time making visits to churches. I'd start walking and just go and go and go. That would be heaven!

ÁNYA: Listen to the birds in the orchard! What time is it?

VÁRYA: It must be almost three. You should get some sleep, darling.

(She goes into Ánya's room) Yes, that would be heaven!

(Enter Yásha with a suitcase and a lap robe. He walks with an affected manner.)

YÁSHA: I beg pardon! May I intrude?

DUNYÁSHA: I didn't even recognize you, Yásha. You got so different there in France.

YÁSHA: *I'm* sorry—who are you exactly?

DUNYÁSHA: When you left, I wasn't any higher than this. *(She holds her hand a distance from the floor)* I'm Dunyásha. You know, Dunyásha Kozoyédov. Don't you remember me?

YÁSHA: Well! You sure turned out cute, didn't you? *(He looks around carefully, then grabs and kisses her; she screams and drops a saucer; Yásha leaves in a hurry)*

VÁRYA: *(At the door, annoyed)* Now what happened?

DUNYÁSHA: *(Almost in tears)* I broke a saucer.

VÁRYA: *(Ironically)* Well, isn't that lucky!

ÁNYA: *(Entering)* Somebody should let Mama know Pétya's here.

VÁRYA: I told them to let him sleep.

ÁNYA: *(Lost in thought)* Father died six years ago, and a month later our little brother, Grísha, drowned. Sweet boy, he was only seven. And Mama couldn't face it, that's why she went away, just went away and never looked back. *(Shivers)* And I understand exactly how she felt. I wish she knew that.

(Pause.)

And Pétya Trofímov was Grísha's tutor. He might remind her . . .

(Enter Firs in his old-fashioned butler's livery. He crosses to the table and begins looking over the coffee things.)

FIRS: The missus will have her breakfast here. *(He puts on a pair of white gloves)* Is the coffee ready? *(To Dunyásha, crossly)* Where's the cream? Go get the cream!

DUNYÁSHA: Oh, my God, I'm sorry. . . . *(Hurries off)*

FIRS: *(He starts fussing with the coffee things)* Young flibbertigibbet . . . *(He mumbles to himself)* They're all back from Paris. . . . In the old days they went to Paris too . . . had to go the whole way in a horse and buggy. *(He laughs)*

VÁRYA: Firs, what are you talking about?

FIRS: Beg pardon? *(Joyfully)* The missus is home! Going to see her at last! Now I can die happy. . . . *(He starts to cry with joy)*

(Enter Liubóv, Gáyev, Lopákhin, and Semyónov-Píshchik, who wears a crumpled linen suit. As Gáyev enters, he gestures as if he were making a billiard shot.)

LIUBÓV ANDRÉYEVNA: How did it go? I'm trying to remember.... Yellow ball in the side pocket! Bank shot off the corner!

GÁYEV: And right down the middle! Oh, sister, sister, just think ... when you and I were little we used to sleep in this room, and now I'm almost fifty-one! Strange, isn't it?

LOPÁKHIN: Time sure passes....

GÁYEV: *(Beat)* Say again?

LOPÁKHIN: I said, time sure passes.

GÁYEV: *(Looking at Lopákhin)* Who's wearing that cheap cologne?

ÁNYA: I'm going to bed. Good night, Mama. *(She kisses her mother)*

LIUBÓV ANDRÉYEVNA: Oh, my darling little girl, my baby! Are you glad you're home? I still can't quite believe I'm here.

ÁNYA: Good night, Uncle.

GÁYEV: *(He kisses her)* God bless you, dear. You're getting to look so much like your mother! Liúba, she looks just like you when you were her age. She really does.

(Ánya says good night to Lopákhin and Píshchik, goes into her room, and closes the door behind her.)

LIUBÓV ANDRÉYEVNA: She's tired to death.

PÍSHCHIK: Well, that's such a long trip!

VÁRYA: Gentlemen, please. It's almost three; time you were going.

LIUBÓV ANDRÉYEVNA: *(Laughs)* You're the same as ever, Várya. *(Hugs and kisses her)* Just let me have my coffee, then we'll all be going.

(Firs puts a pillow beneath her feet.)

Thank you, dear. I've really gotten addicted to coffee; I drink it day and night. You old darling, you! Thank you.

VÁRYA: I'll just go make sure they've got everything unloaded. *(Goes out)*

LIUBÓV ANDRÉYEVNA: I can't believe I'm really here! *(Laughs)* I feel like jumping up and waving my arms in the air! *(Covers her face with her hands)* It's still like a dream. I love this country, really I do, I adore it. I started to cry every time I looked out the train windows. *(Almost in tears)* But I do need my coffee! Thank you, Firs, thank you, darling. I'm so glad you're still alive.

FIRS: Day before yesterday.

GÁYEV: He doesn't hear too well anymore.

LOPÁKHIN: Time for me to go. I have to leave for Hárkov at five. I'm really disappointed; I was looking forward to seeing you, have a chance to talk. . . . You look wonderful, just the way you always did.

PÍSHCHIK: *(Breathes hard)* Better than she always did. That Paris outfit . . . She makes me feel young again!

LOPÁKHIN: Your brother here thinks I'm crude, calls me a money grubber. That doesn't bother me; he can call me whatever he wants. I just hope you'll trust me the way you used to, look at me the way you used to. . . . My God, my father slaved for your father and grandfather, my whole family worked for yours; but you, you treated me different. You did so much for me I forgot about all that. Fact is, I . . . I love you like you were family . . . more, even.

LIUBÓV ANDRÉYEVNA: I can't sit still; I'm just not in the mood! *(Gets up excitedly, moves about the room)* I'm so happy I could die! I know I sound stupid—go ahead, laugh. . . . Dear old bookcase. . . . *(Kisses the bookcase)* My little desk . . .

GÁYEV: Did I tell you Nanny died while you were away?

LIUBÓV ANDRÉYEVNA: *(Sits back down and drinks her coffee)* Yes, you wrote me. God rest her.

GÁYEV: Stásy died too. And Petrúsha Kosói quit and moved into town; he works at the police station. *(Takes out a little box of hard candies and puts one in his mouth)*

PÍSHCHIK: Dáshenka—you remember Dáshenka? My daughter? Anyway, she sends her regards. . . .

LOPÁKHIN: Well, I'd like to give you some very good news. *(Looks at his watch)* Afraid there's no time to talk now, though; I've got to go. Well, just to make it short, you know you haven't kept up the mortgage payments on your place here. So now they foreclosed, and your estate is up for sale. At auction. They set a date already, August twenty-second, but don't you worry, you can rest easy. We can take care of this—I've got a great idea. Now listen, here's how it works: your place here is fifteen miles from town, and it's only a short drive from the train station. All you've got to do is clear out the old cherry orchard, plus that land down by the river, and subdivide! You lease the plots, build vacation homes, and I swear that'll bring you in twenty-five thousand a year, maybe more.

GÁYEV: What an outrageous thing to say!

LIUBÓV ANDRÉYEVNA: Excuse me ... Excuse me, I don't think I quite understand. ...

LOPÁKHIN: You'll get at least twenty-five hundred an acre! And if you start advertising right away, I swear to God come this fall you won't have a single plot left. You see what I'm saying? Your troubles are over! Congratulations! The location is terrific; the river's a real selling point. Only thing is, you've got to start clearing right away. Get rid of all the old buildings. This house, for instance, will have to go. You can't get people to live in a barn like this anymore. And you'll have to cut down that old cherry orchard.

LIUBÓV ANDRÉYEVNA: Cut down the cherry orchard? My dear man, you don't understand! Our cherry orchard is a landmark! It's famous for miles around!

LOPÁKHIN: The only thing famous about it is how big it is. You only get cherries every two years, and even then you can't get rid of them. Nobody buys them. It's just not a commercial crop.

GÁYEV: Our cherry orchard is mentioned in the encyclopedia!

LOPÁKHIN: *(Looks at his watch)* We have to think of something to do and then do it. Otherwise the cherry orchard will be sold at auction on August twenty-second, this house and all the land with it. Make up your minds! Believe me, I've thought this through; there isn't any other way to do it. There just isn't.

FIRS: Back in the old days, forty, fifty years ago, they used to make dried cherries, pickled cherries, preserved cherries, cherry jam, and sometimes—

GÁYEV: Oh, Firs, just shut up.

FIRS: —sometimes they sent them off to Moscow by the wagonload. People paid a lot for them! Back then the dried cherries were soft and juicy and sweet, and they smelled just lovely; back then they knew how to fix them. ...

LIUBÓV ANDRÉYEVNA: Does anybody know how to fix them nowadays?

FIRS: Nope. They all forgot.

PÍSHCHIK: Tell us about Paris. What was it like? Did you eat frogs?

LIUBÓV ANDRÉYEVNA: I ate crocodiles.

PÍSHCHIK: Crocodiles? Really! I don't believe it!

LOPÁKHIN: You see, it used to be out here in the country there were only landlords and poor farmers, but now all of a sudden there are summer people moving in; they want vacation homes. Every town you can name is surrounded by them—it's the coming thing. In twenty years they'll expand and multiply! Right now maybe they're only places to relax on the weekend, but I bet you eventually people will put down roots out here, they'll create neighborhoods, and then your cherry orchard will blossom and bear fruit once again—and even bring in a profit!

GÁYEV: *(Indignantly)* That's outrageous!

(Enter Várya and Yásha.)

VÁRYA: Mama, a couple of telegrams came for you. *(Takes a key and opens the old bookcase; the lock creaks)* Here they are.

LIUBÓV ANDRÉYEVNA: They're from Paris. *(She tears them up without opening them)* I'm through with Paris.

GÁYEV: Liúba, have you any idea how old this bookcase is? Last week I pulled out the bottom drawer, and there was the date on the back, burned right into the wood. A hundred years! This bookcase is exactly a hundred years old! What do you say to that, eh? We should have a birthday celebration. Of course, it's an inanimate object, any way you look at it, but still, it's a ... well, it's a ... a bookcase.

PÍSHCHIK: A hundred years old! Really! I don't believe it!

GÁYEV: Yes, yes, it is. *(He caresses the bookcase)* Dear old bookcase! Wonderful old bookcase! I rejoice in your existence. For a hundred years now you have borne the shining ideals of goodness and justice, a hundred years have not dimmed your silent summons to useful labor. To generations of our family *(almost in tears)* you have offered courage, a belief in a better future, you have instructed us in ideals of goodness and social awareness. ...

(Pause.)

LOPÁKHIN: Right. Well ...

LIUBÓV ANDRÉYEVNA: Oh, Lonya, you're still the same as ever!

GÁYEV: *(Somewhat embarrassed)* Yellow ball in the side pocket! Bank shot off the center!

LOPÁKHIN: Well, I've got to be off.

YÁSHA: *(Gives Liubóv a pillbox)* Isn't it perhaps time for your pills?

PÍSHCHIK: No, no, no, dear lady! Never take medicine! Won't do any good! Won't do any harm either, though. Watch! *(Takes the pillbox, dumps the contents into his hand, puts them in his mouth, and swallows them with a swig of beer)* There! All gone!

LIUBÓV ANDRÉYEVNA: *(Alarmed)* Are you out of your mind?

PÍSHCHIK: I have just taken all your pills for you.

LOPÁKHIN: What a glutton.

(Everybody laughs.)

FIRS: He was here over the holidays, ate half a crock of pickles. . . . *(Mumbles)*

LIUBÓV ANDRÉYEVNA: What's he mumbling about?

VÁRYA: He's been going on like that for the last three years. We're used to it by now.

YÁSHA: He's getting senile.

> *(Enter Carlotta, in a white dress with a lorgnette on a chain. She starts to cross the room.)*

LOPÁKHIN: Oh, excuse me, Carlotta, I didn't get a chance to say hello yet. *(Tries to kiss her hand)*

CARLOTTA: *(Takes her hand away)* I let you kiss my hand, first thing I know, you'll want to kiss my elbow, then my shoulder . . .

LOPÁKHIN: This isn't my lucky day.

> *(Everybody laughs.)*

Carlotta, show us a trick!

LIUBÓV ANDRÉYEVNA: Yes, do, Carlotta—show us a trick!

CARLOTTA: Not now. I'm off to bed. *(Leaves)*

LOPÁKHIN: Well, I'll see you in three weeks. *(Kisses Liubóv's hand)* Goodbye now. I've got to be off. *(To Gáyev)* Goodbye. *(Hugs Píshchik)* So long. *(Shakes hands with Várya, then with Firs and Yásha)* I sort of hate to leave. *(To Liubóv)* Think over what I said about subdividing the place. You decide to do it, let me know, and I'll take care of everything. I'll get you a loan of fifty thousand. Think it over now, seriously.

VÁRYA: *(Angry)* Will you please just go?

LOPÁKHIN: I'm going, I'm going. *(Leaves)*

GÁYEV: What a bore. Oh, excuse me, *pardon,* I forgot—that's Várya's boyfriend. He's going to marry our Várya.

VÁRYA: Uncle, will you please not talk nonsense?

LIUBÓV ANDRÉYEVNA: Oh, but Várya, that's wonderful! He's a fine man!

PÍSHCHIK: One of the finest, in fact . . . the very, very finest . . . My Dáshenka always says . . . she says . . . she says a lot of things. *(Snores, but immediately wakes up)* Dear lady, yes, always respected you, hmm. . . . You think you could lend me, say, two hundred and forty rubles? Mortgage payment, you know, due tomorrow . . .

VÁRYA: *(Terrified)* We can't; we don't have any!

LIUBÓV ANDRÉYEVNA: I'm afraid that's the truth. We haven't any money.

PÍSHCHIK: I'll get it somewhere. *(Laughs)* I never give up hope. There was that time I thought I was finished, it was all over, and all of a sudden—boom! The railroad cut across some of my land and paid me for it. You'll see, something will turn up tomorrow or the next day. Dáshenka will win two hundred thousand in the lottery; she just bought a ticket.

LIUBÓV ANDRÉYEVNA: Well, the coffee's gone. We might as well go to bed.

FIRS: *(Takes out a clothes brush and brushes Gáyev's clothes; scolds him)* You've got on the wrong trousers again. What am I supposed to do with you?

VÁRYA: *(Softly)* Ánya's asleep. *(Quietly opens the window)* The sun's coming up; it's not as cold as it was. Look, Mama, what wonderful trees! Smell the perfume! Oh, Lord! And the orioles are singing!

GÁYEV: *(Opens another window)* The whole orchard is white. You remember, Liúba? That long path, stretched out like a ribbon, on and on, the way it used to shine in the moonlight? You remember? You haven't forgotten?

LIUBÓV ANDRÉYEVNA: Oh, my childhood! My innocence! I slept in this room, I could look out over the orchard, when I woke up in the morning I was happy, and it all looked exactly the same as this! Nothing has changed! *(Laughs delightedly)* White, white, all white! My whole orchard is white! Autumn was dark and drizzly, and winter was cold, but now you're young again, flowering with happiness—the angels of heaven have never abandoned you. If only I could shake off this weight I've been carrying so long. If only I could forget my past!

GÁYEV: Yes, and now they're selling the orchard to pay our debts. Strange, isn't it?

LIUBÓV ANDRÉYEVNA: Look! There ... in the orchard ... it's Mother! In her white dress! *(Laughs delightedly)* It's Mother!

GÁYEV: Where?

VÁRYA: Oh, Mama, for God's sake ...

LIUBÓV ANDRÉYEVNA: It's all right; I was just imagining things. There to the right, by the path to the summerhouse, that little white tree all bent over ... it looked just like a woman.

(Enter Trofímov. He is dressed like a student and wears wire-rimmed glasses.)

What a glorious orchard! All those white blossoms, and the blue sky—

TROFÍMOV: Liubóv Andréyevna!

(She turns to look at him.)

I don't mean to disturb you; I just wanted to say hello. *(Shakes her hand warmly)* They told me to wait until later, but I couldn't. . . .

(Liubóv stares at him, bewildered.)

VÁRYA: It's Pétya Trofímov. . . .

TROFÍMOV: Pétya Trofímov—I was your little boy Grísha's tutor. . . . Have I really changed all that much?

(Liubóv embraces him and begins to weep softly.)

GÁYEV: *(Embarrassed)* Liúba, that'll do, that'll do. . . .

VÁRYA: *(Weeps)* Oh, Pétya, I told you to wait till tomorrow.

LIUBÓV ANDRÉYEVNA: Grísha . . . my little boy. Grísha . . . my son . . .

VÁRYA: Oh, Mama, don't; it was God's will.

TROFÍMOV: *(Gently, almost in tears)* There, there . . .

LIUBÓV ANDRÉYEVNA: *(Weeps softly)* My little boy drowned, lost forever . . . Why? What for? My dear boy, why? *(Quiets down)* Ánya's asleep, and here I am carrying on like this. . . . Pétya, what's happened to you? You used to be such a nice-looking boy. What happened? You look dreadful. You've gotten so old!

TROFÍMOV: Some lady on the train called me a high-class tramp.

LIUBÓV ANDRÉYEVNA: You were only a boy then, just out of high school, you were adorable, and now you've got glasses and you're losing your hair. And haven't you graduated yet? *(Goes to the door)*

TROFÍMOV: I suppose I'm what you'd call a permanent graduate student.

LIUBÓV ANDRÉYEVNA: *(Kisses Gáyev, then Várya)* Time for bed. You've gotten old too, Leoníd.

PÍSHCHIK: *(Follows Liubóv)* Time for bed, time to go . . . Ooh, my gout! I'd better stay the night. Now, dear, look, look . . . Liubóv Andréyevna, tomorrow morning I need . . . two hundred and forty rubles. . . .

GÁYEV: He never gives up, does he?

PÍSHCHIK: Two hundred and forty rubles; my mortgage payment's due. . . .

LIUBÓV ANDRÉYEVNA: Darling, I simply have no money.

PÍSHCHIK: But, dear, I'll give it right back. . . . It's such a *trivial* amount. . . .

LIUBÓV ANDRÉYEVNA: Oh, all right. Leoníd will get it for you. Leoníd, you give him the money.

GÁYEV: I should give him money? That'll be the day.

LIUBÓV ANDRÉYEVNA: We have to give it to him; he needs it. He'll give it back.

> (*Exit Liubóv, Trofímov, Píshchik, and Firs. Gáyev, Várya, and Yásha remain.*)

GÁYEV: She still thinks money grows on trees. (*To Yásha*) My good man, will you leave us, please? Go back to the barn, where you belong.

YÁSHA: (*Smirks*) Leoníd Andréyich, you're the same as you always were.

GÁYEV: What say? (*To Várya*) What did he just say?

VÁRYA: (*To Yásha*) Your mother came in from the country to see you. She's been sitting in the kitchen for two days now, waiting.

YÁSHA: Oh, for God's sake, can't she leave me alone?

VÁRYA: You are really disgraceful!

YÁSHA: That's all I need right now. Why couldn't she wait till tomorrow? (*Goes out*)

VÁRYA: Mama hasn't changed; she's the same as she always was. If it were up to her, she'd give away everything.

GÁYEV: Yes. . . . (*Pause*) Someone gets sick, you know, and the doctor tries one thing after another, that means there's no cure. I've been thinking and thinking, racking my brains, I come up with one thing, then another, but the truth is, none of them will work. It would be wonderful if somebody left us a lot of money, it would be wonderful if we could marry off Ánya to somebody with a lot of money, it would be wonderful if we could go see Ánya's godmother in Yároslavl, try to borrow the money from her. She's very, very rich.

VÁRYA: (*Weeps*) If only God would help us!

GÁYEV: Oh, stop crying. She's very, very rich, but she doesn't like us. Because in the first place, my sister married a mere lawyer instead of a man with a title. . . .

> (*Ánya appears in the doorway.*)

She married a lawyer, and then her behavior has not been—how shall I put it?—particularly exemplary. She's a lovely woman, goodhearted, charming, and of course she's my sister and I love her very much, and there are extenuating circumstances and such, but the fact is, she's what you'd have to call a . . . a loose woman. And she doesn't care who knows it; you can feel it in every move she makes.

VÁRYA: *(Whispers)* Ánya's here.

GÁYEV: What say? *(Pause)* Funny, I must have gotten something in my eye: I can't see too well. . . . Did I tell you what happened Thursday, when I was at the county courthouse?

(Ánya comes into the room.)

VÁRYA: Why aren't you asleep?

ÁNYA: I tried. I couldn't sleep.

GÁYEV: Kitten . . . *(Kisses Ánya's cheek, then her hands)* My dear child . . . *(Almost in tears)* You're more than just my niece, you're my angel, you know that? You're my whole world, believe me, believe me. . . .

ÁNYA: I believe you, Uncle. And I love you; we all love you. . . . But, Uncle dear, you should learn not to talk so much. The things you were saying just now about Mama, about your own sister . . . What were you saying all that for?

GÁYEV: I know, I know. . . . *(Covers his face with her hand)* It's awful, I know. My God, a few minutes ago I made a speech to a piece of furniture. . . . It was so stupid! The thing is, I never realize how stupid I sound until I'm done.

VÁRYA: She's right, Uncle. You just have to learn to keep still, that's all.

ÁNYA: If you do, you'll feel much better about yourself, you know you will. . . .

GÁYEV: I will, I will, I promise. *(Kisses Ánya's and Várya's hands)* I'll keep still. Only right now I have to talk a little more. Business! On Thursday I was at the county courthouse; there was a group of us talking—just this and that—and it turns out I might be able to arrange a promissory note for enough money to pay off the mortgage.

VÁRYA: If only God would help us!

GÁYEV: I'm going in on Tuesday, I'll talk to them again. *(To Várya)* Don't whine! *(To Ánya)* Your mother will talk to Lopákhin; he can't refuse to help her. And you, as soon as you're rested, you go to Yároslavl, go talk to your godmother. There. We'll be operating on three fronts at once; we're sure to succeed. We *will* pay off this mortgage, I know we will.... *(He pops a hard candy into his mouth)* I swear by my honor, I swear by anything you want, the estate will not be sold! *(Excitedly)* I swear by my own happiness! Here, you have my hand on it. You may call me ... dishonorable, call me anything you will, if I ever let this estate go on the auction block! I swear by my entire existence!

ÁNYA: *(Her calm mood has returned; she is happy)* You're so smart, Uncle! You're such a wonderful man! *(Hugs Gáyev)* Now I feel better! So much better! I'm happy again!

(Enter Firs.)

FIRS: *(Reproachfully)* Leoníd Andréyich, why aren't you in bed, like decent God-fearing people?

GÁYEV: I'm coming, I'm coming. You go to bed, Firs. I can get undressed by myself. All right, children, nighty-night. We can talk about the details tomorrow; now it's time for bed. *(Kisses Ánya and Várya)* I am a man of the eighties, you know. People don't think much of that era now, but I can tell you frankly that I have had the courage of my convictions and often had to pay the price. But these local peasants all love me. You have to get to know them, that's all. You have to get to know them, and—

ÁNYA: Uncle. You're at it again.

VÁRYA: Just be quiet, Uncle.

FIRS: *(Angrily)* Leoníd Andréyich!

GÁYEV: I'm coming, I'm coming.... Go to bed now. Yellow ball in the side pocket! Clean shot! *(Goes out; Firs follows him, limping)*

ÁNYA: I feel much better. I don't much want to go to Yároslavl, I don't like my godmother, but I feel better now. Thanks to Uncle. *(Sits down)*

VÁRYA: We've got to get some sleep. I'm going to bed. Oh, there's something came up since you left. You know we've got all those old retired servants living out back—Paulina, old Karp, and the rest of them. And what happened, they started inviting people in to spend the night. Well, it's annoying, but I never said a thing. Then what happened was, they started telling everybody all they were getting to eat was beans. Because I was so cheap, you see. It was that old Karp was doing it. So I said to myself, All right, that's the way you want it, all right, just wait, and I sent for him *(yawns)*, and in he comes, so I say, Karp, you're such an idiot—*(Looks at Ánya)* Ánya!

(Pause.)

She's asleep. *(Lifts Ánya by the arms)* Come on, time for bed. . . .
Come on, let's go. . . . *(Leads her off)* My angel fell asleep! Come
on. . . . *(They start out)*

*(In the distance, beyond the orchard, a shepherd plays a pipe.
Trofímov enters, sees Ánya and Várya, stops.)*

VÁRYA: Shh! She's asleep. . . . Come on, darling, let's go. . . .

ÁNYA: *(Softly, half asleep)* I was so tired. . . . All those bells . . . Uncle
dear . . . and Mama. Uncle and Mama.

VÁRYA: Come on, darling, come on. . . . *(They go off into Ánya's room)*

TROFÍMOV: *(Deeply moved)* My sunshine! My springtime!

CURTAIN.

ACT TWO

*An open space. The overgrown ruin of an abandoned chapel.
There is a well beside it and some large stones that must once have
been grave markers. An old bench. Beyond, the road to the Gáyev
estate. On one side a shadowy row of poplar trees; they mark the
limits of the cherry orchard. A row of telegraph poles, and on the
far distant horizon, on a clear day, you can just make out the city.
It's late afternoon, almost sunset. Carlotta, Yásha, and Dunyásha
are sitting on the bench; Yepikhódov stands nearby, strumming his
guitar; each seems lost in his own thoughts. Carlotta wears an old
military cap and is adjusting the strap on a hunting rifle.*

CARLOTTA: *(Meditatively)* I haven't got a birth certificate, so I don't
know how old I really am. I just think of myself as young. When
I was a little girl, Mama and my father used to travel around to
fairs and put on shows, good ones. I did back flips, things like
that. And after they died this German woman brought me up,
taught me a few things. And that was it. Then I grew up and had
to go to work. As a governess. Where I'm from . . . who I am . . .
no idea. Who my parents were—maybe they weren't even married—no idea. *(Takes a large cucumber pickle out of her pocket and
takes a bite)* No idea at all.

(Pause.)

And I feel like talking all the time, but there's no one to talk to.
No one.

YEPIKHÓDOV: *(Plays the guitar and sings)*
"What do I care for the rest of the world,
   or care what it cares for me . . ."
Very agreeable, playing a mandolin.

DUNYÁSHA: That's not a mandolin, it's a guitar. *(Takes out a compact with a mirror and powders herself)*

YEPIKHÓDOV: When a man is madly in love, a guitar is a mandolin. *(Sings)*
"As long as my heart is on fire with love,
   and the one I love loves me."

(Yásha sings harmony.)

CARLOTTA: Oof! You people sound like hyenas.

DUNYÁSHA: But it must have been just lovely, being in Europe.

YÁSHA: Oh, it was. Quite, quite lovely. I have to agree with you there. *(Yawns, then lights a cigar)*

YEPIKHÓDOV: That's understandable. In Europe, things have already come to a complex.

YÁSHA: *(Beat)* I suppose you could say that.

YEPIKHÓDOV: I'm a true product of the educational system; I read all the time. All the right books too, but I have no chosen directive in life. For me, strictly speaking, it's live or shoot myself. That's why I always carry a loaded pistol. See? *(Takes out a revolver)*

CARLOTTA: All done. Time to go. *(Slings the rifle over her shoulder)* You're a very smart man, Yepikhódov, and a very scary one. Ooh! The women must adore you. *(Starts off)* They're all so dumb, these smart boys. Never anyone to talk to ... Always alone, all by myself, no one to talk to ... and I still don't know who I am. Or why. No idea. *(Walks slowly off)*

YEPIKHÓDOV: I should explain, by the way, for the sake of expressivity, that fate has been, ah, *rigorous* to me. I am, strictly speaking, tempest-tossed. Always have been. Now, you may say to me, Oh, you're imagining things, but then why, when I wake up this morning—here's an example—and I look down, why is there this spider on my stomach? Detrimentally large too. *(Makes a circle with his two hands)* Big as that. Or take a beer, let's say. I go to drink it, what do I see floating around in it? Something highly unappreciative, like a cockroach.

(Pause.)

Have you ever read Henry Thomas Buckle?

(Pause.)

May I design to disturb you, Avdótya Fyódorovna, with something I have to say?

DUNYÁSHA: So say it.

YEPIKHÓDOV: Preferentially alone. *(Sighs)*

DUNYÁSHA: *(Embarrassed)* All right. . . . Only first get me my wrap; it's by the kitchen door. It's getting kind of damp.

YEPIKHÓDOV: Ah, I see. Yes, get the wrap, of course. Now I know what to do with my gun. *(Takes his guitar and goes off, strumming)*

YÁSHA: Double Trouble. He's an idiot, if you ask me. *(Yawns)*

DUNYÁSHA: I hope to God he doesn't shoot himself.

(Pause.)

I get upset over every little thing anymore. Ever since I started working for them here, I've gotten used to their *lifestyle.* Just look at my hands. Look at how white they are, just like I was rich. I'm different now from like I was. I'm more delicate, I'm more sensitive; everything upsets me. . . . It's just awful how things upset me. So if you cheat on me, Yásha, I may just have a nervous breakdown.

YÁSHA: *(Kisses her)* Oh, you little cutie! Just remember, though: a girl has to watch her step. What I'm after is a *nice* girl.

DUNYÁSHA: I really love you, Yásha, I really do. You're so smart, you know so many things. . . .

(Pause)

YÁSHA: *(Yawns)* Yeah. . . . But my theory is, a girl says she loves you, she's not a nice girl.

(Pause.)

Nothing like smoking a cigar out here in the fresh air. . . . *(Listens)* Somebody's coming. . . . It's them. . . .

(Dunyásha hugs him impulsively.)

YÁSHA: Go on back to the house. Go back the other way, make believe you've been swimming down by the river, so they don't think we've been . . . we've been getting together out here like this. I don't want them to think that.

DUNYÁSHA: *(A little cough)* That cigar smoke is giving me a headache. . . . *(Goes out)*

(Yásha sits beside the chapel wall. Enter Liubóv, Gáyev, and Lopákhin.)

LOPÁKHIN: You have to make up your mind one way or the other; time's running out. There's no argument left. You want to subdivide or don't you? Just give me an answer, one word, yes or no.

LIUBÓV ANDRÉYEVNA: Who's been smoking those cheap cigars? *(Sits down)*

GÁYEV: Everything's so convenient, now that there's the railroad. We went into town just to have lunch. Yellow ball in the side pocket! What do you say—why don't we go back to the house, eh? Have ourselves a little game . . .

LIUBÓV ANDRÉYEVNA: Let's wait till later.

LOPÁKHIN: Just one word! *(Imploringly)* Why don't you give me an answer?

GÁYEV: *(Yawns)* To what?

LIUBÓV ANDRÉYEVNA: *(Rummages in her purse)* Yesterday I had a lot of money, today it's all gone. My poor Várya feeds us all on soup to economize, the poor old people get nothing but beans, and I just spend and spend. . . . *(Drops her purse; gold coins spill out)* Oh, I've spilled everything. . . .

YÁSHA: Here, allow me. *(Picks up the money)*

LIUBÓV ANDRÉYEVNA: Oh, please do, Yásha; thank you. And why I had to go into that town for lunch—that stupid restaurant of yours, those stupid musicians, those stupid tablecloths; they smelled of soap. . . . Why do we drink so much, Lyónya? And eat so much? Why do we talk so much? The whole time we were in the restaurant, you kept talking, and none of it made any sense. Talking about the seventies, about Symbolism. And to who? The waiters! Talking about Symbolism to waiters!

LOPÁKHIN: Yes.

GÁYEV: *(Makes a deprecating gesture)* I'm incorrigible, I suppose. . . . *(To Yásha, irritably)* What are *you* doing here? Why are you always underfoot every time I turn around?

YÁSHA: *(Laughs)* Because every time I hear your voice it makes me laugh.

GÁYEV: Either he goes or I do!

LIUBÓV ANDRÉYEVNA: Yásha, please . . . just go 'way, will you?

YÁSHA: *(Gives Liubóv her purse)* I'm going. Right now. *(Barely containing his laughter)* Right this very minute . . . *(Goes out)*

LOPÁKHIN: You know who Derigánov is? You know how much money he has? You know he's planning to buy your property? They say he's coming to the auction himself.

LIUBÓV ANDRÉYEVNA: Who told you that?

LOPÁKHIN: Everybody in town knows about it.

GÁYEV: The old lady in Yároslavl promised to send money.... But when, and how much, she didn't say.

LOPÁKHIN: How much will she send? A hundred thousand? Two hundred?

LIUBÓV ANDRÉYEVNA: Ten or fifteen thousand. And we're lucky to get that much.

LOPÁKHIN: Excuse me, but you people ... I have never met anyone so unbusinesslike, so impractical, so ... so *crazy* as the pair of you! Somebody tells you flat out your land is about to be sold, you don't even seem to understand!

LIUBÓV ANDRÉYEVNA: But what should we do? Just tell us what we should do!

LOPÁKHIN: I tell you every day what you should do! Every day I come out here and say the same thing. The cherry orchard and the rest of the land has to be subdivided and developed for leisure homes, and it has to be done right away. The auction date is getting closer! Can't you understand? All you have to do is make up your mind to subdivide, you'll have more money than even you can spend! Your troubles will be over!

LIUBÓV ANDRÉYEVNA: Subdivide, leisure homes ... excuse me, but it's all so hopelessly vulgar.

GÁYEV: I couldn't agree more.

LOPÁKHIN: You people drive me crazy! Another minute, I'll be shouting my head off! Oh, I give up, I give up! Why do I even bother? *(To Gáyev)* You're worse than an old lady!

GÁYEV: What say?

LOPÁKHIN: I said you're an old lady! *(Starts to leave)*

LIUBÓV ANDRÉYEVNA: *(Fearfully)* No, no, no, please, my dear, don't go. Please. I'm sure we'll think of something.

LOPÁKHIN: What's there to think of?

LIUBÓV ANDRÉYEVNA: Please. Don't go. Things are easier when you're around....

   (Pause.)

I keep waiting for something to happen. It's as if the house were about to fall down around our ears or something....

GÁYEV: *(Meditatively)* Yellow ball in the side pocket ... Clean shot down the middle ...

LIUBÓV ANDRÉYEVNA: We're guilty of so many sins, I know—

LOPÁKHIN: Sins? What are you talking about?

GÁYEV: *(Pops a hard candy into his mouth)* People say I've eaten up my entire inheritance in candy. *(Laughs)*

LIUBÓV ANDRÉYEVNA: All my sins ... I've always wasted money, just thrown it away like a madwoman, and I married a man who never paid a bill in his life. He was an alcoholic; he drank himself to death—on champagne. And I was so unhappy I fell in love with another man, *unfortunately*, and had an affair with him, and that was when—that was the first thing, my first punishment, right down there, in the river, my little boy drowned, and I left, I went to France, I left and never wanted to come back, I never wanted to see that river again, I just closed my eyes and *ran*, forgot about everything, and that man followed me. He just wouldn't let up. And he was so mean to me, so cruel! I bought a villa in Mentón because he got sick while we were there, and for the next three years I never had a moment's peace, day or night. He tormented me from his sickbed. I could feel my soul dry up. And last year I couldn't afford the villa anymore, so I sold it and we moved to Paris, and once we were in Paris he took everything I had left and ran off with another woman, and I tried to kill myself. It was so stupid, and so shameful! Finally all I wanted was to come back home, to where I was born, to my daughter. *(Wipes away her tears)* Oh, dear God, dear God, forgive me! Forgive me my sins! Don't punish me again! *(Takes a telegram from her purse)* This came today, from Paris. ... He says he's sorry, he wants me back. ... *(Tears up the telegram)* Where's *(listens)* ... where's that music coming from?

GÁYEV: That's our famous local orchestra. Those Jewish musicians, you remember? Four fiddles, a clarinet, and a double bass.

LIUBÓV ANDRÉYEVNA: Are they still around? We should have them over some evening and throw a party.

LOPÁKHIN: *(Listens)* I don't hear anything. *(Sings to himself)*
"Ooh-la-la ...
   Just a little bit of money
   makes a lady very French ..."
(Laughs) I went to the theater last night, saw this musical. Very funny.

LIUBÓV ANDRÉYEVNA: I doubt there was anything funny about it.

You ought to stop going to see playacting and take a good look at your own reality. What a boring life you lead! And what uninteresting things you talk about.

LOPÁKHIN: Well ... yeah, there's some truth to that. It is a pretty dumb life we lead. . . .

   (Pause.)

My father was a ... he was a dirt farmer, an idiot, never understood me, never taught me anything, just got drunk and beat me up. With a stick. Fact is, I'm not much better myself. Never did well in school, my writing's terrible, I'm ashamed if anybody sees it. I write like a pig.

LIUBÓV ANDRÉYEVNA: My dear man, you should get married.

LOPÁKHIN: Yes. . . . Yes, I should.

LIUBÓV ANDRÉYEVNA: And you should marry our Várya. She's a wonderful girl.

LOPÁKHIN: She is.

LIUBÓV ANDRÉYEVNA: Her people were quite ordinary, but she works like a dog, and the main thing is, she loves you. And you like her, I know you do. You always have.

LOPÁKHIN: Look, I've got nothing against it. I ... She's a wonderful girl.

   (Pause.)

GÁYEV: They offered me a position at the bank. Six thousand a year. Did I tell you?

LIUBÓV ANDRÉYEVNA: Don't be silly! You stay right here where you belong.

   (Enter Firs, carrying an overcoat.)

FIRS: Sir, sir, please put this on. It's getting damp.

GÁYEV: *(Puts it on)* Firs, you're getting to be a bore.

FIRS: That so? Went out this morning, didn't even tell me. *(Tries to adjust Gáyev's clothes)*

LIUBÓV ANDRÉYEVNA: Poor Firs! You've gotten so old!

FIRS: Beg pardon?

LOPÁKHIN: She said you got very old!

FIRS: I've lived a long time. They were trying to marry me off way back before your daddy was born. *(Laughs)* By the time we got our freedom back, I was already head butler. I had all the freedom I needed, so I stayed right here with the masters.

(Pause.)

I remember everybody got all excited about it, but they never even knew what they were getting excited about.

LOPÁKHIN: Oh, sure, things were wonderful back in the good old days! They had the right to beat you if they wanted, remember?

FIRS: *(Doesn't hear)* That's right. Masters stood by the servants, servants stood by the masters. Nowadays it's all mixed up; you can't tell who's who.

GÁYEV: Shut up, Firs. . . . I have to go into town tomorrow. A friend promised to introduce me to someone who might be able to arrange a loan. Some general.

LOPÁKHIN: That's never going to work. Trust me, you won't get enough even for the interest payments.

LIUBÓV ANDRÉYEVNA: He's imagining things. There's no general.

(Enter Ánya, Várya, and Trofímov.)

GÁYEV: Here come our young people.

ÁNYA: Mama's resting.

LIUBÓV ANDRÉYEVNA: *(Tenderly)* Here we are, dears, over here. *(Kisses Ánya and Várya)* If you only knew how much I love you both. Come sit here by me . . . that's right.

(They all sit down.)

LOPÁKHIN: Our permanent graduate student seems to spend all his time studying the ladies.

TROFÍMOV: Mind your own business.

LOPÁKHIN: Almost in his fifties, he's still in school.

TROFÍMOV: Just stop the silly jokes, will you?

LOPÁKHIN: Oh, the *scholar* is losing his temper!

TROFÍMOV: Will you please just leave me alone?

LOPÁKHIN: *(Laughs)* Let me ask you a question: You look at me, what do you see?

TROFÍMOV: When I look at you, Yermolái Alexéyich, what I see is a rich man. One who will soon be a millionaire. You are as necessary a part of the evolution of the species as the wild animal that eats up anything in its path.

(Everybody laughs.)

VÁRYA: Forget biology, Pétya. You should stick to counting stars.

LIUBÓV ANDRÉYEVNA: I want to hear more about what we were talking about last night.

TROFÍMOV: What were we talking about?

GÁYEV: About human dignity.

TROFÍMOV: We talked about a lot last night, but we never got anywhere. You people talk about human dignity as if it were something mystical. I suppose it is, in a way, for you anyway, but when you really get down to it, what have humans got to be proud of? Biologically we're pretty minor specimens—besides which, the great majority of human beings are vulgar and unhappy and totally *un*dignified. We should stop patting ourselves on the back and get to work.

GÁYEV: You still have to die.

TROFÍMOV: Who says? Anyway, what does that mean, to die? Maybe we have a hundred senses, and all we lose when we die are the five we're familiar with, and the other ninety-five go on living.

LIUBÓV ANDRÉYEVNA: Oh, Pétya, you're so smart!

LOPÁKHIN: *(With irony)* Oh, yes, very.

TROFÍMOV: Remember, human beings are constantly progressing, and their power keeps growing. Things that seem impossible to us nowadays, the day will come when they're not a problem at all, only we have to work toward that day. We have to seek out the truth. We don't do that, you know. Most of the people in this country aren't working toward anything. People I come in contact with—at the university, for instance—they're supposed to be educated, but they're not interested in the truth. They're not interested in much of anything, actually. They certainly don't *do* much. They call themselves intellectuals and think that gives them the right to look down on the rest of the world. They never read anything worthwhile, they're completely ignorant where science is concerned, they talk about art and they don't even know what it is they're talking about. They take themselves so seriously, they're full of theories and ideas, but just go look at the cities they live in. Miles and miles of slums, where people go hungry and where they live packed into unheated tenements full of cockroaches and garbage, and their lives are full of violence and immorality. So what are all the theories for? To keep people like us from seeing all that. Where are the day-care centers they talk so much about, and the literacy programs? It's all just talk. You go out to the parts of town where the poor people live, you can't find them. All you find is dirt and ignorance and crime. That's why I don't like all this talk, all these theories. Bothers me, makes me afraid. If that's all our talk is good for, we'd better just shut up.

LOPÁKHIN: I get up at five and work from morning to night, and you know, my business involves a lot of money, my own and other people's, so I see lots of people, see what they're like. And you just try to get anything accomplished: you'll see how few decent, honest people there really are. Sometimes at night I can't sleep, and I think: Dear God, you gave us this beautiful earth to live on, these great forests, these wide fields, the broad horizons ... by rights we should be giants.

LIUBÓV ANDRÉYEVNA: What do you want giants for? The only good giants are in fairy tales. Real ones would scare you to death.

(Upstage, Yepikhódov strolls by, playing his guitar.)

(dreamily) There goes Yepikhódov. . . .

ÁNYA: *(Dreamily)* There goes Yepikhódov. . . .

GÁYEV: The sun, ladies and gentlemen, has just set.

TROFÍMOV: Yes.

GÁYEV: *(As if reciting a poem, but not too loud)* O wondrous nature, cast upon us your eternal rays, forever beautiful, forever indifferent. . . . Mother, we call you; life and death reside within you; you bring forth and lay waste—

VÁRYA: *(Pleading)* Uncle, please!

ÁNYA: Uncle, you're doing it again.

TROFÍMOV: We'd rather have the yellow ball in the side pocket.

GÁYEV: Sorry, sorry. I'll keep still.

(They all sit in silence. The only sound we hear is old Firs mumbling. Suddenly a distant sound seems to fall from the sky, a sad sound, like a harp string breaking. It dies away.)

LIUBÓV ANDRÉYEVNA: What was that?

LOPÁKHIN: Can't tell. Sounds like it could be an echo from a mine shaft. But it must be far away.

GÁYEV: Or some kind of bird . . . like a heron.

TROFÍMOV: Or an owl.

LIUBÓV ANDRÉYEVNA: *(Shivers)* Makes me nervous.

(Pause.)

FIRS: It's like just before the trouble started. They heard an owl screech, and the kettle wouldn't stop whistling. . . .

GÁYEV: Before what trouble?

FIRS: The day we got our freedom back.

(Pause.)

LIUBÓV ANDRÉYEVNA: My dears, it's getting dark; we should be going in. (To Ánya) You've got tears in your eyes, darling. What's the matter? (Hugs Ánya)

ÁNYA: Nothing, Mama. It's all right.

TROFÍMOV: Someone's coming.

(Enter a Homeless Man in a white cap and an overcoat; he's slightly drunk.)

HOMELESS MAN: Can anyone please tell me, can I get to the train station this way?

GÁYEV: Of course you can. Just follow this road.

HOMELESS MAN: Much obliged. (Bows) Wonderful weather we're having ... (Recites) "Behold one of the poor in spirit, just trying to inherit a little of the earth ..." (To Várya) Listen, you think you could spare some money for a hungry man?

(Várya is terrified; she screams.)

LOPÁKHIN: (Angrily) Now hold on just a minute!

LIUBÓV ANDRÉYEVNA: (Panicked) Here ... here ... take this. (Fumbles in her purse) Oh, I don't seem to have anything smaller. Here, take this. (Gives him a gold piece)

HOMELESS MAN: Very much obliged! (Goes out)

(Everybody laughs.)

VÁRYA: Get me out of here! Oh, please get me out! Mama, how could you! We can't even feed the servants, and you go and give him a gold piece!

LIUBÓV ANDRÉYEVNA: I know, darling, I'm just stupid about money. When we get home I'll give you whatever I've got left; you can take care of it. Yermoláí Alexéyich, can you lend me some money?

LOPÁKHIN: Of course.

LIUBÓV ANDRÉYEVNA: My darlings, it really is time to go in. Várya dear, we've just gotten you engaged. Congratulations.

VÁRYA: (Almost in tears) Mama, that's nothing to joke about!

LOPÁKHIN: Amelia, get thee to a nunnery!

GÁYEV: Look how my hands shake. I don't know if I could play billiards anymore. . . .

LOPÁKHIN: Nymph, in thy horizons be all my sins remembered!

LIUBÓV ANDRÉYEVNA: Please, let's go. It's almost suppertime.

VÁRYA: He scared me half to death. I can feel my heart pounding.

LOPÁKHIN: But keep in mind, the cherry orchard is going to be sold. On August twenty-second! You hear what I'm saying? You've got to think about this! You've got to!

(They all go off except Ánya and Trofímov.)

ÁNYA: *(Laughs)* I'm so glad that tramp scared Várya off. Now we can be alone.

TROFÍMOV: Várya's afraid we're going to fall in love; that's why she never leaves us alone. She's so narrow-minded; she simply can't understand that we are above love. Our goal is to get rid of the silly illusions that keep us from being free and happy. We are moving forward, toward the future! Toward one bright star that burns ahead of us! Forward, friends! Come join us in our journey!

ÁNYA: *(Claps her hands)* Oh, you talk so beautifully!

(Pause.)

It's just heavenly out here today!

TROFÍMOV: Yes, the weather's been really good lately.

ÁNYA: I don't know what it is you've done to me, Pétya, but I don't love the cherry orchard anymore, not the way I used to. I used to think there was no place on earth like our orchard.

TROFÍMOV: This whole country is our orchard. It's a big country and a beautiful one; it has lots of wonderful places in it.

(Pause.)

Just think, Ánya: your grandfather, and his father, and his father's fathers, they *owned* the people who slaved away for them all over this estate, and now the voices and faces of human beings hide behind every cherry in the orchard, every leaf, every tree trunk. Can't you see them? And hear them? And owning human beings has left its mark on all of you. Look at your mother and your uncle! They live off the labor of others, they always have, and they've never even noticed! They owe their entire lives to those other people, people they wouldn't even let walk through the front gate of their beloved cherry orchard! This whole country has fallen behind; it'll take us at least two hundred years to catch up. The thing is, we don't have any real sense of our own history; all we do is sit around and talk, talk, talk, then we feel depressed, so we go out and get drunk. If there's one thing that's clear to me, it's this: if we want to have any real life in the present, we have to do something to make up for our past, we have to get over it, and the only way to do that is to make sacrifices, get down to work, and work harder than we've ever worked before. Do you understand what I mean, Ánya?

ÁNYA: The house we live in isn't our house anymore. It hasn't ever been, really. And I'll leave it all behind, I promise you I will.

TROFÍMOV: Yes, you will! Throw away your house keys and go as far away as you can! You'll be free as the wind.

ÁNYA: *(Radiant)* I love the way you say things!

TROFÍMOV: You have to understand me, Ánya. I'm not thirty yet, I'm still young; I may still be in school, but I've learned a lot. Winter comes, sometimes I get cold and hungry, or sick and upset, I don't have a cent to my name; things work out or they don't. . . . But no matter what, my heart and soul are always full of feelings, all kinds . . . I can't even explain them. And I feel happiness coming, Ánya, I can feel it, I can almost see it—

ÁNYA: *(Dreamily)* Look, the moon's rising.

(The sound of Yepikhódov's guitar, still playing the same mournful song. The moon rises. Somewhere beyond the poplar trees, Várya can be heard calling.)

VÁRYA: *(Off)* Ánya! Ánya, where are you?

TROFÍMOV: Yes, the moon is rising.

(Pause.)

It's happiness, that's what it is: it's rising, it's coming closer and closer, I can hear it. And even if we miss it, if we never find it, that's all right! Someone will!

VÁRYA: *(Off)* Ánya! Ánya, where are you?

TROFÍMOV: *(Angrily)* That Várya! Why won't she let us alone!

ÁNYA: Don't let her bother you. Let's take a walk by the river. It's so nice there.

TROFÍMOV: All right, let's go.

(They leave. The stage is empty.)

VÁRYA: *(Off)* Ánya! Ánya!

CURTAIN.

ACT THREE

A sitting room, separated from the ballroom in back by an archway. The chandeliers are lit. From the entrance hall comes the sounds of an orchestra, the Jewish musicians Gáyev mentioned in Act Two. Evening. In the ballroom, everyone is dancing a grande ronde. Semyónov-Píshchik's voice is heard calling the figures of the dance: "Promenade à une paire!" *The dancers dance through the sitting room in pairs in the following order: Píshchik and Carlotta, Trofímov and Liubóv Andreyévna, Ánya and the Postmaster, Várya and the Stationmaster, etc. Várya is in tears, which she tries to wipe away as she dances. The final pair includes Dunyásha. As the dancers return to the ballroom, Píshchik calls out:* "Grande ronde, balancez!" *and* "Les cavaliers à genoux et remercier vos dames." *Firs in his butler's uniform crosses the stage, carrying a seltzer bottle on a tray. Píshchik and Trofímov come into the sitting room.*

PÍSHCHIK: I'm prone to strokes, already had two of 'em, I really shouldn't be dancing, but you know what they say: When in Rome. Besides, I'm really strong as a horse. Speaking of Romans, my father—what a joker he was—he used to claim our family was descended from the emperor Caligula's horse—you know, the one he made a senator? *(Sits down)* The only problem is we have no money. *(His head nods, he snores, then immediately wakes up)* So the only thing I ever think about is money.

TROFÍMOV: Your father was right. You do look a little like a horse.

PÍSHCHIK: Nothing wrong with horses. Wonderful animals. If I had one, I could sell it. . . .

(From the adjacent billiard room come the sounds of a game. Várya appears in the archway.)

TROFÍMOV: *(Teases her)* Mrs. Lopákhin! Mrs. Lopákhin!

VÁRYA: *(Angrily)* High-class tramp!

TROFÍMOV: Yes, I'm a high-class tramp, and I'm proud of it!

VÁRYA: *(Bitterly)* We've hired an orchestra! And what are we supposed to pay them with? *(Goes out)*

TROFÍMOV: *(To Píshchik)* All the energy you've used trying to find money to pay your mortgage, if you'd spent that energy on something else, you could have moved the world.

PÍSHCHIK: Nietzsche, you know, the philosopher—a great thinker,

Nietzsche, a man of genius, one of the great minds of the century—now Nietzsche, you know, says, in his memoirs, that counterfeit money's just as good as real. . . .

TROFÍMOV: I didn't know you'd read Nietzsche.

PÍSHCHIK: Well . . . actually, Dáshenka told me. And I'm desperate enough. I'm ready to start counterfeiting. I need three hundred and ten rubles, day after tomorrow. All I've got so far is a hundred and thirty. . . . *(He feels in his pockets anxiously)* It's gone! My money's gone! *(Almost in tears)* I've lost my money! *(Joyfully)* Oh, here it is! It slipped down into the lining of my coat! God, I'm all in a sweat!

(Enter Liubóv and Carlotta.)

LIUBÓV ANDREYÉVNA: *(She hums a dance tune)* Why is it taking so long? What's Leoníd doing all this time in town? He should be back by now. *(Calls to Dunyásha in the ballroom)* Dunyásha, tell the musicians they can take a break.

TROFÍMOV: They probably postponed the auction.

LIUBÓV ANDREYÉVNA: I suppose it was a mistake to hire an orchestra. Or to have a party in the first place. Oh, well . . . what difference does it make? *(Sits down and hums quietly)*

CARLOTTA: *(Hands Píshchik a deck of cards)* Here's the deck. Pick a card, any card. . . . No, no, just think of one.

PÍSHCHIK: All right, I'm thinking of one.

CARLOTTA: Good. Now shuffle the deck. Very good. Now give it to me. Observe, my dear Píshchik! *Eins, zwei, drei!* Now look in your jacket pocket, and you will find your card.

PÍSHCHIK: *(Takes a card from his jacket pocket)* That's it, the eight of spades! *(Amazed)* Really! I don't believe it!

CARLOTTA: *(Holds out the deck to Trofímov)* Quick, what's the top card?

TROFÍMOV: The top card? Oh . . . uh . . . the queen of spades.

CARLOTTA: Correct! *(To Píshchik)* Now which card's on top?

PÍSHCHIK: Ace of hearts!

CARLOTTA: Correct! *(Claps her hands, and the deck disappears)* Well, isn't this a lovely day we're having?

(A mysterious woman's voice answers; it seems to come from the floorboards: "A lovely day indeed. I couldn't agree more.")

Whoever you are, I adore you!

(The voice: "I adore you too!")

STATIONMASTER: *(Applauds)* Bravo! A lady ventriloquist!

PÍSHCHIK: *(Amazed)* Really! I don't believe it! Carlotta, you are amazing! I'm completely in love with you!

CARLOTTA: In love? *(Shrugs her shoulders)* What do you know about love? *Guter Mensch aber schlechter Musikant.*

TROFÍMOV: *(Slaps Píshchik on the shoulder)* You're just an old horse!

CARLOTTA: All right, everybody, watch closely! One more trick! *(Takes a lap robe from a chair)* See, what a lovely blanket! I'm thinking of selling it. *(Shakes out the lap robe and holds it up)* Who wants to buy?

PÍSHCHIK: *(Amazed)* Really! I don't believe it!

CARLOTTA: *Eins, zwei, drei! (Quickly raises the lap robe)*

(Ánya appears behind the lap robe; she curtsies, runs to her mother and kisses her, then runs back into the ballroom. General applause and cries of delight.)

LIUBÓV ANDREYÉVNA: *(Applauding)* Bravo! Bravo!

CARLOTTA: Now one more! *Eins, zwei, drei!*

(She raises the lap robe; Várya appears; she takes a bow.)

PÍSHCHIK: Really! I don't believe it!

CARLOTTA: That's all. The show is over. *(Throws the lap robe to Píshchik, takes a bow, goes through the ballroom and out)*

PÍSHCHIK: *(Goes after her)* Enchanting! What a woman! What a woman! *(Goes out)*

LIUBÓV ANDREYÉVNA: Leoníd still isn't back from town yet. I don't understand what could be taking him so long! It's got to be all over by now: either the estate has been sold or they've postponed the auction. Why does he have to keep us in suspense like this?

VÁRYA: *(Tries to comfort her)* Uncle bought the estate, I'm sure he has.

TROFÍMOV: *(Ironically)* Oh, I'm sure.

VÁRYA: Ánya's godmother sent him a power of attorney to buy the estate in her name; she agreed to take over the mortgage. She did it for Ánya. So God *has* helped us. Uncle has saved the estate.

LIUBÓV ANDREYÉVNA: The old lady in Yároslavl sent us fifteen thousand to buy the place in her name—she doesn't trust us—but that's not even enough to pay the interest. *(Covers her face with her hands)* My fate . . . my entire life . . . It's all being decided today.

TROFÍMOV: *(Teases Várya)* Mrs. Lopákhin! Mrs. Lopákhin!

VÁRYA: *(Angrily)* And you're a permanent graduate student! Who's been suspended twice!

LIUBÓV ANDRÉYEVNA: Don't get so angry, Várya; he's only teasing you. What's wrong with that? And what's wrong with Lopákhin? If you want to marry him, do; he's a nice man. Interesting, even. If you don't want to marry him, don't; nobody's forcing you.

VÁRYA: It's not a joking matter, Mama, believe me. I'm serious about him. He is a nice man, and I like him.

LIUBÓV ANDRÉYEVNA: Then go ahead and marry him! I don't understand what you're waiting for!

VÁRYA: Mama, I can't propose to him myself! For two years now everybody's been telling me to marry him, everybody, but he never mentions it. Or he jokes about it! Look, I understand, he's busy getting rich, he doesn't have time for me. Oh, if I had just a little money—I don't care how much, even a couple of hundred—I'd get out of here and go someplace far away. I'd go join a convent.

TROFÍMOV: Now, there's an exalted idea!

VÁRYA: *(To Trofímov)* I thought students were supposed to be smart! *(Her tone softens; almost crying)* Oh, Pétya, you used to be so nice-looking, and now you're getting old! *(To Liubóv, in a normal tone)* It's just that I need something to do all the time, Mama; it's the way I am. I can't sit around and do nothing.

> *(Enter Yásha.)*

YÁSHA: *(Barely controlling his laughter)* Yepikhódov broke a billiard cue! *(Goes out)*

VÁRYA: What is Yepikhódov doing here? Who asked him to come? And what's he doing playing billiards? I just don't understand these people. . . . *(Goes out)*

LIUBÓV ANDRÉYEVNA: Pétya, don't tease her like that; you can see she's upset already.

TROFÍMOV: Oh, she's such a busybody, always poking her nose into other people's business. She hasn't left Ánya and me alone the whole summer; she's afraid we're having a . . . an *affair*. What business is it of hers? Besides, it's not true. I'd never do anything so sordid. We're above love!

LIUBÓV ANDRÉYEVNA: And I, I suppose, am beneath love. *(Upset)* Why isn't Leoníd back yet? I just want to know: has the estate been sold or not? The whole disaster seems so impossible to me, I don't know what to think, or do.... Oh, God, I'm losing my mind! I want to scream, or do something completely stupid.... Help me, Pétya! Save me! Say something, say something!

TROFÍMOV: Whether they sell it or not, does it make any difference, really? You can't go back to the past. Everything here came to an end a long time ago. Try to calm down. You can't go on deceiving yourself; at least once in your life you have to look the truth straight in the eye.

LIUBÓV ANDRÉYEVNA: What truth? You seem so sure what's truth and what isn't, but I'm not. I've lost any sense of it, I've lost sight of the truth. You're so sure of yourself, aren't you, so sure you have all the answers to everything, but darling, have you ever really had to live with one of your answers? You're too young! Of course *you* look into the future and see a brave new world, you don't expect any difficulties, but that's because you know nothing about life! Yes, you have more courage than my generation has, and better morals, and you're better educated, but for God's sake have a little sense of what it's like for me, and be easier on me. Pétya, I was born here! My parents lived here all their lives; so did my grandfather. I love this house! Without the cherry orchard my life makes no sense, and if you have to sell it, you might as well sell me with it. *(She embraces Trofímov and kisses his forehead)* And it was here my son drowned, you know that.... *(Weeps)* Have some feeling for me, Pétya, you're such a good, sweet boy.

TROFÍMOV: I pity you. *(Beat)* I do, from the bottom of my heart.

LIUBÓV ANDRÉYEVNA: You should have said that differently, just a little differently.... *(Takes out her handkerchief; a telegram falls to the floor)* You can't imagine how miserable I am today. All this noise, and every new sound makes me shake. I can't get away from it, but then when I'm alone in my room I can't stand the silence. Don't judge me, Pétya! I love you like one of my own family; I'd be very happy to see you and Ánya married, you know I would, only, darling, you must finish school first! You have *got* to graduate! You don't do anything except drift around from place to place—what kind of life is that? It's true, isn't it? Isn't that the truth? And we have to do something about that beard of yours; it's so scraggly.... *(Laughs)* You've gotten so funny-looking!

TROFÍMOV: *(Picks up the telegram)* I have no desire to be good-looking.

LIUBÓV ANDRÉYEVNA: The telegram's from Paris. I get a new one every day. One yesterday, now again today. That madman is sick again and in trouble. . . . He wants me to forgive him, he wants me back . . . and I suppose I should go back to Paris to be with him. Now see, Pétya, you're giving me that superior look, but darling, what am I supposed to do? He's sick, he's alone, he's unhappy, and who has he got to look after him? To give him his medicine and keep him out of trouble? And I love him—why do I have to pretend I don't, or not talk about it? I love him. That's just the way it is: I love him. I love him! He's a millstone around my neck, and he'll drown me with him, but he's *my* millstone! I love him and I can't live without him! *(Grabs Trofímov's hand)* Don't judge me, Pétya, don't think badly of me, just don't say anything, please just don't say anything. . . .

TROFÍMOV: *(Almost in tears)* But for God's sake, you have to face the facts! He robbed you blind!

LIUBÓV ANDRÉYEVNA: No, no, please, you mustn't say that, you mustn't—

TROFÍMOV: He doesn't care a thing for you—you're the only person who doesn't seem to understand that! He's rotten!

LIUBÓV ANDRÉYEVNA: *(Gets angry but tries to control it)* And you, you're what? Twenty-six, twenty-seven? Listen to you: you sound like you'd never even graduated to long pants!

TROFÍMOV: That's fine with me!

LIUBÓV ANDRÉYEVNA: You're supposed to be a man; at your age you ought to know something about love. You ought to be in love yourself! *(Angrily)* Really! You think you're so smart, you're just a kid who doesn't know the first thing about it, you're probably a virgin, you're ridiculous, you're grotesque—

TROFÍMOV: *(Horrified)* What are you saying!

LIUBÓV ANDREYÉVNA: "I'm above love!" You're not above love; you've just never gotten down to it! You're all wet, like Firs says. At your age, you ought to be sleeping with someone!

TROFÍMOV: *(Horrified)* What a terrible thing to say! That's terrible! *(He runs toward the ballroom, covering his ears)* That's just horrible. . . . I can't listen to that; I'm leaving. *(Goes out, but reappears immediately)* All is over between us! *(Goes out into the entrance hall)*

LIUBÓV ANDRÉYEVNA: *(Calls after him)* Pétya, wait a minute! Come back! I was just joking, Pétya, don't be so silly! Pétya!

(A great clatter from the entrance hall; someone has fallen downstairs. Ánya and Várya scream.)

What happened?

(Ánya and Várya suddenly howl with laughter.)

ÁNYA: *(Runs in, laughing)* Pétya just fell headfirst down the stairs! *(Runs out)*
LIUBÓV ANDRÉYEVNA: Oh, what a silly boy!

(The Stationmaster in the ballroom gets on a chair and begins declaiming the opening lines of "The Magdalen" by Alexei Tolstoy.)

STATIONMASTER:
"The splendid ballroom gleams with gold and candles,
a crowd of dancers whirls around the room;
and there apart, an empty glass beside her,
behold the fallen beauty, the lost, the doomed.

Her lavish gown and jewels make all eyes wonder,
her shameless glance bespeaks a life of sin;
young men and old cast longing glances at her—
see, how her fatal beauty draws them in!"

(Everyone gathers to listen, but soon the orchestra returns and the strains of a waltz are heard from the entrance hall. The reading breaks off, and everybody begins to dance. Trofímov, Ánya, and Várya come in from the entrance hall.)

LIUBÓV ANDRÉYEVNA: Pétya ... oh, darling, I'm *so* sorry. . . . You sweet thing, please forgive me. . . . Come on, let's dance. *(Dances with Trofímov)*

(Ánya and Várya dance together. Firs enters, leans his walking stick against the side door. Yásha appears and stands watching the dancers.)

YÁSHA: What's the matter, pops?
FIRS: I don't feel so good. The old days, we had a dance, we had generals and barons and admirals; nowadays we have to send out for the postmaster and the stationmaster. And they're none too eager to come, either. Oh, I'm getting old and feeble. The old master, their grandfather, anybody got sick, he used to dose 'em all with

sealing wax. Didn't matter what they had, they all got sealing wax. I've been taking sealing wax myself now for nigh onto twenty years. Take some every day. That's probably why I'm still alive.

YÁSHA: You're getting boring, pops. *(Yawns)* Time for you to crawl off and die.

FIRS: Oh, you . . . you young flibbertigibbet. *(Mumbles)*

(Trofímov and Liubóv dance through the ballroom, into the sitting room.)

LIUBÓV ANDRÉYEVNA: *Merci.* I need to sit down and rest a bit. . . . *(Sits.)* I'm so tired.

(Enter Ánya.)

ÁNYA: *(Upset)* There was a man in the kitchen just now, he said the cherry orchard's already been sold!

LIUBÓV ANDRÉYEVNA: Who bought it?

ÁNYA: He didn't say. And he's gone now. *(Dances with Trofímov; they dance off across the ballroom)*

YÁSHA: That was just some old guy talking crazy. It wasn't anybody from around here.

FIRS: And Leoníd Andréyich still isn't back. All he had on was his topcoat; you watch, he'll catch cold. He's all wet, that one.

LIUBÓV ANDRÉYEVNA: I'll never live through this. Yásha, go out and see if anybody knows who bought it.

YÁSHA: It was just some old guy. He left long ago. *(Laughs)*

LIUBÓV ANDRÉYEVNA: *(Somewhat annoyed)* What are you laughing at? What's so funny?

YÁSHA: That Yepikhódov. What a dope. Old Double Trouble.

LIUBÓV ANDRÉYEVNA: Firs, suppose the estate is sold—where are you going to go?

FIRS: I'll go wherever you tell me to.

LIUBÓV ANDRÉYEVNA: What's the matter? Your face looks so funny. . . . Are you sick? You should go to bed.

FIRS: Yes. . . . *(Smirks)* Yes, sure, go to bed, and then who'll take care of things? I'm the only one you've got.

YÁSHA: Liubóv Andréyevna, there's a favor I have *got* to ask you; it's very important. If you go back to Paris, please take me with you. Please! You've got to! I positively cannot stay around here. *(Looks around, lowers his voice)* You can see for yourself this place is hopeless. The whole country's a mess, nobody has any culture, it's

boring, the food is lousy, and there's that old Firs drooling all
over the place and talking like an idiot. Please, take me with
you—you've just got to!

(Enter Píshchik.)

PÍSHCHIK: Beautiful lady, what about a waltz? Just one little waltz!
(Liubóv crosses to him) You dazzler, you! And what about a loan,
just one little loan, just a hundred and eighty, that's all I need.
(They begin to dance) Just a hundred and eighty ... *(They dance
off into the ballroom)*

YÁSHA: *(Sings to himself)* "Can't you see my heart is breaking ..."

*(In the ballroom, a figure appears dressed in checkered trousers and
a gray top hat, jumping and waving its arms. We hear shouts of
"Bravo, Carlotta!")*

DUNYÁSHA: *(Stops to powder her nose)* The missus told me to dance—
there's too many gentlemen and not enough ladies—so I did, I've
been dancing all night and my heart won't stop beating, and you
know what, Firs? Just now, the postmaster, you know? He said
something almost made me faint.

(The orchestra stops playing.)

FIRS: What did he say?

DUNYÁSHA: That I was like a flower. That's what he said.

YÁSHA: *(Yawns)* What does he know about it? *(Goes out)*

DUNYÁSHA: Just like a flower. I'm a very romantic girl, really. I just
adore that kind of talk.

FIRS: You're out of your mind.

(Enter Yepikhódov.)

YEPIKHÓDOV: *(To Dunyásha)* Why are you deliberating not to notice
me? You act as if I wasn't here, like I was a bug or something.
(Sighs) Ah, life!

DUNYÁSHA: Excuse me?

YEPIKHÓDOV: Of course, you may be right. *(Sighs)* But if you look at
it, let's say, from a ... a point of view, then you're the faulty
one—excuse my expressivity—because you led me on. Into this
predictament. Look at me! Every day something awful happens
to me. It's like a habit. But I can look disaster in the face and
keep smiling. You gave me your word, you know, and you
even—

DUNYÁSHA: Do you mind? Let's talk about it later. Right now I'd rather be left alone. With my dreams. *(Plays with a fan)*

YEPIKHÓDOV: Every day. Something awful. But all I do—excuse my expressivity—is try to keep smiling. Sometimes I even laugh.

(Enter Várya from the ballroom.)

VÁRYA: *(To Yepikhódov)* Are you still here? I thought I told you to go home. Really, you have no consideration. *(To Dunyásha)* Dunyásha, go back to the kitchen! *(To Yepikhódov)* You come in here and start playing billiards, you break one of our cues, now you hang around in here as if we'd invited you.

YEPIKHÓDOV: Excuse my expressivity, but you have no right to penalize me.

VÁRYA: I'm not penalizing you, I'm telling you! All you do here is wander around and bump into the furniture. You're supposed to be working for us, and you don't do a thing. I don't know why we hired you in the first place.

YEPIKHÓDOV: *(Offended)* Whether I work or not or wander around or not or play billiards or not is none of your business! You do not have the know-it-all to make my estimation!

VÁRYA: How dare you talk to me like that! *(In a rage)* How dare you! What do you mean, I don't have the know-it-all? You get yourself out of here right this minute! Right this minute!

YEPIKHÓDOV: *(Apprehensively)* I wish you wouldn't use language like that—

VÁRYA: *(Beside herself)* Get out of here right this minute! Out! *(He goes to the door; she follows him)* Double Trouble! I don't want to see hide or hair of you, I don't want to lay eyes on you ever again! *(Yepikhódov goes out; from behind the door we hear him screech: "I'll call the police on you!")* Oh, you coming back for more? *(Grabs the stick that Firs has left by the door)* Come on . . . Come on . . . Come on, I'll show you! All right, all right, you asked for it—*(Swings the stick; the door opens, and she hits Lopákhin over the head as he enters)*

LOPÁKHIN: Thanks a lot.

VÁRYA: *(Still angry, sarcastic)* Oh, I'm so sorry!

LOPÁKHIN: S'all right. Always appreciate a warm welcome.

VÁRYA: I don't need appreciation. *(Walks off, then turns and asks gently)* I didn't hurt you, did I?

LOPÁKHIN: No, I'm fine. Just a whopping big lump, that's all.

(Voices from the ballroom: "Lopákhin! Lopákhin's here! He's back! Lopákhin's back!" People crowd into the sitting room.)

PÍSHCHIK: The great man in person! *(Hugs Lopákhin)* Is that cognac I smell? It is! You've been celebrating! Well, so have we. Join the party!

LIUBÓV ANDRÉYEVNA: It's you, Yermolái Alexéyich. Where have you been all this time? Where's Leoníd?

LOPÁKHIN: He's coming; we took the same train.

LIUBÓV ANDRÉYEVNA: What happened? Did they have the auction? Tell me!

LOPÁKHIN: *(Embarrassed, afraid to show his joy)* The auction was all over by four this afternoon, but we missed the train. We had to wait for the nine-thirty. *(Exhales heavily)* Oof! My head is really spinning....

(Enter Gáyev; he holds a wrapped package in one hand, wipes his eyes with the other.)

LIUBÓV ANDRÉYEVNA: Lyónya, what's the matter? Lyónya! *(Impatiently, beginning to cry)* For God's sake, what happened!

GÁYEV: *(Weeps and can't answer her; makes a despairing gesture with his free hand and turns to Firs)* Here, take these ... some anchovies ... imported. I haven't eaten a thing all day. You have no idea what I've been through! *(The door to the billiard room is open; we hear the click of billiard balls and Yásha's voice: "Seven ball in the left pocket!" Gáyev's expression changes; he stops crying)* I'm all worn out. Firs, come help me get ready for bed. *(Goes through the ballroom and out; Firs follows him)*

PÍSHCHIK: What about the auction? Tell us what happened!

LIUBÓV ANDRÉYEVNA: Is the cherry orchard sold?

LOPÁKHIN: It's sold.

LIUBÓV ANDRÉYEVNA: Who bought it?

LOPÁKHIN: I did.

(Pause. Liubóv is overcome; she would fall, if she weren't standing beside a table and the armchair. Várya takes the keys from her belt, throws them on the floor, crosses the room, and goes out.)

I did! I bought it! No, wait, don't go, please. I'm still a little mixed up about it, I can't talk yet.... *(Laughs)* We get to the auction, and there's Derigánov, all ready and waiting. Leoníd Andréyich only had fifteen thousand, so right away Derigánov

raises the bid to thirty, that's on top of the balance on the mortgage. So I see what he's up to, and I bid against him. Raise it to
forty. He bids forty-five. I bid fifty-five. See, he was raising by five,
and I double him, I raise him ten each time. Anyway, finally it's all
over, and I got it! Ninety thousand plus the balance on the mortgage. And now the cherry orchard is mine! Mine! *(A loud laugh)*
My God, the cherry orchard belongs to me! Tell me I'm drunk,
tell me it's all a dream, I'm making this up— *(Stomps on the floor)*
And don't anybody laugh! My God, if my father and my grandfather could be here now and see this, see *me*, their Yermolái, the
boy they beat, who went barefoot in winter and never went to
school, see how that poor boy just bought the most beautiful estate
in the whole world! I bought the estate where my father and my
grandfather slaved away their lives, where they wouldn't even let
them in the kitchen! My God, I must be dreaming—I can't believe
all this is happening! *(Picks up Várya's keys; smiles gently)* See, she
threw away her keys; she knows she isn't running the place anymore. . . . *(Jingles the keys)* Well, that's all right.

(The orchestra starts tuning up again.)

That's it, let's have some music—come on, I want to hear it!
Everybody come watch! Come on and watch what I do! I'm
going to chop down every tree in that cherry orchard, every goddamn one of them, and then I'm going to develop that land!
Watch me! I'm going to do something our children and grand-
children can be proud of! Come on, you musicians, play!

*(The orchestra begins to play. Liubóv curls up in the armchair and
weeps bitterly.)*

LOPÁKHIN: *(Reproachfully)* Oh, why didn't you listen to me? You
dear woman, you dear good woman, you can't ever go back to the
past. *(With tears in his eyes)* Oh, if only we could change things, if
only life were different, this unhappy, messy life . . .

PÍSHCHIK: *(Takes his arm; quietly)* She's crying. Come on, we'll go in
the other room, leave her alone for a while. Come on. . . . *(Leads
him into the ballroom)*

LOPÁKHIN: What's the matter? Tell the band to keep playing!
Louder! *(Ironic)* It's my house now! The cherry orchard belongs
to me! I can do what I want to! *(Bumps into a small table, almost
knocking over a candlestick)* Don't worry about that: I can pay for
it! I can pay for everything! *(Goes out with Píshchik)*

(The sitting room is empty except for Liubóv, who sits tightly clenched and weeping bitterly. The orchestra plays softly. Suddenly Ánya and Trofímov enter. Ánya goes and kneels before her mother. Trofímov remains by the archway.)

ÁNYA: Mama! Mama, you're crying. Mama dear, I love you, I'll take care of you. The cherry orchard is sold, it's gone now, that's the truth, Mama, that's the truth, but don't cry. You still have your life to lead, you're still a good person. . . . Come with me, Mama, we'll go away, someplace far away from here. We'll plant a new orchard, even better than this one, you'll see, Mama, you'll understand, and you'll feel a new kind of joy, like a light in your soul. . . . Let's go, Mama. Let's go!

CURTAIN.

ACT FOUR

The same room as Act One. The curtains have been taken down, the pictures are gone from the walls, and there are only a few pieces of furniture shoved into a corner, as if for sale. The place feels empty. By the doorway, a pile of trunks, suitcases, etc. The door on the right is open; we hear Ánya and Várya talking in the room beyond. Lopákhin stands waiting. Beside him, Yásha holds a tray of glasses filled with champagne. Through the door we see Yepikhódov in the front hall, fastening the straps on a trunk. The sound of murmured voices offstage; some of the local people have come to say goodbye. Gáyev's voice: "Thank you all, good people, thanks, thanks very much for coming."

YÁSHA: It's some of these poor yokels, come to say goodbye. I'm of the opinion, you know, these people around here . . . ? They're okay, but they're . . . they're just a bunch of know-nothings.

(The murmur of voices dies away. Liubóv and Gáyev come in from the entrance hall; she has stopped crying, but she is shaking slightly, and her face is pale. She cannot speak.)

GÁYEV: You gave them all the money you had, Liúba. You can't do that! You can't do that anymore!

LIUBÓV ANDREYÉVNA: I couldn't help it! I just couldn't help it!

(They both go out. Lopákhin follows them to the door.)

LOPÁKHIN: Wait, please. How about a little glass of champagne, just to celebrate? I forgot to bring some from town, but I got this one bottle at the station. It was all they had.

(Pause.)

No? What's the matter, don't you want any? *(Comes back from the door)* If I'd known that, I wouldn't have bought it. I don't feel like any myself.

(Yásha carefully puts the tray down on a chair.)

Go on, Yásha, you might as well have one.

YÁSHA: *Bon voyage!* And here's to the girls we leave behind! *(Drinks)* This is not your real French champagne, I can tell.

LOPÁKHIN: Cost me enough.

(Pause.)

It's cold as hell in here.

YÁSHA: They figured they were going away today anyway—they decided not to heat the place. *(Laughs)*

LOPÁKHIN: What's with you?

YÁSHA: I'm laughing because everything worked out just the way I wanted.

LOPÁKHIN: It's October already, but the sun's out; it feels like summer. Good weather for home builders. *(Looks at his watch, then at the door)* Listen, everybody, you got forty-six minutes till train time! And it's twenty minutes from here to the station, so you better get a move on.

(Enter Trofímov from outside; he's wearing an overcoat.)

TROFÍMOV: It must be time to go. The carts are here. Where the hell are my galoshes? I've lost them somewhere. *(At the door)* Ánya, where are my galoshes? I can't find them anyplace!

LOPÁKHIN: I'm off to Hárkov. I'll be taking the same train as you. Off to Hárkov, spend the winter there. I've been hanging around here too long, doing nothing; I can't stand that. I got to keep working, otherwise I don't know what to do with my hands; if they're not doing something, they feel like they don't belong to me.

TROFÍMOV: So. We're leaving, and you're going back to your useful labors in the real world.

LOPÁKHIN: Have a glass of champagne.

TROFÍMOV: No, thanks.

LOPÁKHIN: So you're off to Moscow?

TROFÍMOV: Yes. I'll go into town with them today, and then leave tomorrow for Moscow.

LOPÁKHIN: Sure. I'll bet all those professors are waiting for you to show up, wouldn't want to start their lectures without you!

TROFÍMOV: Mind your own business.

LOPÁKHIN: How long you say you've been at that university?

TROFÍMOV: Come on! Think up something new, will you? You're getting boring. *(Pokes around, looking for his galoshes)* You know, we probably won't ever see each other again, so you mind my giving you a little advice? As a farewell present? Don't wave your arms around so much. Bad habit. And this development you're putting in out here—you think that's going to improve the world? You think your leisure home buyers are going to turn into yeoman farmers? That's a lot of arm waving too. Well, what the hell. I like you anyway. You've got nice hands. Gentle and sensitive. You could have been an artist. And you're like that inside too—gentle and sensitive.

LOPÁKHIN: *(Hugs him)* Goodbye, boy. Thanks for everything. Here, let me give you a little money. You may need it for the trip.

TROFÍMOV: What for? I don't need money!

LOPÁKHIN: What *for*? You don't have any!

TROFÍMOV: I do too. Thanks all the same. I got paid for a translation I did. I have money right here in my pocket. *(Worried)* I just wish I could find my galoshes!

VÁRYA: *(From the next room)* Here they are! The smelly things ... *(Throws a pair of galoshes into the room)*

TROFÍMOV: What are you always getting mad for? Hmm ... These aren't my galoshes.

LOPÁKHIN: This past spring I planted a big crop of poppies. Three hundred acres. Sold the poppy seed, made forty thousand clear. And when those poppies were all in flower, what a picture that was! So look, I just made forty thousand, I can afford to loan you some money. Why turn up your nose at it? Because you think I'm just a dirt farmer?

TROFÍMOV: So your father was a dirt farmer. Mine worked in a drugstore. What does that prove?

(Lopákhin takes out his wallet.)

Forget it, forget it. Look, you could give me a couple of hundred thousand, I still wouldn't take it. I'm a free man. And you people, everything you think is so valuable, it doesn't mean a thing to me. I don't care whether you're rich or poor; you've got no power over me. I can do without you, I can go right on past you, because I am proud and I am strong. Humanity is moving onward, toward a higher truth and a higher happiness, higher than anyone can imagine. And I'm ahead of the rest!

LOPÁKHIN: You think you'll ever get there?

TROFÍMOV: I'll get there.

(Pause.)

I'll get there. Or I'll make sure the rest of them get there.

(From the orchard comes the sound of axes; they've started chopping down the cherry trees.)

LOPÁKHIN: Well, boy, goodbye. Time to go. You and I don't see eye to eye, but life goes on anyway. Whenever I work real hard, round the clock practically, that clears my mind somehow, and for a minute I think maybe I know what we're all here for. But God, boy, think of the thousands of people in this country who don't know what they're doing or why they're doing it. But . . . I guess that doesn't have much to do with the price of eggs. They told me Leoníd Andréyich got a job at the bank, six thousand a year. He won't last; he's too lazy.

ÁNYA: *(At the door)* Mama asks you to please wait until she's gone before you start cutting down the orchard.

TROFÍMOV: I agree. That isn't very tactful, you know. *(Goes out into the front hall)*

LOPÁKHIN: All right, all right, I'll take care of it. God, these people . . . *(Goes out after him)*

ÁNYA: Have they taken Firs to the nursing home?

YÁSHA: I told them about it this morning. So I imagine they have.

ÁNYA: *(To Yepikhódov, who crosses the room)* Yepikhódov, could you please go and make sure they've taken Firs to the nursing home?

YÁSHA: *(Offended)* I already told them this morning! Why keep asking?

YEPIKHÓDOV: The aged Firs, in my ultimate opinion, is beyond nursing. They ought to take him to the cemetery. And I can only envy him. *(Sets a suitcase down on a cardboard hatbox and crushes it)* There. Finally. Wouldn't you know. *(Goes out)*

YÁSHA: *(Snickers)* Old Double Trouble.

VÁRYA: *(From the next room)* Have they taken Firs to the nursing home?

ÁNYA: They took him this morning.

VÁRYA: Then why didn't they take the letter for the doctor?

ÁNYA: They must have forgotten. We'll have to send someone after them with it.

VÁRYA: Where's Yásha? Tell him his mother is here; she wants to say goodbye.

YÁSHA: *(With a dismissive gesture)* What a bore! Why can't she just leave me alone?

> *(Dunyásha has been drifting in and out, fussing with the baggage; now that she sees Yásha alone, she goes to him.)*

DUNYÁSHA: Oh ... oh, Yásha, why won't you even look at me? You're going away ... you're leaving me behind.... *(Starts to cry and throws her arms around his neck)*

YÁSHA: What are you crying about? *(Drinks some champagne)* Six days from now, I'll be back in Paris. Tomorrow we get on the express train, and we're off! And that's the last you'll ever see of me! I can't hardly believe it myself. *Vive la France!* I can't live around here anymore; it's just not my kind of place. They're all so ignorant, and I can't stand that. *(Drinks more champagne)* What are you crying about? If you'd been a nice girl, you wouldn't have anything to cry about.

DUNYÁSHA: *(Powders her nose in a mirror)* Don't forget to send me a letter from Paris. Because I loved you, Yásha, I really did. I'm a very sensitive person, Yásha, I really am—

YÁSHA: Watch it, someone's coming. *(He starts fussing with the luggage, whistling quietly)*

> *(Enter Liubóv, Gáyev, Ánya, and Carlotta.)*

GÁYEV: We should be going. We're already a little late. *(Looks at Yásha)* Who smells like herring?

LIUBÓV ANDRÉYEVNA: We've only got ten minutes; then we absolutely must start out. *(Glances around the room)* Goodbye, house! Wonderful old house! Winter's almost here, and come spring you'll be gone. They'll tear you down. Think of everything these walls have seen! *(Kisses Ánya with great feeling)* My treasure, look at you! You're radiant today! Your eyes are shining like diamonds! Are you happy? Really happy?

ÁNYA: Oh, yes, Mama, really! We're starting a new life!

GÁYEV: She's right—everything worked out extremely well. Before the cherry orchard was sold we were at our wit's end—remember how painful it was?—and now everything's finally settled, once and for all, no turning back, and see? We've all calmed down. We're even rather happy. I'm going to work at the bank, I'm about to become a financier! Yellow ball in the side pocket . . . And you look better than you have in a long time, Lyúba; you do, you know.

LIUBÓV ANDRÉYEVNA: I know. My nerves have quieted down. You're quite right.

(Someone holds out her hat and coat.)

And I sleep much better now. Take my things, Yásha, will you? It's time to go. *(To Ánya)* Darling, we'll see each other soon enough. I'm off to Paris—I kept the money your godmother in Yároslavl sent to buy the estate. *(A hard laugh)* Thank God for the old lady! That ought to get me through the winter at least. . . .

ÁNYA: And you'll come back soon, won't you? You promise? I'll study hard and get my diploma, and then I'll get a job and help you out. We can read together the way we used to, can't we? *(Kisses her mother's hands)* We'll spend long autumn evenings together; we'll read lots of books and learn all about the wonderful new world of the future. . . . *(Dreamily)* Don't forget, Mama, you promised. . . .

LIUBÓV ANDRÉYEVNA: I will, my angel, I promise. *(Embraces her)*

(Enter Lopákhin. Carlotta hums a tune under her breath.)

GÁYEV: Carlotta must be happy; she's singing!

CARLOTTA: *(Picks up a bundle that looks like a baby in swaddling clothes)* Here's my little baby. Bye, bye, baby . . .

(We hear a baby's voice: "Wah! Wah!")

Shh, baby, shh, shh . . . good little children don't cry. . . .

(Again: "Wah! Wah!")

I feel so sorry for the poor thing. *(Hurls the bundle to the floor)* You will find me a job, won't you? I can't go on like this anymore.

LOPÁKHIN: Don't worry, Carlotta; we'll take care of you.

GÁYEV: Everybody's just thrown us away. Várya's leaving. . . . All of a sudden we're useless.

CARLOTTA: How can I live in that town of yours? There must be someplace I can go. . . . *(Hums)* What difference does it make . . . ?

(Enter Píshchik.)

LOPÁKHIN: Here comes the wonder boy.

PÍSHCHIK: *(Panting)* Ooh, give me a minute . . . I'm all worn out. Good morning, good morning, good morning. Could I get a drink of water?

GÁYEV: *(Sarcastic)* You're sure it isn't money you want? You'll all have to excuse me if I remove myself from the approaching negotiations. *(Goes out)*

PÍSHCHIK: I'm so glad to see you all. . . . Dear lady . . . I've been a stranger, I know. *(To Lopákhin)* And you're here too. Delighted, delighted, a man I admire, always have. . . . Here. Here. This is for you. *(Gives Lopákhin money)* Four hundred. And I still owe you eight hundred and forty.

LOPÁKHIN: *(A bewildered shrug)* I must be dreaming. Where did you get money?

PÍSHCHIK: Wait a minute; let me cool off. Well, it was an absolutely extraordinary thing. These Englishmen showed up, they poked around on my land, found some kind of white clay. . . . *(To Liubóv)* Here . . . Here's the four hundred. You've been so kind . . . so sweet . . . *(Gives her money)* And you'll have the rest before you know it. *(Takes a drink of water)* You know, there was a young man on the train just now, he was saying . . . there was this philosopher, he said, who wanted us all to jump off the roof. "Jump!" he said. "Jump!" That was his whole philosophy. *(Amazed)* Really! I don't believe it! Give me some more water. . . .

LOPÁKHIN: What Englishmen are you talking about?

PÍSHCHIK: I gave them a lease on the land, the place where the clay is, a twenty-four-year lease. And now excuse me, but I'm off. Lots of people to see, pay back what I owe. I owe money all over the place. *(Takes a drink of water)* Well, I just wanted to say hello. I'll come by again on Thursday.

LIUBÓV ANDRÉYEVNA: But we're leaving for town today. And tomorrow I'm going back to Paris.

PÍSHCHIK: What? *(Astonished)* Leaving for town? Oh, my . . . Oh, of course; the furniture's gone. And all these trunks. I didn't realize.

(Almost in tears) I didn't realize. Great thinkers, these English . . . God bless you all. And be happy. I didn't realize. Well, all things must come to an end. *(Kisses Liubóv's hand)* I'll come to an end myself one of these days. And when I do, I want you all to say: "Semyónov-Píshchik . . . he was a good old horse. God bless him." Wonderful weather we're having. Yes. . . . *(Starts out, overcome with emotion, stops in the doorway and turns)* Oh, by the way, Dáshenka says hello. *(Goes out)*

LIUBÓV ANDRÉYEVNA: Now we can go. There are just two things still on my mind. The first is old Firs. *(Looks at her watch)* We've still got five minutes. . . .

ÁNYA: Mama, they took Firs to the nursing home this morning. Yásha took care of it.

LIUBÓV ANDRÉYEVNA: . . . And then there's our Várya. She's used to getting up early and working around here all day long, and now she's . . . out of a job. Like a fish out of water. Poor thing—she's so nervous, she cries, she's losing weight . . .

(Pause.)

You know, Yermolái Alexéyich—well, of course you know—I'd always dreamed . . . always dreamed she'd marry you; you know we all think it's a wonderful idea. . . . *(Whispers to Ánya, who nods to Carlotta; they both leave)* She loves you, you like her. . . . I don't know why, I just don't know why the two of you keep avoiding the issue. Really!

LOPÁKHIN: I don't know why either. It's all a little funny. Well, I don't mind. If there's still time, I'll do it. . . . All right, *basta*, let's just get it over with. But I don't know, I don't think I can propose without you—

LIUBÓV ANDRÉYEVNA: Of course you can. All it takes is a minute. I'll send her right in. . . .

LOPÁKHIN: We've even got some champagne all ready. *(Looks at the tray of empty glasses)* Or at least we did. Somebody must have drunk it all up.

(Yásha coughs.)

Guzzled it down, I should say.

LIUBÓV ANDRÉYEVNA: Wonderful! We'll leave you alone. Yásha, *allez!* I'll go call her. *(At the door)* Várya, leave that alone; come here a minute, will you? Come on, dear! *(Goes out with Yásha)*

LOPÁKHIN: *(Looks at his watch)* Well . . .

(Pause. A few stifled laughs and whispers behind the door. Finally Várya enters.)

VÁRYA: *(Examines the luggage; takes her time)* That's funny, I can't find them. . . .

LOPÁKHIN: What are you looking for?

VÁRYA: I packed them myself, and now I don't remember where.

(Pause.)

LOPÁKHIN: What . . . ah . . . where are you off to, Várya?

VÁRYA: Me? I'm going to work for the Ragúlins. I talked to them about it already; they need a housekeeper. And look after things, you know. . . .

LOPÁKHIN: All the way over there? That's fifty miles away.

(Pause.)

Well, looks like this is the end of things around here. . . .

VÁRYA: *(Still examining the luggage)* Where are they . . . ? Or maybe I put them in the trunk. You're right: this is the end of things here. The end of one life—

LOPÁKHIN: I'm going too. To Hárkov. Taking the same train, actually. I've got a million things waiting for me. I'm leaving Yepikhódov, though. Hired him to take charge here.

VÁRYA: You hired *who?*

LOPÁKHIN: Last year this time it was snowing already, remember? Today it's still sunny. Nice day. A little chilly, though . . . It was freezing this morning; must have been in the thirties.

VÁRYA: I didn't notice.

(Pause.)

Anyway, the thermometer's broken.

(Pause. A voice from outside calls: "Lopákhin!")

LOPÁKHIN: *(As if he'd been waiting for the call)* I'm coming! *(Goes out)*

(Várya sits down on the floor, leans her head on a bundle of dresses, and cries. The door opens; Liubóv enters carefully.)

LIUBÓV ANDRÉYEVNA: Well?

(Pause.)

We have to go.

VÁRYA: *(Already stopped crying, wipes her eyes)* Right, Mama, we have to go. I can get to the Ragúlins' today, if I don't miss the train.

LIUBÓV ANDRÉYEVNA: Ánya, get your coat on.

> *(Enter Ánya, Gáyev, Carlotta. Gáyev wears a winter overcoat. Servants and drivers come in to pick up the luggage. Yepikhódov directs the operation.)*

Well, we're ready to start.

ÁNYA: *(Joyfully)* Ready to start!

GÁYEV: My dear friends, my very dear friends! On this occasion, this farewell to our beloved house, I cannot keep still. I feel I must say a few words to express the emotion that overwhelms me, overwhelms us all—

ÁNYA: *(Pleads)* Uncle, please!

VÁRYA: That's enough, Uncle.

GÁYEV: *(Crushed)* All right . . . Yellow ball in the side pocket . . . I'll keep still.

> *(Enter Trofímov, then Lopákhin.)*

TROFÍMOV: Ladies and gentlemen, time to go! You'll be late!

LOPÁKHIN: Yepikhódov, get my coat.

LIUBÓV ANDRÉYEVNA: Let me stay a little minute longer. I never really noticed these walls before, or the ceilings. I want a last look, one last long look. . . .

GÁYEV: I remember when I was six, I was watching out that window, right over there. It was a holy day, Trinity Sunday, I think, and I saw Father on his way to church. . . .

LIUBÓV ANDRÉYEVNA: Have we got everything?

LOPÁKHIN: I guess so. *(To Yepikhódov, who helps him on with his coat)* You keep an eye on things, Yepikhódov.

YEPIKHÓDOV: *(Loud, businesslike tone)* You can count on me, Yermolái Alexéyich!

LOPÁKHIN: Why are you talking like that all of a sudden?

YEPIKHÓDOV: I just had a drink—water. . . . It went down the wrong way.

YÁSHA: *(With contempt)* Dumb hick!

LIUBÓV ANDRÉYEVNA: We're all going away. There won't be a soul left on the place. . . .

LOPÁKHIN: But wait till you see what happens here come spring!

> *(Várya grabs an umbrella from the luggage, as if she were going to hit him. Lopákhin pretends to be terrified.)*

VÁRYA: Don't get excited. It was just a joke.

TROFÍMOV: You've all got to get moving! It's time to go! You'll miss your train!

VÁRYA: Here's your galoshes, Pétya, behind this suitcase. *(With tears in her eyes)* Smelly old things . . .

TROFÍMOV: *(Puts them on)* It's time to go!

GÁYEV: *(Deeply moved, afraid he'll start crying)* Yes, the train . . . mustn't miss the train . . . Yellow ball in the side pocket, white in the corner . . .

LIUBÓV ANDRÉYEVNA: Let's go!

LOPÁKHIN: Everybody here? Nobody left? *(Closes and locks the door, left)* Got to lock up; I've got a few things stored here. All right, let's go!

ÁNYA: Goodbye, house! Goodbye, old life!

TROFÍMOV: No, hello, new life! *(Goes out with Ánya)*

(Várya looks around the room again; she's not eager to go. Yásha goes out with Carlotta and her little dog.)

LOPÁKHIN: So. Until next spring. Come on, let's go, everybody. Goodbye!

(Liubóv and Gáyev are left alone. It's as if they'd been waiting for this moment. They throw their arms around each other and burst out crying, but try to keep the others outside from hearing.)

GÁYEV: *(In despair)* Oh, sister, sister . . .

LIUBÓV ANDRÉYEVNA: Oh, my orchard, my beautiful orchard! My life, my youth, my happiness, goodbye! Goodbye! Goodbye!

(Ánya's voice, joyful: "Mama!" Trofímov's voice, joyful, excited: "Yoo-hoo!")

These walls, these windows, for the last time . . . And Mama loved this room . . .

GÁYEV: Oh, sister, sister . . .

(Ánya: "Mama!" Trofímov: "Yoo-hoo!")

LIUBÓV ANDRÉYEVNA: We're coming! *(They leave)*

(The stage is empty. We hear the sound of the door being locked, then the carriages as they drive away. It grows very quiet. In the silence, we hear the occasional sound of an ax chopping down the cherry trees, a mournful, lonely sound. Then we hear steps. Enter Firs from the door, right. He wears his usual butler's livery, but with bedroom slippers. He's very ill.)

FIRS: *(Goes to the door, tries the handle)* Locked. They're gone. *(Sits on the sofa)* They forgot about me. That's all right; I'll just sit here for a bit. . . . And Leoníd Andréyich probably forgot his winter coat. *(A worried sigh)* I should have looked. . . . He's still all wet, that one. . . . *(Mumbles something we can't make out)* Well, it's all over now, and I never even had a life to live. . . . *(Lies back)* I'll just lie here for a bit. . . . No strength left, nothing left, not a thing . . . Oh, you. You young flibbertigibbet. *(Lies there, no longer moving)*

> *(In the distance we hear a sound that seems to come from the sky, a sad sound, like a string snapping. It dies away. Everything grows quiet. We can hear the occasional sound of an ax on a tree.)*

CURTAIN.

THE CHERRY ORCHARD: NOTES

Page 337. Várya's longing to start walking and make visits to churches is a desire to become a religious pilgrim. There were hundreds of these pilgrims in old Russia, older people mostly, who walked from town to town, sometimes in groups, to visit shrines and holy places. They depended for food and lodging on the monasteries and the kindness of the local populations, which was generally given freely.

Page 339. "Yellow ball in the side pocket." Gáyev's constant references to billiard shots are a kind of nervous tic, to cover confusion or embarrassment. The dramatic payoff, of course, comes in Act Three, when Gáyev returns from the auction, weeping. Then Chekhov says: "The door to the billiard room is open; we hear the click of billiard balls and Yásha's voice: 'Seven ball in the left pocket!'" When he hears the detestable Yásha playing his game on his table, Chekhov says: "Gáyev's expression changes; he stops crying." This is the last straw for Gáyev, and he leaves the room.

Page 339. "I've really gotten addicted to coffee." Liubóv's addiction to coffee, together with the pills that Yásha gives her a few moments later, give us a clue to her physical condition and the state of her nerves.

Page 345. "Trofímov . . . dressed like a student." All students in prerevolutionary Russia wore uniforms, as did their teachers and professors, and all members of the civil service and the government.

Page 348. "A man of the eighties." The 1880s in Russia were a period of extreme reaction under the emperor Alexander III. Gáyev presumably tries to identify himself with the populist idea of befriending the oppressed peasantry.

Page 350. Yepikhódov's song is an example of the ballads the Russians called "cruel romances." It is not a folk song but a popular song from a more urban environment.

Page 351. Henry Thomas Buckle (1821–62) was an English historian, author of *A History of Civilization in England*. Yepikhódov's reading list is eclectic, to say the least.

Page 354. "Ooh-la-la . . ." The lines Lopákhin sings are presumably from the musical he saw the night before. There is no record of a tune.

Page 355. "By the time we got our freedom back . . ." Czar Alexander II abolished serfdom in Russia in 1861. The declaration said nothing about giving land to the peasants, and pressures from landowners made the transition endlessly complicated.

Page 387. "Remember, human beings are constantly progressing . . ." Because of Trofímov's long speech here and later in the act, he is sometimes—in Soviet productions, always—played as a revolutionary firebrand. He isn't; he's merely "socially aware" and eager for change, as were the majority of university students in Russia at the time. He was suspended twice from the university, but this was the common fate of many liberal-thinking students. In February and March of 1899, for example, an enormous student strike spread across the country and was brutally put down by the authorities. On March 15, both Moscow and Saint Petersburg universities were shut down and occupied by the police. As Simon Karlinsky notes: "To resume their studies, students were required to supply evidence of their political reliability, and those who refused were dismissed." There exists a letter from Mikhail Lavrov, a student whose views echo those of Trofímov:

> The strike at Moscow University began on Saturday the 13th. Everyone was expelled and is now signing statements of repentance. As soon as the university is reopened, the strike will resume, and this will keep up until the students' demands have been satisfied. . . . It's time to set up a boundary between practical knowledge and faith in broad theories of the future. It is time to recognize the necessity of human sacrifice, for only so doing can we live for the distant future, glorifying and idealizing those who sacrifice themselves. There are very few students with a clear understanding of the full import of the present events, and you will find even fewer people outside the university who understand them. But that only serves to bolster our confidence, enthusiasm, and sense of invincibility. This is a time when life is on its way to becoming pure pleasure. This is what the new age is like.

Trofímov has a keen sense of injustice but little will to do anything about it. His call to "get down to work, and work harder than we've ever worked before" doesn't seem to apply to him, the permanent graduate student and drifter. He is a visionary, if you will, but an ineffectual one, proud of his poverty; and he probably *is* a virgin, as Liubóv suggests. It is telling that he is involved in a platonic relationship with a teenage girl twelve years younger than himself.

Page 359. "Amelia, get thee to a nunnery." Lopákhin's garbled quotes from *Hamlet* are part of his joking avoidance of the subject of marriage. As Várya says in Act Three, when Liubóv questions her about marrying Lopákhin: "he never mentions it. Or he jokes about it!"

Page 364. *"Guter Mensch aber schlechter Musikant."* German: "A good man but a bad musician." The line is a quote from *Ponce de Leon,* a play by Clemens Brentano.

Page 368. "The splendid ballroom gleams with gold . . ." The use of this poem by Alexei Tolstoy, recited to a crowd upstage while Liubóv remains seated alone downstage, is one of Chekhov's most theatrical moments.

Page 0373. "I'm going to chop down every tree . . ." One of the most interesting things about this play is Chekhov's balance of sympathy between Liubóv and her way of life, and Lopákhin and his. The cutting down of the cherry trees is equivocal: the orchard is, in a sense, not part of the natural environment that Chekhov so fiercely defends in *Uncle Vanya*, but an artificial creation that has become the dying emblem of a disappearing era.